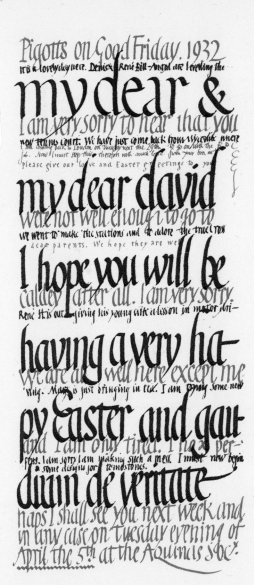

LETTER TO DAVID JONES

LETTERS OF
ERIC GILL

Edited by

WALTER SHEWRING

JONATHAN CAPE
THIRTY BEDFORD SQUARE
LONDON

FIRST PUBLISHED 1947

PRINTED IN GREAT BRITAIN IN THE CITY OF OXFORD
AT THE ALDEN PRESS
BOUND BY A. W. BAIN & CO. LTD., LONDON

CONTENTS

ILLUSTRATIONS

CORRESPONDENTS AND JOURNALS
ADDRESSED

Numbers are those of the Letters

6

PREFACE

I HOPE that the letters collected here will increase the general understanding of the life, work and thought of one of the greatest men of our time; that they will illuminate the memory they preserve.

The *Autobiography* has already given an authentic portrait of its author. Those who knew him best see his character whole in it, and will find no novelty here – at most, an express confirmation of things they discerned as implied before. To others, new aspects may be disclosed, and for all there will be fresh details of his inward and outward history – some particularities of his earlier outlook on men and things, a clarification of his approach to the Catholic Church, an ampler account of his movements and travels in England and abroad.

For those who consider him chiefly as an artist – as a master of lettering, as sculptor, engraver, typographer, designer of many familiar things – the letters provide a variety of information on the circumstances in which particular works were begun and the way in which they were carried out. As an assistance to future writers upon his life and work, I have sometimes included otherwise trivial letters which furnish some date or useful detail. His activities at any given time were in general too varied to allow of grouping letters by subjects, but those who have interest in a special part of his work will find, I hope, that the general index meets their needs; philatelists may consult the entry 'stamps', typographers 'lettering' and 'printing', and so forth.

There are others (I believe they will prove an increasing number) who find in his thought, in his philosophy – the word is not misplaced – his most valuable contribution to the life of our time, overshadowing in its importance and influence his great achievement in the field of the visual arts. And here, I think, the letters will be especially serviceable. They not only show the progress of his ideas — in general by logical development, in a few points by a real change of view; they should do much to remove uncertainties on what he actually held and taught. His thought has been much misunderstood, and for many reasons. Perhaps the most fundamental is the opposition of his whole view of life to the notions current in our time — an opposition so radical that to certain minds it appears as unbelievable. His teaching on poverty, for example, is as hard for the Communists he so often befriended as for the Capitalists he so often inveighed against. That anyone should desire to see England 'poor and needy'[1] is to either party an equal stumbling-block — a position not only un-acceptable but incomprehensible. Yet this was no paradox; he did desire that. And to those who most keenly feel such difficulties his letters will only bring help obliquely, calling out perhaps a sufficient respect and general sympathy to induce a return to the beginning and a frank resifting of ideas which have been too long accepted as axioms.

Other obstacles are less formidable, and arise from the manner of his writing.[2] In stating a thesis which he had much at heart he often would over-simplify it (sometimes con-sciously, sometimes not), disregarding side-issues and failing to make concessions which he was in fact willing to make and perhaps had expressly made elsewhere. In Letter 289 he explains his deliberate use of this procedure. In haste, at times, he wrote with an emphasis that might look like peevishness. ('But you mustn't think I'm cross about it. If I write thus it's only because I haven't time to write other-wise.'[3]) He allowed himself more irony than an English audience was likely to discern, and sometimes presented an opponent's position with a zest and verisimilitude that caused

---

[1] *Last Essays*, p. 64; *It All Goes Together*, p. 156.

[2] I say nothing of careless reading, though this is apparent enough in objections brought by many critics.

[3] Letter 64. Cf. Donald Attwater, *Eric Gill* (James Clarke, 1945), p. 36; *Modern Christian Revolutionaries* (Devin-Adair, 1947), p. 183.

it to be mistaken for his own. Sometimes, though seldom, his wording was actually careless. For all such sources of difficulty (which have their parallels in the works of philosophers by profession) these letters furnish abundance of corrective. His main principles are often and clearly set forth, and in the light of these all details should take their proper place. Objections made to his published writings are often discussed with correspondents. The normal outline should be plain, and small departures on one side or the other — too hasty concessions, too hasty denials — should be recognizable as such.

At the same time, certain sides of his interests and activities remain imperfectly represented. There are gaps in time and gaps in material. Letters of interest have disappeared in the violences of war and the negligences of peace. As will be seen, correspondence begins by being sparse, then by degrees grows ampler; the letters of the last five years outnumber those of the first twenty.[1] Accidental losses apart, in his earlier years he wrote less in any case. It was long before he employed a regular secretary, chiefly to deal with increasing letters of business, though by extension to help with private correspondence. It should also be said that his energy and his industry grew with the years. By common standards his life was always a busy one; at the end it was crowded almost beyond belief. He was then carving, engraving, designing types, writing books and essays and travelling about the country to lecture; but it was precisely then that he wrote and dictated most letters.

Yet even when letters are most frequent, there are many things they fail to bring out. His reading, for instance. A number of books and other writings are mentioned in correspondence, and as a matter of interest I have listed them in the index. But this list is not only incomplete, it is scarcely representative. It gives no hint of his weakness for detective stories, his courteous attention to minor modern verse, his

[1] For this reason I did not attempt to break up the book into chronological divisions. The disproportion would have been far too great.

special regard for Stella Benson's *Tobit Transplanted*, his eager waiting for each new volume of Lady Murasaki; it conceals his great admiration for the history of Christopher Dawson and the theology of Abbot Vonier.

Music, again. There is little said of it in the *Autobiography*, and in these letters scarcely as much; yet it was among the abiding interests of his life. The Gregorian chant was for him quintessential music, and his own singing of it in the chapel at Ditchling has been called the most beautiful sound one listener ever heard.[1] With the chant went folksong, into which he entered as few musicians do, by a connatural understanding.[2] After these he loved best the music of the sixteenth and seventeenth centuries, English and Italian, and a characteristic memory of him is his singing of the *Lachrymae Pavan*, *On a time the amorous Silvy*, or *Amarilli mia bella*, or again his playing on the clavichord a *corrente* by Frescobaldi. (He played simple pieces only, but with a sureness and delicacy that might have abashed a professional pianist.) In his later days, on leisure evenings, the gramophone might be brought in (it never became a permanency), and I remember his keen delight in the chamber music of Bach and Erlebach, Handel and Vivaldi. His respect for Beethoven was tempered by the proper reserves. He was always ready to hear the moderns — the achievement of a Sibelius, the experiments of a Bartók.

I carry such reminiscences no further. I wish only to show that though the letters illustrate much, the record they offer is not complete.

He wrote a very large number of letters to the press — a proceeding one usually associates with men of a different turn of mind. In his case it came from the desire — call it apostolic or propagandist — to present in season and out of season, in

[1] See Hilary Pepler's note in *Blackfriars*, E. G. Memorial Number, Feb. 1941, p. 62.

[2] To amplify this would take me too far afield, but I may add that, unlike most concert-performers, he was really familiar with the modes; and that he was a friend of Herbert Hughes, who lived near him at Ditchling and for some months shared the same house.

all manner of contexts and occasions, a view of life which he held to be socially urgent and intellectually right. Such letters – whether topical applications of his principles or corrections of some misstatement of them – are too characteristic of him and his activities to be simply set aside. But it was out of the question to print them all; they would have overweighted a collection which the reader naturally expects to be of material mainly private. In one of his notebooks he listed some hundred and eighty of them, and I know the list is not complete.[1] I have chosen between fifty and sixty of these as especially important or characteristic. I have also included one document here which is strictly speaking not a letter at all – the account of his ride on the *Flying Scotsman* which he wrote as an article for the *L.N.E.R. Magazine*. In a lively and colloquial way, it relates an experience which gave him great pleasure and which is rather surprisingly unrecorded in his private letters of the time. The Editor of the *Magazine* encourages me to print it here, and I think the reader will acquiesce.

Of private letters sent in to me I have printed by far the greater part. I must thank not only those correspondents who have visibly helped to make the book but also those whose contributions appeared of too limited an interest to be finally included. I have also printed, from copies preserved at Pigotts, a handful of letters to correspondents I could not trace, and would ask the indulgence of those concerned for presuming leave to publish this material.

I have made some omissions of private or merely uninteresting matters. Among private matters I rank certain judgments on men and their work (usually the latter) which though just in themselves might cause offence, and which their author himself would not have wished to receive publicity, at least without some countering praise. I have

---

[1] The journals to which he wrote most were the *Catholic Herald* (1934-40) and the *New English Weekly* (1932-6 and 1938-40); in each case the letters of 1940 are very numerous.

corrected obvious slips of the pen, somewhat strengthened
the punctuation, and reduced recurrent details to uniformity.[1]
I have also made a few insertions — mostly to explain initials,
but once or twice to supply missing words. In the text, the
sign [. . .] denotes omission, ⟨ ⟩ insertion. To complete
this account of my procedure, I should state that for accuracy
of transcription the responsibility is in general mine, but that
Mr. Attwater, Father Desmond Chute and Miss Hall are
responsible for the letters addressed to them, Messrs. Cape
for the letters to Henry Atkinson, George Horsfield, Eric
Kennington and the Rothensteins.

In choosing the illustrations it seemed best to give first place
to portraits and to reproductions of letters themselves; two
drawings of places have been added. The self-portrait facing
p. 172 was made in 1925 for Mr. James Laver's *Portraits in
Oil and Vinegar*; it then belonged to E. G. himself. Long
correspondence has failed to reveal its present owner, and I
hope I have not taken unwarrantable liberty in reproducing it
here from Mr. Laver's book.

The pieces of actual writing photographed invite some remarks on E. G.'s penmanship. Before his contact with
Edward Johnston his writing was, as he says in his first letter
here, 'most eccentric'; there is a specimen facing p. 17.
From 1903 onwards, Johnston's influence is apparent; the
model is good and the pupil apt, but there is some self-
consciousness and 'art-nonsense'. A gradual emancipation
follows, and by about 1912 the writing has most of the
qualities that remained, though I should say that its final form
was not reached in all points before about 1922. But for practical purposes the letter of 1917 facing p. 101 may be taken to
represent his permanent style, with its natural rhythm, easy
rightness and lucid rationality. This letter is written with
some care, but his hand was recognizably a master's even when

[1] Address and date on left and right respectively; no indentation at opening;
postscripts written at top or side transferred to end of letter; all titles of books
and journals italicized.

he was pressed for time or was writing in a railway carriage (as he often did — both letters and lecture-notes). Of formal writing he did little.[1] In the period of first enthusiasm — about 1903 — he wrote out a few texts in the manner of Johnston's pupils; Mrs. Gill has some stanzas of *Rabbi Ben Ezra* and sixteen pages of *Quintus Fixlein*, and his brother Macdonald Gill had a *Cupid and Psyche* in Pater's version. These are accomplished work, the last especially, but the letter-shapes keep elements of the fanciful and archaic such as he afterwards discarded. Both at this time and later he was willing to undertake writing to order,[2] and about 1910 he was using notepaper headed 'A. E. R. Gill, Inscription Carver and Caligrapher'; but his commissions seem always to have been few, and for his period of maturest style I know of none but small examples. When he had more than usual time on hand he might write a postcard or address an envelope with particular care. I reproduce one such card (facing p. 269); and the letter to David Jones (frontispiece) shows him actually trying new pens, not without some small mishaps. His most masterly and most careful penmanship was I think reserved for the season of Christmas and the enrichment of presents made then.

My thanks are due to many co-operators in the production of this book. I must name especially Father Desmond Chute, who in extremely difficult conditions transmitted from Italy an invaluable group of letters and a most admirable portrait. Messrs. Cape have helped me in many ways and have spent much time and trouble in getting letters transcribed. There remain Mrs. Gill and the household at Pigotts. They know my gratitude and will not wish me to attempt to express it.

W. S.

[1] Cf. Letter 317.
[2] A notebook of work for 1903 records among other things 'Writing out *Beautiful Zion* for Uncle Fred'. This took ten hours and was estimated at seven-and-six, which was not paid.

THE LETTERS

I : TO HIS BROTHER EVAN

[At the time of this letter E. G. was eighteen, articled to W. D. Caroë and lodging in Clapham at the Church Club. (See *Autobiography*, p. 108.) Evan Gill was a boy of eight. The letter is in red ink on khaki paper, and the other references to khaki recall the enthusiasms of the time. From the mid-nineteenth century onwards there had been an intermittent use of khaki by some British troops abroad, but its patriotic associations seem to have begun with the South African War.]

Clapham . S.W.   *Sunday . 29-4-1900*

MY · DEAR · OLD · EVAN : THANK · YOU · VERY · MUCH · FOR YOUR · JOLLY · LETTER. I · EXPECT · YOU · ENJOYED · THE PRIM-ROSE-ING · WITH · MAX · DIDN'T · YOU? DO · YOU · LIKE THIS · INK · AND · PAPER? DID · YOU · GET · YOUR · KHAKI CAPS · ALL · RIGHT? I · EXPECT · YOU · AND · VERNON · WOULD LOOK · VERY · NICE · IN · THEM.

I · AM · WRITING · THIS · LETTER · IN · PRINTING · NOT BECAUSE · I · THINK · YOU · CANNOT · READ · THE · OTHER SORT · OF · WRITING · BUT · BECAUSE · I · AM · AFRAID · YOU WOULD · NOT · BE · ABLE · TO · READ · *MY* · WRITING · WHICH IS · MOST · ECCENTRIC · I · AM · TOLD.

I · SAW · A · LITTLE · BOY · THE · OTHER · DAY · DRESSED · UP IN · KHAKI · CLOTHES · JUST · LIKE · A · SOLDIER. I · EXPECT · HE WAS · ABOUT · 6. HE · SEEMED · VERY · PROUD · OF · HIMSELF. NOW · GOOD-BYE · FROM · YOUR · LOVING · BROTHER

ERIC

2 : TO HIS FATHER

Clapham S.W.   *Sunday 24-6-1900*

My dear Father: Thank you very much for your letter received on Monday evening last.

I will endeavour to fulfil all the principles therein laid down.

I have enough cash left to go on to the end of the week at a pinch unless you should be able to send before.

I had a whole day off from the office yesterday to go sketching. I worked at the Abbey all day. I have got three sketches going now.

I sold one little sketch of S. Paul's from Fleet St. on Friday evening to H. E. Seccombe; or perhaps I should say I exchanged it. Because in exchange I got a fine reproduction of one of Rossetti's pictures of Mrs. William Morris.

I am awfully glad to have it.

I played solo whist with Mrs. Seccombe one of the Miss Seccombes Mr. Seccombe and Dr. Codrington all the evening at the Seccombes on Friday last. I also went there last evening and read up Ruskin with Harry S. in their garden.

This morning I went to S. Paul's. I met Mr. Croll there (ask Max who he is please if you don't remember). Archdeacon Sinclair preached – a Hospital Sunday sermon of course.

I came back from the city by the Electric Railway which has just been extended to Clapham Common. If I was going to the city I should certainly go by that on wet days but as I go to Westminster it isn't much use.

My suit of clothes came all right last night from Hammonds Co. I don't know if I told you that Uncle Harry seemed to think a sort of semi-evening dress would be the *most* useful thing.

It has no tails but a fairly *low* waist-coat and roll collar to the coat. I will now go to Max to continue the news such as it is from your loving son   ERIC

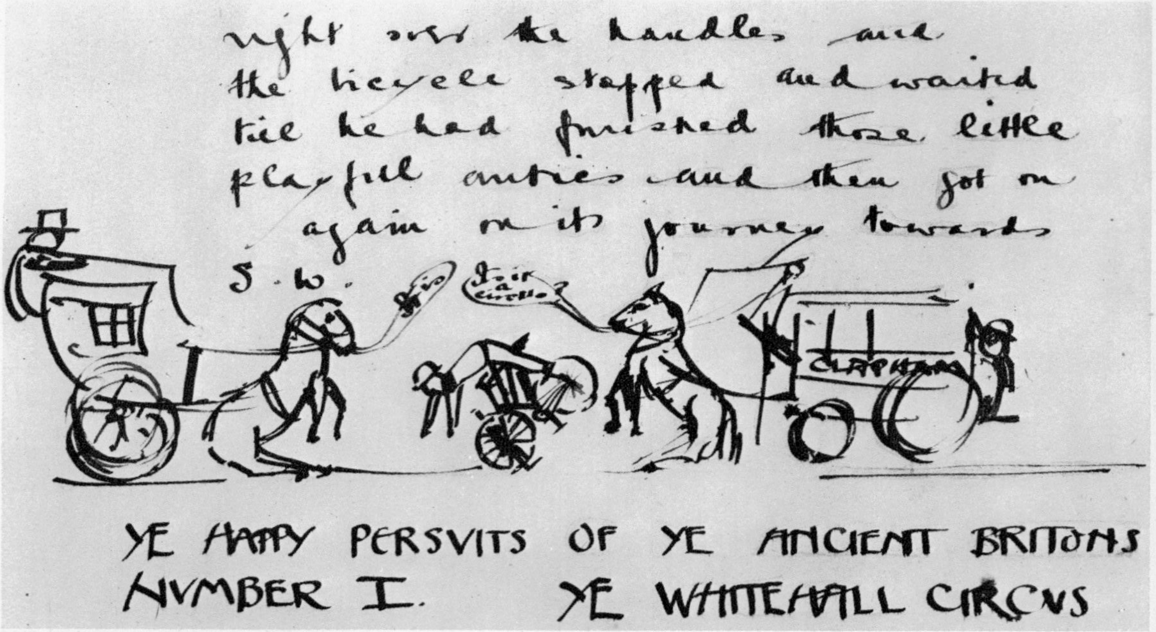

3 : TO HIS SISTER GLADYS

S.W.   24-6-1900

My dear Gladys: Thank you very much indeed for your letter.
    When, as you and Madie were 'carmly' (sic) floating the
other day, and a big wave went into your open mouths; did
all the big wave go in?
    I hope not.
    You ought to have been in a place called Whitehall yester-
day afternoon about 6.30 with a camera, and you would have
had the chance of taking a picture of an idiot falling off a
bicycle, in consequence of his having caught his umbrella in
his front wheel. He looked very funny. He went head first
right over the handles and the bicycle stopped and waited till
he had finished those little playful antics and then got on again
on its journey towards S.W. Now good bye. from the
'circus boy'.

[*Photograph opposite.*]

4 : TO 'THE CHICHESTER OBSERVER'
APRIL 1901

Chichester Market Cross

Dear Sir: With reference to the proposal to restore the
Chichester Market Cross as a memorial to her late Majesty
Queen Victoria, I take the liberty of asking you a few questions and making a few remarks on the subject that have
occurred to me. My chief desire in writing to you is to know
whether it is proposed to restore or to repair the Cross; for
there is a great difference between the two. I take it that
restoration means the renewing of a building stone by stone,
so that it may appear to be again what we suppose it originally
was; whereas to repair a building is to keep it by every means
in our power constructionally secure, both as a whole and as

B

regards detail. To do the first would surely be a mistake. For what satisfaction do we obtain from all the examples which surround us of the restoration of old buildings and monuments which have been done during the last 80 years — the years of the gothic revival? They are certainly not specimens of mediaeval masoncraft, but strike us rather as caricatures of mediaeval inspiration. When we visit the cathedrals of England we are shown the Norman work and the Early English and so on, and we are also informed that this or that portion was restored by some eminent architect in such and such a year; which information spoils the whole thing. We did not go to see copies of Norman work by eminent 19th century architects; but we went to see the masonry of the Normans, stained and worn as it is by time, but none the less the actual work of the men who made Europe famous by their skill as masons.

Now that the desire for restoration is beginning to cool down for want of fresh material to work upon, we are looking around for the real ancient works which were erected so plentifully some 400 years ago and which are now so scarce. Chichester Cross is one of the few remaining specimens of ancient art still left more or less in its original condition.

In Bishop Storey's time (1500) the English mason's craft was perhaps at its highest pitch, and the beauty of the work is astonishing to us. The Cross has suffered much from weather and decay, but so also have the pictures of the 16th century painters, yet who but vandals would think of repainting them? I fear, however, that this is practically what it is proposed to do to Chichester Cross. It is intended to renew or replace all the ornamental parts, which have fallen into decay, with new stone, carved as we suppose it was carved in the year 1500. Is it not absurd to imagine that 20th century workmen can, however skilful they are, transport themselves back into the 16th century and do the work which only exists at all because the 16th century existed? Would not their work remind us somewhat of the sham antiques they sell in Wardour-street?

Of course, it must not be forgotten that, unlike an old painting, a building, as it decays, becomes insecure and is in danger of altogether collapsing. We must at any cost prevent such a fate overtaking our Market Cross. This brings me to my second point, that of repair. The stability of the structure must be repaired by every means in our power. But only those stones should be touched which are necessary to the actual safety of the building. If it be found necessary to replace carved stones, let us cut them to our own design, shaping them so that they will harmonize with and carry on the old weathered stones on either side. Such work would be no deception, and passers-by would be able to see at a glance where repairs had been done. But do not let us try to imitate the inimitable. Do not let us pretend we are Gothic workmen when we are not.

Works of repairs, such as I have suggested above, would have to be executed gradually and under the very careful personal supervision of one who would spare no pains to preserve every stone possible. As regards the beautifully weathered bellcote, which it is proposed to remove, I am of the opinion that, though inferior to the older masonry in beauty and interest, it competes less with the 16th century work than would some structure of fresh stone. It seems to fall in well enough with the Cross, which is more than one can expect of any new and elaborately canopied quasi-Gothic erection such as that shown in Owen Carter's imaginary sketch.

If it is decided that all this work be undertaken as a memorial to her late Majesty Queen Victoria, I would suggest that repair be the first thing, and that after that the memorial find its chief expression in the proposed statuary. They at least cannot harm the Cross itself, and might be very fine pieces of work, and well worthy of the object for which they were erected. But I consider that it would be a very grave mistake for a memorial to our late beloved Queen to be in any way mixed up with such a vexed question as that of restoration.

The form which our memorial shall take must be unanimously approved of, and it must be in no way one which can be disputed over and condemned by lovers of old architecture. I am, dear Sir, yours etc.   A CICESTRIAN IN LONDON

[This drew a supporting letter from Edward Prior the architect (April 27th, 1901), who later wrote twice again (May 15th and perhaps May 22nd) in defence of E. G.'s position against other correspondents. I learn this from a book of early cuttings preserved by E. G., which contains ten letters about the Cross from various writers (all between 1901 and 1903, but few with exact dates). Cf. Letter 5. In recording the matter in the *Autobiography* (p. 116), E. G. seems not to have consulted these cuttings and speaks as if he had written one letter only. The introduction to Prior seems not to have taken place till 1903.]

5 : TO 'THE CHICHESTER OBSERVER'

[Two years after the writing of the last letter, the Market Cross at Chichester was still an object of civic concern. On January 26th, 1903, Mr. Firth Bailey addressed the local *Observer* thus:

Dear Sir, — As the repair of the Market Cross is prominently before the public I beg to make a suggestion that it be carefully taken down and rebuilt either in the Cathedral yard or, failing the permission of the Dean and Chapter, in the centre of the Jubilee Park.

Respecting the first-named site it would I think be singularly appropriate as the Cross was erected by a Bishop of the Diocese and is itself of an ecclesiastical design. As to the practicability, other ancient structures have been taken down and rebuilt, notably Temple Bar, and I believe the Marble Arch has been moved from its original position. Our venerable Cross, although no doubt one of the, if not the chief attraction of the City, is admittedly very much in the way of the traffic in that central spot and its removal for erection elsewhere would I feel sure be hailed with satisfaction not merely by the shop-keepers in the vicinity but by all the drivers of vehicles to whom the Cross is at present a danger and menace.

I believe, Sir, that all the money necessary would be splendidly forthcoming if my suggestion was acted upon. Thanking you in anticipation, I am, Sir, yours truly, FIRTH BAILEY

Helped, apparently, by his friend George Carter (*Autobiography*, p. 116), E. G. replied from London: —]

Sir: Re the letter signed 'Firth Bailey' in your issue of last Wednesday, Jan. 28th, I think the suggestion made therein an exceedingly brilliant one and very feasible indeed. Why, if I remember rightly, a great many fine old buildings have been ruthlessly pulled down, some of which have most certainly been rebuilt and some — not. There was the case of the Bell Tower at Salisbury, demolished because it was in the way. Though I never heard that it was rebuilt in the centre of any Park — Jubilee or other. But if Chichester Market Cross was pulled down and erected in Chichester's Jubilee Park what a useful thing it might become! It might easily be converted into a band stand where the Chichester Brass Band might delight the ear of Cicestrians on a summer's evening, and if it were not considered large enough the upper story might also be used, and with the help of a cast-iron and glass and bric-a-brac canopy supported on atrocious cast-iron columns it might be made a most handsome and edifying spectacle. On the other hand if the Cross was rebuilt within the Cathedral yard it would undoubtedly be a great convenience to visitors to our city — from the point of view of economy — as all photographs of the Cathedral might then have the Cross thrown in.

But, Sir, I have never seen the press of traffic so great as to constitute the Cross a serious obstruction, although I admit it sometimes takes five minutes to get round it — by the clocks. — But are we Cicestrians, as a rule, so pressed for time that we mind that? However, if in the struggle for existence our old Cross must be cleared away, why, having once got it safely down, should the poor Cicestrians go to the expense of re-building it? For having once been pulled down the Cross would have no historical or other interest whatsoever, however carefully rebuilt. Indeed it would then matter little what were done with the materials, whose interest lies in their having been built together on that spot in the centre of the city more than 400 years ago. I am, Sir, yours etc.

A CICESTRIAN IN LONDON

6 : TO HIS BROTHER EVAN

Lincoln's Inn.[1] *W.C.*   *6-4-1903*

My dear boy Evan: How do you like your new school? Which class are you in? Yesterday afternoon Max and I pretended we were bricklayers. The wind had blown the wall on the North side of Dr. Codrington's garden down and it had fallen all over the flower bed. So Max and I helped to clear it off the bed. All in our Sunday meeting clothes. Do you want the crest I am enclosing if not give it to some one who does. I went to the British Museum on Saturday morning. I went to see the Inscriptions, on stone, done by the Romans. In the afternoon Max and I went to the Arts and Crafts Exhibition. I played Ping-pong with Max and Johnston in the evening. I cant write a funny letter as Max can so I think I shall have to give up writing letters. Max and I were going to ride down on our bicycles on Thursday but it was so wet that I left my bike at Petworth last Monday. So I shall not be able to ride down except in the train. Now good bye from your loving brother

ERIC

$$\frac{\text{A.}|\text{.E}}{\text{R}\cdot|\cdot\text{G}}$$

[1] Where E. G. had come to live at the invitation of Edward Johnston (*Autobiography*, pp. 126-30).

7 : TO HIS BROTHER EVAN

Lincoln's Inn, W.C.   *16-6-1903*

My dear boy Evan: I am afraid it is a long time since I wrote
to you last. Isn't it? I was very pleased to get all your letters
yesterday when I saw Max. Harold Shaw is staying with me
just at present. He is going in for an Examination. It has been
very wet here for the last three days but it is fine this morning.
I do not like London in the wet. On Thursday morning before
breakfast I am going to a place called Wormwood Scrubbs to
do some shooting & on Saturday the Queen's W's[1] are going
to be inspected by Lord Roberts! I shall have to go to that
sha'n't I? Please thank Angela, Kenneth, Gladys & Romney
very much for their letters and tell Romney I will write to
him as soon as I can.

Now I must end as I have some more writing to do. Good-
bye from your loving brother   ERIC

8 : TO WILLIAM ROTHENSTEIN

Hammersmith Terrace, W.[2]   *6-12-1907*

Dear Rothenstein: Now I have talked to Johnston. We should
both like to join in the Kessler 'memorial'. But . . . we're
both very impecunious at this present. We suggest: Johnston
would be pleased to write out *the address* in lieu of subscription
(he presumes it would otherwise have to be paid for) — I
should be pleased to carve or engrave inscription, if any,
(either one saying to whom the gift is made or — more
likely — the name or other description of the bronze) in lieu

[1] The Queen's Westminster Volunteer Rifle Corps, to which E. G. belonged.
[2] E. G's. workshop was still at Hammersmith though the household had moved
to Soper's, Ditchling Village, on Sept. 11th, 1907. The workshop was transferred
there on April 1st, 1908 (cf. Letter 10).

of subscription. If these offers are not acceptable we shall be able & willing to subscribe ½ a guinea each, but both of us are practically unable to afford more. We would like to, both because we agree with the motive of the address & present, & because we feel it an honour to have been asked, — but I expect you'll understand — .

I don't think I'll be able to go to the A.W.G. after all to-night as I rather want to go to the Fabian.

Yours sincerely,   A. E. R. GILL

9 : TO WILLIAM ROTHENSTEIN

Hammersmith Terrace, London, W.   *11-2-1908*

Dear Rothenstein: I have this morning had a talk with John-ston about the Kessler address and this is what we suggest subject to your approval & its practicability:— The bronze stands on an ebony (?) stand. This stand is hollow. [. . .] What we suggest is that to the underside of the stand be affixed a *small* engraved brass plate (my part of the affair) & this plate be affixed in such a way that there is room for a *small* (very small) book to be inserted between it & the ebony. In other words we would make a little brass book box & fix it under the stand. [. . .]

You see the little book couldn't fall out it would be too close a fit & *too light*. Another advantage of this idea is that thus the bronze & the address would live in constant prox-imity.

Thirdly the book would have to be small & we think (do you?) that would be good in any case. E. J. goes so far as to say that the German text though right enough in sentiment is so preposterously worded that if he wrote it big he would feel obliged to add what he calls a 'minority report' to it — saying that 'though we agree with the general sentiment expressed we take exception to its form & revise simply to say that we think Kessler's a very decent sort' or words to that effect. [. . .] Yours sincerely   A. E. R. GILL

10 : TO WILLIAM ROTHENSTEIN

Soper's — Ditchling, Sussex   *26-4-1908*

My dear Rothenstein: Thanks for your card and also for the German ms. The mistakes therein were seven in number, two of which were mine & five (!) were in the typewritten draft you sent us in the first place. So E. J. says he'll put a note in as he'll have to correct his ms. in five places!

I heard through Miss Morris of the addition to the Rothenstein family. My wife & I send our congratulations & best wishes. How is Mrs. Rothenstein? & is the baby a boy or girl?

I have now moved my workshop to the above address & am enjoying myself hugely. Hammersmith will see me no more (as inhabitant). I shall be in London from Tuesday afternoon till Friday, *as a rule*, & my address there you know. (Lincoln's Inn, 16 Old Bgs.) We are having the telephone fixed & our number will be *1143 P.O. City* Yours ever   A. E. R. GILL
When is the next meeting?

11 : TO WILLIAM ROTHENSTEIN
                                   [1908?]

My dear Rothenstein: [. . .] Your letter was if possible more welcome than your cheque. For if there's one thing a hard up person needs more than money it's faith, and your encouragement is one of the bulwarks of my faith. Well — I hope to see you to-morrow so will stop. Yours ever   ERIC GILL

12 : TO WILLIAM ROTHENSTEIN

Workshops   *16, Old Buildings*
Ditchling, Sussex   *Lincoln's Inn*
                                               London, W.C.
                                               25-11-1909

Dear Rothenstein: Would you kindly forward the enclosed
letter for me as I do not know the name or address of the man.
I am inquiring particulars of the International Exhibition on the
chance that it may perhaps suit my needs better than the forthcoming Arts & Crafts Exhibn. Not that I love any exhibitions
particularly but that needing under present circumstances to advertize myself I may as well choose the best field and if possible
avoid placing myself again under the A & C banner. The more
so as my article on the Failure of the A. & C. Movement is to
appear in the forthcoming December Number of the *Socialist
Review* published by the I.L.P.! Yours ever   A. E. R. G.

13 : TO WILLIAM ROTHENSTEIN

[On the circumstances in which this letter was written, see *Autobiography*, pp. 179-82.]

Workshops   *16, Old Buildings*
Ditchling, Sussex   *Lincoln's Inn*
                                               London, W.C.
                                               20-1-1910

Dear Rothenstein: I wired to Kessler first thing this morning
as follows: 'Re Marly lease please wait am writing.' This was
because in the enthusiasm of his soul he had been so good as
to say that as he was on the spot he would fix up the house
for us and advance the 1st. quarter's rent. He feared that the
landlord not being over willing to let to a foreign artist I
might have difficulty in working the thing by myself. He

also wanted us to take the house for three years because otherwise we might not get it at all. We wanted to take it for one year only so as to give ourselves a chance of clearing out if we wanted to after one year. Well . . . at five o'clock this afternoon I got the following telegram from Kessler: 'Have signed and paid lease to-day, Kessler'! Now what on earth am I to do? It's really pretty devilish difficult. I don't want to bother you with my affairs but I'd be awfully grateful if you'd tell me if you think there's any way out of it. I thought Kessler might have paid the first rent — hence my wire. But it never occurred to me that he would go and sign the lease for us. I spent the best part of the morning composing a letter to him which is now useless. I'm at my wit's end.

I send you a copy of what I had proposed to say to Kessler. Meanwhile I'll wait. Only just time to catch post now.

The worst of these energetic enthusiasts like Kessler is that they rush you so. What on earth will Kessler say or do? For really I don't think I can face it. I mean I don't think I can face the three years in France. Yours   A. E. R. GILL

I haven't yet written to Kessler & won't till I hear from you. Do forgive me for bothering you so.

———

Soper's, Ditchling, Sussex

Copy

Dear Count Kessler: I'm rather at a loss to know how to begin. I'm very much afraid after all you have done in the matter that I shall seem both rude and ungrateful. Under all my enthusiasm for the projected sojourn in Marly — (in such a beautiful place —starting afresh, as it were, free from the Arts & Crafts Movement —and in the proximity of so splendid a mind as Maillol's —and in his friendship) —there were always misgivings —quite apart from the financial difficulty which you had in your generosity done so much to smoothe over and

quite apart from the difficulty of freeing myself from the
encumbrance of our house in Ditchling and quite apart from
the dangers incidental to a so long absence from all the people
I know in England and the loss of connection resulting therefrom — there were misgivings. These misgivings have now got
the better of me. I can no longer face the prospect. The
attractions which I have mentioned have ceased to weigh with
me. Can you ever forgive me? I will try and explain what I
mean if you will bear with me.

What was I going to Maillol for? Of course it was in order
that I might benefit as a sculptor, and in return for the benefit
received it was hoped that I should prove of some assistance to
Maillol. Well then, in what ways was I to benefit? In the first
place technically and in the second artistically. But it has
gradually been borne in upon me that, Maillol being more of
a modeller than actually a stone carver, technically I should
learn nothing. Was it not even understood that I should learn
'*pointing*' before I went? I have come to the conclusion that
I do not want to learn pointing — that I want to be a stone
carver — that I do not particularly want to know how to
reproduce accurately and expeditiously in stone a clay model.
I want to have only so much to do with modelling as is necessary for that kind of client who wants to know what he's going
to get before he gets it. And even so I should refuse to
guarantee a likeness between the model and the stone. The
inspiration comes with the carving and is an entirely different
inspiration from that which comes with the clay. You see I
feel that splendid as Maillol is it is not the kind of splendid I
can ever be or wish to be. Then you see, that, as a corollary
of the foregoing, that artistically it would be, to say the least,
unsafe for me to work with or for Maillol. The similarity in
our ideas, if I may so presume to speak, would be so seductive
(Oh! this is an awfully difficult point!) that I should cease to
oppose. And one *must* be in opposition. Maillol has a vision
which I feel to be very largely *my* vision. Well then, if I am
to achieve the expression of that vision I must achieve it for

myself, through my own struggles, in my own battle with life. I do hope I am making myself clear to you. Well then, if these things are so, it is obvious that what I need to learn is about tools and the uses of tools —the chisel & hammer and what they are capable of doing. I cannot learn that from Maillol. Infinitely better would it be for me to go and apprentice myself to the most skilful & the most ordinary of monumental masons and learn to hack idiotic angels out of white marble. Then indeed I should be in opposition —and should find out what *I* meant and what *I* should do & say. Do you know I almost feel as if in that brief afternoon at Marly I got as much out of Maillol as I ever should get. I know this sounds horridly conceited. But what I mean is that, in a kind of way, I was allowed to see the vision —and that I cannot forget it. That if, from time to time, I were privileged 'to see Maillol and look at his work I should be more helped than by a continuous stay with him. I have tried to explain one or two points —and there are other aspects —such as my age for instance —which are also weighing with me but which I cannot go into now.

(After this I had written saying how much I hoped he had not yet consummated the lease and so forth. And then I got his telegram!)

I shall send the above letter in any case unless you think it's not the way out. You know Kessler better than I do and also you know better than I do the rights & wrongs of the matter. Anyway it is evident that Kessler has signed a three years lease and paid the first rent! Can I possibly refuse it now? If you think I can —knowing him as you do —I will. Yours A. E. R. G.

14 : TO WILLIAM ROTHENSTEIN

Workshops
Ditchling, Sussex

16, Old Buildings
Lincoln's Inn
London, W.C.
22-1-1910

Dear Rothenstein: I got your letter last night. It was frightfully good of you to write so promptly and your letter was
most helpful and to the point – to say nothing of its kindness.
Well, yesterday morning I got a letter from Kessler, written
before the receipt of my telegram to him, and there is one
part of it that just clinches the matter. I think you will agree
with me that it clinches the matter. I quote the paragraph in
full. I had sent him two unfixed prints of the little statuette
(as he had asked me to do as soon as I had got the thing into
shape) & this is what he says: 'The statuette looks very interesting. I showed the photos. to Maillol who liked them very
well. He says they show great talent; but he rather deplores
you do not work *in clay first*, as it is very difficult, or rather,
impossible to *correct* mistakes in stone. He says you must
learn to work in clay, if you want to develop your art. I
transmit what he said as I think it may interest you.' (The
underlinings are Kessler's). It is rather a coincidence, isn't
it?, that Kessler should refer to the very point, or one of the
very points, on which I had laid stress in my letter to him. I
shall now send my letter off to him (I am glad you think it
clear and right) with another to explain its delay.* I am
looking forward to seeing you next Wednesday morning.
Other aspects equally convincing to me have occurred to me
that I will tell you of. Meanwhile, as you wished, I send four
photographs (very amateurish) of the little figure, and I'll
bring it itself up with me on Wednesday morning if possible.
Yours ever

A. E. R. GILL

* i.e. delayed because of receipt of his telegram and my consequent hesitation as to my actions.

15 : TO WILLIAM ROTHENSTEIN

Soper's, Ditchling   *27-5-1910*

Dear Rothenstein: As I am at present engaged on your India Society job I am sure you will not mind me dictating this as I want to write as soon as possible to tell you how a mere carpet-beater like myself was simply forced to disregard the unutterable beastliness of Messrs —— and Company's Mid-Victorian, Bourgeois, stuffy decorations which on first entering the Gallery gave me a so severe fit of the blues that I thought nothing could possibly live in such an atmosphere. I am sure it does say something for the real strength and sincerity of certain pictures I saw on the walls that after twenty minutes or so Messrs —— & Co were forgotten and are only now with amusement recollected. It is really splendid to consider that so many of the most interesting and inspired men of our time (why are there no women?) have had the good fortune to be placed on record by a pencil which is able to depict so much more than their mere outward appearance, and it is really splendid to consider that so many of the most beautiful and noble works of nature have had the good fortune to be placed on record by a brush which is able to depict so much more than their mere outward appearance —so that in fact the nobility and beauty is brought home to us, (end of peroration). I think the pictures look very well really and the composition suggesting Sorrow still persists in giving me a different feeling of sorrow than that which it inspired in the mind of Mrs K.

I had the unexpected delight of seeing two pictures that I had not seen before.

(Doctor came to vaccinate the baby so must finish this on my own.)

There's no doubt about the portrait of yourself.

It is really splendid & somehow or other all the objections I used to feel on the score of likeness are now disappeared.

I was much impressed by Mrs. Kochler's jewellery —though

I think it varies in splendour. Chiefly I feel very strongly that it lacks sensitiveness (I don't know a better word), I mean I think the workmanship is unfeeling. That is no doubt an inevitable result of the method of execution. It is an enormous pity because fine design demands fine workmanship & not merely a mechanical excellence of finish. On the other hand where the workmanship is *not* mechanical it is rather weak, as, for instance, in the interlacing stems of No. 3 & in No. 9.

Must run to post. Yours ever   ERIC GILL

I do hope the enclosed will do.

16 : TO WILLIAM ROTHENSTEIN

Ditchling, Sussex
London Address:
21 Old Buildings
Lincoln's Inn, W.C.   *25-9-1910*

Dear Rothenstein: Your p.c. to hand. I hope to be able to see you and talk about various things before you go away. I do not know if I shall be able to come to London this week. If I do I will certainly come up to Hampstead.

The fact of the matter is that Epstein & I have got a great scheme of doing some colossal figures together (as a contribution to the world) a sort of twentieth century Stonehenge, and we have been looking out for a piece of land for the purpose. We have now found such a place —about 4 miles southeast of Lewes —and are endeavouring to get it on a lease. It is a plot of about 6 acres, hidden away in a valley in the hills, with a decent-sized house and farm buildings attached. Altogether so ideal a place for our purpose that I do not know what we shall do if we don't get it. We have applied to the owner (or at least *I* have) and can get it on a 14 years' lease. It is empty at present. We should have to do all repairs etc.

But oh! if only we could buy the place outright! Then we should be free to do all we wanted without the fear of hurting anybody's feelings or the risk of being turned out at the end of the 14 years and our figures smashed up by some damned fools who didn't choose to like them. Of course 14 years is a long time and many things may happen before they're up, but I do feel that this is the grandest opportunity and it is increasingly evident that it is no use relying on architects & patrons and dealers. I wish you could come down and see the place. Is that quite impossible? Surely some millionaire could be persuaded to buy the place for us (we could pay him back by instalments). Roger Fry is coming here tomorrow and I'm going to speak to him about it too. But we want everybody interested to support. Besides I should awfully like you to see my sculptures before you go away again. Yours ever

A. E. R. GILL

17 : TO WILLIAM ROTHENSTEIN

Ditchling, Sussex   *15-10-1910*

Dear Rothenstein: Herewith my first letter to you in India. I hope you'll have got there safe and sound. There's no particular news. My brother Max went up and painted the inscription & coat of arms on the Baker portrait yesterday; I wasn't able to go myself as I had to go to Derbyshire this week. I send photo. (not a fearfully good one) of the young woman —I do hope you think her pleasant. (She's better in the real thing).

Our great scheme, Epstein's and mine, is, alas!, hanging fire just at present. The owners want such a devil of a price for the place & we are now running round risking all our friendships by asking for money. I very much fear we shan't pull it off —but on the other hand p'raps we will —I'll let you know how things go as soon as anything's decided.

C

You see they first of all said they'd let the place for £50 per ann. and now they say they'd rather not *let* but want to *sell* and they want £3500! Of course we can't run to that but it remains to be seen if we can beat them down at all. I hope to hear from you some time. Much love from self and Ethel. Yours ever   A. E. R. GILL

18 : TO WILLIAM ROTHENSTEIN

Ditchling, Sussex   *5-12-1910*

My dear Rothenstein: This is to wish you a happy Christmas in India. I was glad to hear from Mrs. Rothenstein that there was good news of you. That is all I've heard so far tho. I send you another copy of the *Highway*. I wonder very much what you thought of the last, for my article, 'Masters & Servants', which appeared in it, seems to be going to have some good results. I am really very anxious to hear from you whether you approve of the line I am taking or not. In fact I wish you weren't in India just now for all sorts of exciting things are happening and I want to talk to you about them. To begin with the least important: — I'm going to have a show of my works at the Chenil Gallery in January. Do you approve of that? And now, apropos of that, I want to make a request. As I have not very many things to show may I borrow your 'Mother and Child'? I'd be very grateful if I could. The show opens on Jan. 12 or 14, probably, so I don't know if you'll have time to reply but I couldn't ask you sooner as I only closed with Knewstubb's offer to-day. If, however, for any reason, and there may be some, you don't want to lend it to the Chenil Gallery would it be awfully expensive to send me a wire? One word, No, would be enough and if I don't get a wire I'll take it I *may* borrow it. Meanwhile I'll mention the matter to Mrs. Rothenstein and see what she says. I am not really keen on having this show but there's the possibility that

through it I may sell something and I happen to be very hard
pressed at present. Which leads me to another subject. You
remember that blooming monument I was doing for a certain
Easton Gibb —the one with the standing figure of a woman
and the sitting child? Well, it's now practically finished & the
man says it's so rotten that he can't possibly have it erected!
Whether I shall get the money or not remains to be seen. He
says the design I showed him led him to expect 'a very different
production'! As a matter of fact he's entirely in the wrong
but it's a damned nuisance anyway. However Fry & MacColl
(not to mention Epstein & John) both back me up in my
contention that I have carried out the design satisfactorily
and am entitled to my pay, so I hope I shall get it, for if I don't
I shall certainly be in an awful hole.

You are missing an awful excitement just now being provided for us in London: to wit: the exhibition of 'post-
impressionists' now on at the Grafton Gallery. All the critics
are tearing one another's eyes out over it and the sheep and
the goats are inextricably mixed up. John says 'it's a bloody
show' & Lady Ottoline[1] says 'oh charming', Fry says 'what
rhythm' & MacColl says 'what rot'. As a matter of fact those
who like it show their pluck and, those who don't, show
either great intelligence or else great stupidity. The show
quite obviously represents a reaction and a transition and so if,
like Fry, you are a factor in that reaction and transition then
you like the show. If, like MacColl & Robert Ross, you are
too inseparably connected with the things reacted against and
the generation from which it is a transition, then you don't
like it. If, on the other hand, you are like me and John &
McEvoy & Epstein, then, feeling yourself beyond the reaction
& beyond the transition, you have a right to feel superior to
Mr. Henri-Matisse (who is typical of the show —though
Gauguin makes the biggest splash and Van Gogh the maddest)
& can say you don't like it. But have you seen Mr. Matisse's
sculpture? . . .

[1] Lady Ottoline Morrell.

There is one thing more I must tell you as it is the most important of all, and yet I don't know how to begin. I almost think I shall have to wait till you come back and yet I don't want to do that because I owe it to you to tell you. The fact is it is really too splendid if it's true and so splendid that I hesitate to write of it. I will just hint it to you:— there is a possibility that religion is about to spring up again in England. A Religion so splendid & all embracing that the hierarchy to which it will give birth, uniting within itself the artist and the priest, will supplant and utterly destroy our present commercial government and our present commercial age. If this is true it is grand, if not then are we of all men most miserable. I'll tell you all when I see you. With much love. Yours ever   ERIC GILL

I did the enclosed engraving for Fry for a Christmas card. Since taking this proof I have made some improvements but have no copy.

19 : TO WILLIAM ROTHENSTEIN

Ditchling, Sussex   *6-1-1911*

My dear Rothenstein: I was awfully glad to hear from you and to know that you were all right and having a good time in spite of loneliness in the evenings (are there no ladies whose acquaintance may be made o' nights?). India must be the most marvellous place. There has lately been appearing in our midst a publication called the *Wonders of the World* (7d. fort-nightly – you know the sort of thing) and, greatest wonder of all!, in it have been quite a large number of photographs of Indian sculptures. So we have been gaining some small notion of the sort of thing you are seeing. Epstein (who, by the way, is staying here at Ditchling doing a large figure in stone) and I agree with you in your suggestion that the best route to

Heaven is via Elephanta, Elura & Ajanta. They must be won-derful places indeed. Several photographs of their sculptures & paintings have appeared in the *Wonders* and we have also had pictures of the carvings at Gwalior which you wrote about. Some day we will follow in your footsteps and go and see the real things. Epstein has decided to do the Wilde monument in stone and to carve it himself too — that is why he is down here — getting into the way of stone carving. He is doing splendid things. I saw Mrs. Rothenstein a week or two ago and asked if I might borrow the little figure for my show and she agreed to let me — subject of course to your being willing too. The show has been postponed a week to allow John's show to remain open an extra week as it is such a success. So my show will open on Jan 20. John has had an immense success with his 'Provençal Studies' having sold nearly every one of them! Which reminds me that the other day he, John, was awakened from his peaceful slumbers by the sound of screams in the next room or somewhere. In a half-asleep condition he rushed to see what was up and found a maid servant who, having been dusting the mantel shelf after lighting the fire, had set herself alight and was all ablaze. The heroic Augustus thereupon embraced her and though successful in smothering and extinguishing the flames got very badly burnt himself in the process. He is now in bed in a bandaged-up condition. Other people say that the embrace took place before the fire and not after it (i.e. that a lamp or something got upset in the struggle) but then some people are so uncharitable.

Epstein sends his love and says he will write to you too. I send another copy of the *Highway* which I hope will amuse you. Mrs. Cornford's little poem is very good isn't it? They, she & her husband, came here for the night last week — delightful couple. Ever so much love from   ERIC GILL

20 : TO 'THE HIGHWAY', FEBRUARY, 1911

A Preface to an Unwritten Book

Sir: In the article[1] referred to by Mr. Goodman in his letter published in your December issue, Mr. Eric Gill did not 'seek to discover' anything, but merely suggested the lines on which his enquiry into modern conditions should proceed. Your correspondent is a little precipitate, therefore, in assuming that Mr. Gill sees an antagonism between commercialism and quality, for whether there is or not is precisely what Mr. Gill, in his suggested book, would endeavour to find out.

However, let us overlook the precipitancy, and answer some of the statements. Commerce, which Mr. Goodman is so concerned to defend, is, of course, a necessary and valuable institution, and is, as he says, 'one of the most potent civilizing powers humanity has yet developed'; but I was not writing of commerce viewed as a means to an end, but of commerce regarded as an end in itself. Commerce is one means by which men render service to one another, but that man exists to render service to his fellows is, I suggest, open to question, and I refer Mr. Goodman to my article in your November issue, wherein I have endeavoured to explain the thing for which man does exist.[2]

Money-making is not the essence of commerce, but is the essence of commercialism, and if Mr. Goodman does 'not identify commercialism with the mere making of money,' that is because he identifies the word 'commercialism' with the word 'commerce,' and thus confuses himself.

Mr. Goodman objects to the statement that 'the qualification for the vote is a property qualification,' and suggests that 'adult masculinity' is a more accurate definition of the qualification. But Mr. Goodman might be hoary with age and as male as anything, and yet without a certain amount of property —if only in the form of credit in lieu of money

---

[1] 'A Preface to an Unwritten Book', *The Highway*, Oct. 1910.
[2] 'The production of fine works and fine men.'

wherewith to pay rent — he would not be qualified to vote. Most grown-up men have votes, but the qualification is not therefore adult masculinity.

But, Sir, your correspondent's worst offence is not a matter of words or of definitions. His is the old and dreadful error of having concern for the conditions of the workers more than for the work they turn out. Because, in his opinion, machinery is capable of relieving drudgery, he overlooks the possibility that machinery has made us a race of dull men, among whom an artist is as rare as a needle in a haystack, and has given us such a supply of cheap and ill-made goods that good materials and good workmanship are now only to be found in the machines themselves, and not always there. I said my enquiry would 'concern itself with the products of a people rather than with the conditions of its being,' and I am promptly told that I ought to admire machinery because it improves the conditions of the workers!

As a matter of fact, I do admire machinery, and said as much, too, in my article, but not because it reduces drudgery. Suppose machinery does diminish drudgery, what is that to me? I am not concerned with conditions. Good conditions will no more produce good work than good tools will make good workmen. I would not spend five minutes trying to reduce drudgery. If Mr. Goodman will say that we are in this year of Grace 1911 producing, as a nation or as individuals, as fine works of art and craftsmanship as they did in the year 2000 B.C. in Egypt, or 400 B.C. in India and Greece, or 1300 A.D. in England, well, then, there's no more to be said, and I must talk to someone else. — Yours, etc.,   ERIC GILL

21 : TO WILLIAM ROTHENSTEIN

at Steyning, Sx   *15-7-1911*

My dear Rothenstein: [. . .] I have been hoping to see you
at Ditchling —or anywhere else. Next Friday I'm due to read
a paper at your A.W.G. on 'Lettering for public purposes' so
I shall be in London on that day. Will you? If you will (& I
will ring you up to find out) I should like to come up & have
tea & Badminton as you suggest. That would be very jolly.
Perhaps, if free, you'll be coming to the Guild. I don't suppose there will be many there tho. I guess I'm rather a 'stop-
gap' lecturer. If I come up on Friday I can then fetch away
your very intriguing 'gift'. I wonder whatever it can be.
Thank you in advance. I'm excited to see it.

Fancy you going to America. I wonder how you'll like that
after India! 'What ho for a bit of a change' as the lift-man at
Chancery Lane Tube Station said when he was shifted to
Tottenham Ct. Rd. From India to America is even more of a
change tho. I expect you'll have a good time & it will be
immensely interesting.

I want you to see my statue of the Virgin —though still very
unfinished. It's doubtful whether Fry will have it. I think
he's frightened of it and, as my brother said, it hardly goes
with strawberries & cream & tea on the lawn at Guildford.
It is either too serious for such like or not serious enough. I
want you to see it. We must discuss the chance of your
coming over to Ditchling when we meet as I hope we shall on
Friday.

We (my wife & I) are having a little walk through Sussex at
present. We started on Thursday from Beachy Head & hope
to get to Bognor to-morrow night. I return to Ditchling on
Thursday. Yours ever   ERIC GILL

2 2 : T O W I L L I A M R O T H E N S T E I N

In train to Bognor   *22-7-1911*

My dear Rothenstein: I am awfully sorry I rushed away so unritually. And I need not have done so neither for the train was very late in starting. This is just to say that I'm most frightfully bucked up by your visit & your enthusiasm. I only hope you will both come again when we're all at home. Life is indeed good when you find someone to whom your vision is credible & worshipful. Yours   ERIC GILL

I've got an inscription to cut on the new British Museum Building during the week after next so I hope to come up & beat you at Badminton one day then.

The enclosed will amuse Mrs. Rothenstein & exonerate *me*.

2 3 : T O W I L L I A M R O T H E N S T E I N

Ditchling, Sx.   *5-11-1911*

My dear W.R.: Thanks awfully for your p.c. from New York — in reply to which: 'let me assure you' that I have been for a long time a devoted adherent of sky scraping and admirer of New York architecture. I only wish I could walk down Wall St. in your shoes as I have done in my own in my dreams. Some day p'raps I will (if you have an old pair). I've wanted to write to you for some little time with reference to our conversation that evening at the Savile Club. I mean about the Roman Catholic Ch. You will remember that you said that, though you could appreciate the motives which led others to become members of this or that church yet, for your part, you thought yourself one of those persons who, like those ordained to bachelor blessedness by nature, are constitutionally unsuited to, having by temperament no need for, such membership. I was unable to answer that argument at the time but after consideration I've come to the conclusion that by that argument you give evidence that I had not made clear to you *my* reasons for wishing it possible that I could join the Church. In fact your argument was beside my point. I remember I took it for granted that you'd understand what I was after in the matter. Of course I shd. have explained. May I try now? I hope it won't bore you —*Assuming* that in the Catholic Church we have an organization regarding itself as the casket in wh. is contained the true explanation of the significance of the Universe and which, by virtue of that regard, should impose not only spiritual but also temporal authority over the minds and acts & policies of men, then in the first place we have to discover whether the church has a right so to regard itself and secondly whether it is anyways possible for it to impose such authority and thirdly whether, in the minds of its responsible governors, it has any desire to do so. If these three things can be discovered then, 'bachelor' or not, it seems to me obvious that we should submit ourselves as members. My difficulty is then 1st: can the Catholic Faith be so exposed as to convince *me*? (not that I matter —but I want to know.) 2nd Can a Church exercise temporal authority? & 3rd Does the Roman Church seek to exercise it?

I cannot answer the 1st question but the 2nd is easy for, in the past, the church has done it and with immense though varying success. As to the 3rd question: again I am in doubt, for though the fact that the Popes, since the fall of Rome in 1870, have always considered themselves prisoners in the Vatican would seem to imply that they resent the usurpation of their temporal power by Victor Emmanuel, yet I have heard of no attempt to rebuild even so limited a state as was the 'Holy Roman Empire'.

You see it is, with me, a question of good politics not of temperament and I can only explain your attitude by reference to your nationality of which of course you are proud. The Jews always have been outsiders —that is part of their genius — and if you explain your attitude in that way I can understand it —but, when you say that there are some people naturally

& therefore rightly unattached to any religious organization, you seem to me to imply 1st that it is not obvious that the world shd. be governed in accordance with its significance, 2nd that, even if the significance of the world were known and even if the world's government were or could be run in accordance therewith, even then it would not be desirable or possible that loyalty to that government should be the duty of every individual. By the same reasoning you presumably hold yourself absolved from loyalty to the country of which it has been supposed you are a citizen! I am only seeking to raise citizenship to a higher power and to impose the same idea and custom of loyalty on men as religious people as is already imposed on them as trades-people. Am I clear? I mean that if loyalty to the State is obviously desirable (is it obvious?): then loyalty to a church is even more so because individual states are subordinate affairs which shd. be run under the tutelage of a church. Wanted that church: Is it, for us as Europeans, the Roman Church? If it is, you, unless by nationality you claim exemption, shd. be a member of it as much as I. Now I'd awfully like to know what you think. Do tell me.

We are getting on all right at Ditchling. I'm working hard at sundry tombstones at present so as to resuscitate my balance at the bank. I do a little carving in between whiles tho.

Alas! my younger apprentice has just died from pneumonia. This is a great loss to me. We were very fond of him & he was becoming a good workman too. And now this last week my wife's father has died — so we are brought to realize things — I hope your mother has recovered.

I have not been in London lately. I hear that Christopher Whall has been elected Master of the A.W.G. I don't know if that's really so — poor A.W.G. — but 'No matter — more was lost at Mohacs field'.

I hope you're having a good time — and that your exhibitions are successful. I'd like to see a press cutting or two if you bring any back. What is the American Press like in that way?
Yours ever   ERIC GILL

24 : TO WILLIAM ROTHENSTEIN

Ditchling   *29-1-1912*

My dear Rothenstein: I was very glad to get your letter of Nov. 30 & thank you very much for it. You say many things which throw light on my problem but I still feel that you miss my main contention: that it is a matter of political loyalty as much as or even more than one of temperament.

That it matters little whether I personally (or you) like the church or need it —because, whether I like it or not, the church is desirable and necessary.

I can quite understand people neither liking nor feeling need of the church but if I am right in thinking that all the ills of modern 'industrialism' are the result of the loss of religion and the powerlessness of religious organizations then I think we are in duty bound to join the church if anyways possible and we are in a bad way if it's not possible.

The fact is I think the church should rule the world like a government. If there were no church it would be necessary to make one. If I am going to live in England under the English government, I want to be a naturalized English citizen and not an outsider. If I am going to submit to the Church's vision of the significance of the universe —and you admit that the Catholic Faith is such that such submission is possible — then I want to be a member of the Church and not an outsider.

The desirability or necessity of submission is a temperamental matter.

The desirability or necessity of membership is a political matter.

(e.g. If I believed in Socialism I shd. not only call myself a Socialist —I'd join a Socialist Society.)

I wonder if my point is clear now. I also wonder if you're still in America. I hope you have had or are having a successful time anyway. When you are back I want to see you and show you some photographs of my latest efforts. Yours ever

ERIC GILL

25 : TO WILLIAM ROTHENSTEIN

Ditchling   *5-3-1912   Good Friday*

My dear Rothenstein: Thank you very much for sending the
telegram which came as a great surprise and was very welcome
news as we were down to our last shilling on Monday last and
had only received a chq. for £2. 2. 0 since then — which wasn't
very hopeful. Now we can at least pay the rent & get on for
a little while. I am very much obliged to you for the trouble
you have taken in the matter. In fact I don't know how to
thank you enough for all your help and encouragement. I shall
come and see you as soon as I can.

I'm glad Coomaraswamy liked the 'acrobatic'. I'm glad for
him to possess it too. He's a respectable person. I shall
certainly write to him.

I hear from Belgium that they cannot take my figure of the
B.V.M. on account of its size & weight — so that's no go.
I'm getting on fast now with Fry's statue & should like you to
see it soon. If you can't manage to run down for a night,
which wd. be splendid, I must get a photograph of it to show
you. But come if you can and will.

Meanwhile, on your suggestion, I'm planning to carve a
series of small polished marble figures — I've got about half a
dozen in my eye. With love from us both. Yours ever

ERIC GILL

26 : TO WILLIAM ROTHENSTEIN

Ditchling   *24-4-1912*

My dear Rothenstein: [. . .] I have to tell you that Fry has
been here to see his statue! I was in London! Wasn't it
unfortunate? He sent no notice of his coming because he
came on the spur of the moment with Warren (of Lewes) in
Warren's motor. (That was last Monday). However he

appears to have been really pleased with his statue, of which I now send you a rough photographic snapshot, so that's all right. What do you think? Warren was greatly taken with the relief group (Man & Woman embracing) and wants to buy it! What do you think of that? Of course he may not have it. I saw him yesterday in Lewes (he asked me to come & see him) and I asked him £60 for it. Do you think that's all right? He said he'd let me know to-day or to-morrow after he'd gone into his affairs (how do you interpret that?).

I wrote to Count Kessler a few days ago (being desperate) and asked him, if he still liked the thing, if he'd buy the little *sea-side panel* with supporting figure for £20 or if he had no place for it to let me know if he knew of any one else who'd care for it. He didn't reply at once but before I heard from him I got a cheque for £20 from his London agent! I have now heard from him and he *appears* very pleased to have it! Am I not in luck?

Listen again –I wrote to J. M. Keynes (of King's, Cambridge) and asked him, as an admirer, if he'd give me a fiver for the *Votes for Women* panel. He sent the fiver by return and I at once dispatched the stone! (Five pounds is pretty cheap I daresay).

Listen again –I sold a small figure of a boy (like the one you admired when I sent a post card to you at Normandy) to my brother-in-law for ten bob! I was sick of the sight of it and thought George's face on a half sov. wd. look prettier – Matter of taste I suppose (some people say George is damned ugly) –Well, anyway –I managed to scrape up –with the help of you and Coomaraswamy –about £50 and have thus been able to pay up about a third of my debts. I only wish Fry hadn't paid me 40 out of 60 in advance. Very good of him – but now I haven't got it to come.

27 : TO WILLIAM ROTHENSTEIN

En route for Ditchling   *Thursday 2.0* ⟨*1912?*⟩

Dear Rothenstein: I've learnt, too late, that to-morrow evening at the Guild 'Apprenticeship' is the subject. I can't go. But I wish I could. This is to say that *Penty* who is to read the first paper is against us. Roughly his view is that Art being largely concerned with form it is chiefly necessary to set up a *standard* for all and sundry to copy. The Trajan Alphabet for instance or what not. He thinks I'm unpractical & idealist. (That may be.) But anyway if you should be going I hope you will feel inclined to speak. The whole subject of the A & C Movement will probably come up, and as the A & C. Exhibition opens next week the time is opportune. Yours   A. E. R. G.

Of course I may be wrong & Penty etc. may be on the right tack, but I doubt it.

28 : TO GEOFFREY KEYNES

Ditchling   *16-9-1912*

I am most awfully sorry to have missed you again. What a nuisance —However I hope you'll be in this part again soon. I am sorry to have missed Rupᵗ Brooke too.

I intend to come to Cowley St. when next I'm in town & take my chance of missing you *there*. (Do you know Tom Bridson who lives in your lane?) Yrs.   ERIC GILL

29 : TO WILLIAM ROTHENSTEIN

Ditchling, Sussex   *17-12-1912*

My dear Rothenstein: I am sorry, I am in many ways so damned an idiot, I did somewhat misunderstand your letter. However it's quite all right. The work is now in full swing and going strong and I hope soon to be able to ask for the drawing of profile.

I am very grieved that you shd. be so depressed. What I can do or say to help I don't know. You have my sympathy very much indeed — but what's that? I'm one of the people that believe in your work, as I understand it, but I really don't see where you come in with the present-day whirlpool. You are not going with any particular current, and instead of circling towards the centre of King Neptune's favours you are running a risk of being cast off, centrifugally, into the outer seas & . . . but this is no good. What with Post Impressionists on the one hand and Orpen, McKennal & Co on the other there's not much chance for anyone decent as the money is all used up. It's different for me — I'm a mere beginner & have got the fly-wheel & safety-valve of letter cutting to hearten me when sculpture & the modern world seem equally bloody. Your work is so much your own &, if I may say so, extremely serious. People now want either to be flattered or fooled — not treated seriously as if they might be the sons of God. I can only say for God's sake don't lose heart — buck up and get into the country & get as well as possible. There — I've talked to you like an equal — which I don't feel to be — but you must forgive me. I should like nothing better than to come & spend a day or two with you presently — sometime after Xmas. Yours ever   ERIC G.

30 : TO WILLIAM ROTHENSTEIN

Ditchling, Sussex   *1-2-1913*

My dear Rothenstein: [. . .] Thank you very much for your letter of the 26th. & invitation to come to you soon. Yes — I will do so. I can't come before the end of February tho. I am very rushed with work at present and also rather hard up. But as soon as I can I will come & will let you know as soon as I know when. Tombstones, Tombstones, Tombstones, also a few quite decent jobs including a design for a new 'Great Seal'! But tho. they (the Ld. Chancellor's office) have done me the honour to ask me to make a design —I bet you a quid they won't take my design when they see it. Is it likely? I think not. Me do a portrait of Georgey on his throne! Did you ever see the Great Seal of Henry III —1230? It's a marvel. Since then things have 'appened. Love from us both to you all —Yrs.   ERIC GILL

31 : TO WILLIAM ROTHENSTEIN

Ditchling   *4-3-1913*

My dear Rothenstein: I want to tell you that my wife and I have now been received into the Catholic Church.[1] We have your blessing I know —and you have our love & prayers. So now I shall jolly well buck up.

I've been wondering if you have seen the tombstone yet and if you liked it all right. This evening I hear from Albert (about an art project he's running) and he says he likes it very much. I'm glad. I also have got an 'art project' and I much want to talk to you about it. When shall I be able to come down to see you! I'm wondering if, supposing I can raise the wind, you'll be at your farm during the weekend beginning Saturday March 22nd. Will you? I can't come this week nor next so if you'll be there I wd. endeavour to come on the 22nd. All news when we meet. Yours ever   ERIC GILL

32 : TO WILLIAM ROTHENSTEIN

Ditchling, Sussex   *20-5-1913*

My dear Rothenstein: Your letter delighted me very much and you give me great encouragement —as indeed you always do. Thank you dearly.

[1] On E. G's. birthday, Feb. 22nd.

D

Yes, I guessed you'd be having a good time this fine weather. It must be specially good for you – but it's good for us all. I wish my aims & objects as an artist were as clear cut to me as yours are to you. The war between the flesh & the spirit is a trial at present. If I wanted either of them to win it would be easier but I don't and that's what makes it difficult. I hope to win through & your encouragement is a great blessing. Right O –I'll send the apprentice later on. Will you let me know when it's convenient? You have only to say the word & I'll pack him off. Love from us both   Yours   ERIC GILL

P.S. By the bye –beastly rude of me –thanks v. much for cheque. But why 15/-? It is at least ½ as much again as I ask for the painted plasters.   E. G.

33 : TO WILLIAM ROTHENSTEIN

Ditchling, Sussex   *31-7-1913*

My dear Rothenstein: I do very much agree with you in your criticisms of the little brass mother & child although I do not feel perhaps quite so strongly the lack of feet. You see it was the attitude of the child against his mother that I was chiefly concerned for and in a sort of way my 'inspiration' didn't run to feet. However I daresay it ought to have feet whether 'inspired' or otherwise and I don't think I'll omit them thus again. As for the execution –there I am wholly with you of course. I can see clearly enough that if I am ever to do a satisfactory bronze I must do all the chasing and finishing myself. But so far I haven't worked on metal at all (barring tin-tacks) & so have tried to get the founders to do the finishing. I am very unhappy about it. They seem to mess the thing up first of all in the casting & then make it worse in the chasing.

As soon as ever I get the chance I'm going to get hold of some tools & do some chasing myself. Everything depends on that. The bronze founders aren't artists, they're only mechanics.

Now about a show in the autumn. As you know I shd. like to have an exhibition with you very much indeed & I hope we'll be able to meet before very long & talk it all over. The *where* is the difficulty. My stuff is so frightfully heavy that it is difficult to find a floor that will take it. Where had you thought of? I've been meeting Marchant several times lately & he seems keen on my having a show with him but I see no chance of that as his place is too difficult to get into altogether even if the floors wd. hold — which I doubt — though of course something could be done by shoring up the floor underneath. Good strong timbers wd. do the trick. Well, so long — for now. I rejoice for you in this good weather. I wish we weren't such leagues apart. Yours ever & love from us both to you all   ERIC GILL

P.S. I must tell you that we are about to buy a little farm near here. No such beautiful house as yours, but a decent little place in a heavenly part. 1¾ miles north of here. *Ethel*'s borrowing the money from an uncle to purchase it. *I* shall pay the interest — I hope.   E. G.

34 : TO WILLIAM ROTHENSTEIN

Ditchling, Sussex   *19-8-1913*

Dear Rothenstein: [. . .] I am glad you are busy & 'serene'. I am pretty much of both myself, though I find things difficulter & difficulter as I get more experience. The mistakes I made without knowing I made them in my first works I cannot now make with the same innocence and as I am less & less inclined to do what I am by nature best fitted to do (i.e. wicked works) things do not get easier.

As for our farm — well it is a matter of two acres only — but enough for us. We haven't paid the money yet because we are still in process of borrowing it, but we have every hope that we shall succeed before long. We are paying a hundred or so too much but want the place & so can't let it slip on that account — But we're awful hard up & shall be more so later I expect. Yours   ERIC G.

I'll let you know when Cribb is coming to do the inscription at Painswick.

35 : TO GEOFFREY KEYNES

Ditchling   *20-8-1913*

My dear Keynes: Of course I'll be only too delighted to do something for you for the sum named. I gather that you want it to be a 'Mother & Child' same (or thereabouts) as R. B.'s. I think I can manage it for you and without very much delay as I hope to have some stone in in the course of a day or two. If it works out at more than £10 I'll let you know but I won't run it up if I can help it.

I was awfully sorry not to be more hospitable on Monday — it just happened like that. I would have liked to have walked to Lewes with you.

Anyway we hope to see you again soon. Perhaps you'll come & fetch your stone away — if you like it well enough — as I hope you may. I'm awfully pleased that you like R. B.'s so much. Yours   ERIC GILL

36 : TO GEOFFREY KEYNES

Ditchling   *30-9-1913*

My dear Keynes: I've made you a carving of a 'Mother & Child'. But following your general instructions to make it as big as possible (in reason) I've made it of such a size and have consequently taken such a time over it as to make me feel that if you can run to the £15 (instead of £10 or £12) you spoke of I'd be glad. I'm sorry but you have only to say so if you don't care to run to the £15 & I'll do another one smaller. Then again you may not like the thing & so not want it at any price. Will you come & see? We shd. be v. glad to see you again. Or wd. you rather I sent it up on spec? Let me know. Do you happen to know Raverat's friend Dudley Ward's address? I've done a carving for him too at J. R.'s instigation & want to communicate with him. Yours

ERIC GILL

Is Rupert B. back from America yet?

37 : TO GEOFFREY KEYNES

Ditchling   *7-10-1913*

My dear Keynes: I was very glad to get your letter this morning. I am very glad you really like the stone and I think it a very good idea to put a little inscription round the bottom on three sides. The cost of such an addition wd. be so little that as in the case of 'this 'ere tortoise' there wd. be no charge for it. As you suggest the Magnificat what do you say to this: — 'ESURIENTES IMPLEVIT BONIS: ET DIVITES DIMISIT INANES.'? There might be many applications in that.

I'm glad you caught your train — yes, it was a wonderful evening. It must have been fine along the hills — and I'm very glad you enjoyed your visit — I did. *She* is getting on very well now. I hope she'll be up by the week end. Yours ERIC GILL

38 : TO WILLIAM ROTHENSTEIN

Ditchling Common,[1] *Sussex*   *11-12-1913*

Dear Rothenstein: Many thanks for your letter. I'm sorry again to have missed seeing you in London but I was in town

[1] On Nov. 11th, E. G. had moved from Ditchling Village to Hopkins' Crank, Ditchling Common.

on Tuesday & could not stay over the night as my wife cannot be left for long yet. However there is plenty of time as far as you are concerned & I hope we shall meet soon to discuss many things. My own difficulty is that I have two large sculptures which I do not wish to take to our new house if I can avoid it. The expense of moving large stones is considerable & I thought, if I was going to have a show, now was the time: for I could move the things straight to London instead of to our place on the Common first & then a second time to London.

As for the Alpine Club: no place could be better —it is a beautiful room & big enough, but then again the difficulty is mine, for I don't believe my heavy stuff would ever be got up the stairs! I fear we may find it impossible to have a show together on that account, for it is imperative that I shd. have an easily accessible ground floor place. I wish it were otherwise, for the Alpine Club, could I only get up there, would be just the thing. Well, anyway, I must do something soon, for the two big stones I speak of must be removed from Ditchling at Xmas, and as I say, if I'm going to move them, I may as well move them to London.

I hear that C. L. R., most kind man, is to be with you this week end.

I now send the dimensions of the new dog collar required for our spaniel. I hope the smith will be able to let us have it before very long. Do you mind if I keep the big one to look at for a bit longer? I am loth to part with it. By the way, what sort of price are these collars? Yours   ERIC GILL

39 : TO GEOFFREY KEYNES

Ditchling Common, Sx.   *31-12-1913*

The exhibition I told you is coming on now. It is to open at the Goupil Gallery on Jan 9th. Can I borrow your stone? You will remember you said I might. Please let me know,

&, if I may, I will arrange for it in Catalogue and call with taxi early next week to fetch it away. Good luck to you in 1914.   ERIC GILL

Please tell me a convenient hour for the fetching away (if I may).

40 : TO ANDRÉ RAFFALOVICH

Ditchling Common   5-7-1914

My dear Mr. Raffalovich: I am delighted that you shd. treat me with the utmost familiarity. Alas! no, my umbrella is safely in the drain pipe (still I do possess one you see).

I have now got safely back home again (on Friday evening) & found your most kind letter awaiting me. I also found the songs. How good & generous you are. I had a most comfortable journey to London from Edinburgh. I enjoyed the experience very much in fact. It was great fun too. Now I must thank you very much for the delightful time you gave me at Edinburgh. What a round of visits & parties — what nice, good people — what a host & hostess! I indeed thank you very much for all.

I shall of course be very pleased indeed to come again & hope that will be soon — though it cannot be just for a month or two. I must now make a great start with the Westminster Station.

As for your commissions — I shall be delighted to execute them. I shall be seeing Siordet soon I expect and will endeavour to get him to let me draw him for you. It will be a very interesting job too. How amusing if he has *two* profiles! I also have your letter about A. B's sister and I shall certainly call upon her the next time I am in London.

Miss Gribbell's most magnificent parcels of cakes & sweets arrived yesterday evening. Were they appreciated? You may say so. What good things, and persons, Edinburgh provides to be sure. The two elder girls have to-day been writing to

Miss Gribbell & I shall post their letters herewith. Again –
thank you and Miss Gribbell very much for all your kindness –
I am yours sincerely   ERIC GILL

Yes, thank you, Ethel, my wife, & the daughters are all very
well indeed & gave me a great welcome home. When you
come South you will come and see us won't you? We look
forward to your doing so.

                41 : TO ANDRÉ RAFFALOVICH

Ditchling Common   *24-9-1914*

My dear Raffalovich: I am really very grateful to you for
sending me Father Gray's encouraging report. Thank you
very much and him also. I am the more pleased because the
architect to the cathedral, one John Marshall, has written to
me in a very different style saying that it must '*now*' be clear
to me that my style of work is neither suitable for the peculiar
light of the Cathedral nor the Catholic public (curious, that
word 'now' – underlined above – as though the blame for the
importation of my work into the Cathedral attached to *me*!).
I have replied to him urging him to forego any decision until
at least three or four more of the panels are erected and
suggesting that the one already fixed should be covered with
a sheet meanwhile. I have pointed out to him, as I wrote to
you, that the 'Stations' are a series and should not be judged
individually and that a panel that may seem unsatisfactory alone
may fall into line well enough with its fellows (and that, if
any particular panel seemed, when all were done, bad or
wrong, that one might be done again perhaps). He has not
replied to me as yet so I am going on steadily with the 2nd
'Station' assuming that things will clear. I do not wish to
inflict bad work on our chief church but I do not think anyone
is yet in a position to judge whether the work is going to be
bad or not. They have definitely given me the 'order' for the

work and they must have the courage to see it through. I hope they will see this. Oh, but the light is bad! There's no doubt of that. The stone looks utterly different from what it did in my shop. I will let you know what happens.

Rheims! What do I say to Rheims? I say nothing at all. I have no words. Louvain, where I went in the summers of 1912 & 1913 and where —at the Benedictine Abbey on Mont César —I received my first instructions,[1] Louvain was bad enough —but this —Rheims, the highest leaping flame of all the Gothic fires —a great fire which curled round the very throne of God —it was alive, it burned, it sparkled, it laughed. I am punished indeed —well are we served! We deserve nothing else. We have made the houses of God mere quarries for sightseers. What was Rheims to us? 'A fine specimen of Gothic,' 'the crowning place of French Kings,' it contained priceless this & priceless that and masterpieces by Tintoretto & Titian, we are 'indignant' & issue protests to all the neutral powers. Good Lord! The thing was a mystery and we measured it. It was a great shout and we sat and listened. And now we are indignant. I have often said we had need to construct a whip of thongs wherewith to drive the money changers out of the Temple of England. God has found a whip of German guns wherewith to deprive the money changers of the temples of France. Why shd. Paris be indignant? What was Rheims to it? A blooming museum —a kind of provincial branch of the Louvre. I do not care. The sculptures of Rheims are gone. Good. If we cannot construct a Christian Europe in this age, we certainly are not fit to be the guardians of the evidences of the Christian Europe of the past. The whole thing shd. be wiped out. It wd. be completely just. When we want an altar we can build one. And when God has finished with this whip He will discard it. May we deserve to be His instruments! [. . .]

We are all back again and well. We hope you are both well also. I am yours affectionately   ERIC GILL

[1] Cf. *Autobiography*, pp. 184-7; U.S.A. ed., pp. 191-4.

42 : TO WILLIAM ROTHENSTEIN

Ditchling Common, Sx.   *10-10-1914*

My dear Rothenstein: Many thanks for returning my funny book and indeed many thanks for the *Mystic Trees*.[1] I am very glad to have this latter (there are good things, very good, in the former for that matter as e.g. 'as music binds into a strict delight' — 'strict delight' is very good — isn't it?) and the more so as I recently got *Songs of Adoration*[1] and admired them much. I don't know what to say about that kind of poetry — as poetry. It is felicitous enough, surely, but that is the least part of it. I think the really moving quality in it is the extraordinary atmosphere of a shrine which it has. To read ten or more of the poems one after the other is to feel that you are — whether or no you have understood or responded to individual lines or words or thoughts — in a place where precious things are ritually preserved & worshipped. Of course they are too special, too withdrawn from the mess and dirt of this admirable world — but how charming — how completely enfolded in the everlasting arms. And now they are both dead and possibly seeing things face to face. R.I.P.

I wonder how things are going with you. I guess you keep at it & find 'no end' to do. Is the house nearly finished or has the war delayed you in that matter? As for us: we are getting on all right more or less. I am fortunate in having this Westminster Work to do, but I am sorry to say the first 'Station', now fixed in the Cathedral, is not a success — not from my point of view. I have nearly finished the 2nd one and hope it will be better — but I am distressed about the 1st. The light in the Cathedral is extraordinarily difficult and makes things look entirely different from what they do in my shop. The expressions of faces (a subtle enough thing in any case) are completely changed or obliterated and the colour I put on the edges of garments is not a success. However, after some

[1] By Michael Field.

worrying correspondence with the architect, and some doubts as to whether or no, after all, the Cathedral authorities wd. not endeavour to back out & get rid of me, I am glad to say things are settling down and I am going ahead with the work hoping to do better each time.

I have got a very nice commission, for a Church in Glasgow (through D. Y. Cameron!), to carve an image of the Madonna & Child, 4 ft high, in red sandstone. This is splendid — red sandstone is most exciting too. I am going ahead with this so soon as ever I get the stone.

A small memorial to George Gissing for Manchester University, just completed, has been a recent & I think successful work.

The farm prospers — tho. lack of rain is a trial. The chickens are well & our first pig (killed on October 1st.) makes excellent eating and will supply us for some time to come. Our potatoes are not bad & the beer in these parts is all that could be wished. Money is short — of course — the war has ruined one client & perhaps killed another — but we have known worse times. I hope *you* are not very hard pressed — tho. I fear you are. The destruction of the evidences of the former Christian civilization of France and Belgium will be followed, I hope, by the destruction of present German atheism and, even more I hope, that of ourselves. May this teach us — but I fear it is too much to hope — not to slobber any more about art. A man I met yesterday promulgated to me a great scheme, as he thought it, by which, after the war, all the 'art' treasures accumulated in German museums shd. as an indemnity be handed over to Belgium and thus make Belgium an 'art' centre for the world. I poured, as I hope, a proper and sufficient scorn upon so damned a proposal. But there you have it — that is the sort of thing everybody will suggest. Another man, I am told, writing to the *Daily Mirror*, from *Streatham*, (Oh! Streatham) suggests that it is a matter for congratulation that modern engineering is capable of such wonderful feats because, after the war, Cologne Cathedral

(Cologne, I say, that German wedding cake) can easily be taken down and removed and rebuilt at Rheims. Oh Lord! Well, well, we all send our love to you all. Yours

ERIC GILL

Another man said to me 'What do you think about Rheims?' I said 'What?' He said 'You know I never was so frightfully keen on the Gothic —now S. Paul's. . . .'

'Oh! hell' I said. Pray for me.   E. G.

43 : TO ANDRÉ RAFFALOVICH

Ditchling Common, Sx.   *4-11-1914*

My dear Raffalovich: Thank you for your letter of the 2nd. [. . .] I have not yet heard anything from Westminster. This is alarming & inconvenient. I finished and sent off the 2nd. 'Station' yesterday. I hope to see it fixed up next week. I am now working on the XIIIth. — a very moving subject — and also on my Glasgow statue. I will bring a drawing of this latter to show you. And we must also discuss what I am next to do for you. Yours affectionately   ERIC GILL

44 : TO ANDRÉ RAFFALOVICH

Ditchling Common   *23-12-1914*

My dear Raffalovich: We thank you very much for all your kind wishes and we also wish you & Miss Gribbell a very happy Christmas and New Year.

I am having an enforced but not regretted holiday this week for, in addition to the hindrance to work involved in the usual preparations for Xmas, my two Canadian brothers and my architect brother are coming down to-day on the way home to Chichester for Christmas (the Canadians are luckily among those whose Christmas leave fell from the 22nd. to 28th.) and are spending the night here and, as a sister is also staying here for a day or two, we shall have a merry party to-night I think. The children are all very excited & happy and the weather is better than of late it has been. We send the enclosed with our united loves & affections.[1]

I have instructed Everard Meynell who keeps the Museum St. Shop to dispatch, at once, the three images as you request. Many thanks for the order. I note that now six images, which equals six guineas, are to be written off our account. Again — thanks. I hope these will be received by their owners before Christmas.

I am very glad to hear that John Duncan liked my drawing of you. That is good. Father Gray wants me to carve a low relief panel on the lines of that drawing. If this may be done — may I make a new drawing for the purpose when I come north again?

I am getting on all right with the work at present. I have nearly finished the Glasgow statue and am well ahead with the next 'Station' for Westminster. By the end of January I hope to be ready to come to Edinburgh, or early in February. The second Station is now fixed up and I await the architect's certificate therefor. I rejoice in continued expressions of approval on the part of respected friends on account of the first one put up. I shall have to approve of it myself in the end it seems!

Now a small request: When I was staying with you last I sequestered a few sheets (you know whence) of paper because it struck me as particularly nice paper for taking proofs of engravings upon. I have since tried it and it is excellent. I enclose sample for identification and illustration. It is beautifully strong and yet thin & yet pleasant. Would you mind telling me where I can get the stuff? I would be glad to know.

I hope you and Miss Gribbell are well. We are so. The war is extraordinarily difficult to follow. I hope all goes well with

[1] Below these words is a tiny ink-drawing of a fish, to which I can find no clue.

our part in it —it seems to be doing so. But the siege of Germany is an immense undertaking. Scarborough, that wanton business, will do them no good & will only serve as a stiffener for us. It is an amazing exhibition of hatred. I am yours affectionately

ERIC GILL

45 : TO WILLIAM ROTHENSTEIN

Ditchling Common, Sx.   *23-12-1914*

My dear Rothenstein: [. . .] I am getting on all right at present. I am blest in having so much work to do. The warning you give me is opportune or at any rate appropriate. I feel the danger of vagueness very much and more and more feel the necessity of asking the question (& demanding an answer too) 'what's it all bloomin' well for' as did the unfortunate giant in Wells' *Food of the Gods*.

I'm sorry I've no photographs to send you at present. Our local photographer has gone to the war and so I haven't bothered to have any made lately. This Westminster work is very difficult & I am far from pleased with the portion already done & fixed. The reflected light from the floor and the conflicting shadows thrown by the electric lights upon all sides are very hard on low relief carvings. But I hope by the time I get to the 14th I shall have achieved some success. (Truly it is a marvellous chance anyway.) And then apart from such technical difficulties there is of course the terrible difficulty of realizing precisely what I am actually doing and what the 'Stations' actually are, complicated as that difficulty is by the absence (apparently) of any but a sentimental (anecdotal as Fry wd. say) attitude upon the part of the Catholics in general —my clients to wit & those for whom I am working & whose approval I do most deeply desire (vainly I fear).

I hope you are well & all your family too. We are. We send our love & all good wishes for Xmas. Yours ever

ERIC GILL

46 : TO HENRY ATKINSON

Ditchling Common, Sx. England   *4-2-1915*

My dear Atkinson: Your letter from Egypt arrived long ago and at last I make attempt to answer it. I was very glad to hear from you and to know that things were going strong with you. When I heard from you before (in April 1914) you were in the middle of bad times and when I called at your office in Q. V. St. I heard no very cheerful news of you. I hope all continues to go well & that you & Mrs. Atkinson and Sheila are all in the best of health.

We were indeed surprised to learn of your flight into Egypt presumably to escape the destroying hand of a modern Herod (if we may believe a small half of what we hear & read of his doings!) However he was not to be done and you are to receive his emissaries in spite of all. We in England see very little of the war and were it not for the presence of a regiment of Territorials who are billeted near here & are training daily on the common we shd. see nothing at all. But of course the newspapers will not let us rest —the swine.—The press alone is vile.

I have got three brothers at the war —two came with the Canadian Contingent and are completing their training on Salisbury Plain —& one is a lieutenant in the 1st. Cambridge-shires —he has only this week gone to 'the front'. Also I have a brother-in-law who enlisted in 'Kitchener's Army'. So you see we are more or less involved. For myself I cannot yet afford the luxury of soldiering tho. I wd. be glad enough to go (and, I dare say, to come back). But my financial affairs here are too difficult to leave and as I am lucky, fortunate or favoured enough to have a lot of work to do I shall endeavour to stick it out at home & wait till they start putting their beastly heads up over our hill-tops before I bestir myself. It must be either one thing or another. I can't do the half-and-half business as some people can and work all day & drill in the evenings. If I can't go into the army I'll go on with my work as near as may be as if nothing were happening. How are things really going I wonder? You cannot judge from what the papers say. Still it seems hopeful on the whole and at any rate I think we may safely say that, whatever *we* may be doing, *they* are not winning yet. But it's the Navy I'm keen on. That's a fine clean warfare* – good gunnery & seamanship & courage & no ruination of the homes & towns & countrysides! To sink a battleship is better than to smash a church. (I think we may say we have now avenged Admiral Cradock – what with the Falklands & last week in the North Sea.) Still of course it must come back to land fighting in the end.

I was very interested to read of your work in Egypt. How rum it seems to think that it could matter whether or no a 'wireless' station could be erected in 5 weeks or 18 months & all the time you saw yourself surrounded by things upon which time seems to have made no impression. That obelisk which you say is over 4000 yrs. old – do you think they rushed the making of it? Perhaps they did – who knows?

Well, as I said above, I'm lucky to have plenty of work on hand – just now. Last May I got a commission to carve 14 panels (each about 6' 0" square) representing scenes from 'the Passion' (generally called the Stations of the Cross – if you understand) for the new Cathedral at Westminster and this is more than two years' work! They are in a stone called Hopton-wood Stone (a fossil limestone – semi-crystallized – from Derbyshire) which though not technically a marble is as good and nearly as hard. So I'm busy. Naturally I was very keen to get this work though the financial aspects of it are not very alluring. It is one of the best sculpture commissions one could have. I wonder if it will last out the war? Apart from this work I have only a few small jobs on hand – I'm hoping to get just enough to make up the necessary 'bread & butter'. We

* Not that the Scarborough business is particularly clean, but that is not our affair & neither is that sort of thing essential to war by sea as it is to war by land apparently.

are all very well & contented in our little farm. The only difficulty is that I can't find enough time to do all that wants doing
out and about. Things are always either growing or wearing
out —and when you have even so little a place as this is there
are always a lot of improvements you want to make —i.e. if
the place is your very own —otherwise it's no use wanting.
First I had to build a workshop for myself, then a cart lodge,
then (the ground being heavy clay) we found it practically a
necessity to have brick paths from the house to the various
outbuildings, then the paddock wanted a fence across one end
to keep animals from straying into the orchard, & so on. But
we shall have to stop improving for a bit now — the war makes
things too difficult. Flour is nearly 10/- a bushel, eggs (not
our own) are 2/6 & 3/- a dozen, bread would be 4d a loaf if
we did not bake our own. However we have not yet got an
education bill to pay —we are managing so far to teach the kids
ourselves. Ethel teaches them reading, writing, sewing &
'tables' & all domestic accomplishments & I do the arithmetic,
drawing, Latin, History & Geography. We are wondering
when the inspector will look in on us! Damn all this state
interference. What about the Insurance Act? As for me I
have not yet seen a stamp and do not intend to do so. You
never were an official socialist —now I am like you —unattached
& free to vote against anything & everything —but what we've
got to do now is to finish this bloody war & then set about
finishing the bloody politicians & their bloodier press. I don't
suppose we shall succeed —the bankers are too clever & we too
timid. I agree very much with a friend of mine who wrote to
me the other day (a frenchman who, to his great chagrin, was,
owing to a slight spinal curvature, struck off the conscript lists
& is now in England) that 'we who cannot die fighting must
live fighting', we must justify our lives & to that end work as
never before.

What a long time it is since the 'House breakers' meetings
and all the societies & meetings we used to go to. I suppose
you are a student of the 'national' question in Egypt. Do you

E

ever hear talk of Wilfrid Scawen Blunt? A cousin of his is a pal of mine (now a dispatch rider in France). I know the politicians think W. S. B. was an overweening meddler –but what do the Egyptians think of him? And what is it like to live in what is, to all intents and purposes, a British Colony? Are we just or are we not? Are we simply out to make money –or have we really an enthusiasm to spread British justice throughout the world? What is the British culture like when seen from the distance?

Well –we all send our love to you all & hope to hear from you again. We hope you will escape a Turkish victory & come home some day & see us all here. Yours very sincerely

ERIC GILL

47 : TO GEOFFREY KEYNES

Ditchling Common, Sx.   *31-3-1915*

My dear Keynes: I have been on the point of writing to you for the last two months and now your second letter comes & puts me to shame. I heard from the Cornfords that you were with the R.A.M.C. & almost wished myself wounded to find myself in your extremely capable hands even tho. the result shd. be that you deprived me of a limb. I expect you are having plenty of bloody experience –at intervals.

Yes, I am going on with my work (what is left of it) and am progressing more or less favourably with the Westminster 'Stations'. The third is now 'up'. Of course I am extraordinarily lucky to have this work to do –for apart from one or two small inscription jobs I have nothing else and several jobs on hand before the war have succumbed. That Great Seal, for instance, is indefinitely postponed.

Ditchling Common is now the scene of military operations. The Territorials, billeted in Burgess Hill & Hayward's Heath, use it daily & many of them come to us for drinks & cake of a morning (cocoa $\frac{1}{2}$d a cup –cake $\frac{1}{2}$d a slice)! I also have put on the armour (i.e. khaki) of home protection & go drilling & shooting – a mixture of fun & boredom. No doubt we look pretty foolish – but you never know and there's always the chance of our coming in useful. I've seen the Raverat's several times lately. Poor Jacques R. seems very shaky tho. he says he's much better. Any way he's full of enthusiasms & high ideals & *she* is doing admirable painting. Their latest scheme is to help me build a chapel here on our plot and then come and paint frescos! I've got out a preliminary plan & am getting estimates from the builder. I hope it will materialize. It wd. be splendid. Wouldn't it? But before I do that I must put up another small workshop. I find it such an incessant nuisance having drawing & writing housed beneath the same roof as carving. Everything gets coated with dust and it gets on my nerves. By the way: or rather to return to war: I've now got three brothers in the trenches. I wonder if you'll come across them or they you! One is a subaltern in the 1st Cambridgeshires (Kenneth) & the other two (Evan & Vernon) are gunners in the 1st Batt^y. 1st Brigade, Canadian F.A. They are twins! They come from Regina, Sas. You might keep an eye open for any wounded Gills therefore. So far (i.e. up to last Wednesday when last I heard) they are unhurt. I don't know whether they were at N. Chapelle or not. They write the most fearfully cheerful letters. This war is amazing. It is grotesque too. Fancy a table & chairs in a gunners' 'dug-out' & upon the table a vase of wild lavender (oh Lord!) & upon the walls pictures – picture post cards, cigarette cards & a picture of 'the Ascension'. – So they write – the Canadians. Aren't they marvellous children? We have some wounded here at Ditchling (branch of the Red X. you know). They've been up here twice & play at shooting with a small rifle I've got. You'd think they'd be tired of the thought of letting off a gun.

Well now, about those boxers – (wrestlers if you prefer it) – of course I'd be delighted to dispose of them to you. It is still painted. I doubt if the paint wd. come off v. satisfactorily. It wd. be sure to stick in the pores of the stone a good deal. However if necessary I cd. have a try. About the price. I don't know what to ask. War is war & I must snatch at any chance of selling things — besides I'd like you to have the stone. At the Goupil Exhib^n. it was priced at £42 but that was absurd. What wd. you think of £20? Let me know. I wd. consider any offer from you.

We all send our love to you & Betty (my eldest unmarried dau.) has done an Easter picture for you which I send herewith. I'm sure you'll like it (I regret parting with it anyway). Good luck to you. Yours   ERIC GILL

(private H.P.B.)
hush!

48 : TO GEOFFREY KEYNES

Ditchling Common, Sx.   *9-4-1915*

My dear Keynes: Your letter and cheque came this morning — very many thanks indeed. How you manage to spend so much in war time, and on something for somebody else, I cannot imagine. However I make no complaint. [. . .]

I am glad you liked B's picture — but I knew you would. It was, inexpertness apart, really first class. The composition & colour were splendid I thought, & I do not remember ever to have seen the rock-hewn tomb better managed. You shd. have given us warning and we would have sent you some (hot) cross buns — the miss'es made some very good ones, well spiced, with sugar crosses on the top.

Last time I wrote I forgot to enclose the photograph of a little (2 foot) stone which I have lately done. I send it now as you asked for photographs of anything of the sort. This is practically the only thing, apart from the 'Stations', I have done recently in the sculpture line. I hope you will like it. It represents an advance in the appreciation of the human body I think. Love from us all. Yours ever   ERIC GILL

49 : TO WILLIAM ROTHENSTEIN

D. Common, Sx.   *12-5-1915*

My dear Rothenstein: I am very glad indeed to have your letter of the 9th. from Moreton and to have the good news that you find the Stations at Westminster so satisfactory. I am delighted and proud. I am really very much encouraged by what you say and feel that I can now go ahead in a much more cheerful frame of mind. I am now doing the first of the Stations: 'Jesus is condemned to death': a difficult subject for me because so much depends on the exact attitude of Jesus. I hope to pull through but I do not feel good at subtleties. Did you have any ideas about colour when you went to the Cathedral? You know I think colour shd. be used. But the architect seems afraid to risk anything and I'm bound to attend to him.

About the Village Cross: I dare say you are right about my design, i.e. I dare say you are right in thinking that the country people are to-day what you say they are. I am very glad you like the design in itself. I do not believe that when carved (after all my drawing is very much of a scribble & paper is not stone) the thing, as conceived of by me, wd. be either so ecclesiastical or poetical or wistful —especially if, as I think wd. be best for a wet climate, the colour were omitted. The thing wd. be quite square & the carvings wd. I think take away from the weight & squareness very little. After all, this is all it is.[1]

I can't help thinking that it is chiefly my pretty sketch which suggests all the trouble. However I'm going to make an alternative design for Debenham & then we'll see what happens. It's a fine job to get, isn't it?

I don't understand what you mean by 'a Religion imported from an alien civilization'. I suppose you mean Christianity — surely its a little late in the day to speak of Christianity as an 'importation'? Any way I don't see any difficulty and I can't imagine why any one shd. do so. I was brought up more or

---

[1] Sketch below, with the marginal note 'Jolly nice lump of stone, eh?'

less Christian & it seems natural enough to me. Of course I understand the trouble of what you call 'moral gymnastics' – but I think that trouble is avoidable. I know that I do far more moral gymnastics in my efforts to escape the dictates of my conscience & the Church (or the Church & my conscience is it?) than I do when I submit.

As for what you say of the country people: Yes, they are like that – exactly – at present. But it is pretty obvious that such an attitude as you describe (Good humour, live & let live, a faith in the ultimate sanity & decency of men) is, though admirable in itself, an attitude rather of despair than of hope, of decay than of a vigorous will to create, of agnosticism than of faith. And I still believe that faith is possible as well as desirable and that country people are as likely to get faith as any other kind. Anyway I don't see why one shd. play down to their level (if one thinks it 'down'). No, I'm not agreeing with you. I think that village cross ought to be as gaudy & scrumptious as possible – to hell with all the dignified expressions, materializations of our present discontent.

In an 'age of faith' a cross like this[1] wd. be all very well. In such an age the plain symbol might be understood to mean all the fullness & riches. But now we must make some attempt (besides I want to) to proclaim the fullness & riches in a manner more seductive and alluring. Do you think the village wouldn't like it? They would – not in so many words of course, but they'd like it – be interested & amused – much more than they wd. in a thing more really expressive of their present jaded & forlorn & enslaved state – and I think too that they wd. like it much more than a cross strong & rude & noble – a cross agnostic however courageously. Do you really think they wouldn't? Yours ever   ERIC GILL

I wish you'd been at Moreton when I was there the other day. I hope we'll meet again soon.

---

[1] Second sketch, of a plain cross.

50 : TO WILLIAM ROTHENSTEIN

Ditchling Common   *13-6-1915*

My dear Rothenstein: I am sorry I've not been able to get to
the answering of your letter before. I think I understand and
agree with what you mean about playing up or down to a
village audience and I daresay I deceive myself in thinking that
there is more of the old spirit of worship and more appreciation of a ritual expression of it than there actually is. However
I do not really of course consider what or how much appreciation there may be in a village, I am leaving such qualms to Mr.
Debenham. If he says to me I don't think my village will
stand the halos & we can't risk that crucifix on the top, I only
have to consider whether such things are essential to my
design or not. I don't suppose they are — though I think all
such definitive signs desirable in these days of vague unbelief.
I am now making a new drawing on the same lines but bigger &
I hope better drawn an'd I am also to make another drawing
showing a plainer kind of thing altogether. I also quite agree
with you about 'colour' at Westminster. I hope it may be
possible to make a bold attack. I have just finished the 'Judgment' panel & it will be fixed up this week. So I shall be up
in London probably on Wednesday. [. . .] Yours ever

ERIC GILL

51 : TO HIS BROTHER EVAN

Ditchling Common,   *15-7-1915*

My dear Evan: At the risk of causing you serious displeasure I
must make an attempt to squeeze in a letter to you. My
activities are such that it is really difficult to find time in which
to write — talk about active service why you chaps are having
a blooming holiday compared with me — a strenuous holiday
and one containing many exciting moments I dare say — thin
red line of 'eroes and all that — I know and frankly (in so far as
my nature is capable of frankness) admit — but for real filled

up days —squashed down and overflowing —I recommend you
to take notice of the life of the British-Sculptor-small-farmer-
&-volunteer-man-of-war. Oh it's awful! 'Arrever' there's
twenty minutes between me and my next drill so I'm jolly
well going to make a start with an epistle to the professional
soldier. [. . .] Last Saturday, having a job to see to at Lincoln
(i.e. Inscription on monument to Bp. King which Herbert
Joseph Cribb is cutting & which I had to go & see —I being
responsible &, besides, I wanted to see Lincoln —Have you
seen that Church? its a marvellous fine thing), I went through
London —Ethel was with me & Petra (the last going on a visit
to Auntie Gladys) —and we all went to Guy's Hospital & went
to see Ken.

Poor old Ken —He did get knocked about a bit —tho. it
might have been worse. (At that moment the bugle went —I
say 'went' rather than 'blew' because it 'went' so far away
that I couldn't be sure if it blew or not —I say at that moment
the bugle . . . I mean, to be brief, that it was time for me to
form fours & so I went & did it and now it's got on to Sunday
evening and I will this time endeavour to finish without further
mishap — which reminds me; after drill I went & had some
bayonet practice —great sport, but the real thing, I am inclined
to believe, must be the devil —you know a gun with a bayonet
on the end of it is a devilish awkward thing to get out of the
way of and you can only hope the other chap finds it even more
difficult still.) Well, we saw Ken and found him, all things
considered, very well & cheerful and very comfortable &
luxuriously besprinkled with good things —kind nurses,
flowers, books & cigarettes & not, I understand, starving. We
had about an hour & a half with him —discussing the war and
things at home. At home! So you and Vernon are to have
some well earned 'leave'. That will be 'great' & if, as you
plan, you can manage to fix it up for Max's wedding day that
wd. be 'a treat'. I guess I'll be there to see. How's Vernon?
I hope he's fit & cheerful. Dear chap —he's, I won't say improved, 'filled out' like anything since living in Canada &

become a fine fellow. These things are 'orrid pathetic if you dwell on them and when we think of all the hard times he (and you too) had as a kid & especially during the year or so immediately before he went to Canada it moves me literally to something very much like tears to see him so fine & big & strong & good & quiet. Give him our love & blessings.

You asked me if I'd seen that about Count Reventlow & Roman Lettering —no I hadn't —very amusing and, as you wd. say, 'crude'. No —I don't know where Count Kessler is. I understand he's 'on the staff' & someone told me they'd seen his name (but there may be & in fact are many other Kesslers) in connection with the Germans in Turkey. I wonder what he thinks of it all. I think he must be pretty sick. I know he belonged to the anti-Kaiser party and had no love for Potsdam —but now I suppose it's a case of 'my country —right or wrong' for him and so he's fixed up & helping God to punish England. It'll be interesting to meet him après la guerre —if he's not killed & I'm not either. The market cross job is now more or less fixed up (also) & I hope to start work on it before long though there's no hurry about it. I'm going down to Dorset next month, all being well, to see the quarries from which the stone is to come —Purbeck stone (not marble). It's to be a fine big thing with a figure of our Lord holding a sheathed sword in his left hand and his right raised in blessing & a niche with a statue of the Madonna & Child. It will be something over 20 feet high I think altogether. I enclose a press cutting for your delectation (as you ask for such) —send it back to Ethel when done with as she does me the honour of liking to keep such things. Now good-bye old boy & God bless you & keep you whole & well to return to 'this little land'. I'll write to brother Vernon very shortly. Meanwhile accept this, both of you, as a greeting of love from us all —your brother

ERIC

We are very glad you liked the bread —will send some more when opportunity offers. (Money's pretty short these days so

I know you'll understand all about that.) Your sporting postcard is much appreciated.

I also enclose a cutting from the *Herald* (a rum sort of rag).
I thought the article v. amusing in parts.

52 : TO HENRY ATKINSON

D. Common, Sx.   *26-8-1915*

[. . .] Of course we'd be v. pleased to see the L.C.C. books
you mention. Like all Catholics it is not science we distrust
but scientists. Their facts are all right — it's the funny conclusions they draw from them that are all wrong. As a description of the Universe that of science is one of many excellent
ones — As an *explanation* . . . well, it isn't an explanation — I
suppose, properly speaking, doesn't profess to be. But more
of this when next we meet wh. I hope will be soon. Yours

ERIC GILL

53 : TO ANDRÉ RAFFALOVICH

Ditchling Common   *24-11-1915*

My dear Raffalovich: I hope you are quite well — and also Miss
Gribbell & Father Gray.

This is just to apologize for not yet having been able to send
you your second acrobat. The fact that I have been and am
very much pressed with work wd. not be any excuse for I wd.
as much wish to do your job as any other. The trouble is
partly that I have had to keep up with the Westminster work
with which I am very much behind and partly that, owing to
the unfortunate fact that that work is far from profitable
financially, I have had to give all the time I have had in between
whiles to the earning of money. You will understand I know.
Things are going to be most awfully difficult soon and I am
getting alarmed. However the work *is* in hand (by the bye

D. Y. Cameron came to see me the other day and expressed great admiration for the thing in its present state —if that is any consolation to you!) and I will get to it again as soon as I can. You will trust me I know.

The enclosed book advertisement will interest you I think. I think you will particularly like Edward Johnston's little book of rhymes.

My brother Kenneth is still at Guy's. They keep on finding fresh pieces of bone to be removed. Poor boy —he's getting pretty sick of it. The two Canadian brothers are still out there and unwounded as yet. One of them was home on leave a fortnight ago. Did you see that Kenneth had been given the Military Cross?

We are all well and cheerful. I am yours affectionately

ERIC GILL

54 : TO ANDRÉ RAFFALOVICH

[The first page of this letter is missing; it seems to belong to the second half of 1915.]

. . . now making or about to make designs for it. It will be about 12 or 15 feet high and is to have carvings representing the nativity (i.e. a crib) & the Good Shepherd upon it. This job is from Ernest Debenham (Debenham & Freebody) who is the squire of a large estate, including two or three villages, in Dorset and is apparently intended by him as a sort of libation to those from Dorset who have fallen in the war and also as a memorial of his ownership. So I am lucky. I have also just got a commission to make a monument for the grave of the late Alfred Lyttelton (the M.P.) but the inscription which is to be cut on this is I think the most fulsome & extravagant thing I have ever read. It is therefore a less pleasing work than it might be. So you see it will be a matter of some difficulty to fit everything in and to keep everything going. But I am the more fortunate to have these additional works on hand in as much as, I am sorry to say, the Westminster work is not at all profitable. The expenses are very heavy. (viz.: — on the first three panels, including preliminary expenses, cartoons, drawings etc.: —

Out of pocket (cash) expenses	£87	9	11
Cash received on account	£141	15	0

Balance for own work	£54	5	1

and, as I did on the first three, according to my working diary, as much as 117 days work, you will see the pay is not excessive. And in addition to the above there was the cost of making that first stone panel which I put up in the Cathedral as a sample before the commission was given to me at all & the cost of that was: —

out of pocket	£11	2	8

& 34 days work of mine! for which of course I received no payment at all. However I still have this sample stone and may someday dispose of it. It is the fifth station (Simon of Cyrene). So if you hear of anyone wanting a stone picture measuring about 4′ 6″ square you will know where there is one to be had. The worst of it is that the longer you keep things the less you like them and very soon I shall be ashamed to sell this particular stone at all. While I am writing I may as well add that, as you will see, in the above summary of expenses, no allowance whatever is made for what the business people call 'establishment charges', i.e. rent, rates, taxes, light & heat, tools, packing cases etc., & this shd. hardly be reckoned at less than say 25% of the total value of a job I think. So all things considered I am not to be considered as making a fortune out of the pious donors, bless 'em. I tell you all this, I know you'll bear with me, because, not only are you kindly interested in my affairs, but so that, shd. you hear of me being 'county-courted' for debt, in spite of all your efforts on my behalf, you'll know that it may not be all my fault. However we are all right so far & will pull through. (I think I am right in saying that we are owed more than we owe so that's as it shd. be. i.e. apart from a certain loan you wot of & apart from our debt to the bankers & the mortgage on this place.)

Now no more of these money affairs.

I hope you and Miss Gribbell & Father Gray are all well. This present weather is truly magnificent and we all enjoy it. The Common is most beautiful & our little estate flourishes. Oh! but what a business it is to keep the chickens out of the garden! I must buy a terrier dog. They say they are better than any amount of wire netting besides being better to look at.

I must stop. We all send our love. I am yours affectionately

ERIC GILL

Please return the Canadian's letter when done with.

55 : TO GEOFFREY KEYNES

Ditchling Common, Sx.   *30-12-1915*

My dear Keynes: This comes, assuming you still to be in the land of the living (and after this morning, when I received a letter informing me that a friend, to whom I sent a Christmas card, had died on January 13th last, and that the writer was his executor, I am feeling nervous about you), wishing you a happy New Year and in belated reply to yours of May 20th.!

I[1] wonder (see how narrowly I missed the Kingly style) how you are and if you are still on No. 10 train. You have not yet, I hope, had the job of patching up any of my brothers tho., as I said before, you are very welcome to it when the need arises. But you missed a chance with one of them (Lieut! Kenneth of the 1st Cambs.) who was badly 'strafed' (as he wd. put it) on June 1st and spent a month or so at your old place at Versailles. Since August he has been at Guy's but I believe they let him

---

[1] An original 'We' has had 'I' written into it; the result looks rather like 'I've', and perhaps E. G. meant to write 'I've wondered'.

out to go home for Christmas. The other two are (or were up to the week before last) still o.k. If you *are* all right and can find the time, do send us a line – a field p.c. wd. be acceptable. Well, we are all well here and I am very busy and have a lot of work on hand. The Westminster Stations are of course still in the forefront of my activities tho. just lately I have been doing wood cuts for that book of which I think I sent you the advertisement.[1] Then I've got a truly magnificent job to do for a village in Dorset. It is a village cross and has two statues (one life size & one a seated figure 2 foot 6 ins.) on it. The whole thing will be 25 feet high. This is a grand opportunity and I hope to take advantage of it. What with all this work (for, in addition to the above mentioned, I have several small things on hand – including a wood cut to go in a reprint of Cobbett's 'Cottage Economy'!) I find volunteering quite impossible and so have chucked the V.T.C. for the present. I now await the call of Conscription but I doubt if that will come.

A week or two ago I went down to Dorset to visit the quarries from which I am getting the stone for that Cross. It is near Swanage – along the coast between that place and Lulworth. Do you know that part? It's pretty good – so to speak. The quarry is in the Cliff near S. Alban's head – just a wild deserted place – nobody about but two or three quarry men working by candle light a hundred yards or so in under the cliffs – the sea roaring outside. Very fine stone – something like Portland but harder. I was going to say 'I've got my work cut out' but, *au contraire*! The job will be to get it cut out, for one of the blocks by itself will weigh over two tons!

A friend of mine has got a cottage at Lulworth Cove. Do

---

[1] *The Devil's Devices* (St. Dominic's Press). E. G's. illustrations to this were in fact *engravings*, and it is interesting to note that at this date he did not trouble to make the distinction. Later he came to distinguish sharply between a wood-cut — made on the 'plank' with a knife — and a wood-engraving — made on the end-grain with a graver. The illustration for Cobbett mentioned below in this letter was also an engraving. E. G.'s true woodcuts were very few, but among them was the big block of 'Animals All' (Letter 62).

you know that place? The cottage is on the east side of the cove away from the village & separated from it by a great high down. It is the remains of an ancient Abbey and the chapel is still useable &, in a private sort of way, used. As I was down in those parts I went on there and spent a couple of nights at the Abbey Cottage. It was jolly good. Only our two selves. Very stormy weather —nothing to do but cook, eat, drink & talk. An ideal 'retreat' —nearly.

I had a brief Christmas note from Jacques R. & he sent a few v. beautiful wood cuts of his & hers. I gather they are well. I wish they weren't so far away. The children had a letter from Frances Cornford. I gather they are well also. We haven't heard from them for some time. But she says he is writing to us shortly.

If and when you get some leave, do steal a day to come and see us if you can. It wd. be fine to see you again.

Well —with love from us both and all. Yours   ERIC GILL

56 : TO GEOFFREY KEYNES

Temple, London   *29-5-1916*

My dear Keynes: Many thanks for your letter of May 6. I was glad to hear of your continued good health. As for me, I am still in civilian attire. How long I shall remain so, I know not. Yus. I'm only 34 at present so have still seven years to serve in the Army. Of course I shall try & get off —no conscientious objections —none whatever —but it wd. be such a rotten mess up for all my work, nationally unimportant tho. it be, were I to be conscripted. I shall try the sole-head-of-business-with-three-children-solely-dependent-thereon lay I suppose. I will let you know if I do shave it off —my beard I mean. At present I'm working at Westminster Cathedral. I've just put up two more Stations & am finishing them in situ. I expect to be up here another fortnight. It's rather a rum job, working at the

Cathedral in the full glare of publicity. E.g. to-day: Voice of lady from below: 'Can you tell me what style these Stations are in?' Self: 'No, I can't.' Lady: 'Can you tell me what style the Stations are in?' Self: 'I'm sorry, I can't tell you.' Lady: 'Are they Italian?' Self: 'I don't know.' Lady: 'They're very ugly, aren't they?' Self: 'I don't know.' Lady desists. Beastly business sometimes, if amusing. It's difficult to work while watched, but I'm getting more oblivious than at first. In between whiles lately I've been making designs for a big monument to commemorate the Colonial Troops. It's to be erected by the Overseas Club. I fear my design will not get the job. The drawings are to be published shortly, I understand, in 'the Graphic'. If you see you'll understand why I don't expect to get the job. It's been worth trying for though and I'm to get 20 quid for the drawings anyway so that's encouraging to the commercial mind. The Dorset Market Cross marks time at present. Can't get any masons —no use trying until I know whether I'm going myself or not. Both my chaps have gone. I'm all alone & find things rather difficult. Can only get on with drawings & light jobs. Lucky I had two Stations well ahead before my chaps left. I can finish them by myself now. Wood engraving & various typographical ambitions occupy the remainder of my time. Pepler (the author of the D. *Devices* you know) who lives at Ditchling in our old house there, has set up a printing press. It's a great step in the right direction & he's doing very good work. I do various things for it from time to time. When do you expect to get leave again? I wish you could come & see us & the press.

July 1st. It's a fact but I haven't had one single chance to finish this epistle since May 29! I'm sorry. I meant to have written it & sent it off straight away.

There's no special news to add. I'm still in 'plain clothes' though as you'll know I am, since June 24, a reservist in the Army. My date for 'falling in' is July 5th. but as I'm putting in for an exemption and as my application has not yet been heard I don't suppose I shall go quite so soon as that. Even if

I don't get off altogether I daresay they'll give me a month or two to clear up my affairs. I shd. be glad of it as I've got a lot I want to do before I can take a holiday.

I heard from one of my Canadian Brothers the other day. He says that they've now retaken all that they previously had lost. So that's cheering for them. Judging by the noise of the guns which we have been hearing pretty continuously lately, you people are busy over there. I hope you'll win through all right.

I saw Jacques R. when he & his miss'es were in London some months ago. He was cheerful & enthusiastic. I've not heard from him since. Is he going to be a paralytic?

I've finished my job at Westminster and am now doing odd jobs. Don't feel inclined to start anything fresh until I know what's going to happen.

Well — I'll send this off. Yours ever   ERIC GILL

I enclose an Easter Card which is now too late even for Whitsun. I hope you'll like it all the same. By the by, did you get Pepler's reprint of Cobbett's *Cottage Economy*? If you did you will have seen my funny wood-cut therein. If you didn't get it you have missed a v. good preface by G. K. C. I'll enclose a copy herewith. Hand it on to some one else when you've read it. It's good propaganding.   E. G.

57 : TO WILLIAM ROTHENSTEIN

Ditchling Common   *22-7-1916*

My dear Rothenstein: Very many thanks for your letter of July 17.

I was amused to learn that my Civic Arts Compn. Design was put second on the ground that it did not follow the conditions. That no doubt was only an excuse for so doing. I am only surprised that, if Rickards & Poole's design is the sort of thing they like, they gave me any prize at all. However I, it

F

goes without saying, most heartily agree with you in all you
say about such Associations. They ain't no bloomin good at
all and I only, I frankly admit it, went in to the competition at
all because you & Debenham were keen on the business and
because there seemed some chance (& in that I was not mistaken) of earning some money.

I am very glad indeed that my design for the L.C.C. Monument meets with your admiration (and I suppose my tablet
design & the alphabet which was its only excuse did not disgust
you). I wonder what Debenham thinks of it and, if he likes it,
how he likes giving his prize to Rickards. (I suppose you know
Rickards? He is the man responsible for that vain-glorious
temple of Baptism opposite to Westminster Abbey —and how
opposite!) Well, it was worth doing and it will amuse &
interest you to know that when you were drawing my portrait
the other day[1] I said to myself 'now what shall I think about
while I'm sitting here?' And the choice was between thinking
about women (in some detail) and thinking what I wd. do for
the L.C.C. Monument design. The former subject of cogita-
tion seemed irresistible & I began on that, but somehow I got
shunted on to the other subject & it suddenly occurred to me
that the act of Jesus in turning out the buyers & sellers from
the Temple as he did was really a most courageous act & most
warlike. You know the difficulty was that I was convinced that
a group on a plain base of stone was the thing demanded for
that site. But I couldn't think what the group should consist
of —what subject —what persons —Britannia handing out rifles
to L.C.C. Clerks —goodness knows what. And even if I could
think of a good subject I couldn't see how it cd. be made into
a group of persons forming a conglomerate mass. So you see I
was very glad when the 'Moneychangers' occurred to me (I
don't know how —the notion came quite of its own accord
apparently) and, as I say, the 'occurrence' occurred during the
time I was sitting to you. So I came back on the Monday very
bucked up —armed with a clear & definite notion & all the

[1] Photograph opposite.

ERIC GILL

Drawing by William Rothenstein

'leader-writer's' difficulties behind me, so to speak; the difficulty of having to design something without knowing what —
an impossible position. So I am glad *you* have got a clear &
definite job for the A. & C. exhibition. You also can go ahead
& let the society & all societies go to hell their own way. I
only hope they won't worry you while you're at it or spoil
your work with their 'architectural' setting.

I go before the local Tribune on Monday — medically, I am
passed fit for garrison duty abroad (not general service) So if
my exemption be not granted, I may get a free trip to India!
By the bye, the designs for the Overseas Monument are appearing in the *Graphic* next Friday (July 28). They will not thus
appear to the best advantage as designs, but I hope the project
will be aided rather than hindered by the publication. I
believe James Bone is going to do something in *his* paper too.
Yours ever   ERIC G.

P.S. I've not yet received the mount from Chenil's.

58 : TO FRANK PICK

30-7-1916

Dear Mr. Pick: Thank you for your letter of the 27th.

It is very kind of your committee to ask me to write an
article on the subject of Tombstones for the Design & Industries Association's *Journal*, but as I do not believe in that
Association I cannot very well do so.

It does not seem to me that modern tombstones are lacking
in 'design', & if it is the opinion of your Association that that
design is of poor quality, as I agree, that seems to me to be the
result of modern conditions & I think that those conditions
require more than an Association concerned with Design
for their remedy. May I add that it seems to me to be the
trouble not so much that modern goods (& tombstones) are
machine made as that being so made they attempt to appear

otherwise? Many fine things are machine made —e.g. guns &
the Forth Bridge —but such things are not 'designed' in the
D. & I. Association's sense of the word. I would like to see
all the productions of our modern commercial system as well
done as are guns & girders & equally 'inartistic'. That is my
propaganda until such time as the modern commercial system
can be scrapped —as scrapped it some day will be.

Please forgive my churlishness & believe me yours faithfully,

ERIC GILL

59 : TO GEOFFREY KEYNES

Ditchling Common   *11-8-1916*

My dear Keynes: V. many thanks for yours of July 13.

My exemption has been granted (conditionally on my
remaining in my present employment!) so now I'm free to
work. [. . .]

We're about to bring out a magazine at the Ditchling Press.
I'll send you a copy of the 1st number.

I hope you're well —we are. Yours ever   ERIC GILL

60 : TO WILLIAM ROTHENSTEIN

Ditchling Common   *12-9-1916*

My dear Rothenstein: *Greetings*. Many thanks for your note.
Re the Brass Font Ewer: Gimson is the man to help you. A
few months ago he sent me an ewer wh. he had made, or got
made, for the same purpose and got me to get an inscription
engraved upon it. So I expect he can do the same for you.
Apart from the ordinary Church Furniture people, to whom
I suppose you don't want to go, I know of no one better than
Gimson & his company. But if you want to go further afield,
what about Harold Stabler? He wd. do it for you I expect.

He has my old workshop in Hammersmith Tce. He is a metal worker. Then there is Edward Spencer of the Artificers' Guild — Maddox St. W., he is also a metal worker. But *all* these people are of the arts, 'arty'. I shd. personally prefer, failing an artist in whom I really believed, to get a plain brass jug from Messrs. Loftus & Co., 18, Tottenham Ct. Rd., W., or some such firm. Messrs. L. are brass & copper & pewter jug & measure manufacturers. They supply Public Houses and have some really good & decent, ordinary machine-made things in their shop. If you get a jug there, supposing they had the sort of article you want, it wd. only be necessary not to say that it came from a Public House outfitter's shop & all wd. be well. Go & see the shop next time you're in London — you'll find some good useful things there.

You astonish me by what you say about the Leeds Monument. I have heard nothing definite as yet from Prof. Sadler. I hope it may be as you say — but I hardly think it has got as far as that yet.

Many thanks for your congratulations. It would be splendid indeed if it came off. I'm looking forward to seeing your R.A. decoration. I shall go to the show, if for that only. It will be most exciting. I hear from Gere that he has finished his. If you are to be in London on the 22nd. perhaps we can fit in a meeting. Yours affectly.   ERIC GILL

61 : TO WILLIAM ROTHENSTEIN

1 Hare Ct., Temple   *22-11-1916*

My dear Rothenstein: I was very glad to get your letter of the 16th. and to know that you did not take my criticisms as presumptuous. The reason why I did not write at once was simply that I had no chance of doing so. I have had no time at all for letter writing for some weeks and I had to wait until I could consider the matter with some care.

And now in spite of what you say I still feel that it is difficult for a rich man to enter into the Kingdom of heaven —that we and you particularly and all men trained in habits of observation & representation and intellectual appreciation of nature are too rich and cannot give up the riches. I think it is absolutely essential to all painting & sculpture (& music) that is not made to stand by itself isolated from its surroundings that the thing as a whole and every unit of it, every line & form (& sound), should be taken for what they are and not for what they represent. As a child who draws a house makes a house of lines, so that it may truly be said not to make an image of a house but actually a house built of lines, so, it seems to me, in *our* work we have to use our materials as things of which to *make* things & not as things by which to *represent* things. I do not believe, at least I find it difficult to believe that it is possible for anyone trained, as you and most artists have been trained, to use materials as means of representation to throw off that training and become again as a little child. Even persons without the artist's training cannot do it. They always use a line (e.g.) to represent something and not to make something. It's a habit of mind as well as a habit of hand. Well —I think the revolution is essential. I don't rule out representation. I simply say it's another game which debars those who play it (unless by some chance or by design they have preserved the habit of making) from playing the other game —they can't *begin* to do it —and if you can't begin you can't end (or is that a fallacy?).

Take this letter: A. That's not a picture of a letter —it *is* a letter.

Take this scribble:[1] That's not a picture of a head —it *is* a head. I wonder how this matter strikes you. Now I must stop as I'm being waited for. With greetings to you all I am yours affectionately   ERIC GILL

[1] Here a pencilled head.

62 : TO GEOFFREY KEYNES

Ditchling Common   *25-1-1917*

My dear Keynes: We send you our most affectionate and hearty congratulations upon the joyful event of your engagement. I hope you will soon get married and, if you make half as much of a success of it as we have made, you will not do badly. I hope we shall soon meet again —you and both of you. I gather from your letter that my last letter has not reached you. I wrote just before Christmas & sent you a copy of a new magazine emanating from Ditchling called *The Game*. I will send you another copy if the first has gone astray.

I am most awfully busy writing a paper wh. I am to read at a Dominican Priory near Birmingham shortly so must not write more now. We are all well and cheerful at present. With love from us both: Yours ever   ERIC GILL

I will tell Pepler to send you his new catalogues as they appear. I'm glad you like the big 'Animals All' block. Of course the extra charge for signed copies is absurd. I must remedy that.

63 : TO WILLIAM ROTHENSTEIN

Ditchling Common   *25-2-1917*

My dear Rothenstein: We must begin again —for I seem to have given you a quite wrong impression of what I think of your work & my own. E.g., I don't think of you as one '*representing a merely accidental appearance*' —nor of myself as attempting to make '*a significant image* of the actual reality the idea of a thing gives you' (me). However whatever I thought I now unreservedly accept & respect the aims which you describe as your own and I am really glad to have been the occasion of eliciting so full & good a description. Now that is clear: you have told me what you are at and I accept the telling and respect the attitude expressed.

I wish I could tell you as lucidly & well what I am at. But I cannot. I do not know nearly as clearly what it is I think or feel about my work and nature and reality. In one aspect I am just the craftsman doing that which is ordered and in another I am just the artist doing what I please, i.e. what pleases me aesthetically.

No, my contention was nothing to do with your conscious aims or mine nor with the respective values or virtues of our two jobs. My contention was simply that our work was different & that that difference was one of kind, not in intellectual or spiritual value (that I don't go into) but in aesthetic & technical form —and that my difference was one inevitably resulting from our different trainings & one, as it seems to me, debarring you from what is called 'decoration' & me from what is called 'representation' (though I think it possible that I might more easily put on a 'representative' manner than you a 'decorative' one —not really but apparently, simply because that manner is the one for which our time stands whereas the other we usually throw off with our 2nd. box of paints). I am speaking only of the actual work —the paint or the stone —and not at all of its significance or meaning or value in the abstract, what it's 'worth to God', but simply what it *is*. On the one side are e.g.: Giotto etc.

> Persian Rugs
> Bricks & Iron Girders
> Tools, Steam engines
> Folk Song
> Plain Song
> Caligraphy
> Toys (not some few modern ones tho.)
> Animals
> Men & Women physically regarded
> Hair
> Lines
> String

                    Plaited Straw
                    Beer
                    & so on.
    on the other are   Velasquez
                    Rembrandt etc.

No, this second list is too difficult — what I wish to convey is that such things as I name in the 1st. list & such things as young children's drawings & the works of savages are themselves actually a part of nature, organically one with nature and in no sense outside her — while, on the other hand, the work of Rembrandt & most moderns (the modern contribution — the renaissance) is not a part of nature but is apart from nature — is in fact an appreciation & a criticism of nature — a reviewing of nature as of something to be loved or hated. Good criticism is an excellent thing — why not? Well, it's no good trying to write all this — I wish we could meet & thrash it out.

    Possibly this modern contribution, this post-Raphaelite conception of art, is a 'higher' thing than that other (it's not exclusively modern of course — individuals have transcended nature in many ages before our own) but I'm not concerned here with 'higher or lower' but only with differences and I think that the qualities which make you so good a painter are not such as can be of use to you as a decorator — you don't use lines & colours as a bricklayer or weaver uses them — I don't think your hand will let you & I don't think your head will let your hand. It is you, not I, who quâ artist is concerned with the significance of things — *I* am only concerned to develop & exploit my consciousness of beauty — to make things which are not only beautiful as a whole but beautiful in their every line & shape & colour. Well — dangers of misunderstanding lurk in every word so I will stop. Yours ever affectionately

                                                ERIC GILL

I hope the copper jug has turned up safely and is considered suitable & seemly.

64 : TO HENRY ATKINSON

Ditchling Common, Sx.   *20-6-1917*

My dear Atkinson, I must send you a short letter to say that I
have read your most valuable description of the utterly damned
system of efficient or scientific management in its particular
aspect of 'Reward' payment. I think the book[1] most valuable
as being a clear & complete exposition of one part of the
subject and I am very glad to have it for reference. I was
recently the guest of a man called Impey who is a partner in a
firm of 'looseleafledger' manufacturers at Birmingham &
whose factory is run on the system you advocate. I went all
over the factory & had opportunities of discussion with both
the masters, 'foremen' (or whatever you wd. call them), &
men, & it was as a result of that visit, followed as it was by a
three days stay at a Dominican Monastery at (or near) Rugeley
(Staffs.), that I invented my famous definitions of Slavery &
Freedom. I sent you those definitions (*The Game*, Easter
Number) & you will see at once how opposed are our principles. You will of course put me down among that absurd
class of idealists who seek to destroy all the benefits of modern
'progress'. I can't help it. I fully admit that you are on the
rising tide. I was going to say 'the winning side' but of course
that is not true, for in the end your side will not win simply
because it bases itself upon a false estimate of human nature.
We say that normally (& by 'normally' we do not mean
generally or on the average at any particular time & certainly
not at this present time) a man finds his greatest interest &
pleasure & enthusiasm in his work; that that work to bear him
that fruit of interest & pleasure must be the work by wh. he
earns his living & not merely work done in his spare time (that
normally men do not desire leisure, spare-time or holidays —
except by way of exception); that such work, to bear such
fruit, must be such as the workman is responsible for, not
merely for its lack of faults but *for its merits*.

[1] *A Rational Wages System.*

But, enough, you know what I'm at — it is just the precise opposite of what *you* are driving at. *You*, as far as England & indeed the whole of our modern civilization is concerned, will win, & I face the fact fully. There is just this weakness in your position: you do not in your heart believe that the factory system of production (I say nothing about machinery — that is neither here nor there & doesn't enter into the discussion) is the best system. Of course you don't. In spite of your (obviously absurd & illogical) contentions that the system you advocate tends to make the work itself interesting to do and (more absurd still) that the knowledge that the greatest quantity is being produced tends to make work less mechanical, you don't really believe that the sort of things of which man is normally desirous can be made under your system. Of course they can't. Why pretend they can? Let us have no more of this hypocrisy about art & beauty. They don't come in. Why shd. they come in? Do you suppose that art can live under such circumstances as you dream of? You really are jolly funny about art & all that sort of extra — something you get in your leisure time — concerts & exhibitions & theatres & culture. No, you don't face the facts properly. You want to eat your cake and have it (or, if you don't do so personally — for perhaps you may justly contend that you don't think art of much importance — many of your colleagues do so). You think you can have a civilization founded upon a quantitative basis with a sort of 'quality' department running along side. Can't be done. Better face the facts & chuck one or the other as I do. I say that you can't have the country run on the factory system & at the same time produce works of art of any kind worth having — i.e. works wh. are not merely a sort of lick-spittle works done to please either the cultured rich or the clamouring factory hands trained in cinemas & municipal art schools. But you mustn't think I'm cross about it. If I write thus it's only because I haven't time to write otherwise. We won't talk any more about art. You don't understand as much about that side of things as I do about the factory system. So you're not capable of judging. You must take it from me therefore as an expert (as I take things from you as an expert) that the sort of civilization wh. you are helping to build is one in which there must be no sort of talk about the word or the thing. Let it be a sensible civilization & not a silly one. Let it be sanitary & comfortable & efficient. (We'll put aside the question 'what's it all bloomin well for'.) It will have a certain grandeur of its own. The Forth Bridge, tho. it may be by now somewhat out of date as an engineering feat, is a splendid thing, so is a type-writer (if only they wd. leave out the 'artistic' slobber on the cover) & so is an aeroplane & so is a loose leaf ledger (if only they wd. leave out the imitation hand-tooling on the leather back –but they daren't, because, so Impey told me, their customers ask for it & they must please their customers or else they'd lose the order & that wd. never do. Damned silly, but there you are) & so, I dare say, is a Ford car (if you can't afford anything better or more durable). In fact the whole show might be a jolly fine show if only we could really make up our minds to be sensible & leave out incompatibles. Now there's my trouble. I don't believe the human race is capable of such a sacrifice. I believe it will still demand wall papers & muck of that sort & patterns on biscuit boxes & frills on chemises & rings on its fingers. So we shall fall between two stools –and it will be jolly well our own fault.

One more point: Suppose all the 'necessary' work of the world to be done in a few hours per day & the remainder of the day given to self culture. Do you suppose every one will amuse *himself*? Will there be no need of organized amusement, i.e. paid amusers –professional spare-time contractors? Why shd. some people have the privilege of being paid to be entertaining while others have to put up with the 'enlightened self-interest' of their masters? If you were a factory hand you wd. look with considerable envy upon the lazy swine who played at work to please you.

Oh yes, one more point. You say we can't afford hand-made goods or small workshops & their products – I forget your words but you know what I mean (Morris books & all that tosh). There again you don't face the facts. The fact is that we can afford to have the best, provided we are prepared to have less of it. We can afford a hand-made saucepan if we are prepared to put up with it for several years. If, on the other hand, we must have a new saucepan every month or so, well then of course we must put up with enamelled iron. You ought to give up running that stunt about 'can't afford'. It's all balderdash. You must know that the real trouble is that we can't make up our minds to have few things instead of many. Of course we are not to blame. The things are in the shops & we buy them. It's the workman that's to blame for selling himself for money. Enough said.

Again thank you very much for your Christmas letter. I am very glad you found my Westminster carvings more or less to your liking.

I'm still going ahead with them.

We are all very well & cheerful. I am not yet 'called up'.

With love to you both from me & my wife I am yrs. sincerely   ERIC GILL

6 5 : TO JOSEPH CRIBB

D. Comm., Sx.   *6-8-1917*

My dear Joseph. Thank you very much for your letter of July 28.

We are very glad you are still o.k. and more or less enjoying life. Things are all serene here. The haystack is now thatched, looks jolly smart. We have a litter of puppies at present, they also are all right. Jolly nice little chaps. Do you want a dog? We shall have four to dispose of. Yesterday Pepler and I went for a walk with a friend on the hills. We went to Mass at Keymer & then, after breakfast at Soper's, up the hills at

Westmeston & along the top to Plumpton & down to lunch of beer bread & cheese at the Half Moon. We then walked home by Streat &, coming across the fields at Blackbrook farm, ran into Mr. Edge. As we had lost track of the footpath he showed us the way and we had a long jaw with him. The worst of it was that the blighter would persist in arguing with us all the time! It stands to reason a man like that can't really be on our side and yet to hear him you'd think he was. P'raps we'll meet again now that the ice is broken and then we'll try being really rude to him & see how that works.

Now for your questions: (I can see you arguing with the other chaps & getting jolly well slated all round. However it's good to think you're with people who are interested in such things & can have a talk.)

1.   *Gothic lettering*. This name is usually given to the manu-
     script lettering of the *late middle ages* in England France
     & Germany. In Italy the nearest approach to it is what
     is called 'Lombardic.' Gothic lettering is a manuscript
     form of Roman lettering, but of course in the course of
     time the Roman forms got very much lost.

     Here is a 'Gothic' M for instance: —
     You can see the Roman M still tho. it is   𝔪
     pretty well changed.

     Gothic lettering of this kind is now-a-days generally un-
     suitable for anything which you want to read easily. It
     is only used for titles (like the titles of newspapers) &
     for the initial words of documents (like the 'Whereas' in
     a lawyer's document).

2.   Apart from the above mentioned uses of 'Gothic' letter-
     ing (& a few others of the same sort) which are tradi-
     tional & therefore allowable, there is no proper use for
     it in the ordinary way (i.e. you can use it for fun if you
     like). 'Gothic' lettering is generally *un*suitable for in-
     scriptions even in Gothic churches because it is un-
     natural to write or inscribe letters in a style which

belongs to another age and which is very illegible compared with the lettering to which we are accustomed.
You might as well ask a munition factory to turn out
bombs of the 1914 pattern because they were to be used
in a trench wh. was dug in 1914! Or you might as well
ask a parson to preach in the English of Chaucer because
he was preaching in a mediaeval church! If you had never
seen 'Gothic' lettering and were asked to do an inscription on the wall of a church & you wanted to invent a
style suitable for the occasion you wd. not get anywhere
near Gothic lettering. The development of Gothic
architecture & the development of Gothic lettering
proceeded upon different lines altogether. The essence
of Gothic art is freedom to do the best you can. It is not
a matter of pointed arches or angular lettering. If you
want to be really Gothic you must follow the tradition
of your own time & be a slave to no-one.

3. Of course it is impossible to put up a Gothic building
now-a-days. That is: it is impossible to put up a *good* one
if by 'Gothic' you mean one having the shapes and
ornaments of the mediaeval buildings. The Gothic style
was a style developed in the middle ages & was the
natural result of the conditions of those times. It was
the style of a time when iron was hardly dreamed of as a
building material —when stone was the ruling material.
When the Church was the ruling spirit & when the trader
and merchant & banker were jolly well subordinate (they
were generally Jews & jolly well hated). Now-a-days the
conditions are quite different. Iron, bricks & concrete
are the ruling materials, the Church is subordinate to the
man of commerce (at least she is in all the commercial
countries) & the banker rules the roost. Building sham
Gothic churches is just about as ludicrous as going naked
to a garden party. The factory-system & the mediaeval
system of production are at opposite extremes. The
modern method is one in which the individual workman

counts merely as a hand —a tool —a cog in the machine. The mediaeval method was like that of a football team. Everyone was bound by the rules & played for his side & not for himself merely, but at the same time everyone counted as an individual with special talents & capabilities & responsibilities. A mediaeval master builder was like a football captain —a man who worked with his men & for the sake of the sport & not a mere man of business with his eye on the till.

4.   The best modern building is done by the engineers —because they make the best use of modern materials & take most advantage of the modern method of production & of the modern style of workman. There is no good modern architecture except that done by men who, like the engineers, recognize the fact that art is a matter of personal devotion to beauty and cannot be imposed on workmen by means of drawings & specifications. Undoubtedly the Westminster Cathedral is one of the best modern buildings (if you leave out of account all the sham Byzantine ornamentation —which is of course bloody rot) because it makes a good use of modern materials & methods. The inside of the building shows this best because it is a naked exhibition of millions of bricks & tons of concrete simply depending on its size & proportions for its effect.

It makes no pretence of being the workmanship of a team of artist-craftsmen such as a mediaeval master-builder had at his command. It says quite frankly 'This is the best that can be done with machine-made materials & an army of men who have no particular interest in the job beyond their Saturday's pay.' Another jolly good building is the Nile Dam at Assouan (for the same reasons) and some of the modern brick railway bridges are splendid too. As for sculptors —well there is none of whom you can say 'he is the finest' because that sounds like the finest of a lot of fine ones and there are not a lot of fine ones of whom one is the finest. Of the Academy sculptors I suppose Auguste Rodin is the boss, but then Academy sculpture is a rum old game and, like George Robey, I shd. say to it 'buzz off.' You see there cannot be a great school of sculpture again until we get a great school of builders again — and that will not happen until after the revolution and even then it will not happen unless, on the ruins of our present godless civilization, we build a state in which poverty, chastity & obedience are the ruling ideas and *that* will not happen unless we all become Christians & THAT will not happen unless we throw away our pride in our own judgment & admit that the Church is the Bride of Christ and that we are all her children & there shall be one fold & one shepherd. So there!

As for *What is Art?*, I suppose you mean the book by Tolstoi, but I don't think it's much use sending you that. It's rather a back number & tarred pretty thick with old Tolstoi's pacificism & puritanism. (It's a good book tho.) To be brief Art is 'showing Beauty.' That is to say an artist is one who shows Beauty & a work of art is a work showing Beauty.

N.B. Art is not skill or cleverness or prettyness or goodness or correctness.

N.B. Beauty is not a picture of the lovely or the lovable, e.g. a picture of your best girl is not a work of art just because she is lovely. The work of art, to be a work of art, must have in it an expression of the artist's own personal devotion to Beauty — his own worship. Beauty is nothing to do with being like anything you like. Beauty is itself something you like. Beauty, like Goodness & Truth, is one of the names of God.

N.B. If you think too much of being good you will be a prig & in the same way if you think too much of doing the beautiful you will be a snob. The great thing is to *love God* & *do what you like* as S. Charles Borromeo said. And so instead of calling ourselves artists we shd. just remember our trades & call ourselves by them — stone-carvers, letter-cutters, potters or whatever it is. Goodbye for now.

We all send heaps of love to you. Yours affectionately
ERIC GILL

G

P.S. What does 'R.C.E. 5' stand for?

P.S. Max (not May) Muriel & John are my brother Max his
wife & his kid! No, Mike is not the father of the pups, tho.
he had a good try at it. We got the bitch to keep the chicks
out of the garden, but she's too old to train so we shall keep
one of the pups instead.

6 6 : TO GEOFFREY KEYNES

In a train to Leeds   *Evening, 27-9-1917*

My dear Keynes: Many thanks for your letter of Sept. 4. I've
had precious little time for letters lately or wd. have written
to you before. I'm glad you are all right so far. So am I.
By heaven! but I've got plenty of work on hand (I'm v. glad
you think me a useful object) and at the present moment
(which partly inspires me to write to you — though I've had
your letter in my bag for a fortnight — I've been in London
away from Ditchling Common a fortnight working at
W'minster Cath! on the vii & viii Stations) I am going to
Leeds upon that very job of which you saw a rotten reproduction in *Land & W⟨ater⟩*. It's really a perfectly magnificent job
&, if I make anything approaching a success of it, it will be a
case of *Nunc dimittis* for me when it's done. The photo. print
you saw showed the original design (done for a competition,
last year, for a monument for the L.C.C. employees — but the
L.C.C. didn't take it on — p'raps they took fright or were
insulted at the awful suggestion that London were a commercial city or that England were a Temple from which a
money-changer or two might not be missed!) wh. was for a
colossal group in bronze. But the present proposal (oh, I
haven't told you that Michael Sadler, vice chanc! Leeds Univ.
you know, has conceived the idea, being taken with the
design & its subject, of putting it at Leeds, in the University
somewhere — I'm going to see the possible sites now, not
necessarily as a war memorial but as a public benefaction —

what ho!) the present proposal is to do it as a colossal high
relief carving in stone. This is my own proposal & I'm v.
glad Sadler approves (he seems to be practically god at Leeds
Univ. & can do what he chooses) because it will keep me clear
of the bronze-founders, whom I know not, & allow me and
my faithful assistants to put the work through entirely on our
own. What a job to do, if it comes off! You see I'm thinking
of making it a pretty straight thing—modern dress as much as
poss., Leeds manufacturers, their wives & servants, don't you
see. Not that I'm thinking to revert to my first stage—the
artist as prophet & preacher—the Chenil Gallery stage—
because there's no need. Here is the sermon given into my
hands, so to say. I didn't invent the notion—I got it from the
Gospels if you'll believe it! I'm only the aesthetic instrument
of the moralists and philosophers. But there's no need to
apologize, is there? Even as artist I may well be enthusiastic
quite apart from the fact that, as 'citizen of this great country'
& member of Christ's Bride, I rather like the job of, the
revolutionary job of turning out the money-changers. Well—
I hope it comes off, that's all. Meanwhile I'm going ahead
with the Westminster job. I've now got ten of the Stations
fixed up—which leaves four, and one of the four is half done
& another begun. So I expect to be through with the 14 by
Easter next year & then I shall be free for 'pastures new'.

Talking of pastures—the 'farm' at Ditchling Common progresses favourably. We have now got 2 pigs, 2 ponies & a cow
besides chickens & other small fry (you don't want a half-bred
sheep-dog pup, do you?) & the cow has a calf—what ho!
We've found the benefit, this last year or so, of having food
on the spot—haven't had to trouble the butcher since before
Xmas—& if the poor devils in London knew 'how they feed
in Sussex' in war time there'd be something said—and it gets
bad if you don't eat it you know. We started brewing beer
too & it was a great success. You wd.n't believe what
thundering good stuff 'home brew' is—knocks the pub. stuff
off the earth. At present we're trying malting 'cause the

brewers, taking fright at the thought of 'home-brew', have got the Gov.ᵗ to stop the sale of malt. But we can get or grow the barley so we'll beat 'em yet. I wish you could come in again soon. It wd. be good to see you. I gather from your letter that you are now married. Is it so? Good luck to you and to her & all the little Keynes that'll 'round the table go'. Where do you live in England? & did you get your leave all right as you hoped? If 'we' thought that they 'might go to Cocking' I hope they enjoyed that beautiful spot. Cocking Down, not that I've seen it since I was 16, is a fine round hill. I've not heard from Jacques Raverat for a long time. Mrs. Cornford is more or less in touch but I've not seen him or her for a long time either.

As a subscriber to *The Game* (you are, aren't you?) did you approve of the Easter tract? I hope you did. If you can write something revolutionary from an army doctor's point of view for the next number we wd. be glad.

Now good bye for the present — Don't fail to see Ditchling Common before you die. Yours ever   ERIC GILL

I'm sorry you're so fed up with idleness, that's partly why I suggest the writing, I only wish it meant that all the 'wastage' was German wastage. All my brothers are home at present. Both the Canadians wounded now. One was run over by a motor lorry — broken pelvis & ruptures poor chap & none of the glory of fighting for it. But he's getting on all right.

67 : TO DR. COOMARASWAMY

Ditchling Common, Sx.   *8-11-1917*

My dear Coomaraswamy: This is in reply to your letter of August 28 last for which many thanks. I liked the poem and have done a woodcut for it. D. P. has the block and is at the earliest opportunity going to set up the poem and print 50

Ditchling Common, Sx. Nov. 8 1917

My dear Coomaraswamy:

This in reply to your letter of August 28 last for which many thanks. I like the poem and have done a woodcut for it. B.P. has the blocks and so the earliest opportunity, going to strike the first and print 50 copies for you. I hope you will get them before Christmas.

I hope you will like the 'picture.' Here is a drawing thing. The next number of the Game is in preparation — I hope that will come to you too. By the way which is no. 3 & after? Did you not get no. 3 — The Easter number? — with a sort of article on Slavery & Freedom?

Any matter whatsoever is nursing my attention at last. I shall be there with it.

Eric next sheet. I have got a lot of fresh work coming in too, so I shall be fully employed for some years to come! Yes, the Miners have been to Ditchling aged sure. They are trying to get a piece of land here & build a workshop & settle down here. Manie (the young man, but accomplished up with various pictures — sophies as present) has finished all the summer working on a farm so he can again set to learn all of him. Mrs. M. has settled down from time to time. I'm a place to learn that you had got a card for a son at the Boston museum. I wonder if you will ever come over to England. We may in for the devils own time if it after the war. Things unfortunately have from a religious point of view. The war does it seem to have Christian or so it is. I hope you are one and Mrs. Coomaraswamy also & the children also as we are. From yours all through.

Yours sincerely,
Eric Gill

LETTER TO DR. COOMARASWAMY

copies for you. I hope you'll get them before Christmas & I hope you will like the 'picture'. Here is a tracing thereof![1] The next number of *The Game* is in preparation —I hope that will soon be out too. But you say 'when is No. 3 to appear?' Did you not get No. 3 —the Easter number? —with a sort of article on 'Slavery & Freedom'? My work at Westminster is nearing completion at last. I shall be thro. with it by Easter next I hope. I have got a lot of fresh work coming in too, so I shall be full of work for several years to come! Yes, the Mairets have been at Ditchling a good deal. They are trying to get a piece of land here & build a workshop & settle down in it. Mairet (nice young man, but too much mixed up with curious philosophies at present) has been here all the summer working on a farm so I've seen a good deal of him. Mrs. M. has been down from time to time. I was pleased to learn that you had got a good job at the Boston Museum. I wonder if you will ever come back to England. We are in for the devil's own time of it after the war. Things look extremely black from a religious point of view. The war doesn't seem to have chastened us at all. I hope you are well and Mrs. Coomaraswamy also —& the children. Have you got them all with you? We are all well and flourishing on our little tiny farm. Yours sincerely,   ERIC GILL

68 : TO JOSEPH CRIBB

D. Comm.   *6-2-1918*

My dear Joseph: What pigs we were to let your birthday pass without writing to you —we did think about you on the day & we did and do wish you many happy returns of it. I hope at any rate that you heard from your spouse —that wd. make up for a whole forgetful world. But we didn't forget —I'll only speak for myself —I had no chance to write.

[1] Photograph opposite.

Thank you very much for your letter of Jan. 10. We were glad to hear that you got back safe and sound after your adventurous holiday. What a fine time you must have had one way and another. Well you deserved it and now we are all looking forward to your next homecoming and as you said yourself we hope it will be a fixture next time.

Things are going on much as usual since you left except that we've at last made up our minds to be a more methodical household. We've got a housebell and a time table —what they call, in the places where they really live proper lives, a 'horary'. I'm going to rig up a proper bell on the outside of the house on the wall & then the whole neighbourhood will know the time. The children are bucking up like anything and it makes things go like one o'clock. To amuse you I'll enclose a time table herewith —my time table —but each of the children has one —so everyone knows what to do at every hour of the day —and night.

I'm now working on the last 'Station' but one & have nearly finished the claw work. I shall begin the last next week I hope & then fix the two together. So I think the whole job will be finished by Easter! Then I shall be able to begin to earn my living again what ho!

I've recently written an article for the *Westminster Cathedral Chronicle* on the subject of the Stations. I will send you a copy when it comes out. It was rather amusing writing it because I wrote it under a pseudonym as if I were an outsider criticizing someone else's work.

My sister Angela has been staying with us for the last ten days. She's going again to-morrow —alas. It's been ripping having her and she's helped no end with the children & the time table business. On Joan's birthday she got up a cinematograph entertainment with our children and the Peplers. It was great sport. They had the back part of the living room for a stage and it did very well indeed with the curtains across. All the audience sat in the other half. The acting was awfully good and the play was most melodramatic and cinematographicalistical. Poor old Joan unfortunately had a toothache off and on all day —but she enjoyed herself pretty well on the whole I'm glad to say. I quite agree with all you say about the Tommys and the Path to Rome. We must all do our bit to bring in as many as we can reach. Spread the news for all you're worth. I send herewith a copy of the *N. Witness* wh. will interest you. G. K. C.'s article in the middle & the *N.W.* War aims are splendidly right. And Fr. Vincent's article (tho. too personal for my taste) will interest you too. Pass it on to your pals.

I went to Leicester on Jan. 19th. & lectured on Slavery & Factories to the Art School students etc. It was a pretty good fight —the manufacturers were there in force —I must tell you more when I see you next. After Leicester I went on to Hawkesyard again with Pepler —he was lecturing there on Education. H'yard you may remember is the Dominican Priory where Fr. Vincent Mc.Nabb is. We are great friends there and they are the right stuff —not half. Well cheeri ho! With heaps of love from me and from us all & I will try and write again soon. (I hope you have good news of little Agnes.) Yours affectionately   ERIC GILL

Angela says give him my love & salaāms. She's a dear.

69 : TO HIS BROTHER ROMNEY

At the George Inn.
77 Boro' High St., S.E.1   *6-3-1918*

My dear old R. C. G.: Thank you very much for your birthday greetings & letter (N.B. 'the enclosed is for my sub.' them's your words but there weren't no bloomin enclosed!)

Very glad *The Game* interested you. When an officer & a gentleman (not to mention a public sch. & varsity man!) condescends to argue it takes my breath away —I'm not used to it. However, to answer your letter:—

In the article referred to it said: 'a factory workman (I quote from memory) may show the l⟨ove⟩ of G⟨od⟩ in his *life* or in his *thought*; he cannot show it in his work.' You reply 'if he does his work well for the honour of his side (as at football) or for the love of his country (as in an aeroplane factory) he may show the l. of G. in his work.'

But suppose he did his work well (i.e. in a thoroughly efficient manner — so that the foreman could find no fault in it) not for the honour of his side or for patriotism but because the organization of the factory was such that 'bad' work earned the 'sack'? What then? You couldn't tell the difference, neither by looking at them nor using them, between a propeller made by your 'l. of G.' man and one made by my 'hatred of sack' man. 'Efficiency for its purpose' is a thing obtainable by force. Slave labour, especially if you are reasonably kind to your slaves ('one loves one's men' — you know the phrase — it is used in the factory as much as in the army!), will produce perfectly efficient aeroplanes. No — it's not what can be forced out of a man wh. is evidence of the l. of G. Paying taxes is not *charity* however willingly & patriotically it is done. Charity is free — gratuitous — a free-will offering — a sacrifice — an oblation. In workmanship this oblation of the workman to God is Beauty — something not asked of him or demanded but given — for love.

'But,' you will (or may) say, 'Beauty may be demanded — as when a man is *paid* to put filigree on a watch cover.' True — but that's why I distinguished between Beauty & loveliness — between Beauty & adornment. It may not always be possible or easy to tell the real from the counterfeit — but in the long run Truth will out & hence in the long run the factory is doomed because in a factory you pay taxes all the time (however willingly) and can never give in *Charity*. Hence the saying that 'the essential perfection of man is in Charity'.

But don't worry yourself about Beauty or imagine I want a world in which every workman is self-consciously an artist making things of beauty — any more than I want a world full of prigs consciously going about 'doing good' —*I* have to worry about Beauty because its more or less in my day's work. I suggest that you approach the matter from the philosophic side —what is freedom? What is servility?

Is a factory organized like a football team? Yes, like a professional football team (Chelsea v. Hotspurs, you know). The players are paid the lowest they can be got for & the directors take the gate-money & arrange the fixtures. Organization is all right —but it's one thing to organize, another thing to be organized. 'The workers haven't the power (brain-power being meant) to organize' they say. Quite true, & so you can take your choice & have Free & Catholic Galway or else the factories of protestant Belfast. The working man can run a small farm or a small workshop —he can't stand up to our merchant princes & run Manchester & Liverpool. He hasn't got the tradition or the training or the *inclination*. But there's v. little hope for him in England or Germany (we copy everything from G.!), he's lost even his own tradition of freedom just as he's lost his property & his appetite for property. Hence the only remedy suggested in *The Way Out* q.v.

My love to Cecil & to yourself too. It's good news that you & Lulu are so soon to be married. Ap. 6th. Right ho!

What a great time you two must be having —only five more weeks. Your loving brother   ERIC

P.S. If you find yourselves anywhere near *Far Oakridge*, which is a mile or so from Sapperton (along the canal), which is a mile or so from Cirencester, go and see Wm. Rothenstein at Iles Farm; he wd. welcome you. Give him my dutiful love & greetings. I am up in town, except for week ends, working at W'minster Cath., till Easter or after. Give us a look up if you're in London.

70 : TO WILLIAM ROTHENSTEIN

Ditchling Comm. Sx.   *7-7-1918*

My dear Rothenstein: Your letters of June 28 & July 4 reached me yesterday. Thank you very much for them. It is very good of you, in the midst of your own difficulties, to have troubled to write at all. I am astonished, almost incredulous, to hear that you are called up & perhaps will be gone before this can reach you. I wd. have answered at once but a visit from Debenham yesterday morning and the necessity of helping with the making of our haystack in the afternoon & evening prevented me. I, like you, am Grade I. Debenham seems to think I might get another month's exemption by putting a letter which he is going to write to me before the head of this Recruiting District. He says he *will* word it pretty harshly to the effect that he doesn't see why he shd. pay 2 or 3 hundred pounds for a half finished monument. I suppose he will pay whether I finish it or not (at least something on account), in fact he said as much, but it's a pity not to finish the job now its so nearly done. The Westminster job is done! I finished at Easter. So there's nothing to be got out of that. Otherwise I've got on hand *three* 'Wayside Calvaries' —one a big one to be put up at Marlow-on-Thames. And, apart from small jobs, there was to have been the Leeds job as soon as Sadler returned from India. I understand that More Adie is trying to do something on my behalf. I know nothing as yet & expect that I shall join up as a private. I rather hope that. I understand quite well your feelings as to that. I hope my friends will not get some horrible job for me which as the father of a family I shall feel bound to take. Please don't worry about me. Your own affairs must be quite enough to worry about. I hope Mrs. R & the children are all well. We are all well & send our united loves. Yours ever   ERIC GILL

7 1 : TO GEOFFREY KEYNES

Ditchling Comm. Sx.   *25-7-1918*

My dear Keynes: Your letter of November last year has lain on
my desk ever since I received it reminding me from time to
time to write to you when an opportunity came and now I'm
'called up' and am to 'join up' next Thursday Augst 1 and
have been most awfully rushed during the last few months
trying to get as much done as possible before going so the
opportunity has never turned up. Even now I cannot tell you
all the news for it is 3.30 a.m. and I am supposed to be doing
a drawing and get to it again before dawn if I am to get it done
to-night which is my desire. I will try & let you know where
I get sent to after Aug 1st [. . .] Westminster Stations are
finished ('ence, I understand, the withdrawal of my exemption), Dorset Cross is nearly finished but cannot be quite done
before Aug 1st Many other jobs (including that Leeds affair
of wh. I told you) must be left. I hope you are well & flourishing. It seems that things are looking up a bit in France — but!
wait till I get there. Love from us both   Yours ever

                              ERIC GILL

Has your infant by now arrived?

    We hope all is well with Mrs. Keynes & him or her (if he
or she is here).

7 2 : TO DESMOND CHUTE

In hospital   J.M. ✠ J.D.[1]   *Sunday 6 p.m.*
                                        22-9-1918

My dear Desmond: I hope you are quite well & getting on all
right. I am getting on fairly well but am suffering horribly
from homesickness. There isn't much news to give you — nor
is it possible adequately to describe this army life. Mary will
have told you that I failed in the drawing test owing to my

    [1] That is: Jesus, Mary, Joseph, Dominic.

not having any mechanical knowledge. So they asked me what I wd. like to do. I said I didn't know. So the officer asked if I wd. like to be a motor driver. I said 'yes'. So that's what I am put down as, and now I am waiting to be sent away to some squadron. This camp is only a distributing centre. It's an enormous place — covering about eight square miles! Life is absolutely mechanical and brutal here & I shall be jolly glad to leave it. I hope it will be soon. I am jolly glad to be having a day or two in hospital. I have felt rotten during the last three days. The orderlies here are decent friendly men & I am very comfortable. The Catholic chaplain comes every day — so that's all right. I hope to have some talk with him. He is going to bring me Communion to-morrow. I got Mass this morning. It was said in a huge canvas building (originally an air-ship shed) which is used for a cinema during the week. There seems to be no proper accommodation for Catholics. Considering the large number of Irish Catholic soldiers here, this is extraordinary. But there seems to be a general attitude of scorn and sneering towards the Catholics in the camp — and I think they do as little for them as they can. [. . .]

It is the greatest possible blessing having the office to say & so far I have found it quite easy to fit in. There is a terrible lot of waiting about in the army & as I don't talk to the other men much I find the beads very good. It is rather a treat being in hospital for one thing & that is that I can *read* the office regularly.

How goes it with the work? It seems years since I left. What a ripping day we had that Wednesday & wasn't it jolly fine having all the children up to supper?

Have you started lessons yet?

I enclose a memorandum of various things which I shd. be glad if you wd. attend to. Some of them are things you already know about & may already have done but I've made the list as complete as I know. How is Albert? I am longing to hear from Ditchling Common. Perhaps there are letters for me at the hut to-day & if I were not in hospital I shd. have them. I hope they will forward them. But I don't suppose I shall be here more than a day or two.

Now good-bye. I can't write much now. It's rather a job in bed & I don't feel up to much yet. But oh Lor! I am getting hungry. I've had nothing to eat since 8.30 this morning & then I only had one piece of bread & butter or margarine rather. I'm not supposed to have anything to eat to-day —so they say. From your loving friend   ERIC JOSEPH

73 : TO DESMOND CHUTE

In hospital,   J.M. ✠ J.D.   *27-9-1918*
Blandford Camp   *Friday, 10.15 a.m.*

My dear Desmond: The doctor hasn't come round yet —but as I am really nearly well (except for the 'dire rear') I shd. not be surprised if I am turned out to-day for the orderly says there are 150 pneumonia cases in the camp detention huts awaiting admission to hospital. There are 2 or 3 in the ward! The wet cold weather & the continuous standing about at parades is cruel. I don't know what they think they are doing. The organization of the place from the point of view of the men's health & spirits is scandalous —However I won't bore you with that. I will begin by answering questions, as well as I can:—(Wo! the post man has just come. Any for me? Yes, 3. One from Hilary —written on the 13th! forwarded here from Dixon's, one from my father & one from D. Common —a little package from Joanna —the darling —some sweet lavender & a picture & letter. How ripping.) And now the Doctor has been too & owing to the need of this ward for specially bad cases I & half a dozen others are transferred to *No. 5 ward.* We have just packed our odds & ends & now are waiting to go. I wonder how long I shall stay *there.*

1)   I am glad Baines has done the Attree tomb [. . .] That shd. be rather a nice little Inscript. when done and shd.

lead to more churchyard work for Albert. This I think
wd. be good. [. . .]

3)   I'm glad Ernest Collings wants a brass. (He's a nice
man — Secy. (did he tell you?) of the Mestrovic Purchase
fund) — Yes, I'm sorry you didn't give him food — Never
mind. Why didn't you offer him the brass from the
shelf? or do you think we ought to keep one? I got them
cast by Alex^r. Parlanti — Albion Works, Parsons Green
Lane, Fulham, S.W. He charged £3. 10. last time I think.
The original is in the cupboard with the coloured
Madonnas. I am under agreement with Marchant not to
sell more than one dozen — I don't know whether the
agreement also includes price — I shd. think it did.
Anyway as other people have paid £15 I fear Collings
must — if he is willing. [. . .]

4)   I'm glad Baines is letting a cross into that panel for you.
I shd. like to see *all* those panels used up.
How I long to see the workshop again & my tools.

5)   *Gough Stone*. I hope Albert is getting on all right with this
and not hurrying it. I hope he is keeping the thin strokes
nice & thin & the thick strokes not too fat. I want it
cut as neatly as poss. Please note (generally), keep
rubbings of all inscriptions done but I expect you naturally
would. I told you about the Gough *Colour* last time —
didn't I?

6)   *I rejoice about Complin*. I only hope the singing practices
don't take too much of your time. But if the children
are keen that's half the battle. Dear Betty — she makes a
most useful cantor & I believe Dame Laurentia wd. be
quite pleased with her if she went to Stanbrook. I v.
glad you've learnt the Saturday *Te Lucis*. The 2nd ending
of Tone VIII is good — when is it used — ad lib.? [. . .]

8)   Vespers at H.H. I told you it was good to be there.
Isn't it marvellously beautiful to hear & yet not to see —
except an occasional lay sister trimming a candle — &
yet to be so near the Bd. Sacrament. How wonderful it

wd. be in a really beautiful church. Oh —if some day we
got the chance of building a monastic church! What tone
did they sing *Jesu Corona Virginum* to? Don't the lay
sisters (if they are such) look lovely in their habit —Oh —
but there's something about Sunday afternoons & Vespers
& *Lucis Creator* that's not explainable in words —& the
In Exitu (Ton. peregrinus). . . .

9) I like you to call me Master. It gives me great satisfaction —but what am I to call *you*? [. . .]

13) Light in workshop. I should buy a packet or more for
    workshop use out of workshop money —& enter it in
    cash book. You can buy them from the house if you
    wish —if Mary will sell!

14) How —jolly fine to be going to H'yard for Rosary Sunday.
    I wish I could be there —better luck next year. How
    marvellous to think it is a whole year since Hilary was
    received.

I am glad you will have a good chance of having a real
consultation with Fr. Vincent. For I don't feel myself com-
petent to advise you —I am too much an interested party.
There are two main points (as I see it) in your difficulty —
(This v. moment I've suffered a ridiculous humiliation —about
shaving —I give it to you —with my love.) [. . .]

You remember one day discussing S. Ben^t. J.[1] I said he
stood for apostolic poverty and I would stand for apostolic
riches. You understood what I meant, didn't you? I consider
that at Ditchling we are rich —but there is a certain apostolic
value in such riches isn't there? Take Saturday afternoon tea
for instance —the hot new bread from our own oven, baked
by our own women folk —it is holy bread.

The little land —the workshop —the stone —the animals &
garden —all are riches —but if we give God the praise and have
compassion on our fellow-men I believe God blesses such riches.
(I have been greatly tempted to self-praise and self-pity here —
but it is my daily watch-word: 'Praise *God* & have *compassion*!')

[1] St. Benedict Joseph Labre.

As to your money: —I am but a little older & more worldly
wise than you —but I say (until you've talked to Fr. Vincent)
go easy with your conscience in that matter — thro. no fault of
your own you are not yet able to earn your living for certain.
Your health and upbringing have made difficulties hitherto.
At our trade a man should start earlier in life than you are
doing. You ought to have been apprenticed at 15 or earlier.
But you have great gifts to bring —not to be despised —wh.
will be of great use in the cause. How great a blessing have
you been to me! (*Donum Dei*!) You have some small capital —
well, keep it as God's gift —until He gives you that other: the
power to do without the capital.

Did you explain to B. P. and J. about 'the handmaiden's eyes
on the hands of her mistress'? Albert also —How great a
blessing it is for the pupil to love his master and the handmaiden her mistress —they will only know when they are
masters & mistresses themselves. But the whole 122 Psalm is
great & holy as indeed they all are, only some hit you in the
eye quicker. How splendid to sing hymns —there are none
here —but in my heart I sing them. I sang the *Salve* one night
in the dark outside the tent lines —but I could hardly do it for
tears. Sing *Jerusalem the Golden* too —I love it & it is a Catholic
hymn —also *Veni Emmanuel*, the grand thing!

Good bye —God bless you —my friend & loving brother in
S. Dominic.   ERIC JOSEPH

74 : TO DESMOND CHUTE

R.C. Chaplain's Room   J.M. ✠ J.D.   *5-10-1918*
B'ford Camp

for S. Francis' Day

My very dear Desmond: I had no chance to write to you
yesterday. I was in the middle of a letter to Hilary (q.v.) and
couldn't even finish that. Now I will try and deal faithfully
with you —in this peace and quietness. It's awfully nice of the

R.C. Chaplain (Fr. McCabe)*—he's given me the run of his room for reading and writing and that is a great blessing. Well, I'm getting on a bit better now. But I'm not at all well I'm sorry to say & the stomachic complaint from wh. I have the honour to be suffering takes it out of me & makes me rather tired —and sanitary 'fatigues' do the rest. However I am greatly blessed as usual —God's darling is my name.

1) Thank you very much for all your letters. I hope you aren't tiring yourself too much with all the affairs of 'the firm' & the home. You must be strict and go to bed at a regular and proper time. Thank you very much for the rubbing of the 'Pietà'. I think it is beautiful and I am very glad to have it. You are getting on jolly well with the letter cutting (whatever is the language?) and I am very pleased about it. It is true as you say that you haven't yet quite got the 'modern' touch. The thick strokes shd. be a trifle thicker in proportion but it isn't only that for you can have quite modern lettering with no difference of thick & thin at all. [. . .]
I like the 'pietà' very much. You must certainly do it in the round. I amuse myself sometimes to think of all the things I will do when I get back! That Madonna and Child I've got to do for my Edinburgh friend —don't you think it wd. be beautiful in half relief in white marble *polished* (one of those biggish blocks in the yard —so don't use *all* the stone up —save a bit for me!)

2) Yes, I shd. think I do know the Crusaders' song. It is one of the very grandest things I know. It wants a lot of breath to sing properly. We must go through it together and learn it when I come home.

3) The Apocalypse: Oh —do send it to me. I've not got it here, but can you get it separate? Yes —it was fine —that reading of it together down at Bryantspiddle.

* C. SS. R. (Do you know anything about the Redemptorists? I don't.)

H

4) I do hope (I think I do) understand now what you mean by 'positive' poverty. I hope you are now at Hawkesyard & that this will reach you & Hilary there. I hope you will have a really straight talk —putting all these things before him —with Fr. Vincent. I wish we could meet & talk —it is so difficult in writing. You can make statements in writing but you can't *discuss*. When —where will it be? Never mind, I must wait patiently. God is blessing me here with very high blessings & I mustn't ask to be allowed to have my pudding as well as eat it. I want, e.g., to know more what your view (and it is mine too when I put myself in your circumstances) actually involves in practice. But it must wait. Let's get on with the war and meanwhile Praise God. [. . .]
You mustn't starve your shop. On the other hand many an artist has ruined his work by having too good tools. I think you must apply the 'apostolic riches' rule to your shop even tho' you apply the 'holy poverty' rule to your life. Do you agree? [. . .]

6) I am very glad you've been having good talks with Hilary. He has written very lovingly to me. I think he misses me —I am glad & sorry. How good it will be to join hands again. Meanwhile we must all keep in touch as best we can —in prayers & praises & spiritual communications. Oh what a marvellous beautiful epistle to-day (29th. Sunday). [. . .]

8) I am very glad the Gough tablet looks well. Dear little Albert —simple child. He will do well —and what a blessing he's 'under instruction'. What jolly good pupils God has given me. I'm glad you got the wood from N. and B. all right.

9) Music —good —that is splendid. [. . .]

11) Yes, do enter your carvings into the ledger (& also into the list of jobs book so as to get a number on each). I shall be very glad if you do this & honoured by it too. You might put a star in the number book by the side of

the first new number you make and in the margin write to this effect: J.M.✠J.D. —here begins record of work done by E. J. G. cum D. B-M. C.

12) *Insurance:*—Opinions differ about this. It is a form of saving money & not necessarily condemnable. There is a lot of competition among Insurance companies & to get clients they outbid one another in offering benefits — bonuses —easy payments & all sorts of tricks for making the payment of the premium seem a pleasure —& for making people think they are getting something for nothing. There are good, old-established companies who do good sound business & no trickery & with them insurance is simply a sort of wordly prudence. In so far as, by insurance, you can say you are doing away with the possibility of becoming (in illness or through accident) a burden upon friends or relatives —well —it may be a good thing. But why thus obliterate family charity or even collective charity? I feel personally that insurance is an infringement of the command of our dear Lord (I agree with you & think we must plagiarize our dear Fr. Director) that we take no thought of the morrow. I think a good case can be made out for insurance on the part of public trustees. Thus I think the W'minster Cathedral chapter wd. be well advised to insure Arch-bishop's House against fire —I don't *know* but I think a good case cd. be made out where the thing insured is not a personal possession but is held in trust. But personal insurance I think smells of the devil —too canny by half for Christians. 'Mothers are different —Mothers are darlings' as Wilde said & I don't want to urge you, against your own conscience, to run counter to her wishes. Mothers are generally a bit worldly-wise. They have to be so. I am not insured in any way myself — (the home is insured against fire & air attacks —but this because the mortgager insisted on it —there again I think a good case can be made out. He lent us £450 on the property —

why shd. *he* suffer if by *my* fault or misfortune the house were destroyed?) So there you are. I think insurance incompatible with Holy Poverty — but — mothers are mothers.

13) Eliz. has sent me two rosaries for show purposes. (Black & violet & red yellow & green). [. . .]

15) *Money matters* [. . .] In general pay when the money comes in — not before unless urgently necessary, principally because we have not much capital to play with. But when the creditor is poor and wants his money then, if I can, I pay him at once. [. . .]

17) Yes you can put your letters to me in the file. . . Please read what you will — but beware of my awful past! [. . .]

20) The Dinner was grand to read of. Here we are not ill fed (see Hilary's letter) but I could eat more — & I miss a drink at dinner. [. . .]

22) *Albert's drawing.* He's very slow I know. He ought to draw say 50 $1\frac{1}{2}''$ 'letters' in $\frac{1}{2}$ an hour easily — i.e. well enough for cutting purposes — for there's no occasion to draw serifs or to get a very high degree of sharpness in edges of forms. Still it wd. be good for him sometimes to draw letters (with brush) on paper — so as not to be incapable of good and finished drawing.

23) I agree — let all his orders be from you if Mary agrees. I'm glad he's doing the Attree Inscript. [. . .]

Now good bye & God bless you & guide you. From your loving friend & brother in S. Dominic.

ERIC JOSEPH

I may have news for you in a day or two.

Let me know when you are returning to Ditchling —
N.B. my address need only be: Pte AER Gill 295744
H Section R.A.F.,
Hut 17,
Blandford Camp.
(leave out all that about Petrol Driver.)

[A pencilled fragment]

Sandown Pk.   J.M. ✠ J.D.   *23-10-1918 9.30 p.m.*

My dearest Desmond: I will at last begin a letter to you to-day
—but, I feel a horrid pig, I went out & got some supper at a
cookshop in Esher this evening and so spent the last part of
my spare time! But I thought you wdn't mind (all the urgent
points in your last letters being I think already answered) and
it was rather a treat to be 'out of the army' for an hour & a
half. She was a nice fat motherly woman in the cookshop too —
& I got her to air the scarf which Mary sent (she said it needed
airing!) —tell Mary this.

Well, Hawkesyard was a great success —I knew it wd. be &
I rejoiced all the time to think of you & Hilary in that house &
habit. I must be going there myself v. soon [. . .]

Sandown Park,   J.M. ✠ J.D.   *Sunday*
Esher.   *10-11-1918 3.0 p.m.*

My dear Desmond: I did not write on Friday because in the
evening I went hunting for a Catholic Church in Surbiton and
could not find one. The nearest is Kingston. The complete
irreligion of this life amazes me. Here is another Sunday and
no Mass. The C. of E.'s had a church parade; the R.C.'s and
the Nonconformists were put on fatigues. I was put on dining
room fatigue —washing tables and dishes. We are now free
for the rest of the day. Of course, apart from missing Mass, I
do not mind. I am inwardly contented —thanks be to God.
But four Sundays without Mass! and Holy Communion not so
much as dreamed of by those in authority. Last Sunday I complained to the Sergeant Major and he said 'you can go to
Church this evening'; I said 'as a Catholic I want Mass'; he
said 'well there's no Church parade for Catholics to-day'.

They don't care a scrap – Why shd. they? They have no conception of the Catholic idea of the Church.

Well, well – but what are the priests of the neighbourhood doing – not to have made any arrangements for us? They must know that we are here. That was why I tried to find a church. I will try again and see the priest and ask about it.

Yesterday afternoon I went up to London & went to Vespers & Complin at the Cathedral. It was a great blessing & to hear the *Salve* sung again (simple tone) was marvellous. I spent several hours in the C.W.L. hut (by the Cathedral) writing letters. It is a very nice comfortable place & quite blessedly devoid of the wretched Y.M.C.A. undenominational flavour. I also went to the Admiralty & learned that the War-Office had approved my transfer from the R.A.F.S. I suppose that will now go through – sometime. There is nothing fresh to tell you about army life. I am getting on slowly with the motor-driving. I do not find it over easy – the big lorries take a bit of managing, especially on hills.

I look forward to our next meeting. You will let me know when you are coming in good time won't you & I will write to you at 'the George'. I am very glad you had a good & fruit-ful talk with Mrs. Chute. I hope you are now having a really good threshing out of your affairs at Hawkesyard. I feel very much the difficulty you are in. It is a crisis. I pray earnestly that you may be guided & strengthened by the Holy Ghost. The war is marvellously ending and in a few months I shall be home again, I hope. It will be a wonderful thing for me – the ending of this exile. But what a mercy too the exile has been and, I pray, may yet be. Shall I fall again into my old self-indulgent ways? I also need your prayers that I may be guided & strengthened. There will be so much to do in the future & the real war is only just beginning. The war with Germany has done no more than clear the decks for a much larger battle. God bless you – my dear Desmond. Pray for me as I pray for you. Your loving brother in S. Dominic

ERIC PETER JOSEPH

77 : TO DESMOND CHUTE

Sandown Pk.   J.M. ✠ J.D.   *18-11-1918*

My dear Desmond: I was exceedingly disappointed not to be able to get to Haverstock Hill on Saturday or Sunday. Just as I was starting off I was informed that all leave to London was cancelled until further notice! (I suppose on account of the crowds & excitements.) I only hope you guessed that I was unavoidably prevented. It was a great disappointment on another ground too — I very much wanted to make the acquaintance of the Haverstock Hill House — and your presence there seemed an admirable opportunity. However, though I could probably have gone to London with v. little risk (or none) of being stopped (several men went and returned safely) I am in the army for religious as much as patriotic reasons & make it my practice to render unto Caesar what is his without complaint or subterfuge. So now I suppose you are back at the Crank & I wd. I were too. You will have heard of my flying visit (oh, but it was great!)

Now to business: —

Albert: Keep him continuously employed and let me know, without reserve, how he works. It is good for you that you shd. have this little experience of mastership. Keep an eye on him as much as poss. in a friendly way & let him see that idleness won't do & is disloyal and dishonest. [. . .]

Your workshop. Have you come to any decision as to your future? If so, does it involve staying at D. Common or leaving us? If the former — then the workshop is urgently necessary — & must be begun at once. A temporary wooden hut wd. do you for a start. I have no idea when I shall be released but when I am I must start work — and shall need a clear shop.

I feel I can't write much without meeting you & learning the results of your visit to Hawkesyard.

Meanwhile God bless you. I am your loving brother in S. Dominic   E. P. J. G.

LOVE TO ALL

Has Nic returned? I was sorry not to see him. Have you got any coke in for the workshop fires? I have *The Game* from Hilary this evening. I had no idea I was going to take up so much of it. Your roundel[1] is beautiful and 'the Apple' makes a most splendid tail-piece.

78 : TO DESMOND CHUTE

Hurst Park Camp Canteen J.M. ✠ J.D.   *Evening 29-11-1918*

My very dear Desmond: Here is Friday — our day and Our dear Lord's day &, as he has willed it, the day of my release (potentially) from Caesar's Service. Before you get this, you will have heard from Mary of the good news. Many days I have hoped to hear & now it has come in the most unexpected manner. But I will tell you all the amusing details of the manner when I get home, as I hope, next week. It has been most exciting & amusing. Well, now I have a free evening & so will write to you as promised. To-morrow morning early I go off to Blandford & there, presumably, I shall finish off the business. To-night I am here because it was too late, after I had been medically inspected etc., to get to B. to-night.

I have rejoiced to hear that you have been steadily getting well. I hope I shall be home before you go away home. I have an idea that in some ways it will be an exile for you — your home going. (By Jove! I know a little about exiles — if only a little.) But — cheer up and come back quite well & strong for the coming work. I hear from Hilary that Mrs. Chute is quite willing to advance the money for the workshop. I am hoping to hear from her as to terms — & I hope they, the terms, will be such as I can manage — or as you & I can manage between us. I will leave a good deal of what I want to say to you until I come home — much depends on what you yourself have to say to me — as to e.g. your visit to Hawkesyard & the decisions you have come to as a result of that visit.

[1] 'Every leopard lark or rose.'

'Fortunately' my release has come just in time so that I can get home to manage things without there being a gap between your stewardship and my return. Albert I am writing to.

Nothing presses in the way of work — & I shall soon get started again & make things hum.

I am very grateful for all the blessings of this life. I only wish you & Hilary had been with me to share it — but then it wd. have been so much less of an exile as to have lost much of the value it has been for me. But how short a time is 3 months (& barely that) when you think of the many who have borne it for 3 years! But I wd. have borne it for 3 years if necessary & I think I wd. have continued to praise God.

Now good night — God bless you & make you strong & well — & guide you. Blessed Dominic — pray for us all. Your loving brother   ERIC JOSEPH PETER

P.S. Of course I may find that I have to report at the Admiralty — but even in that case I shall be free to come home & see to things at frequent intervals, so all will be well.

79 : TO DESMOND CHUTE

In train from   J.M. ✠ J.D.   *21-12-1918*
Maidenhead to London

My dear Desmond: [. . .] I am now on my way back from Bisham. I've been to see the Cross. It doesn't look half bad & the site is most beautiful. It will be a marvel to see a Crucifix in such a place. I'm now going home & after Christmas I'm jolly well going to start the carving. (I must tell you, by the way, Marchant has given me a commission to carve him a crucifix in black marble — gilded like the wood cut! That's a fine job isn't it? It is to be 2 feet high — as for an altar.)

Well — I reported at the Admiralty on Thursday & was told that, as they are still able to struggle on without my assistance, I could go home till called for! & get on with my own work.

So I gave thanks ✠ & departed. Yesterday I did various jobs in London — got the 2 little brasses from Parlanti among other things — I took them to the Goupil Gallery. I also took Bro. Richard's M & C & left it there for him. Thus he & Collings can both care for their images in person. [. . .] I also got the welcome news from Dixon that Stanley Spencer is home again (they meet at the Slade). [. . .]

I'm seeing about the wood engraving tools for Sister Werburg. Have you got *yours* with you? Send me Spencer's address. I wd like to write to him. God be with you & O.L. & St D. pray for us both. Yours loving bro.   E. P. J. G. O.S.D.

80 : TO WILLIAM ROTHENSTEIN

Ditchling Comm. Sx.   J.M. ✠ J.D.   2-1-1919

My dear Rothenstein: This lettercard has lain ready addressed on my table for several weeks waiting an opportunity for writing but what with Christmas, visitors and a mass of work & correspondence & general straightening up of my affairs necessitated by my three months absence from home I have had no chance until now — and now I have only a chance because the advent of your letter this morning determines me to make one! Well — well . . . Three months as a motor driver (learner of course) in the Ryl. Air Force is an experience which can hardly be described in writing. I must really wait until we meet to tell you about it. I am very well & was getting even fat. Idleness is not the word for it — but then of course it was the tail end of the war and we were not really wanted as at an earlier stage we shd. have been. Motor driving is great sport but, like everything else in the army (anyway in the R.A.F.), it is made a punishment and every man a criminal.

However as things stand at present I am 'on leave' indefinitely! I was transferred in December to the Anti-Submarine Div. of the Admiralty (as a draughtsman — through the influence of a client of mine who is a friend of Capt. Fisher (brother to the Educ^n. Minister) who is director of that Division.) But as they had no need of my services there — the armistice being signed & work slack — I was told I could go on with my own work until called upon. Technically therefore I am still an 'airman' lent to the Admiralty & by the latter given indefinite leave! Meanwhile I have put in for my discharge & I am now growing a beard again!

I am v. glad you liked our Christmas booklet. Yes, I was home in time for Christmas and am busy with work of all sorts. I am hoping soon to hear of Sadler's return & that I can put that Leeds job in hand.

And you? Did you escape altogether? Was the Y.M.C.A.'s job a possible one? Oh! the Y.M.C.A. as seen from the private's level! Oh! the Y.M.C.A. buns & lady helpers!

I hear from C.L.R. from Harrogate. I am sorry he has been ill. We are all well here & the little farm, though muddy, is flourishing. [. . .]

We both send our love to you all. I hope we may meet soon. If you are to be in London soon let me know. Yours affectly.

ERIC GILL

81 : TO DESMOND CHUTE

J.M. ✠ J.D. Dom. in Oct. Epiph. 1919 (Incip. in Sabb. 11-1-1919)
Ditchling Common, Sx.   *9.0 p.m. 11-1-1919*

My dear Desmond Bernardin-Mary. Greetings & blessings.

At last I am about to write to you, partly because it is becoming indecent — this prolonged silence — & partly because I really have an opportunity! [. . .]

Well, I'll begin with your letters & go through them. In the first place I think you know that they let me off at the Admiralty and told me I could go on with my own work till called upon. I have since heard officially that the termination of my engagement there has been approved. This means that

if the R.A.F. chooses, it can now claim me again. What ho!
I'm not worrying because I don't think they will claim me.
But suppose they do! Anyway I'm behaving as if I were home
for good and have not shaved since Dec. 19th. (I believe I am
beginning to look respectable again.) Furthermore Mr.
Baines has come back! He is now in Ireland fixing the Gough
Tablet. Lady Gough only wanted to see it to discuss with me
the addition, on the badge, of the words 'Life Brigade'. But
she decided to leave them out. I have since been in correspondence with her about the Government Report on 'War
Graves'. She, as a mourning widow, is very indignant. I,
as an artist and an opponent of the Servile State & in several
other capacities am equally indignant.' [. . .][1]

Now about the workshop. [. . .] The times are too difficult at present for the launching of any new scheme. I have
got to get to work again —a thing I have not yet succeeded in
doing. Building operations seem impossible at present. So
you must be patient and come back on the old lines for a time.
I had a long talk with Fr. Vincent when he was here and he
seemed quite to agree with me. [. . .]

It was very good having Fr. Vincent here, tho. of course I
did v. little work in consequence. However the conferences
I had with him were invaluable so I'm not complaining. Mary
& Hilary & I went into Brighton on the Sunday (S. Thos.) and
heard him preach a very good sermon on the subject of New
Year resolutions —the excitements to be expected from a
deliberate attempt to put one's soul *first*! Incidentally he let
fall an excellent definition of a genius: he who puts the first
thing first! When you think of it, that is precisely what those
who are not what are called geniuses don't do. Of course
anyone can put the first thing first if he tries hard enough &
knows the first thing when he sees it! But the genius is he who
knows the first thing & puts it first without oceans of tears &
hours of regret. Fr. V. was here from the Monday (Dec. 30)
to Saturday morn. (Jan. 4.) Another excellent saying he left

[1] Cf. Letter 84.

behind: Scrupulosity is as inexcusable in a man as agnosticism in a woman —or vice versa. (i.e. a in w is as inexcusable as s in m). That comforted me —for I've been quite worried to think I was not scrupulous enough — . . . On the Friday before Fr.V. went, he and I went for a walk on the hills.

It was a beautiful though showery day. Hilary met us on the Beacon at 1.30 & brought a lunch of bread & cheese & chocolate & a bottle of beer & an orange for Fr. V. It was jolly good & we sat in the rain, in the very centre of a marvellous rainbow, on the side of the hill overlooking the Weald. Then we walked home, via Westmeston, discussing the question of the publication of his book on the *Rerum Novarum*. But we will tell you about that and other matters when you come back. Next Saturday Hilary & I are going to Hawkesyard till the following Wednesday. Then we go to Leeds & Bradford (for one night) & then on to Edinburgh (for one night) & then on to Glasgow. We are to be at Glasgow from the 24th. to the 27th. and have got (both of us) to give lectures. Have you heard of the Glasgow people? —Dr. Pat. Flood & Co. —great enthusiasts apparently for the policy of a magazine run by two gents in Sx.! Fr. Vincent seems to have boomed it —&, alas!, us. The titles of the lectures (chosen by Hilary) are:

    'Education at the Bench' by Hilary,   Jan 24 evening
    'Revolution or Servility' by us both,   Jan 26 afternoon
    & 'A Grammar of Industry' by E. G.   Jan 26 evening

It sounds like a fairly exciting time if, by the Grace of God & the prayers of S. Dominic, we don't muck it up. In Glasgow too —a real stormcentre. So pray hard for us —or, shall I say, continue to do so. But had you not better come to Hawkesyard yourself? Why not, if you are well enough now again? Then we can have a fine talk & without delay. This wd. fit in with your proposal to come back here next week. You could meet us H'yard on Saturday (we hope to arrive by Complin time) & stay on after we have left —meeting us in London on Jan. 27th. (Unless you can come to Glasgow too — but that's an expensive business.) So unless I hear from you

to the contrary, we'll expect you next Saturday at H'yard!
What ho! [. . .]

I have written to Stanley Spencer. I write primarily because
I want to meet him now he's back. 2nd. because we want his
permission to print that description of 'Cookham' which he
sent you from Salonika (in *The Game*). I suppose you approve.
I gather from Hilary that he discussed it with you. 3rd. at
Hilary's suggestion (you can see the Hilarious finger in it)
to suggest *his coming to Hawkesyard with us next Saturday*! [. . .]
If you can say that *you* will be there too it wd. very likely
clinch the matter. [. . .] I rely on you to do that & I hope . . .
that we shall all meet next Saturday. What sport it wd. be
[. . .] I have hardly begun work. I've had so many interrup-
tions. But I've begun on that 'torso' again & hope to finish it
this week, D.V. But — is at B'Hill with — & the baby &
he wants to come here & do wood engraving this week —
that looks like trouble. And another young man brought some
drawings to show me yesterday & he wants to do wood engraving too! I wish my workshop were in the wilds of Central
Africa & fifteen lions chained up outside. [. . .]

Now I must say good bye, really I must. My dear Desmond
I am your loving friend & master   ERIC JOSEPH GILL

82 : TO DESMOND CHUTE

Hawkesyard   J.M. ✠ J.D.   *20-1-1919*

We are here and Stanley S. is with us. He met us at Euston
on Saturday determined not to come after all —but we persuaded him and he came just as he was with his hands in his
pockets & no luggage at all. [. . .] I am trying, in between
talking bouts, to think about Glasgow next Friday and Sunday.
We wish you were here. The habit is an admirable institution.
We go to Bradford on Wednesday & on Thursday to Edinburgh. I hope to meet Fr Blessing at B. & also Fr O'Connor.
                                        E. P. J. G.

83 : TO GEOFFREY KEYNES

At 'The George', 77 Boro High St., S.E.   ⟨*12 Feb. 1919*⟩

Your letter forwarded to me here. I am working in London for abt. 10 days (at Havard Thomas' Studio in Chelsea cutting inscript on Rupert B's Rugby Chapel Mem. Tablet!). I am out of the Army & have not shaved (or saluted anyone) since Dec. 19th. Now as we are so near surely we can meet & then I can tell you the news and all about all. This 'ere pub is a jolly good place to meet. Can you manage an evening and have supper with me? If so let me know the day. [. . .]
Yours   ERIC GILL

84 : TO 'THE BURLINGTON MAGAZINE'

APRIL, 1919

War Graves

Gentlemen: Sir Frederic Kenyon's report[1] to the Imperial War Graves Commission calls for public protest. We are all aware that to be effective such protests must come from the millions of men and women whose sons and husbands and fathers are buried in foreign lands, rather than from anybody of specialist opinion. I am, however, convinced that something will have been gained if the Government's proposals can be discredited upon technical and artistic grounds alone.

In the first place, and generally, it seems clear that the principal mistake is the placing of the matter of war graves in the hand of architects. Architectural *advice* is possibly desirable, but *leadership* by architects in such a matter is a mistake on two grounds, *viz*:; 1. The provision and erection of monuments, whether central monuments or headstones, is the

---

[1] *War Graves.* Report to the Imperial War Graves Commission by Lieut.-Colonel Sir Frederic Kenyon, K.C.B., Director to the British Museum (H.M. Stationery Office, 3d. net).

principal business under discussion, and this is not an architect's job, but a sculptor's and a tombstone-maker's. 2. The architect is, by the nature of his profession, one who directs the work of builders —he is not himself a maker of things. The designing of monuments is properly the business of those who *make* monuments.

In this matter of war graves there is, upon the one hand, the department of government concerned, *viz.*, the Imperial War Graves Commission, and, upon the other, there are the various classes of workers and makers of things, among whom we are here only concerned with those who make monuments.

The business of the War Graves Commission is, in this matter of monuments, to decide what form, if any, the national or central monuments shall take, having regard, not at all to the artistic views of architects, but solely to the sentiment of the nation, poor as well as rich, if ascertainable, and to the funds at its disposal. If it should decide that headstones should be placed upon every known grave (i.e., if it should conclude that such is the nation's wish, and the French or other foreign governments, *mirabile dictu*, do not object), then it is its business to ascertain and declare the number of headstones required, and, calling together a representative body of headstone-makers (small firms rather than big, because the heads of small firms are generally themselves working masons and not merely business managers, however cultured by acquaintance with architects), to discover the best method of production.

This method has not been followed by the War Graves Commission, which, impressed, as most people are at the present time, by the commercial success of organized production and, probably, quite ignorant, as rich people generally are, of the evils resulting from modern industrial methods, naturally allowed itself to be led by architects —the artistic counterparts of business managers.

This would be the less deplorable were it not that the making of tombstones is still in a very large degree in the hands of small firms which, scattered up and down the country (there is probably hardly a town without a small mason's yard), are quite capable of supplying all the headstones or crosses required, and that in a manner which, if not up to the artistic level of former times (and that cannot be expected in an age concerned more for the *volume* of international trade than for the good *quality* of the product), would certainly have the merit of being representative of the national culture or lack of culture, and not representative merely of the ideas of a few individual architects.

The commission's attitude in the matter is the more easily understood inasmuch as it is the whole trend of our time to impose the ideas of the few upon the many while being careful to hide the process under a guise of democratic sympathy and social reform. Thus the idea that half a million headstones should be made according to the ideas of a few architects (an idea worthy of the Prussian or the Ptolemy at his best) instead of according to those of several thousand stone-masons and twenty million relatives is not surprising, and under the plea of commemorating 'the sense of comradeship and common service' and 'the spirit of discipline and order', *etc.* (*vide Report*), it is hoped that the very widespread desire of relatives to have some personal control of the monuments to their dead will be overcome.

If the graveyards in France and elsewhere, and the bodies buried in them, are the absolute property of the government (a legal question as to which I am ignorant), then the wishes of relatives need not be considered, and the government has only to discover how best to provide, if such be its desire, a permanent memorial, and, if only from that point of view, the idea of erecting over half a million headstones from the designs of a few architects stands condemned, for, by such a method, nothing will be commemorated but the ineptitude of a commercial nation blind to the fact that good workmanship is a personal achievement and cannot be ordered, like coal, by the ton.

But few successful architects, still less men of business and

I

administrators, can see the truth of these contentions, and the hypocrisy becomes appalling when, on the strange contention (*vide Report*) that 'we are a Christian empire', it is proposed not only to put up crosses as central monuments but even sham altars. The central doctrine of Christianity is the freewill and consequent responsibility of the individual. Yet here is a nation calling itself Christian which refuses responsibility to the workman, and under the cloak of culture denies to mourners even the unfettered choice of words! (*Vide Report.*)

I assume that the administration decides that any known grave shall have a headstone (whether or no this is really desirable or desired).

I assume that the administration has the right, and it has the power, to make certain regulations (we are not anarchists) as to the size of headstones.

I assume that the administration has *not* the right, though it has the power, to enslave, intellectually, morally, aesthetically, or physically, even one man, and certainly not a very large number of men.

I assume that, provided certain regimental particulars (name, date, regiment, *etc.*) be inscribed upon each stone, the administration has not the right to dictate to relatives as to what shall or shall not be inscribed upon the stone, and this in spite of all that may be said (*vide Report*) about 'the sentimental versifier or the crank'.

Now, an ordinary small monumental mason could, without turning his shop into a factory, easily and without hurrying, supply, say, six hundred small headstones in three years at the cost of a few pounds each (say between £3 10s. and £5). Presumably a thousand other small workshops could do the same, and it would be desirable and seemly to distribute the work so that, as far as possible, the stones commemorating men of a certain locality should be made in that locality — Brighton masons doing stones for Brighton men, Marlow for Marlow, and so on — placing the work always in the hands of 'small' men and not big firms.

In this way a certain local quality would result, and the graveyards would gain the desirable quality of variety. Anything in addition to the regimental particulars could be paid for by the relatives and not by the government. What would it matter if the lettering and mason's work varied between one stone and the next —some good, some bad? That variety would be better than a uniform mediocrity, however quasi-artistic (*vide* Postscript to this letter). Why should not the inscriptions be as varied as the men they commemorate — some good, some bad? If we are, as we are, a nation without a strong tradition of good worksmanhip, why hide the fact under a pretentious scheme of architectural origin as do the Prussians in Berlin?

It is suggested in Sir Frederic Kenyon's report that the rows of headstones will be like a regiment on parade. But a regiment on parade is, though uniformed, not composed of men all of one size and shape and colour and kind.

It is said that the existing wooden crosses are very impressive, and they well may be. But they were not made all at one time by the thousand from the design of an architect! A crowd in Trafalgar Square is very impressive; but if you were to replace it by an equal number of tailor's dummies it is not certain that the result, however architectural, would be equally impressive.

In conclusion, I would urge that the government should take the advice of those who have some respect for individuality and responsibility instead of that of persons whose whole outlook is coloured by the notion that good work can be produced by proxy. —I am, yours faithfully,   ERIC GILL

P.S. —I understand that, for the actual doing of inscriptions, the government is employing several architects and assistants to experiment with a process by which acid shall be used to 'bite' the lettering into the stone. Even if the result were not bound to be a failure upon artistic grounds (as all methods must be which have their *origin* in the desire to save money), and it is, to say the least, unlikely that the repetition upon many thousands of headstones of the same rather feebly artistic lettering (we have seen specimens), made more or less worse by the acid process, will be a success, it is clear that such a process would never have been thought of if the government were not inspired by quantitative rather than qualitative notions. If a single firm should have the job of turning out 600,000 headstones, naturally it would cast around for cheap and quick processes, and it is, I think, not the least merit of the counter-proposal suggested above that the temptation to sacrifice quality to quantity would be reduced to a minimum. A man who has got three years in which to make six hundred small headstones has (provided the payment be reasonable) no need to hurry himself, and he can put his best into the work — always supposing that he is himself a workman and not merely the master of other workmen with no interest in the work but the profit to be got out of it. —   E. G.

85 : TO GEOFFREY KEYNES

Ditchling Common   J.M. ✠ J.D.   *30-10-1919*

My dear Keynes: Thank you for your letter of Oct. 19th. We are very glad to hear of the event of Aug. 14th, and to know that young Richard is doing well. We congratulate you both. Gordian is getting on fine and although he cannot say more than half a dozen words he is quite strong on the mouth organ.

I am glad to hear of the imminence of the Raverats' second. I hope all will go well. I hear that she is to have some engrav-ings on view at the Adelphi, I also a few, but I do not like the gallery very much. We have not heard from them for a long time, and wish we and they and you and the Cornfords were more within meeting distance. I will come and see you in S. John's Wood when you are there. I expect to be here up to Christmas. I have just got back from a three weeks' tour in Ireland and Scotland where Pepler and I have been giving some lectures on art and industry and such like matters. We had a great time — a week in Dublin, 5 days in Galway, 3 days in Glasgow and Dumbarton. Ireland was decidedly exciting, and secret meetings with Sinn Fein leaders 'on the run' added to the gaiety. Have you been to the Arran Islands and seen a civilisation entirely unspoiled by the factory system? Have you been to Glasgow and seen a civilisation entirely unspoiled by religion?[1]

We are all well here and have just purchased the adjacent farm of 160 acres (borrowed money, of course). We do not want it all, so if you want a few acres of land, here's your chance — average price £50 per acre. Yours ever, ERIC GILL

86 : TO WILLIAM ROTHENSTEIN

Ditchling Common   J.M. ✠ J.D.   *3-11-1919*

Dear Rothenstein: [. . .] I am sorry it is so long since we met or corresponded. I find it very difficult, as I expect you do, to keep in touch as I should wish, and after this lapse of time there is so much to say and so many things to tell you of that it is very difficult to know where to begin.

Both my life and work are centred upon the Church, and that necessarily means that our spheres of activity are separate. If you lived next door it would be different, and I wish it were so for I should very much like a renewal of the old discussions.

As far as my work is concerned, I mean my stone work, I look upon it less and less as having any value but as a means of livelihood, and so we endeavour, as far as possible, to insure against the future by getting a firm footing on the land.*

*For stone carving of my sort is only wanted by the few & cultured and I object to being absolutely dependent upon such. A Revolution is coming — I try to meet it 1°, by living or learning to live as much as possible upon my own resources as

[1] Cf. 'A Diary in Ireland' (*In a Strange Land*, pp. 27-49).

I hope you and all the family are well, we are all well. I suppose John is pretty nearly grown up by now. What is he doing?

The Leeds monument which Prof. Sadler wants me to do is still a possibility but the work is not in hand yet. That wd. be a magnum opus! I hope it may come off. Christ turning the money changers out —such a subject carved upon such a scale would satisfy all my ambitions — both as man & artist. Yours affectionately   ERIC GILL

Please excuse my dictating part of this. A friend of mine does some secretary work for me and thus many letters are replied to promptly which otherwise might be put off for 'when I've got some leisure'.

87 : TO THE REV. JOHN O'CONNOR

Ditchling Common   J.M. ✠ J.D.   *6-11-1919*

My dear Father O'Connor: I hear that you want Stations for your church! Is this really the case? If so, do you want me to submit design and estimate of cost? In that case please say *size* required. I could do a set in the same manner (i.e. low relief) as those at Westminster, coloured or uncoloured, about 30 ins. square, for about £350. Is that anywhere near the possibilities?

Have you heard from Bro. Hilary about Ireland & Glasgow?

Bro. Desmond has been ill again & is now away for a week's holiday. Yours affectly.   ERIC GILL

---

a small landed proprietor and 2°, by doing what I can to propagate the Faith so that the Revolution may be guided in a direction consonant with the fundamental facts of human nature and man's essential perfection. It is a forlorn hope but one not nearly so forlorn as reform by Parliamentary legislation, Civic Arts Association, Design & Industries, Arts League of Service & so forth —such things merely whitewash sepulchres.

88 : TO THE REV. JOHN O'CONNOR

Ditchling Common   J.M. ✠ J.D.   *13-11-1919*

Dear Father O'Connor: Thank you very much for your letter of Nov. 8th. I was considerably bucked up by it. I will consider the order booked. Meanwhile, I agree, I ought to see the place, especially as you are considering decoration as well. I am not likely to be up your way yet awhile, but our profession as Tertiaries is, as at present arranged, to take place about Christmas time or soon after and it is to be at Hawkesyard. This suggests that I should come to Bradford then. Would that be soon enough, or too soon?

I am interested to hear that you have heard of that crucifix at the Goupil Gallery. It very nearly satisfied me, but I hear that the exhibition is very mixed affair, and Desmond says that our things look very out of place on a red brocade wall with gold-framed frivolities above, below and on all sides.

Father Kelly, of Dumbarton, wants me to do S. Michael for him. Father Finbar Ryan, O.P. of Dublin, wants S. Vincent Ferrer. You want Stations. Lord Howard de Walden wants a colossal bas-relief of a soldier (this I am now doing). *I* want round nudity. Perhaps it is as well that I am too busy to attend to my own wants — God knows. Yours affectionately

ERIC GILL

89 : TO THE REV. JOHN O'CONNOR

Ditchling Common   *17-11-1919*

Dear Father O'Connor: Thank you for your letter of the 15th. I will come on to Bradford from Hawkesyard & I am looking forward to the event.

The crucifix at the Goupil is already sold — I do not know to whom. I am sorry, I should have liked you to have it. I do not know whether it would be possible for me to do the crucifix in olive wood as you suggest. It would be a splendid thing to do, but like the statues of Our Lady and S. Joseph which you want, it must wait, at least until I have got S. Michael and S. Vincent Ferrer off my chest. It is all jolly fine for Wordsworth to talk about 'emotion remembered in tranquillity' — I wonder where he got the tranquillity from.

The stone has come for S. Antony at last and I hope to put it in hand very soon. It should not be a very long job.

I am glad you will be saying Mass for the Stations. Of your charity please put up a prayer for the unworthy sculptor. Yours affectionately   ERIC GILL

90 : TO MRS. WINGATE

Ditchling Common   J.M. ✠ J.D.   *15-3-1920*

Dear Mrs. Wingate: Thank you for your letter of the 7th inst. and for returning the scale drawing.[1] The price I gave you (about £400) was the price for which, if I were in a position to do so (but I am not, having too much work on hand at present), I would do the work throughout exclusive of carriage to Cambridge and fixing.

If the work were done locally, as I suggest, you would, of course, have to get an estimate from the local mason, and if the lettering and moulding were left to me and the carving of the figures, my charge would be about £100, I suppose, for Portland stone — that is, 4 carved panels, inscriptions and moulding.

I hope this is the information you want. Meanwhile, I will make a model as you request as soon as possible. Yours very sincerely   ERIC GILL

[1] Of the proposed war memorial at Trumpington.

91 : TO PAUL COOPER

Ditchling Common, Sx.   *28-5-1920*

Thank you v. much for your letter of the 24th. I hope you'll
print the article.[1] I will try & alter it in proof to temper the
wind. By the word 'designing' I do not at all mean designing
on paper but in the mind. I merely wish to distinguish between
art & a *work* of art. Obviously they *are* distinct. As for your
Persian Carpet example: —you say the design 'is a family heir-
loom'. In this case you mean of course a design actually transmitted to paper (or some such means of record). Right; but
unless the succeeding generations actually themselves appreciate the family design &, so to say, make it their own (just
as a Christian receives a creed and yet it is his own creed or
he is no Christian) the work done from the design is not a
work of art. Love is essential. The Persian carpet makers do
in fact put love into the job. The family design is simply a
springboard from which to jump. Is this clear? The living
quality of their work shows their love. When a family design
has outstayed its welcome the work goes dead. This has often
happened. Yrs. sincerely   ERIC GILL

92 : TO WILLIAM ROTHENSTEIN

Ditchling Common   J.M. ✠ J.D.   *10-6-1920*

Dear Rothenstein: Herewith I enclose short note about Mr.
Cobden-Sanderson.[2] I hope it will serve your purpose. Yours
affectionately   ERIC GILL

If you approve, I think it wd. be desirable to show this to
T. J. C-S. I don't want to say things he wd n't approve of or
agree with.   E. G.

[1] I have failed to trace this article, which was evidently written for a publication of which Mr. Cooper was editor.
[2] Printed opposite the portrait of Cobden-Sanderson in William Rothenstein's
Twenty-Four Portraits (1920).

I am sorry not to have been able to come to the marionette show. I shd. have liked to do so v. much indeed. But I am very much tied by work here at present. Did I reply to your last letter? I don't believe I did. I am most interested to hear of your appointment to the R.C. of A. I think you can do great good there. I want to talk to you about all these things. E. G.

93 : TO ANDRÉ RAFFALOVICH

Ditchling Common   J.M. ✠ J.D.   16-6-1920

Dear Raffalovich: I was very glad to get your letter of June 6th and to know that S. Sebastian[1] had arrived and had been received with 'enthusiasm'.

I am very glad that you and Father Gray are pleased and that it meets with approval from your artistic friends. I shall look forward to seeing it again some day.

You will be amused to hear that the study from which I did the carving was made from myself in a mirror. I think the chest and arm-pits are the best part certainly. I think the head is good though not, perhaps, in quite the same style. The tree is rather out of keeping being much more conventional than the figure. I think the legs are the weak part, at any rate from the knees downwards.

[. . .] We are all very well here and Antoninus Gordian is growing a fine boy, much loved by all. We are in great difficulties at present with regard to the affairs of the little Catholic community which is growing up around us. The difficulties are largely financial, of course, but I may have more to say about it at some later date. Please do not be alarmed.

Five of us here are Dominican Tertiaries and we are trying to build a little chapel. We are also putting up a crucifix on a hill at the corner of the Common. We are also proposing to build our workshops in a group in one field and to form a little

[1] Reproduced in John Rothenstein's *Eric Gill* (1927), Plate 20.

guild of Christian workmen. One workshop is already up and another begun. I wish you could come here when you are down South.

I hope Miss Gribbell is now quite well. Please give my love to Father Gray. I am yours affectionately,   ERIC GILL

94 : TO THE REV. ARCHIBALD
MCSPARRAN

Ditchling Common   J.M. ✠ J.D.   *20-8-1920*

My dear Father McSparran: Thank you very much for your letter of Aug 16 and for the notes for £15 in payment for the Madonna & Child carving. I am very glad it arrived safely at Dumbarton and that you are still pleased with it. [. . .]

I suppose we shall be hearing from Dr. Flood soon with reference to the land business. I quite understand that it is hardly to be expected that your people will see the fun of owning land in Sussex. The house idea originated in Dr Flood's remark that it seemed foolish for your people to lend money to one Bank & for us to borrow from another. We are all very well and have just finished haying. Next week I go to North Wales to finish off that great monument. We are expecting Fr. Austin Barker here this week end and hope to have some good talks with him. Thomas Shore since his engagement has hardly been near the place! However I still hope for his conversion. Hilary's printing shop is nearing completion — at least the roof is now going on & to-day he gave me a loaf made with flour grown, ground & baked on the estate! That is a bit of a triumph isn't it? We got some malt this week — the first since 1917. So now we shall start brewing again. Next time you come South I hope to give you better beer than what you had last time.

We all send our love and I hope I shall see you soon. Yours affectionately   ERIC GILL

95 : TO MRS. WINGATE

Ditchling Common   J.M. ✠ J.D.   *10-9-1920*

Dear Mrs. Wingate: Thank you for your letter of Sept. 8th.
I am glad to hear that the Trumpington War Memorial Committee have approved of my design.

I am very sorry I am unable to undertake the work myself
as I think it is the only way to get the most satisfactory results,
but at the present time that is quite impossible as I have too
much to do already.

In order to make the work as much as possible the work of
the people who actually execute it, that is, to avoid the usual
results of working merely to drawings, I think it will be best
for me not to make any full-sized details but merely to pay
a visit to the people whom you employ and explain to them
by word of mouth what is wanted. I think it is a mistake to
get estimates from various firms. I think you ought to choose
from among those known to you the man you think most
suitable to do the work, either on account of his having some
connection with the place or on account of his being the best
workman.

With regard to the carving of the panels and the lettering,
I will do these either myself or have them done by one of my
pupils, which comes to the same thing, and we can do the
work either in the mason's yard or when the cross is fixed,
whichever turns out to be the most convenient.

With regard to the moulding, this ought to be done by the
mason, and as they are quite simple there should be no difficulty. The whole cross should be left from the chisel and not
rubbed smooth.

It is not possible for me to come to Cambridge during the
next two or three weeks as I am going down to North Wales
next week to finish some carving I am doing there, but I will
let you know as soon as I can manage it. Will you be in
Cambridge during October?

I do not know Clipsham stone, but personally I think it

would be desirable to use stone from a quarry as near Cambridge as possible rather than Portland which is not only expensive but has to be carried a long way. I should like Red Mansfield if it could be got. I suggest that you get the local mason to submit samples of stone from the neighbourhood. Yours very sincerely,   ERIC GILL

96 : TO HIS FATHER AND MOTHER

Ditchling Common   J.M. ✠ J.D.   *24-12-1920*

My dearest Father and Mother: We all send our love and hope you will have a happy Christmas.

I had hoped to write a long and controversial letter but have not been able to get at it & Christmas Eve is as you know a difficult day. So I must wait. The Harting Cross is still unfinished but now only requires about a week's work so my visit to W. Sussex cannot now be far off and then I'll come to W.W. and spend a night.

We are all well and the children are happy and excited. We killed a goose for the occasion and Uncle Len has kindly sent a Christmas tree as usual. I have also brewed some beer which is at least a wholesome drink.

We shall think of you to-morrow — Bless you both from your loving son   ERIC

97 : TO WILLIAM ROTHENSTEIN

Ditchling Common   J.M. ✠ J.D.   *29-12-1920*

My dear Rothenstein: Thank you very much indeed for the excellent print of the excellent drawing of that excellent man. I am very glad to have it. I think my note reads quite kindly as printed but of course I tried to say too much. However T. J. C-S seems pleased & I am very glad of that. I am very glad you like my Adam and Eve carving. I wish you could have it. So far as I have heard nothing has been sold of mine at that hotch potch of an exhibition. This is disappointing —for the usual reason. I am glad too that John is pleased with his book-plate & I hope you approve of it. I hear from Oxford that he is to meet Father Martindale (that very remarkably discrimin-ating & enormously learned & versatile Jesuit) next term. I hope such a meeting will meet with your approval. I am very busy here —just about to begin a set of Stations of the Cross for a Church in Bradford and a black marble crucifix for Canada. I still intend to come & visit you when I come to London & hope it will be soon. Yours ever affectionately & with best wishes for the New Year from us all to you all

ERIC GILL

98 : TO THE REV. JOHN O'CONNOR

Ditchling Common   J.M. ✠ J.D.   *8-2-1921*

Dear Father O'Connor: Yet another question: What about the titles on the Stations? On the first one I have inscribed '*1. Jesus is condemned to death*' and I hope this is right but I should be glad if you would send me a list of the titles you wish put on the others and I should be glad if, as far as possible, they do not contain more letters than the above.

Are there any texts which you would like inscribed on the backgrounds of the panels as at Westminster? Of course, it may not always be possible to find space. On the other hand an empty space is sometimes improved by lettering. Yours very sincerely   ERIC GILL O.S.D.

99 : TO 'THE GAME', MAY 1921

[*The Game* had been printing in parts the essay on *The Song of Solomon* afterwards published as *Songs Without Clothes* and reprinted in *Art Nonsense*, pp. 27-58. In a letter to the Editor, Mr. Geoffrey Rhoades protested against the phrase 'that last dying flare of the idolaters,

Impressionism' and named Giorgione, Velasquez, Old Crome, Manet and Whistler as painters who would be 'down and out' if the standards expressed in this essay were applied to them. (Pp. 43-4 in *The Game* — p. 37 in *Art Nonsense*.)]

Sir: Your correspondent, Mr. Geoffrey Rhoades, expresses one of the common difficulties, but I think if he will read pages 43 and 44 again he will see that the giants of the Renaissance are not without their meed of praise.

I do not think I am blind to the high spiritual qualities of the work of those artists whom your correspondent mentions. Nevertheless, the note of post-Renaissance art until quite recent times has certainly been idolatry, and the idol has been man. It was, indeed, the boast of the Renaissance that it discovered man!

It is true that the comment Impressionism makes upon God's work may be, and often is, a 'Hymn of praise', but I am reminded of those people who claim superiority to what they feel to be ecclesiastical fetters and the fetters of the creeds, who boast that for their part they can worship God just as well in the fields as in churches, and that they do so. There are also people who say that they have no need of the confessional. There is truth in both contentions but the experience of the last three centuries gives overwhelming proof that in fact those who do not go to church do not worship any God, and those who do not confess to a priest do not confess to any sin.

Human nature is compounded of matter and spirit, and while in this world man is bound to respect both.

Applying this to 'Impressionism', my argument is that though exceptional individuals have in fact rendered praise to God in their works, the general result of the Renaissance attitude of mind has not been man's worship of God, but a worship of himself, and that, therefore, the bulk of such work is a more or less presumptuous criticism (even if appreciative criticism) of creatures rather than worship of the Creator.

Perhaps this point will be made clear in the latter part of the article referred to. —Yours, etc.,   E. G.

100 : TO MRS. WINGATE

Ditchling Common   23-6-1921

Dear Mrs. Wingate: Herewith I enclose, as promised, a new setting-out of the names on the war memorial.[1] I have placed the longer words in the lower parts of the panels and have given two lines to each name. This means that the lettering is slightly smaller but not enough to make any difference.

I also return the former setting-out so that you may compare them.

The following is the text we cut on the monument at Stanway, in Glos.: 'For your to-morrow we gave our to-day'.

Here is another one that seems to me a good one: 'Let your work be a fight, your peace a victory.' That is an address to the passer-by, but if it were desired to make it apply to those whose names were inscribed it might be better to say: 'Their work was a fight, their peace a victory.' [. . .] Yours very sincerely,   ERIC GILL O.S.D.

101 : TO THE REV. JOHN O'CONNOR

Ditchling Common   J.M. ✠ J.D.   14-7-1921

Dear Father O'Connor: Thank you very much for your letter of July 12th. Desmond is away until next Monday. I will write again on his return. I hope to persuade him to come with me when I come.

The hymn is splendid and I like the music, the translation is as quaint and cunning as the bliss it describes.[2] Please send me as many copies as the enclosed P.O. will cover. Yours affectionately   ERIC GILL O.S.D.

P.S. Your further letter of the 14 recd. this morning. Thank you for it. I note that you will put the wall work in hand.

[1] For Trumpington.
[2] Father O'Connor's translation of Abelard's *O quanta qualia*; 'What quaint and cunning bliss', stanza 2; music by Dom Alphege Shebbeare.

My Stations go thus: Start at Sanctuary end of *epistle* side, proceed down church, up gospel side & finish at Sanctuary end of *gospel* side. I've got to go to Oxford on the 22nd. so cannot get to Bradford before the 23rd. I gave a lecture on 'children's drawings' at the Viennese children's show when it was in London. I'd like to talk to you about that. My view is that most of the work exhibited was, though done by genuine children, not genuine child work but precocious in kind —very wonderful but no better than grown ups can do in the same line of business whereas . . . the 'child', properly, draws in a less naturalistic & less sentimental manner than those Viennese marvels —i.e. more in the manner of barbarians & primitives & of post-impressionists & Chutes & Gills! More anon: but this is a thesis I will burn for. The Viennese phenomenon is easily explainable without denying either its marvellousness or the veracity of its admirers.   E. G.

102 : TO THE REV. JOHN O'CONNOR

Ditchling Common   J.M. ✠ J.D.   *8-8-1921*

Dear Father O'Connor: I arrived home safely last Tuesday feeling very grateful to you for all your kindness both spiritual and material. I found Father Austin here and he has done a very good work helping us with the internal troubles of which I told you.

The children were delighted with the 'speculations' and also with the sewing encyclopaedia. I enclose pro forma account which I hope you will find in order. There will be perforce a lull in the work for a bit as I must now finish the New College inscription and some other jobs but I hope to visit Bradford again with the next batch of three before the end of the year.

I will return *Orpheus in Mayfair*[1] anon. It is very delightful,

1 By Maurice Baring (1909).

K

but I spent most of the time in the train writing a poem beginning 'What is it to the Sussex shore that Alfred's bones lie buried there and how shall Egypt's bleached sands remember Cleopatra's violet veins' and leading on to the thought that even my mistress' corpse will forget that her heart ever beat! Yours very affectionately,   ERIC GILL O.S.D.

[The poem begun thus was completed later, and I print it here as it appeared (unsigned) in *The Game*, March 1922.]

CAELUM ET TERRA TRANSIBUNT

What is it to the Sussex shore
   That Alfred's bones lie hidden there?
And how shall Egypt's parchéd sands
   Remember Cleopatra's hair?

No memory indelible of man's frail life
   Can earth in earthy prison set.
Even the pulsing of conjoinéd love
   Shall your own corpse forget.

But coals of fire shall still be piled
   On earth's unheeding land;
And men shall not forget the rounded hills
   Or leave deserted even desert sand.

And oh! my Lover, when your grave shall give
   His long embrace, and all your parts disdain,
Love still shall keep our love imprisoned,
   And bless your breast whereon my breast has lain.

103 : TO DR. WINGATE

Ditchling Common   J.M. ✠ J.D.   *Nat. B.V.M. 8-9-1921*

Dear Dr. Wingate: I think when you were here we agreed that when I had made the designs for the four panels of the Cross[1] I shd. send them to you to place before the Memorial Committee if necessary. I now send them and hope you will like them and see the possibilities of them as carvings. You will of course see that they are designs for carvings & not finished naturalistic drawings. I hope the committee will be willing to trust me as a sculptor & will not ask for naturalism in a thing which obviously calls for symbolism. However I won't purposely set out to give offence — you may be sure of that.

As to the designs in detail:—

*(3) S. Mary. Mother with baby & cradle. Lily on shelf.

(4) S. Michael slaying the dragon, i.e., the Devil. The devil a combination of various vices: especially unbelief (*non est deus*), deceit (the serpent), avarice (the breasts with mouths instead of nipples, for he devours & gives no nourishment). Flames behind.

(2) S. George slaying the dragon who would destroy the Church: i.e. St. George the Christian champion. Hand of God in the sky.

(1) The soldier, very tired, heavily burdened, walking towards the setting sun. Broken tree stumps.

When you write will you please say if the enclosed plan is correct for the disposition of the carvings & inscriptions. *I shall be able to go straight ahead with the carvings now.* We finished the Oxford (New College) inscription on Tuesday last. It has taken every available person & every available minute for the last month to get it done. It was promised for

*These numbers correspond with those on the drawings & plan.   E. G.

[1] At Trumpington.

the end of August but Sept. 6th. was the nearest we could get.
I am sorry Trumpington has been delayed in consequence. I
will go on with it as fast as possible now. Nevertheless of
course you do not want it spoiled by hurry.

I hope you & Mrs. Wingate & the children are well. I am
yrs. very sincerely   ERIC GILL O.S.D.

104 : TO THE REV. JOHN O'CONNOR

Ditchling Common   J.M. ✠ J.D.   *13-9-1921*

Dear Fr. O'Connor: Thank you very much for your chq. rec^d
in the nick of time this a.m. Marvellous precision with which
Omniscience & Heavenly Fatherhood replenishes overdrawn
accounts! We are all hard pressed by contrary winds but
keeping eyes glued to compass. Great hopes of making port.
We are delighted about David[1] & hope he'll come back afore
long (then we'll have to keep him up to the mark & knock
some corners off him D.V.) Thank you v. much re Eliz. her
portrait. I go to Switzerland, if poss., with her on Oct. 1st.
Desmond also travels then. I return home in a week or ten
days. Did David tell you that she's been taken on as domestic
in small hotel in Gruyères —help in house, learn French, Swiss
cooking & la vie Catholique —neither pay nor be paid.
Desmond stayed there last winter & says Mme. Ruffieux is very
holy woman & leads v. holy life and all. We hope this will do
her good & solve some problems. Meanwhile work in plenty
here & much else. Am now doing four panels for Trumpington
Village Cross. After that I return to the Stations. I will send
Desmond's design for Xth. It's good but too feminine. In
any case I shd. alter it. You will see what you think. The
pony was a sad loss —broken fet-lock —probably kicked —past
mending. Yesterday our pet Magpie drowned himself in a
rain water tub! I feel this v. much —a most friendly bird.

---

[1] David Jones, who had just been received into the Catholic Church.

I am v. glad Frs. J-B. & B. D. are to be with you. My greetings
to them. [. . .] I hope you will have a good rest. I pray
for my next visit to Bradford. May it be soon. Yours affectionately   ERIC GILL O.S.D.

105 : TO THE REV. JOHN O'CONNOR

Ditchling Common   J.M. ✠ J.D.   *30-11-1921*

Dear Father O'Connor: Thank you for your letter of Nov.
11th and for the Children's Mass. Thank you also for the
inscriptions for the next three Stations.* I am now about to
begin these and will report progress in a few weeks' time.

I expect you have heard that, in the absence of definite
prohibition from you, David made up his mind, with the
encouragement of his headmaster at Westminster, to come
here without further delay, and he arrived on Monday. I
think we can keep him employed and for myself I promise you
that I will do my best to see that he gets from us normal and
'no new-fangled popery'. Yours affectionately,

                                             ERIC GILL O.S.D.

* I note that in a former letter you gave me for the Vth.
Station *Quid non potuistis?* Which will you have? That or
Tantae molis erat?

106 : TO DESMOND CHUTE

D. Common, Sx.   J.M. ✠ J.D.   *13-12-1921*

My dear Desmond: At last I'm able to begin a letter to you.
It's just 9.0 & supper's finished and Petra is sewing & David J.
is reading *Twelfth Night* to her! As for me I've done nothing
at all but letters & accounts & sorting things out since I got
back from Trumpington a fortnight & more ago. You see

when I got back from Switzerland I had to put all possible time into finishing the carvings & then when it actually went off I went to London & spent a week doing the Memorial Inscrip. on the British Museum. Albert came with me. I stayed at Denis T's. It was very pleasant. I went down to David's home at Brockley for one night & enjoyed it very much. His father & mother were most kind & hospitable. Another night I spent at Will Rothenstein's & gave an informal lecture to the students at R. Coll. of Art on wood engraving. Well then the following week I went to Cambridge & took Petra with me. She stayed at the Cornfords' & I at Trumpington one night & in Cornford's room at Trinity the next 2 nights. While I was there I drew the Cornford children's portraits —passable likenesses but indifferent drawings. Petra enjoyed her outing v. much. [. . .]

(13.12.'21. 7.0 p.m.) Evening again & a few minutes before going home. I mustn't be late because Hilary & David, Major & Minor, are coming to supper (Clare being away for a few days).

Well, things are going pretty well here at present. We've all got plenty of work. I'm about to start the IVth Bradford Station. David J. & I have been grinding colours all the afternoon to fill up various paint boxes & make stock. We've got a fine show done. To-morrow we'll do some more. I hope shortly to start the Leeds sculpture. Hilary & Co. are very busy one way & another & David Jones is kept hard at it. It's a great pleasure having him with us. Lately we've been doing figures for a Christmas Crib. We've been doing them in card & cutting them out & putting stands behind. David has done our Lady, S. Joseph, & S. Dominic. I have done the Child. Joseph is doing dog, pig, cow, & cock & hen. Hilary is making a big tree, cut out of wood, to have candles on it, & to stand behind the altar against the wall and the Crib will be under the altar!¹ There will be straw on the floor to fill up. But don't

¹ A drawing of crib below, with the annotation: 'Black sky behind with silver stars.'

tell anybody as we are doing it for a surprise for the kids. It's going to be seen at Compline on Xmas afternoon. I hope it will turn out good. David's figures are jolly good anyway. [. . .]

(14.12.'21) Here is another evening come! We had a good supper party & a glorious blaze in the kitchen & a glorious pork pie. Now I must really finish this letter or at least post it! I have so much to say — but how can I write 14 or more pages and tell you all that's going on & all we are doing & saying & thinking? We must just go on praying in general &, in particular, for one another. So now good bye. You'll get this just before Christmas. May you have a most happy feast dear brother. We all send you our love — do we not? And we shall meet again, after all, before many months have gone D.V. I am your most affectionate brother in S. Dom.

ERIC P.   J. G. O. S. D

P.S. Have you read or heard of Dean Inge's *Plotinus*? Francis Cornford lent it to me. Most useful & illuminating on the Beauty stunt. (Item) — & — are more & more alien now-a-days. Quite friendly (so far as I do know) but alien. — says 'the arts are an embellishment to civilization' (so they are, E. G.) '& not civilization a frame for the arts'. In this saying he says he sums up his position! I said in reply that if he found my art an embellishment to his civilization he was lucky & if I found his civilization a frame for my art *I* was lucky. So everybody's 'appy.

(Item) Have you heard the latest form of greeting?:— 'How d'you frightfully do old thing?'

(Item) Geo. Maxwell is *all right*. He's now with wife (most good & beautiful) & 2 children in Joseph's end of army hut. H. J. C. & family are now at Miss Wall's cottage. (Item) Miss Hinde's cottage is roof high. It is to be thatched. (Item) Though rougher & crookeder it is much better than any building Chisholm & I ever did. Oh that George M. had been here 18 months ago!   E. G.

107 : TO DESMOND CHUTE

D. Common, Sx.   J.M. ✠ J.D.   *18-2-1922*

My dear brother Desmond B-M: Your very welcome letter
came the day before yesterday and found me in bed with
inflammation of the intercostal muscles — what ho! and I am
still there tho. much better. Mary has been poulticing with
linseed all the week. Luckily it's not lungs at all but only
muscles. However the unfortunate thing is that we've *all* got
whooping cough (the six of us). So we are in a bad way though
cheerful. (Incidentally to have a violent cough & inflam^n of
chest muscles at the same time is a . . . penance.) Everybody
in the 'Community' is catching it. Fragbarrow has got it and
the Army hut. I, even I, was the first to get it — where from
I do not know — and never having had it before I didn't
recognize it & therefore took no precautions & nor did anyone
else . . . 'My God, I am annoyed'[*]. But, don't worry — 'we
shall recover by and by'.

Well, I have passed your admirable letter on to Hilary so
will wait until I get it back to answer it in detail. I am very
sorry it is so long since you heard from D. Common. We
were overjoyed to get your letter from Gruyères and to know
that you found Eliz. as well & happy as her own letters lead
us to suppose. She writes such splendid & cheerful letters
& most regularly. It is a weekly event — Thursday morning —
reading the news from furrin parts. There is no doubt but
that Gruyères is a holy and admirable institution & that dear
Eliz. is profiting by her life there. (Item: her spelling is
greatly improving in quality — more intelligent —) Mary and
I look forward to paying her a visit & we purpose going for
June 1st. (don't tell Eliz.!). By that time, I am in hopes, I

---

[*] Extract of letter from Bengali officer who wrote to his
C.O. explaining why he had not returned to his regiment:
'My absence is impossible. Someone has stolen my wife.
My God, I am annoyed.'

shall have got four more Stations set up at Bradford and shall have made a beginning with the Leeds 'Money Changers'.

I have made a model $\frac{1}{4}$ full size of the figure of Our Lord (in Beer stone) so as to acquaint myself with the problem & to discover the amount of relief required. (Result: $4\frac{1}{2}''$ relief for figures about 4' 6" high.) I sent Eliz. a photo of the model. She will show it to you when you go to G. I sent one to Sadler and he seems gratified. The stone is on order. As to Bradford: The fourth Station is finished save for colouring — only illness has prevented my being by now half way through the fifth. The fourth looks well, I think. Our Lady's figure is very good — thanks to D. M. C. Talking of illness — this is my second whole week in bed! I think the rest will have done me good. Christmas time utterly tired me out and I never really got over it. Now, I think I shall do well. I do feel less tired. As for the work — well, as usual I have all sorts of extras to attend to. Item. On Jan. 14. I went to B'ton and gave a lecture to the United B'ton Arts Club & Sx. Women's A.C. The substance of this was Beauty is . . . well, you know the Beauty Stunt! They said it was (the lecture) above their comprehension & indeed I do believe it was, and that not at all because I was learned or obscure, but, as I realized almost for the first time, because the non-Catholic is almost entirely unacquainted with & unused to the consideration of anything of ultimate moment. It was like talking about Electricity to those who though very familiar were *only* familiar with the steam engine. I expect you understand the situation. Well, anyway the lecture is being printed and will be in Feb. & March numbers of *The Game*. I hope you will approve of it. I particularly hope this because in fact several important advances are made in its elucidations and collations. I sent the proofs to Fr. Vincent and he returned them with a covering letter of approval — saying that to the Greeks (i.e. the artistic folk) it wd. be folly & to the Hebrews (the financial folk) a stumbling block. He made no criticisms — so, as we had most pointedly asked him to read it 'theologically' we presume to take it that he found nothing definitely wrong in it. Which reminds me, I am at present reading *The Ideal of the Monastic Life* by Germain Morin, o.s.b. Have you read it? It was lent to us by Dom Pepin of Parkminster in response to our appeal for enlightenment on certain matters connected with the difference between modern and ancient spirituality. The book is very interesting and most useful and is a very good comment upon our thesis: that modern spirituality suffers in a way precisely parallel to that in which mod. art suffers. That what may be called (i.e. to you, who understand the phraseology) 'Representative' prayer has ousted 'Conventional' prayer from its proper place — That it has come to be supposed that the conventional, the hieratic, the formal, is a dead thing and that there is life only in the naturalistic & idiosyncratic. I doubt if I can explain the whole of this matter to you in a letter. You can guess the drift and the point of it. You will see where the Jesuits come in — and where they don't. You will see that just as you cannot certainly paint a good picture by going to an art school and learning a 'method', but must fall in love with God first and last — that it is not 'art' you can be taught but only technical things (e.g. to keep your hand & brushes clean & your lines clear . . .) — so you cannot certainly walk with God by following a 'method' but must wait upon Him as upon a lover — singing beneath his window — waiting for him in the snow — & that the only things you can be taught are again technical things — to keep clean. . . .

We went over to Parkminster at the end of January (Sat. Jan. 28), Hilary, David, George Maxwell (of whom more anon) and I, and we spent the night there. We went to the night office — very grand and holy . . . (no use my telling you about that) and in the morning Hilary and I had a long talk with the Prior while David & George M. went round the place with Father Hugh Weld. (David J. 'got the wind up' properly and has hardly yet got over the feeling that as he is single and without ties . . .) The Prior was most kind and helped and seemed very much on our side in all that we are doing or trying to do here. He said among other things that he thought it wd. be a good thing if we were to write at length to the Bishop and put before him more or less formally a statement of our history and intentions so that his Lordship's information shd. not be entirely from unsympathetic sources. I have since written a part of this and we shall be sending you a copy.

Another thing you wd. find v. interesting reading is Fr. Devas' book of the correspondence between Lacordaire & Jandel relative to the restoration of the order[1] in France. This makes most exciting reading and extraordinarily apposite in many ways to our own affairs. As to these last: We are maintaining the enterprise and I think it is progressing favourably. Certainly God's blessings seem to be poured upon it. The office is more firmly established and in this matter Bro. Thomas (George Maxwell) is a very great Godsend. He is a man of great simplicity & humility — a wheelwright or rather a coachbuilder from Birmingham full of enthusiasm for the faith and for the order. He is not a convert (except, as he says, in the sense in which many are converts who, born Catholic, are slack & unenthusiastic up to a certain age — at which they receive grace to see what they have hitherto had without seeing) and he was a Tertiary of S. Dominic before he came here. He is a friend of Fr. Vincent and an enthusiastic — well, modesty forbids me to say — no it doesn't — I mean an enthusiastic supporter of what we are trying to support. Dear good man — his beautiful & intelligent humility — very different from the attitude of some people . . . Joseph and Agnes & Co. have now moved into Miss Wall's Cottage so the Maxwell's have the west end of the Hut. Mrs. Max. is also the right kind of Christian woman — no intellectual highbrowism about her. They have 2 children (2 girls) (Teresa & Winifred, 5 & 2) and another due in March. [. . .] You will be pleased to hear that we had Mass for Candlemas and a grand blessing of Candles in the chapel. The priest was Fr.

[1] The Order of Preachers. (Raymund Devas, O.P., *Ex Umbris*, 1920.)

Lopes from London (a member of the Soc. of the Mission), a friend of George M. He came down at George's invitation. An excellent man & most good & enthusiastic on our account. A convert Anglican clergyman. (Age 45 approx) The day before George and I were in London —I on various businesses & G. to be professed at Haverstock Hill. We also bought a store of candles for the morrow. I went with G. to H. Hill and assisted at the rite. Fr. Fabian Dix was not well so it was performed in his room. [. . .]

We shall of course visit you at Fribourg when we come out and we hope you will be able to spare a few hours. You must let us know what times are best for visitors. I was to have been in Birmingham to-night, lecturing to the B. Craftsman's Club. But pleuridinia is a diriment impediment to acrimony — and so I am still in bed. I was going on to Hawkesyard to-morrow in hopes of seeing Fr. Austin. My subject at Brum was to have been (at request of Mr. Bloye) Applied sculptuah! (David J. remarks — 'as tho. there were any other kind') I was going to have at the Brummy architects of whom I understand there are many in the *Craftsman's* Club. Now good bye —God bless you.

We pray for you —pray you for us. Your loving brother in S. Dominic.   ERIC P. J. G.   O.S.D.

P.S.

1) I don't mean of course that electricity is Catholic thought or ultimate things & steam is the opposite, but simply that the things are so different that understanding one is no guarantee of understanding the other.

2) A dead conventionalism is of course the devil (*corruptio optimi*). A living convention is not, as modernly supposed, a sort of approved regimental drill. It is the necessary form of any work undertaken with God clearly in view —because with God in view any other form is paltriness. The long extempore prayer of the Nonconformist minister, with its 1st head 2nd. head & so on, is,

one may suppose, the one extreme, as the prayer of the man simply kneeling with arms outstretched & no word but 'Jesus, Jesus', is the other.

Also the analogy of art, consider the drawing of children & of all unsophisticated peoples —how they go straight to the real business & how antithetic such are to the work of 'art students' with their life class methods.

3) Don't think I mean that J. & A. are the people I had in mind in the previous sentence. [. . .]

23.2.'22. Thank you very much indeed for your birthday greetings. I had a very happy day indeed tho' I spent it in bed. [. . .] Yes, Denis was received on *Feb. 18*. Your news was correct but previous! And finally, yes, & many thanks, we should be very glad to have the *Rerum Novarum*, Latin-French. Please send 2 copies or 3.

E. P. J. G.

108 : TO ERIC KENNINGTON

Ditchling Common   23-2-1922

Dear Kennington: Thank you for your letter of Feby. 13th. I am interested to hear that you have got the chance of doing a large piece of sculpture and although in a normal age I should say it would be wrong for you to undertake so big a thing without experience, still, at the present time, the blunders you may make will certainly be less objectionable than the expert beastliness of — — and Co.

(1) Certainly, £800 should be plenty. (2) You cannot do better than use Portland stone which you can procure from Messrs. F. J. Barnes, Ltd. Isle of Portland, Dorset at the price of about 10/- per cube foot F.O.R. (3) It depends on the design whether you should do it in France or in England. If you did it in France I should use a French stone of which there are several similar to Portland but I do not know their names or quarries.

Yes, I have finished the Trumpington cross but did not eventually make use of your drawing because I found it was too full of particularities for my skill and besides I wanted a more symbolic kind of figure. Yours very sincerely

ERIC GILL O.S.D.

109 : TO THE REV. JOHN O'CONNOR

D. Comm. Sx.   *31-8-1922*

Dear Father O'Connor: Thank you very much. I got yr. letter yesterday. And I was relieved to hear, 1°, that the drawing was acceptable. You are a Godsend to this little one. I hate secrets and you make them unnecessary. 2°, that the crosses arrived and are fitted in. 3°, that you have got a maid at last and that so Miss Dot is relieved.

I hope Fr. Shebbeare was well. Abbot Butler, who was here for the night of Tuesday and said Mass for us on Wednesday (yesterday to wit), told me that Fr. Sh. was not in good nervous condition. It was a great event the Abbot's mass – we did him as well as we could & as episcopally. His visit was a great blessing. His friendship & support – he gives us his support without stint! – are a great asset. We are reading his book (B⟨enedictine⟩ *Monachism*) at present – he left us a copy. It is very much to the point. Of course he doesn't see eye to eye with us aesthetically – but we are in process of convincing him that what we are doing or trying to do in ART is on all fours with what is attempted in the Religious life as understood by 'the older Religious orders'.

Jacques Maritain would help *him* – which brings me to the point: – Herewith the transcription of Notes 1-24.[1] Tull says no one could read his shorthand (this I can well believe) and that ∴ the longhand must also be his! He will send it to you batch by batch from now onwards. We take your advice.

[1] For Father O'Connor's translation of Maritain's *Art et Scolastique*.

We will not do it via *The Game*. It shall come out in book form at once. We are issuing announcement – that it will be out by Xtmas! Yours affectionately   ERIC GILL O.S.D.

110 : TO HIS BROTHER EVAN

⟨*21-10-1922*⟩

Your good news gave us joy. We send very loving congratulations to you both and to him. Both Peter and Francis are names of good omen –the one for obedience no less than poverty & the other for poverty no less than obedience and both for chastity. We all send you our love. Your brother

ERIC P. J. G.   O.S.D.

111 : TO THE REV. JOHN O'CONNOR

Ditchling Common   *31-10-1922*

Dear Father O'Connor: Thank you very much indeed for chq. It came at the exact moment of need –the cash box [and I have now no bank acc.–a great relief and a great simplification of life –I cannot now be 'overdrawn at the bank'] being emptied last Saturday. I have credited your acc.

If you have got a Watteau (and who shd. doubt it?) for 23/-, well –that is probably about the sum the said Watteau got for it; so you have the satisfaction of having done the dealers. I rejoice.

We have been working hard to get our big Crucifix (for the bank by the Railway) finished. I have finished the carving – it is now being painted. The figure is 14′ 6″ high –head to heel. Arms 6 feet from the shoulder –some crucifix. I hope you will like it when you see it.

Yes, you are right. Eliz. is home. I fetched her at the beginning of the month –it cost £20 to do it one way and another altho. we travelled 3rd! I visited Beauvais on the way out —what a church! What a people that had the enthusi- asm (alas! at that date fast merging into pride) to put up such a height of stone. Eliz. is very well and full of beans. She is working like anything. The forthcoming *Game* will, I hope, amuse you —the incident took place in May after you'd gone home.[1]

Hilary is at present in Ireland! We *expect* him back this week.

I hope your window was bearable . . . the Leeds sculpture progresses. It is to be finished & 'opened' by May next. We all send you our love —yours ever affectionately

ERIC GILL O.S.D.

1 1 2 : TO THE REV. JOHN O'CONNOR

Ditchling Common   J.M. ✠ J.D.   *10-2-1923*

Dear Father John: Thank you very much for your letter of Feb. 2nd. *We* had Hy. Mass on that day & blessing of Candles in our Chapel at the 'hands' of your friend (so I understand) Fr. H. E. G. Rope! His visit was a great success & we feel we have gained a real & holy friend in him. I shd. have replied to your letter before, especially re Marchant & the Ivory Madonna & Child. However you did give me breathing space by saying: 'Write by return or —stay, I will write him . . .' I have 'stayed'. I've been very rushed with work of all sorts & particularly, I am putting in all available daylight on to the Leeds business which now approaches the critical stage both as to carving (those wretched money changers!) and as to its acceptance by the University. As to the latter point: Sadler has asked for (& by now received —I have his acknowledge- ment this morning. He says thanks for photos . . . 'I share your hope that the Council may deal with the matter as *we*

1 Cf. 'Idiocy or Ill-Will' (reprinted from *The Game*), *In A Strange Land* (pp. 50-62); *It All Goes Together*, pp. 3-13.

wish' —my underlining of the significant word —significant as implying that *he* makes no adverse criticism of the work as shown on the photo. By Jove! will they stick that cornice inscription?) photographs of the stone in its present state to give to the members of the Univ. Council so that they may accept or refuse the gift! I enclose one of the pictures herewith. What price James, v.i.? If they stick that they'll stick anything.* To-day is v. wet so I'm in, doing arrears of letters. [. . .]

No, I've not done any more 'Stations' yet. When Leeds is done then I shall do them. Is that all right? Leeds is to be finished & fixed by June. As for D. C.'s designs. I'm not bound to them in the least —on the whole I think them very admirable & am v. glad of them. I employed him because he has a gift for that kind of illustrations & I have not —my gift, so I imagine it, is more physical, more objective, more sensual. I lay it on the altar —before you, my father.

Apropos: I've done a crucifix, nude, in ebony (6 inches only) and am doing another (in ebony also) 1 ft. 9″ high. The wood is cut out to size ready for me (but I've no time to do it at present). Query: shall it be nude? Is there any practical place for such a thing? Please tell me. [. . .] Yours affectionately   ERIC G. O.S.D.

* on the stone it begins with AGITE NUNC.

113 : TO DESMOND CHUTE

D. Common, Sx.   J.M. ✠ J.D.   *14-5-1923 Deo Gratias*

My dear Desmond: I've delayed & delayed writing to you in the hope that we'd be able to send you a supply of money. Alas! none is forthcoming yet & the whole community is dry as bone & without a halfpenny. (20.5.'23) Again I had to put this by! The very morning I began it I got a letter from Leeds saying that the sculpture was in place & ready for me to finish the carving. So Joseph and I went off at half an hour's

notice & spent the best part of the week at Leeds. I took this
letter with me but as I had promised to give a lecture at the
London Univ. Cath. Student's Club on Friday (the 18th.) I
had to spend all available spare time collecting my wits &
witticisms & so wrote no more of this 'ere till now. We are
just back from Mass —It's Sunday —& Whitsunday too and all
is well. The *Deo Gratias* at the head of this refers particularly
to the blessed event you wot of. Oh God be praised indeed —
and now everybody's 'appy —a penurious 'appiness —the best
kind —except for you and how we are going to get funds for
you, I don't know [. . .] The Guild is very hard up, and
Hilary is at the very bottom of his fortunes & Joseph, with 'St.
Anthony' on his shoulders, is stony as can be too . . . Angelus
bell now ringing . . . I must finish later (22.5.'23) Two more
days gone —this is becoming a diary. On Sunday I was unable
to continue as we had to go driving Gipsies off the Common
in the afternoon (quite exciting at times & much cursing &
threatenings) and after that I had an engagement to tea with
David J. & S. Lawson to give them a 'Cantor' instruction.
They have both become T.O.S.D. so now they take their
turns as Cantor in choir! Yesterday we had a surprise visit
from Fr. Austin & that took up the morning & half afternoon.
After that I had to set to and write letters to various newspaper
editors re the Leeds sculpture. There is a bit of a furore at
Leeds & the London papers are taking it up too. We hope to
have a little sport over it. They can't make out why Christ &
the money changers should be a subject of a war memorial.
As for the job itself —it's a veritable 'curate's egg' and I shd.
say rather a failure on the whole. Weathering will do it
good —but the University Students will very likely smash it
up as being an insult to 'the glorious dead' & so it won't get
weathered. I stayed at Bradford with Fr. O'C. while working
at Leeds. He was very well & affectionate.

To continue re money: [. . .] You burned all your boats
when you came to D. Common and now you want a new
Navy. Enough . . . .

Re book plate: I did you an engraving, 'Sedes sapientiae', ever so long ago and thought Hilary had sent you a packet of prints. I hope you are pleased with it and that it will serve your purpose.

Re B'ford Stations. I enclose tracing of portion of your design for No. IV. If you compare it with the photo. as the stone is finished you will see that I made the man thrust the nail into Our Lady's face so to say. What I lost in facial expression I tried to gain in expressive attitude.

Your long letters from Rapallo gave us all great joy & instruction. It was very good indeed & enlightened our darkness very considerably. It was good for you to have such a fine time. This week Elizabeth goes back with Octavie to Sierre. She will stay 3 mths. only. I hope it will enable her to get more below the surface with her French. She will probably revisit Gruyères & hopes to see you there. I wish I could come with her.

Now I must to work. I've got a design to make for a monument —Madonna & Child with group of children round her —all on top of a little pillar:[1]

We all send you our love. I myself shall shortly write again & send you cash (so soon as Leeds pays up . . . unless the civic uproar determines them to refuse payment!) Your affectionate brother in S. Dominic: ERIC GILL O.S.D.

Art et Scholastique is in last stages of proofs.

114 : TO 'BLACKFRIARS', MAY 1923

Sir: Mr. G. K. Chesterton, in his article in the April number of *Blackfriars*, makes great sport of Mr. H. G. Wells, and there would be no harm in that if Mr. Wells had really said about Buddhism what Mr. Chesterton made out. But there seems to be a regrettable misunderstanding.

[1] Here a small drawing.

Mr. Wells, as quoted by Mr. Chesterton, says: 'There are three principal forms the craving of life takes, and all are evil . . . The second is the desire of personal immortality'; and again: ' . . . Nirvana does not mean extinction but the extinction of all the futile personal aims that necessarily make life base . . .' Hereupon Mr. Chesterton rides off on his gloriously high horse and has a fine time showing how illogical is Mr. Wells to maintain that there is no personal immortality and yet that Nirvana does not mean extinction. By some astonishing oversight Mr. Chesterton failed to notice that Mr. Wells did not say that Buddhism taught that there was no personal immortality. Mr. Wells said precisely the contrary, viz., that the Nirvana of Buddhism does *not* mean extinction. But, says Mr. Wells, Buddhism does teach that the *desire* (my italics) of personal immortality is evil. Here is the thing which Mr. Chesterton missed. There is personal immortality (Nirvana) but the *desire* for personal immortality is evil. Now that word 'desire' is the whole point, and the doctrine is not so very difficult after all. For example: we Catholics do not deny that a Christian state may be rich and that its riches may be enjoyed by all; yet we do teach that 'the desire of riches' (*cupiditas*) is the root of all evil (St. Paul, 1 Tim. vi, 10). Is there a discrepancy? Certainly not. Both statements are true. Riches are good and the desire of riches is evil.

In the same way the Buddhist says there *is* personal immortality of a sort (*Nirvana*), nevertheless the desire of personal immortality is evil. And so it is, even for us Catholics, if we think of heaven simply as the place where *we* are glorified. Is this not precisely the sense of Matthew xx, 20-23? When Our Lord rebuked the mother of the sons of Zebedee surely the whole point of His rebuke was that she was desiring heaven as a place of personal glorification for her sons. Heaven is not such a place. The Catholic doctrine of the Beatific Vision implies, as the Buddhist doctrine does, that in heaven we shall be beyond the desire of personal glorification and shall delight only in the glory of God.

It is true that among Catholics it is not commonly said that the desire of immortality is evil. But that is simply because among Catholics the desire of immortality is taken to mean the desire of the Beatific Vision — union with God. It may be supposed that the desire of immortality is called evil by the Buddhist simply because he is 'up against' a conception of heaven as a place of merely personal glorification and gratification. And perhaps Mr. Wells may be forgiven for viewing with sympathy the Buddhist doctrine for, as a person brought up by and living among the Protestants, he is properly revolted by the fact that the same degraded conception of heaven is the one commonly held by his neighbours. Of course, there is personal glorification in heaven — the glorified body of the Resurrection, the glory of all the Saints and all the other glories. But these things flow out from the Beatific Vision and are, so to say, its panoply. They are not the substance but the accidents of immortality.

Buddhism and Christianity are widely divergent religions — the one a false religion and the other the true religion. What we desire, therefore, is that non-Catholics shall see the truth and deny falsehood. More particularly we desire that 'men of good will' shall find the peace of God. Is it not regrettable then that such should be 'put off' by mere misunderstanding? Yours, etc.   ERIC GILL, O.S.D.

Ditchling Common, Sussex. 16/4/23.

P.S. When I say that riches are good and the desire of riches is evil, of course an inordinate or disordered desire is understood. And when the Buddhists say that the desire of personal immortality is evil, of course an inordinate or disordered desire is understood.[1] For the word *cupiditas* means an in-

[1] It may naturally be asked whether this statement would be accepted by Buddhists themselves. I consulted Mr. Marco Pallis, who most kindly sent me the following commentary. 'To a Buddhist, this use of the word "inordinate" would sound somewhat equivocal. Should it be taken in the sense of a personal desire which is inordinate through excess or is it inordinate because it remains personal? The same question, *mutatis mutandis*, would apply to the word "futile"

ordinate desire of riches, and the mother of the sons of
Zebedee, like most Indians and Red Indians and like most
Protestants (and, I suggest, like not a few Catholics, including
myself, alas!) had a disordered desire of heaven. The doctrine
of Nirvana is the Buddhist attempt, however inadequate, to
counter this disorder. It is necessary, if we wish to convert
the Buddhists (and Mr. Wells), to show that the Catholic
doctrine of the Beatific Vision beats the doctrine of Nirvana,
and at its own game!   E. G.

115 : TO THE REV. JOHN O'CONNOR

Ditchling Common   J.M. ✠ J.D.   *19-5-1923*

My dear Father John: Thank you very much indeed for all
your kindness. I enjoyed my visit very much and put several
pearls of great price in my pocket. You will be gratified to
learn that, after *missing* the 9.28 at the Midland Station, I
caught the 9.35 at the G.N. Sta^n! Great ovation from the
guards & ticket collectors —much shouting & *despectio superbis*.
So I got to London at 2.0 & did a few useful jobs before going
to the University at 4.30 for my lecture to the Cath. Students.
Fr. V⟨incent⟩ took the chair which was a great blessing & all
went as well as could be expected. Maritain was v. useful but
I did not use him in extenso. The atmosphere was not quite
suitable and I think I did the right thing though clumsily.

---

as used by Wells. According to the Buddhist view any kind of wish for an
experiencing of fruits personally, by "this man So-and-so", is futile and inordinate by definition: futile, because a lingering attachment to the ego, however
purified in its form, fatally involves the being concerned in the round of becoming, of mortality, from the very fact that the empirical ego itself is a compound,
the result of causes, and subject to eventual dissolution; inordinate, because true
order, in the most universal sense, can only be realized by one who has been
freed from all particular desires whatsoever. To borrow a Sufi phrase, it may
be said that there is no desirable excepting only The Desirable, with Which
nothing whatsoever may be associated. In general Buddhist usage, therefore,
"desire" is always referred to in a privative sense.'

This afternoon a reporter chap has been over —sent by the *Sunday Express* —to ask what means the Leeds War Memorial! He says there is discussion in the Leeds papers. What, already? I saw nothing of it. If you come across anything interesting please do send it along to your affectionate penitent

ERIC GILL O.S.D.

Mary is delighted with the ivory.

The enclosed is for Gertrude to buy sweets withal.

116 : TO DESMOND CHUTE

Ditchling Common   J.M. ✠ J.D.   *19-6-1923*

Dear Desmond: [. . .] There was a great to do in Leeds over that sculpture. Much opposition in the local press & among local financiers. As usual in English Universities, the Students were largely on the side of the fallen angels. I had a happy four days staying with Fr. O'C. while finishing off the carving. My next job is to do Fr. O'C.'s Stations.

You must have been surprised to see Eliz.! She no doubt told you that we came en masse to Dieppe with her. We went on to Beauvais for the Sunday & returned by the Sunday night boat. Beauvais at High Mass was very grand & splendid & worshipful. The Bp. was there and the choir of ecclesiastical students sang the chant very finely —accompanied quite nicely on a small choir organ. (The big organ let itself go every now & then on its own —e.g. in between the verses of that great hymn, *Lauda Sion*, it played a sort of thundering echo of the melody —very glorious effect & converted me to Catholicism every time. Clare also became a Christian . . .) I hope you are very well. I hope you are not *starving* or going short of clean linen. We all send you our love. I am your affectionate brother in S. Dom.   ERIC P. J. G. O.S.D.

117 : TO THE REV. JOHN O'CONNOR

Ditchling Common   *11-10-1923*

Dear Father O'Connor: Herewith 12/6 in payment for the
tusk. [. . .]

You will be interested to hear that we went to meet
Elizabeth coming back from Switzerland and had an interview
with Maritain in Paris and have established an entente. I wish
you had been there for he does not speak English. However
Eliz. shone with much effulgence & Hilary made good by
understanding what was said. [. . .] Love from all

ERIC G.   O.S.D.

118 : TO WILLIAM ROTHENSTEIN

Ditchling Common   J.M. ✠ J.D.   *27-10-1923*

Dear Rothenstein: Thank you very much for your letter & the
cutting and all the kind things you think well to say of me.
I am most pleased to know the Leeds sculpture gave you
satisfaction. I shd. like to see it again myself now that, being
a thing of the past, I might more easily see it freshly. And I
am glad you liked *Autumn Midnight*[1] –tho' I don't think it a
great success myself –too spotty & scrappy and the initial to
the 20" baby[2] is absurd (as F. C. herself thinks). It wd. be
very nice to have a long talk –but I am very seldom in London
& when I am it is rarely that I have time for visits of affection.

I hope Rachel is well again. I've heard no news for a long
time. We are all well and busy. I'm still doing 'Stations' for
Bradford besides tombstones for the Rich & Great –but I'm
seriously thinking of emigrating to a land 'where falls not hail
nor rain nor any snow' & where there are no Rates. If I do
I shall certainly come & say good bye. Yours affectly.

ERIC GILL   O.S.D.

Have you seen our new book on *The Philosophy of Art*?

[1] By Frances Cornford, illustrated by E. G.
[2] 'When I was twenty inches long' (p. 8).

Caldey   J.M. ✠ J.D.   *12-1-1924*

My dear Desmond: Here beginneth . . . at last, and the first
decent opportunity too! The envelope in wh. I propose to
put this was packed with pretty pictures 2 or 3 days before
Xmas. I hoped to have written then & posted before the feast.
But, no luck. Now here I am at Caldey. George Maxwell is
with me. Hilary was coming but owing to a feverish cold
could not come at the last moment. What on earth, you will
say, are we at? Well, well, to put it short we are on an
exped^n. of inquiry into the affairs of the island—to see whether
a marriage can be arranged & perhaps shortly take place
between the Tertiaries of D. Common, spinsters (stone-
carvers, printers, carpenters & what not —not to mention
farm labourers) children of S. Dominic & S. Joseph, and the
Benedictines of Caldey —monks and priests —Sons of S.
Benedict (hitherto doing their own housekeeping on rather
amateurish lines & badly needing a wife). I shd. think you can
see the possibilities of such a marriage. The young woman
needs a husband as much as 'he' needs a wife —obviously.
But, of course like all modest christian females she is anxious
not to be jilted nor unhappily married. [. . .] The young
man is very keen on the marriage but is in very serious
financial difficulties & has been flirting not too wisely with
other rather less virtuous (!) females —& probably they will
hang round his neck rather tightly. But he is penitent & in
hopes of throwing them off. [. . .] To return to plain
language —the conferences with Fr. Prior are satisfactory & on
Monday next (Jan. 14) we go with him to Llanthony to see
the estate & buildings there with a view to seeing whether or
no that place might be an interim place of sojourn —i.e. a
place of honeymoon for the time during which the husband
will be getting the home in order for the bride. But why
leave D. Common? But why not? Is it not possible that we
are living beyond our means there? Have we the Bd. Sacra-

ment? (I grant you we do not claim to deserve It —but we must *desire* It —as a bride her bridegroom.) There are many things. But we don't *want* to leave & shall not except to go to a good home. [. . .] Fr. Provincial o.p. is coming to D. Comm. next Tuesday. We are racing to get back to meet him. Well, —that's that. Now, first I crave forgiveness for so long not writing. I have had no chance at all. Life gets fuller & fuller & letters, not having a regular place in the curriculum, get left for months. I'm very sorry. [. . .] Yes, Leeds was an amusing business. How they did take on! It's 'all quiet' now, apparently. The carving was really good in parts —but I found it difficult to be very enthusiastic about it myself. It seemed a failure —lacking much beauty as a whole —how much better if the figures had filled the panel to the top thereof.

Item: R. L. has gone (to-day) to Quarr —to try his vocation as a lay brother! I think he found & we found that we had not quite the authority to guide & lead a stray sheep at D. Comm. David J. wd. have been in the same boat but that he, unlike R. L., is a man with a definite trade & a definite vocation to that trade —& so has pulled through. [. . .]

¶ Item: Did you get the tonsure in July?

Item: V. interested to know that you've been lectured to by Père Allo. Fr. Martindale in his S. John (*Apoc.*) makes great use of him. [. . .]

We had a very happy Christmas. I hope you did too. Your letter came on the very prick of the feast. Alas, that you have yet got no letter from us. Indeed you were much thought of & prayed for. The carol party was again a much enjoyed affair. We learnt several new ones —an excellent Basque one & a fine Latin one, *Jure plaudunt omnia*. We went all round the Common night by night. How good to have Clare with us too. . . .

On Jan. 5 & 6 we had a Nativity play (Chester), the 4 Shepherds. That was some sport I may say. The old Vic's been doing it & P. A. M. being one of the four he suggested coming & doing it at the Common. We to supply the 'hall', and Our Lady & S. Joseph & S. Gabriel & 4 Shep. boys & a chop & a hill etc. These things we did. Petra: O. L.; David P.: St. J.; Philip Baker (you don't know the excellent lad): S. Gabriel; Mark, Joanna, Susan & another boy: the 4 shep. boys. Also we supplied a *Gloria* for the angelic choir (ourselves took the part!). The kids did their parts (oh, most admirable words —most dear) in a splendid monotone. St. Gabriel was fine —monotone with intonations. The pros. from the old Vic. were by comparison abominable with their mouthings. But it were a fine game none the less & Costick's ironing room was crowded by 100 people! [. . .]

Yes, I've had a good year as H. says, and —praise be —we're out of debt for a time —even in funds. I'm still doing Bradford Stations. I hope to fix them all by Easter. Otherwise, since Leeds, I've had nothing on of any size (sounds like the garden of Eden). I've been doing tombstones & inscriptions without stopping. I've no photos.

Item: The bally election —no, we saw nothing of it. But I hear the result is embarrassing to the politicians. [. . .]

Item: On the way here I went to Quarr —that great abbey. (There is still a community of about 30 & the chant is still very very good). There I met Bro. Richard Anson! I had news of Caldey from him you may be sure. Nevertheless, he only says *if* the marriage could be arranged, he has no doubt of the result —the good result. Only he says its imposs —that their difficulties are too great. We shall see.

Item: Fr. Prior comes to Ditchling for the night next Wednesday! So then we shall talk to him on our own quarter-deck. You shall hear if anything happens. Now good bye — God bless you. I am your affectionate brother in St. Dom.

ERIC GILL   O.S.D.

Rain & wind ever since we've been here (we came on Thursday).

But it's a marvellous island —N'est-ce pas? Good land too.

The abbey buildings are not so bad as I'd expected — but the picturesque pinnacles — turrets & what nots — the gothic tit-bits — oh God, oh Caldey.

P.S. (Sunday eve) Have had an hour's talk with Dom Theodore — v. satisfactory — & he very good & affectionate & receptive. He wd. be pleased to see *you* again.   E. G.

120 : TO THE REV. JOHN O'CONNOR

Strictly 'secret & confidential' vide letters of P.M.G.
                    & Dep. Master of Mint.

Ditchling Comm. Sx.   *24-1-1924*

My dear Father John: I have finished at last all other work in hand & have started again on the Stations. All seemed to augur well for an uninterrupted run home. But alas by consecutive posts came letters from H.M. Government officials inviting me 1, to make designs for new 1^d & 1$\frac{1}{2}^d$ postage stamps & 2, to make designs for new silver coinage. Appropriate honorariums are offered — but apart from that it seems clear that I ought to have a go at it (of course I'm not the only one they've invited). Drawings of the stamps are to be sent in by Feb. 18 & of the coins by Mar. 27. It's not many days work as far as I can see, but I'm letting you know in case it spells delay for the Stations. I feel sure you'll agree that I ought to do these things & will forgive me if my project for delivering 7 Stations by Easter proves imposs. Yours very affectly.   ERIC GILL O.S.D.

P.S. The Mint seems genuinely concerned that it shan't leak out that a new coinage is proposed. So there you are — more confessional stuff.

ERIC GILL

Self-portrait (1925)

121 : TO DESMOND CHUTE

D. Comm. Sx.　　　　J.M. ✠ J.D.　　　　*20-2-1924*

My dear Desmond: [. . .] Thomism at Ditchling —most vital.
Agreed. But Thomism anywhere —most necessary and particularly in a secular community living under the wing of a
contemplative community — the one string it needs. [. . .]
Love from all. Your affect. bro. in S.D.　　ERIC G.　O.S.D.

122 : TO THE REV. JOHN O'CONNOR

D. Comm. Sx.　　　　　　*22-2-1924*
　　　　　　　　　　　　viz: my birthday
　　　　　　　　　　　　the 11th. anniversary of Mary's
　　　　　　　　　　　　and my Reception
　　　　　　　　　　　　the feast of S. P. Ant. etc.

Dear Father John: Your letter of the 20th. came this auspicious
morn. I'd like to see your medal & coins but I'm a bit off
heroics in my mind in the matter of H.M. Gov. and, as the
Mint says that they're prepared to abandon heraldry & St.
Georges in the new coins, I'm thinking of symbols of money-
making & such, more or less thinly veiled. (e.g.[1] what could
be better than the 3 balls or some such device . . .)

It is good news that you can come for the Easter Sunday &
M & T. We hail the suggestion with enthusiasm — It's a fixture.
As you'll be away in Holy Week there's no point in my rushing
to get the Stations finished for Good Friday —that relieves the
situation.

Your titles are absolutely it. viii & xiii shall not be altered
for any one not divinely guarded from error. In 1921 you
gave me (your own handwriting) the title for viii: 'the women
weep for him'. I wasn't keen on it but *cut* it the week before
last! So now I must cut it all away & cut the new one![2] But

---

[1] Here a small drawing of three balls on a coin.
[2] HE TELLS WOMEN HOW TO WEEP.

it must be done & shall. The worst of it is that whereas the carving is rather better than your 1921 words, *now* it is beaten by the new words —annoying I call it. It's like being caught up a yard from the winning post & beaten by 3 lengths.

I think I can make out the Greek. I'll let you know if I can't. I hope the Leeds lecture was a success. Love from

ERIC G.   O.S.D.

123 : TO WILLIAM ROTHENSTEIN

D. Comm. Sx.   *22-2-1924*

My dear W. R.: Fr. V. McNabb is proposing to give a course of 4 lectures upon Art & Philosophy (on the lines of Maritain's book). He wants a responsible chairman & has appealed to me to help him. He would be very glad indeed if *you* could do it for him and I told him I wd. write to you. You wd. I know approve of the *stuff* & your name wd. greatly help to bring the right young people to feed. I hope you will agree. If you do, could you write to Fr. V.* & tell him & he will arrange dates to your mutual satisfaction.

As to *place*: He is at present lecturing in the Army Hut (next to Westminster Cathedral) on the philosophy of St. Thomas Aquin. And the same place wd. *do*, though it is not v. large. But if there is a lecture theatre at S.K. which you could commandeer for such a course of lectures —perhaps that wd. be better still. You will understand, of course, that the lectures are in no sense to be regarded as propagandist in the controversial sense. It's Truth that's at stake. Love from

ERIC G.   O.S.D.

I hope Rachel's better.

P.S. The present lectures at W'minster are under *London University* auspices —not R.C., so that may help you (I mean, help you in dealing with 'the Board')

* address: Very Rv. Fr. Vincent McNabb O.P., St. Dominic's Priory, Southampton Rd., London, N.W.5.

124 : TO THE REV. JOHN O'CONNOR

D. Comm.   *16-3-1924*

Dear Fr. John: Many thanks for Greek texts. They shall be inscribed. [. . .]

I was in S. Wales (Brecknock) last week looking at a farm. We may buy it! 14 m. from Abergavenny. Capel y ffin's the name and just describes it. 2000 feet of mountain wall on both sides & to north of it —no outlet but to the South. 4 m. N. of Llanthony Abbey Ruins. Benedictine monastery 400 yards away —B^d Sacrament & Dy Mass. Good land —fair price —nice little house & 107 acres with some timber & two rushing streams. Sheep run on mountains & stone galore, both for carving & building, *no extra charge.* 10 miles to Ry. Station. Postman on horse-back once a day. Doctor on horseback, from Hay, once a week. Any complaints? 400 yds. approx. to Monmouthshire border! London in 3½ hrs. from Abergavenny. Exciting prospect. We may *all* trek. Say goodbye to Burgess Hill. Why not? Love from us all. ERIC G. O.S.D.

P.S. I hope C. L. R. liked the Stations.

125 : TO DESMOND CHUTE

Ditchling Common   J.M. ✠ J.D.   *8-6-1924*

My dear Desmond: I expect you are at home by now. I hope you had a pleasant and health-giving voyage. I wish we could meet. There is so much to say & discuss & more than can be done by writing. We are in various throes —financial (of course) & 'political'. . . .

1. Here are some photographs of the last seven Bradford 'Stations'. I hope you will be pleased with the work. N.B. Father O'C wishes to buy the set of designs you originally made for the said Stations. Therefore will you write to me naming your price & that right soon?

2.   How long will you be at Bristol, and while you are there
could you come on a visit to Capel y ffin —which is 14 m.
from Abergavenny, which is something under an hour in
Ry. train from Newport, Mon., which is not so unget-
atable from Bristol.

3.   Thank you very much for the picture postcards received
at various times & especially from Lucca & Pisa.
Sundry pars.
    § Father Vincent is coming here on Whit. Mon. & leaves
on Tuesday & Fr. Prior from Caldey is coming on Tuesday
morn. early, just in time to meet & I hope have some talk
with Fr. V.
    § The mountain air at Capel y ffin is just the thing for your
trouble.
    § Capel . . . is in the Diocese of Menevia.
    § David Jones and I are going to Bradford on Wednesday
next week to finish & colour the last seven stations. We
shall be there some ten days. [. . .]

Did Mrs. Chute or you ever meet Maggie Albanesi? I am
doing a tablet (portrait & inscript) to go in St. Martin's
Theatre (entrance hall). She was an R.C. so that is a solace.
[. . .] Yours affectionately in St. Dominic,   ERIC GILL O.S.D.

126 : TO G. K. CHESTERTON

Ditchling Common   *6-8-1924*

Dear Mr. Chesterton: Forgive my presumption. I wrote the
enclosed notes for *The Game* some time ago. But the Game,
though still being played, is no longer being played in print
and, rather than merely put the m.s. in the drawer, I thought
you might as well see it first —if you wd. so far honour me.
I hope you will. I hope you'll overlook the annoying personality business —Mr. Chesterton this & Mr. Chesterton that —I
think there is some sense in the view put forward —I do think
you make a bit of a bloomer in (1) supporting Orpenism as

against Byzantinism & (2) in thinking that the art of painting *began* with Giotto — whereas Giotto was really much more the end.

We are leaving Ditchling Common & after this week my address will be *Capel-y-ffin, nr. Abergavenny, S. Wales.* Yours very affectionately   ERIC GILL O.S.D.

G. K. C., The New Jerusalem p. 242

'There is no sort of reason why their [mediaeval] sculpture should not have become as perfect as their architecture; there is no sort of reason why their sense of form should not have been as finished as their sense of colour.

A statue like the St. George of Donatello would have stood more appropriately under a Gothic than under a Classic arch.'

Truly there is no sort of reason except that it *was* as perfect, it *was* as finished. Donatello's St. George is a fine statue, but it stands appropriately exactly where it does stand. Mr. Chesterton has perhaps never seen the sculptures of Chartres. If he has seen them he has remained blind. He has remained blind because he has sought what was not there & so has seen nothing but the glass above them — oh! what glass — yes, to be sure! But the sculptures are as good.

Controversy

Mr. G. K. Chesterton (in 'Our Note Book', Illustrated London News, Mar. 10, 1923.)

Here are cuttings from a whole page of almost incredible misunderstanding! Why should we bother about it? Because Mr. Chesterton is, as he deserves to be, widely read & because he is, as also he deserves to be, widely honoured. Though we have always suspected him to be, like Mr. Belloc, something of an iconoclast, we have never caught him 'at it' so openly until now. For it is possible to be an iconoclast without having Puritanism for one's religion or Knox for one's surname. A man may be an iconoclast simply because he does not like the art of the imagemaker — because he thinks the whole proper business of art is comprised in the art of the illustrator. It is as

M

though he had no use for any music but 'programme' music. It is as though he had no use for any literature but story telling. It is as though he had no use for creation but for criticism. Mr. Chesterton has been a champion of mediaeval civilization. Yet he is so far a child of the Renaissance that he is ready to join company with a merely dextrous portrait-painter in spurning a great creative period and to suggest that Christian art only began with Giotto! Giotto, alas! was the end, not the beginning. But he is hailed as the beginning because he was the first great illustrator, and illustration, portraiture, criticism are the only functions of art honoured in an age in which men are no longer 'partners with God in the *making* of beauteous works', in which artists are a class apart, spoiled & petted so long as they are able to purvey the lovable to their employers.

(1. 2. 3 & 4) When we got to the words 'ironical presence of modern art' we said 'ha! now he's going to give old Orpen beans —now the R.A.'s going to cop it —Now the chocolate box is going through the hoop!' What was our astonishment therefore when we read on & discovered that the onslaught was upon the poor little futurists & cubists —those fighters of the forlorn hope against mammon who have never heard of God —teetotalers who have never heard of Temperance? We thought he was going on to say 'How can we have the face to condemn Byzantine art as hard, abstract & mathematical in the presence of modern art which, for the most part, is soft as slime, sentimental as Cocoa, & illogical as angry women! Would to God modern art had a little Byzantine hardness; would that modern artists had, every now and then at least, a remembrance that the distinctive difference between men and animals is that man has power to deal in abstract ideas; oh that the 'T' square were as much a part of the equipment of a studio as a milk-sop model. And, as all art is not studio art, would to God the modern variety of house furniture were a little harder & less cushioned; would that divorce court reports were a trifle more reticent, not to say abstract; oh that jerry builders could work on the square . . .' But no, Mr. Chester-

ton is so modern of the moderns that he is oblivious to all the mass of filth & vulgarity of industrialism & when you say 'modern art' to him he sees only Picasso & Marinetti — as if *they* were typical — as if *they* cut any ice — as if *they* made any difference to the manufacturers of Birmingham or Bradford. Besides it is so ungenerous of him. Here we are enmeshed, engulfed, squashed flat by the vilest tyranny of money-making ever known on earth, and when a few men are found who have the heart to stand up against it (what if they are belauded by a clique of fashionable fools calling themselves connoisseurs?) &, however crankily, set to work in opposition to all the tyrants' most cherished notions of art, they are hailed as buffoons and, what is more odd, as representative of modern art! At most they are merely cranky (who wouldn't be cranky in Birmingham rather than play the Birmingham game?) at best they are honest and intensely unworldly experimenters who think that form in the abstract is more important than verisimilitude, that creation is more worth while than photographic effects, & that God is more to be worshipped than Man. But of course if you go to a cricket match & complain because the players play bad football, nothing can be done until the misunderstanding is dispelled & even then nothing can be done if you have a rooted dislike of cricket.

(5 & 6) It wd. not be possible for Sir William Orpen or even Mr. Chesterton to explain 'the ugliness & dullness of Byzantine art' simply because it is neither ugly nor dull. And that it shd. be called ugly and dull is precisely the trouble. It shows the depths of our self-love. It is not possible here to write at great length an essay on aesthetics. We may refer our readers to the advertisement printed herewith of a forthcoming book which deals with the subject in dispute[1] & we shall have great pleasure in sending Mr. Chesterton a complimentary copy. There is however one salient aspect of the difficulty to which we may here call attention. This is an age in which the glories are shared by the money makers & the

[1] Father O'Connor's translation of Maritain.

literary men. It is an age of money & an age of print. This is inevitable (vide *Game*, Dec. 1922, article 'Idiocy or Ill-will')[1] & one of the results is that the literary critic of works of art always seeks for and belauds only 'literary content' in such works &, where he finds none, weeps or howls. The painting of Giotto is admirable and the more remarkable because it is great painting in spite of his preoccupation with illustration or story telling. The painting of Cimabue is upon a higher plane, a more exalted plane, a plane more removed from representation & one upon which the painter finds himself face to face with God. It may well be maintained that the great Byzantine school deserves even greater honour for here was not simply one individual bathing in the vision of God but, as it seems, a whole people, & for several centuries, filled with the Holy Ghost. Their works are indeed the evidence – to the Jews a stumbling block, to the Gentiles foolishness, & to Mr. Chesterton & Sir William Orpen ugliness and dullness. (E. G.)

23.4.'23

127 : TO DESMOND CHUTE

Capel-y-ffin, Abergavenny

11.9.24. SS. Protus & Hyacinth reminded us that to-day is your birthday & me that I have not yet written to you since our arrival at Capel, at least not a letter worth calling such. I will write without fail before Sunday becomes Monday –so there! Until this week I have hardly done a stroke of work except the work of house arranging & fitting etc. Now, at last I am able to start again & must keep at it henceforth like anything. I've got plenty to do I am glad to say. I've a carving to finish this month & a good many engravings at hand, including 3 portraits! [. . .] We are all well and we all send you much love and wish you every blessing & very many happy returns of SS. P. & H. I hope you are well –blessings on you – *This place is A 1.*   ERIC G. O.S.D.

[1] Cf. Letter 111.

Capel-y-ffin, Abergavenny   *14-9-1924*

My dearest Desmond: It is Sunday morning and a fine fresh
sunny cold windy morning and all is pretty well. I will make
attempt to write to you then. And first I will answer your
letter. I got it at Ditchling a day or so before we left. We
departed in good order and without heartbreakings. [. . .]
Well the net result is this: —

1. Hilary and George M. remain at Ditchling & carry on as
   heretofore! Joseph is determined to come to Wales next
   Spring. David J. is coming before Xmas.

2. I resigned my membership of the *Guild*. [. . .] They
   wanted me to reconsider my decision but I stuck to it.
   (Philip H. & David J. concur with me and are also resign-
   ing). I said that I hoped it wd. be poss. to start another
   Guild at Capel and that I hoped the two Guilds might be
   affiliated and have mutual sympathy & identical aims. I
   think they might arrange an annual meeting & so on.
   That's how it stands at present. [. . .]

After all there is no antagonism, quite the contrary, between
St. Dominic & St. Benedict. Fr. Austin B. agreed with me
when I put it to him that the mission of St. Dominic might be
described as having for earthly objective the bringing back of
the world, collectively & individually, to St. Benedict —and
from my point of view, bearing in mind the general objective
of the restoration of all things in Christ, our life here and at
Ditchling is much more, or intends to be much more, con-
structive than propagandist. But no doubt you see the whole
problem clearly enough & will lend us the aid of your prayers
that whatever we do it may not be for the satisfaction of personal fancy. Well, we have been here a month and are now
comfortable and in many respects settled. 'Us' & the Hagreens
have (with the Attwaters, whom I do not think you know) the
Monastery building to ourselves. One whole side of the
ground floor is Chapel pro tem. (i.e. until we can put the big

Church built by 'Fr. Ig^s.' into repair). Fr. Joseph Woodford
O.S.B., who is permanently here, lives in the house next door
(the 'Grange!') with a Brother Michael Davies & a Brother
Augustine from Caldey. At present Dom Theodore B. is
staying there also. He is very quickly advancing in good works
& straight thoughts. I like him v. much anyway. He is going
back to Caldey this week to return, for a month or two, after
Christmas.

I am at last able to start work again —tho. my workshop
accommodation is very bad at present. I am carving a black
marble torso of Our Lord (a 'Deposition')[1] & I am doing a
set of wood engravings for a book of poems for a 'Lady in
London'. Also I am doing 3 wood-engraved portraits, the
Lowinsky family. I hope you are well and happy and getting on
well with your 'studies'. We have been v. pleased to have the
postcards from you lately. Please go on thus keeping in touch
& we also will . . . The children are of course much occupied
with the work of this new life, but they are writing to you
also.

Everyone in this Valley is most kind & friendly. We have
been astonished at the welcome they have given us —and the
place is marvellous. You will be in England in a year or two
no doubt and you will certainly be at Bristol. Therefore you
will surely come to Capel. We look forward to that meeting.
Dear Desmond, God bless you & give you the health & strength
you need for His work. I am your ever loving brother in St.
Dom.   ERIC P. J. G.   O.S.D.

129 : TO DESMOND CHUTE

Capel-y-ffin   *15-11-1924*

My dearest Desmond: Thank you very much indeed for your
repeated greetings and now especially for the Papal Blessing
and your letter and photographs from Rome. The P.B. came

[1] A small drawing of this at side.

at a most opportune moment for, altho. I know it is far from being a unique privilege, it is an imprimatur of a sort and gives me a sort of feeling that whatever happens me and the Pope are pals —fiat, fiat. Moreover it almost makes me wish to hasten the day whereon I shall be born, as even I may hope, into the better life. I say the moment was opportune for up here in this Valley in the black mountains one's nose is to the grindstone more than it was . . . elsewhere. It is as tho. we had been living, formerly, in a more or less comfortably camouflaged villa residence and now we have nought but a bed —a good bed but full of fleas. I wish you were here for a talk. I'm a bit lonely —sometimes v. much so. Philip H. is v. good, but he's too ill to discuss much [. . .]. Mary as usual is good as gold and 'all will be well —all manner of thing shall be well'. Are we downhearted? No, but . . . However I've got plenty of work to do — my only serious trouble is lack of peaceful workshop accommodation. That will come in time —meanwhile I'm much heartened by the P.B. Herewith I enclose intaglio print of M & C. with much love & also some for your amusement & comment. They are all *wood* engravings. The one of 'The Deposition' is a failure obviously but I went on & on with it to see what depth of black one could get & by what means. As I write this your postcards from Orvieto have arrived. Many thanks indeed.* Also by same post a set of new wood cuts from Dom Theodore —a very great improvement on anything he's done before —praise be —I feel he's now really getting on to the right road. Ask him to send you some [. . .]

Well good bye for now. I hope you are well & strong again & fit for study. Blessings on you & may you come through safe & sound even here below. Bristol Diocese touches Cardiff do. [. . .] I am your loving brother in St. Dominic.

ERIC P. J. G.   O.S.D.

* What a superb St. John's eagle.

Sir: Mr. Thorp, in your second issue, states exactly what I
had always supposed the D.I.A. to stand for.

As an example of the D.I.A. way of thinking, he suggests
that a cheap ash-tray might be 'stamped with a die cut by
Cellini or Gill.' He asks whether an artist 'can't so use and
control the various machines [used in book-production] that
a lovely (sic) whole is produced at a tithe of the cost of a hand-
wrought book' (he always says 'wrought'). He ends up by
stating, as the D.I.A. basis, that things, whether hand or
machine made, should be 'first fit for their purpose, then
pleasant to use, then so far as possible beautiful', —and, as
though it supported him, he quotes Prof. Lethaby's dictum
that 'Art is not the Sauce but the cooking itself, so it be good.'
Now this is a very clear statement of the D.I.A. muddle.

First let me say that the quotation from Prof. Lethaby,
though good, is not quite perfect, for it would be an improvement to say 'the thing cooked' rather than the 'cooking'
merely, and also because Prof. Lethaby implies that a work of
art properly so called is never bad, whereas the Queen Victoria
Memorial is undoubtedly a work of art however bad one may
think it, and a man-made clock is a work of art even if it keep
time badly. But, perfect or not, the saying is contrary to
the D.I.A. point of view as enunciated by Mr. Thorp, for the
whole point of the saying is that art is not an extra but an
inherent quality in things; whereas, according to Mr. Thorp,
the enthusiasm of the D.I.A. is expended upon the addition of
Cellini or Gill art-sauce to otherwise undesirable ash-trays and
such like.

Moreover, and more fundamental still, Mr. Thorp clearly
teaches that a thing fit for its purpose may or may not be
pleasant to use! or that a thing fit for its purpose and pleasant
to use may or may not be beautiful!

Now that is the muddle which Mr. Thorp so clearly exposes. On the contrary: the truth is that a thing fit for its purpose is necessarily pleasant to use and also beautiful (beautiful, *i.e.*, seen as being in itself delightful to the understanding). And that is why we find the D.I.A. a superfluous institution: because we think that an artist as such is not a person who makes things beautiful, but simply one who deliberately makes things as well as he can — whether he be clock-maker or picture-painter; because we think that machine-made things are very much better when no 'designer' has had anything to do with them — *i.e.*, when they are just plain serviceable things as, for instance, are the machines themselves; because we think that if you look after goodness and truth, beauty will take care of itself.

Designer! Of course there must be a designer, a person, a mind, who thinks and contrives how things shall be made; but just because there *must* be there is no need to talk about him unless — and here's the trouble — you mean, not the person or persons really responsible for the production of the article, but a person called in from outside and paid to add something. To add what? Ah! what? Why just that extra quality which Mr. Thorp and his friends call 'beauty' or 'comeliness' or 'the seemly'. If the designer isn't going to add something, why call him in? If he is merely to restrain the vulgar manufacturer from lathering his goods with what Mr. Thorp thinks ugly, why not call it the R.I.A., that is, the *Refined* Industries Association? I would join the society then with pleasure, for my one complaint against machine-made goods, as such, is that they too often hide their light under a bushel of 'design'. Think how decent alarum clocks might be if they were just as plain and well made outside as they often are inside! But for that consummation you don't need a D.I.A. You need my R.I.A. You don't need 'Designers'; you need mere intelligence and fortitude. But there is no money in it, for clock manufacturers largely depend upon the 'attractiveness' of their outsides to make the insides 'go'. So there you are and there is the D.I.A.; and it simply isn't convincing to tell us that certain 'magnates' don't think it good business. How touchingly innocent Mr. Thorp must be and must imagine your readers to be! Yours, etc.,   ERIC GILL, O.S.D.

131 : TO WILLIAM ROTHENSTEIN

Bradford   *2-2-1925*

Dear Rothenstein: This is the first opportunity I have had of writing to you since I saw you last Wednesday morning. Since then I have turned the matter over and over and have come definitely to the conclusion that the job, in spite of its attractions, is not for me. I cannot expect you to sympathize with my reasons so do not see why I shd. annoy you by giving them. I am much honoured by your invitation and very much regret my inability to accept. The appointment would have been economically a great help to me and, socially, it would have kept me in touch with many people whom I like to meet. So you will believe me when I say that my refusal has nothing to do with the terms of pay or the physical conditions. In a word, it is simply that I am not of one mind with you in the aims you are furthering at the Ryl. College, and, may I whisper it?, I think there are too many women about.

Thank you very much indeed for your kindness in making me the offer. I am very sorry to disappoint you. Yours affectly.   ERIC GILL O.S.D.

132 : TO DESMOND CHUTE

Capel-y-ffin   *23-5-1925*
London Address: c/o Goupil Gallery
5 Regent St., S.W.

My dear Desmond: Is it poss. that I'm writing to you at last? Well, I am very very sorry to have neglected you so long. Indeed we did wish you a happy Christmas though we did not tell you so —and a happy Easter also —and we do thank you for your welcome postcard messages —they served at least to let us know that in spite of all we were not given up as hopeless. I have eight on my desk as I write! The last one came this morning from Assisi —the one with the unmistakable Craig scenery. I hope you sent him one too. What a magnificent place, and that tower at Arezzo —yes, it's absolutely the right way to build —no architect hath done this. And the picture of Our Lady from Siena —most beautiful —most perfect —and the superb S. John, his eagle, in bronze. You have seen some fine things. I hope you are well & getting on fine with the work. When will you be ordained —is the day visible yet? I shd. like to see Mrs. Chute when she gets back and hear all about you. I wish she could come and visit us up here. Is that poss? But if it isn't I could, on my way to or from London one time, visit her at Bristol. Also I want to talk to her about Ditchling — alas! an unhappy subject at present. I am still exactly where I was when I left August as regards any settlement [. . .]

Item: I have arranged with Mr. Marchant of the Goupil Gallery to be my agent in London. I don't know how that will work, but I had to have a *pied à terre* somewhere (hence this note paper). I've sold a good many prints since I left Ditchling — every now & then there's a bit of a spurt and it's quite a business. Doing my own printing is great sport & I've got a large & a small printing press here and a copper plate press too. Copper engraving is a great game. I hope to do something in that line. But for the last few months I've been absolutely rushed with lettering work of all sorts & have neither done a stone carving nor an engraving (except lettering). I'm aching to do something in both lines of business. At present I haven't a single sculpture commission —not one. A few tombstones that's all. We finished the Stations at Leatherhead all right. They are really quite a good set and were a jolly good experience for Joseph. As for him he's well & loyal. He hopes to be down here before very long. That will be good for it's very difficult to run our joint business from such widely separated bases. We were working together last week cutting inscriptions on a monument by Epstein in Hyde Park [. . .]

Item: I'm doing a set of alphabets for the Army & Navy Stores —for them to use for all their notices & signs! This is an interesting job —for it is: how to do 1, good letters, 2, absolutely legible-to-the-last-degree letters, 3 letters which any fool can copy accurately & easily. So I'm doing them simple block letters. It's rather fun cutting out great big letters out of white paper & sticking them on big black sheets —they don't half stare at you —fine test for astigmatism . . . Supper time —Mary's calling —will continue if poss. tomorrow, Sunday.

24.5.'25

I continue. *Item:* The Hagreens, brother & sister, are 'no longer with us'. Poor Philip got iller & iller. [. . .] They have gone to Ramsgate to his mother's. We hope Joseph & family will take their place. Agnes is coming down shortly to inspect.

Item: Petra has left Mrs. Mairet's —she comes here next week for good.

Item: My old workshop, your old workshop, at Ditchling has been taken by one Val Kilbride, a weaver & dyer. A very good fellow —friend of Fr. O'Connor's. He, V. K., hopes to join us here if all goes well, in a year or two. He's engaged to a girl at Caldey —the farmer's daughter (Celia McHardy). *Item:* great changes for the better seem imminent at Caldey. We hear strange rumours of the Cistercians having bought the island & paid all debts —but we have heard nought officially yet. May it be so! If that has happened we gather the present Community will move elsewhere. Fr. Prior is expected up here very shortly —then we shall know. Till then we aren't believing anything, but I tell you for fun —don't take it as Gospel. Dinner bell —I'll continue later . . . *I continue!* You'll be annoyed to hear that Gordian developed the measles a fortnight ago! He only had them very mildly but he had a touch of 'congestion' with them which made the situation ticklish for a day or two. However prayers soon dispelled the congestion & he's downstairs again to-day for the 1st time. But now both Eliz. & Joanna have got 'em! They're both in bed with temp^s & looking all blotchy so I think there's no doubt of it. What a business! Mary is very well fortunately.

Laurie Cribb is here working for me at present. He's a great help and also to Mary too —lighting fires etc. He's too good to live by a long way.

Item: No further developments in the matter of the T.O.S.D. and I shall still sign myself your very affectionate brother in S. Dominic   ERIC P. J. G.   O.S.D.

P.S. re your letter of last November:

Item: The Crank was eventually sold to Mr. Hacker (a stranger to us) for £1850. As we had spent, of our own money, on the place something over £1500 & there was a mortgage of £900, you will see it was not exactly a profitable deal. But just as in your own case, we built at the money time, so that's that. We hear that Mr. Hacker is putting in electric light plant, garage, baths etc. *Item:* Hilary has sold Frag. House to Mr. Richmond! He & the boys are living in the 'Sorrowful Mysteries'. Clare & the girls are in France for the summer. but no doubt you get the news from Clare. We hear very little of Ditchling here. David J. is at Caldey —he's been there since beginning of Lent —painting & engraving. I don't know what'll happen to him. He's so determined to earn his living off his own bat —but he's so incapacitated by his temperament & unworkmanlike training.

Item: But this is too much to write about really —I must just hint & wait till we meet again. It is this: Dom Theodore Bailey & I have begun to start a *Confraternity* —a Guild if you like but we're not thinking of so calling it —to bind Christian artists: 1st. in prayer, 2nd. in work. I can't tell you more at present for there's no more to tell, but I can invite you to pray, and if you like to, to pray with us thus: *before the day's work: Pater, Ave, Gloria, Dñe ostende . . . faciem tuam & salvi erimus, Ste.*

Thoma, Ste. B. J. Labre, o.p.n. En ego, Ave. I'll tell you more when there's more to tell. Are you coming to England this summer? If you are, then of course we shall meet, for Bristol is near. [. . .]

Item: I heard no more of the Exhibition in Rome.

Item: Are you still expecting to be here in *July*? Let me know betimes, so that I may not be away.

Item: No, I don't know Evan Morgan.

Item: I enclose some engravings.

I long to see you again. I told the girls & Mary I was writing. They one and all exclaimed: 'Give him our love' —it sounded like '& heaps of it'. I enclose the girls' Christmas cards (copper-engraved by me from their designs.) And much love from me also —

E. G.

133 : TO G. K. CHESTERTON

Capel-y-ffin   *5-6-1925*

Dear Mr. Chesterton: I was overjoyed to get your letter yesterday & I have hastened to comply with your request, by which I am honoured, for an article more or less round about the Hudson Memorial (on which, by the way, I cut the inscriptions —so I have inside knowledge). I hope you will be able to use it. Your allusion to me was certainly a tempting draw and I have tried to play the game. But is it the game you are willing to play? For, I begin by saying, I'm not going to hear of any disagreement between us. If you think you don't agree with *me*, that's 'all a horrible mistake' — due to clumsiness on my part —both as a writer & as an engraver or stone carver or what not. And if you think I don't agree with *you* — well you're mistaken & the mistake is due merely to the fact that we've never met to thrash out differences of terminology or differences of opinion upon what I might call the *politics* of exposition —e.g. we might put slightly differing emphasis on this or that. Well, the point is that I don't intend to write for you as an outsider (have I not put almost my last quid into your blooming company? – 7% or not). You've got to accept my 'doctrine' as the 'doctrine' of *G.K.'s Weekly* in matters of art –just as I accept yours in other matters. If you say this is a bit thick –rather a tall order –well, I *know* what I'm saying is what is in harmony with your propaganda just as I know that both are in harmony with the Faith. (Your suspicions, & Belloc's, are groundless –it's only because we've not had it out face to face) and I know that no one else is doing it at the moment. God forbid that you shd. have an art critic who'll go round the picture shows for you & write bilge about this painter & that –this 'art movement' and that. We've got to keep right off that. I'm not suggesting that I shd. write a regular weekly or even annual 'art' article. I haven't time (thank heaven) & you wouldn't wish it. Moreover it's not what's wanted. What is wanted is the attitude of mind of that decent person who says 'he doesn't know anything about art but he knows what he likes', but . . . in our case it's to be because what we like is what we *know* to be likeable –because we know in Whom we believe. I am sure that the two ground notions for us 'Distributists' (I say, it is an awful word though!) are the ones I've put into the article I'm sending herewith – viz: 'a work of art is simply a thing well made' & 'Look after Goodness & Truth, & Beauty will take care of itself'. We can push those notions in all departments & rescue art from the snobbery & worse which kills it –i.e. kills all good workmanship.

Well, please forgive me for thus rushing at you.

And please forgive, if you find it objectionable, the slangy tone of my article. I did it thus because, 1st, you must have it straight off the reel – while the topic's hot, 2nd, at the risk of flippancy, I think we've got to let it be clear that we're not on the high aesthetic stunt & 3rd, I think it won't be read unless it's a bit light hearted –after all we aren't downhearted. Yours affectly.　　　　　　　　　　　　　　ERIC GILL O.S.D.

P.S. I hope you did get that other article labelled 'Responsibility'. & I hope you approved of it & will be able to use it –

you see the 'Machinery' business is really too difficult to dispose of until we get certain lower, more bed-rock things settled. Penty & Co. will beat the air . . . They *can't* decide about machinery until it's decided who's responsible for using it.

134 : TO 'G.K.'S WEEKLY', 7 NOV. 1925

The Control of Machinery

Sir: With reference to the letter of Mr. W. S. Roe in your issue of October 17. The matter of machinery is one to which no doubt you will be giving your official attention before very long, and I do not wish to anticipate. There is one point, however, which might as well be stated without delay, for it is one which has been missed by all your correspondents hitherto.

Mr. Roe says: 'Learn how to control machinery and we shall get a much better result from that we already have, etc. . . .' Now before we can say *How* to control anything we must decide *who* is to control it — this is the fundamental point. Imagine an unruly child. People ask themselves how to control it. Is it not obvious that the problem wears an entirely different aspect directly we put it to ourselves, as we should do in the *first* place, in terms of *who*. Thus, is the father to control, or the schoolmaster, or the superintendent of the reformatory? The mere mechanism of control is entirely different according as it proceeds from one or the other.

I do not propose now to write at length upon the question as to *who* should control machinery. I merely wish to point out that this question is antecedent to the question of *how* we should control machinery, and I think it is obvious that when the question of who is decided, the question of how will be much less difficult.

Mr. Roe's letter ends with the sentence: 'To persuade a man to use a spade when he can employ a plough — well, I think it is a hopeless job.' Mr. Roe implies that the cultivator he envisages is able to choose his tool. Before we can make an implication as delightfully simple as that, let us ask ourselves, for example, whether the linotype machines used in Fleet Street are chosen by the compositors, or whether it is not possible that those machines are chosen by persons whose trade is money-making rather than 'comping.' Yours, etc.,

ERIC GILL

P.S. —Mr. Roe quotes Carlyle's saying that man is 'a tool-using animal.' It is at least doubtful whether Lord Beaver-brook can justly be said to use the linotype machines he controls.

135 : TO DESMOND CHUTE

Capel-y-ffin   .   *13-12-1925*

My dear Desmond: Here I wish you a very happy Christmas & New Year & all good health. I hope you are quite well now. We heard that you were better than ever. *D.G*ˢ. Before saying more I must tell you that Mary & I & Miss Bill (you know, Miss Fennell's friend) are going on the Christmas Pilgrimage to Rome . . . We leave here next Sunday & reach Rome on the 23rd. evening. We're supposed to leave Rome on the 26th. & arrive back on the 28th. A frightful rush, but it seems very important that all who can, should. Now look here:—
* on the way out we reach *Genoa* at 6.55 a.m., Tuesday 23rd. & leave again at 9.55 a.m. (3 hours wait)
* on the way back we reach *Genoa* at 4.12 p.m., Saturday 26. & leave again at 4.22 p.m. (10 minutes wait only.)
Is it conceivable that you could come to Genoa & spend that 3 hours with us on the 23rd.? It wd. be splendid if you could. It's awful early —but I gather that Rapallo isn't far away & I don't expect we even stop at R. Do, if you possibly can. A talk wd. be so much better than a letter. We'll look

N

out for you anyway. It says in our 'itinerary' that breakfast
will be served in the station buffet at Genoa 'after which
pilgrims will hear Mass in Genoa'. So now you know the
worst — what about it?

I've got a job coming on at Bristol. Your mother will tell
you how we've failed to meet so far. If the job comes off, I
shall be able to visit her quite a lot 'cause it'll involve 2 or 3
weeks' stay in Bristol. It's to carve a niche, & figure therein,
in the Highbury Chapel! [. . .]

I'm sending you a book.[1] I hope you'll approve of it.
[. . .] I think p. 36 is too much of a bad thing, but —
wished it to stand — so that's that. I'd much appreciate your
criticism both of pictures & text — & preface. [. . .] I'm
now about to begin pictures to illustrate Matt. 26 & 27 to
come out in March next uniform with the S. *of* S. Also I'm
doing copper plate illustrations (*à la* Laboureur) for a wedding
hymn, by a poet called Powys Mathers, uniform with Enid
Clay's poems in size. I've no carving jobs on hand at present
but in addition to the Bristol job I may have a fine big job at
Fleetwood (Rossall School) Lancs — an oak panel to go over
an altar (7.0 × 3.9) with the Adoration of the 3 Kings in low
relief. I've got to go & see the site this week & then send
design — pray for me I beg.

I'm keeping busy one way and another. I hope you approved
of the thing I had in *B'friars* in October — did you? I've just
written another entitled '*Id quod visum placet* — a practical test
of the beautiful'. I hope you'll approve this also.

V. many thanks for p.c. from Verona (smiling man in
armour — jolly fine) & for your letters during the year —
shamefully unanswered. I do hope we can meet in Genoa on
the 23rd. Anyway I hope you'll be in England this summer &
we shall demand nay seize you for a week in the Black Mountains. Meanwhile good bye — God bless you dear brother in
St. Dominic. Yours   ERIC G. O.S.D.

[1] The Golden Cockerel Press *Song of Songs*.

136 : TO 'THE ARCHITECTS' JOURNAL'
27TH. JANUARY, 1926

'The Superfluous Architect'

Sir: You invite me to reply to the criticism with which you honour me in your issue of January 13. May I take it point by point?

First of all I must complain (I am sorry) of misquotation. Your leader writer might have taken a little more trouble, if it was worth his while to take any notice of my words, to get them transcribed correctly. He makes complete nonsense of his first quotation. My words were 'architecture is the imposition . . . upon building of the notions of beauty possessed by the architect and favoured by his clients.' Your contributor makes me say: 'architecture is the imposition . . . of the notions of *building* (my italics) possessed by the architect.' Thus the point of my words is lost. Of his next and longer quotation my only complaint is that, though he gets the sense very nearly, he has apparently quoted from memory, for the punctuation and incidental words are different.

In his third quotation he makes me say of Chartres Cathedral that 'no architect and no contractor considers her.' What I did say was: 'No architect nor no contractor consider*ed* her.' In the misquotation the implication is that no architect of to-day and no modern contractor thinks much of Chartres which, whatever may be the case with Sir Robert McAlpine and such like, is certainly not true of architects; whereas the implication of my own words is that at the time of the building of Chartres Cathedral there were not the kinds of person we now call architects and contractors. This, whether good or bad, happens clearly to be true, for whatever sort of man they had to boss the work of planning and building, he was very certainly as different in kind from him we now call 'architect' as his work is different in kind from what we now call 'architecture.' And whatever sort of man they had to boss the work of supplying and controlling materials and labour he was certainly as different in kind from him we now call 'contractor' as the person called 'merchant' is different from the person called 'financier' and as the thing called 'Guild' is different from the thing called 'Trades Union.' Why, then, pretend otherwise and, any way, why misquote?

But now let us get to the business, and first let me say that I did not say nor do I say that the architect is *at the present moment* superfluous. This is the kind of thing we are always meeting. Suppose I say: 'We must find a way to abolish "industrialism." ' Immediately I hear all round me murmurs of: 'What should we do without steamships . . . ?' and if the thing got into the newspapers it would be sarcastically headed: 'The Superfluous Steamship.' That's the way the trick is done — consciously or unconsciously. The ultimate issue is shelved, the immediate convenience alone is insisted upon, and the wild 'Bolshy' is shown up once more as 'an enemy of the people.'

Now, of course, *at the present moment*, neither the architect nor the contractor is superfluous. Both are necessary *to-day*. Neither of them is actually a builder in the old sense, but between them they are necessary to the production of buildings. What has happened to the old-fashioned builder? He still exists, of course, in a small way, but he becomes more and more merely a man of business whose test of success is not his work, but his bank balance. Hence he tends, when 'successful,' to become less and less a builder, and more and more a contractor — that is, he becomes less and less concerned with the job of building, and more and more concerned with the business of buying and selling materials and labour. Under such circumstances it is natural enough that he should lose what little he had left of a sense of either honesty or beauty. What have they to do with him? If he can get shoddy materials on to the job, so much the better for him (now don't let's be sentimental — of course, we know contractors aren't wholly vile — they are often kind husbands, good fathers, and what not — but, their job being primarily money-making, we mustn't expect them to forget that business is business), and if he's asked to contract for a sham Chinese or a sham Gothic or a sham Mudejar building — what odds is it to him? Style? What is style? That's no business of his. It makes a difference to the price, that's all.

Hence, plainly enough, the sphere of the architect. He exists, and must exist for a long time to come, first of all to protect his client from the rapacity of the commercial building contractor. That's clear. That's not exactly how he came into existence. He came into existence to satisfy the appetite for classical architecture at a time when cultured people could not get anything but a more or less degraded 'Gothic' from the ordinary builders. Why they wanted Classic and why the Gothic had become degraded are questions involving the whole business of religion and politics, and are not my immediate concern. But the thing once started had to run its course. The designing of buildings, except in a small way and in the provinces, ceased to be the concern of the 'builder,' and became the exclusive job of the cultured person. The business of buying and controlling materials and labour ceased to be the job of the designer, and became the exclusive job of the 'builder' and he, in his turn, becomes 'contractor.' Hence, to-day you must employ both. The one has no knowledge of 'labour,' the other no knowledge of 'design.' But from the client's point of view the architect is the chief — naturally — because he can *design* something and can protect his client, while the contractor cannot design, and if not watched will probably rob. Moreover, in the case of really big jobs, the thing is utterly beyond the powers of well-meaning 'arty' people. In such cases even your architect becomes entangled in 'business' considerations, or else, as in the case of Norman Shaw and the Piccadilly Hotel or Gaiety Theatre (as he wrote to me himself), the architect merely makes a striking 'elevation' and hands it over to more business-like people to 'put it across,' as the Americans say.

No, indeed! the architect and contractor are not superfluous. Nevertheless, it is still possible that the system of which they are a necessary part may be a bad system. What is that system? Must I describe what we all live in? Shall I describe war to those who lived four years in the trenches? Are we as blind as all that?

Well, let us give a look at Waterloo Bridge —that bone of contention. I didn't know Ruskin had written about it. I just brought it in as a very well-known object of the countryside, and one much admired by people of culture —God bless them. We all know it by sight —its row of level arches and its double Doric (?) columns. Now, I ask: Why is there what you call rustication to the masonry? Why are there Doric columns? Why are they in couples? Why that balustrade to the footway? Why, in fact, any of the particular architectural devices and ornaments? God be praised there are much fewer of such things on the Waterloo Bridge than in most architectural works. God be praised that from a reasonable distance it looks like, almost like, a reasonable building —which is more than you can say of the Tower Bridge, however far away you get — but why shouldn't it be reasonable close up? Don't mistake me. I like stage scenery and architectooralooral fallals as much as anyone, and admire the good taste of whoever designed Waterloo Bridge as much as any F.R.I.B.A. But I don't see why I should blind myself to the facts. I simply prefer, as building, the old Lambeth chain Bridge, or the Nile Dam at Assuan, or the north transept of Chartres, or the Pyramid of Cheops, or the B.S.A. building at Smallheath, or the Roman aqueduct at Nîmes, or the railway viaduct at Brighton, or the power station at Lots Road.

It is a pity to make a bother about words, and yet words are very important things. Not for nothing is it said: 'In the beginning was the Word' —and I think the words 'architect' and 'architecture' have a certain special significance which should not be denied them. There *is* a difference between the methods employed in building to-day and those of, say, 1200. There *is* a difference between the work done. But there isn't much difference between the methods of to-day and those of Rome in the year 100, and if there is a considerable difference in the work turned out, that is due to the fact that with all their slave-owning and slave-driving (the Coliseum was built entirely by Jews enslaved after the destruction of Jerusalem) the Romans had not invented machinery. Therefore, we do well to-day when we confine ourselves to such things as can rightly be demanded of servile workmen. We do ill when we demand of them stylistic ornamentation or any ornament at all. The younger men are coming to see this well enough, and there is consequently a laudable plainness in some of the more recent work. I hope we shall see the tendency carried farther still – but that depends largely on the clients. They want the 'architecture' very often for business or sentimental reasons. Thus, can you imagine Liberty & Co. putting up anything remotely resembling the B.S.A. building at Smallheath (an admirable work)? Can you imagine a parson putting up anything like the nave of Sta. Sabina (that most reasonable of all churches)? Upon the other hand, why did not Messrs. Bishop and Etherington-Smith leave out the stone cornices on their Nine Elms brewery (illustrated in your issue of January 13)? Now, why? And why those three round windows at the top of the elevation to railway, and the windows below in groups of three? Why? And this brings me to the main issue. Your leader writer suggests that my quarrel with the architect is 'that he presumes to plan his buildings beforehand . . .' No, if your architect confined himself, or was forcibly confined by his client, to *planning* (in however wide a sense of that word) we should have no quarrel with him, provided he planned according to reason. But no – he must have his cornices, pillars, pilasters – God knows what – to get his *effect*. Cut it out. Let us have the inevitable results that arise from really reasonable plans, whether for breweries, bridges, or banks, shops or churches.

I'm not saying things which apply only to the job of building, though the fact that building demands the co-operation of many hands places builders more at the mercy of the modern degraded workmen bred by commercialism and industrialism. What I am saying applies as much to painting and sculpture, to preaching and praying – to the making of anything whatsoever. We've got to be reasonable all the time and ride our sentiments on the curb. We haven't got to think of style (style is a thing to be discovered in a building after completion – not determined beforehand) – we haven't even got to think of beauty. We've got to make things *right*. Beauty consists in due proportion. We have got to give things the proportion that is *due* to them. It's a matter of justice. 'Justice is truth in action.' This is not 'Utilitarianism.' The utilitarian is unjust. He denies to things their due proportion in order to save money or to avoid mere physical discomfort.

Now, one thing more. What about Exodus, chapter 25? Well, not to be too long about it: 'The service of God is perfect freedom,' and that's more than can be said of the service of contractors, whatever may be that of architects! But surely there should be no difficulty in answering your leader writer on that point. He calls in the Bible to support him, and uses the detailed instructions given to the makers of the Tabernacle★ (instructions given by God Himself, mind you, and not by an F.R.I.B.A.) as an argument in favour of architects! He adds: 'Not the smallest liberty is given to the craftsman to express his individuality in any particular.' Now, on this point two things: First, to give a workman (architect, artist, statesman, anyone) detailed instructions is an admirable habit. I wish it were always done. Suppose you came to me and said: 'I want you to carve me a crucifix,' and, being a

★ Your leader writer gives the impression that he thinks 'the Tabernacle' was a permanent architectural structure. He writes: 'A certain building of even greater spiritual prestige than Chartres Cathedral.' But the *Tabernacle* was a thing of wood, with rods and curtains to be folded up and carried from place to place by the Israelites.

heathen, suppose I said: 'What's that?' Would you say: 'Oh, any old thing —just some sort of a human being on a cross'? Suppose I said: 'On a cross —what's that?' Would you tell me? You might, of course, go to some one else who didn't need so much telling, but, supposing for the sake of argument that I were a really first-rate stone carver, you might think it worth while to give me detailed instructions. Cross, such and such dimensions —man's attitude so and so —so many nails — crown of thorns or otherwise. Should I complain? Should I have any right to complain? On the contrary it's just what I like. The more details the better. Then my job begins — putting the instructions into material shape. Should I say that I wasn't given any opportunity to express my individuality? Expressing my individuality on purpose isn't my job or anyone else's. But, all the same, such things will out —and this brings me to the second point about that Temple. I looked it up to see. The instructions given are marvellously precise and embracing, but to say that, given those instructions, *therefore* the workmen were deprived of any opportunity for self-expression —well, it simply doesn't follow —simply because it can't. You can tell a man as much as you like, you don't fetter him a bit. You only start fettering him when what you've told him to do is something he doesn't believe in, and yet you make him do it or else give him the sack. Now, what is there to show that the Israelites didn't believe in their Tabernacle job? And the saying that the service of God is perfect freedom has just that meaning —for His is a job in which a man *can* believe, and, therefore, the most detailed instructions cause no servility, and impose no unjust privation of individuality.

[May I say that it strikes me as a trifle comic, not to say impudent, to imply that because God gave detailed instructions as to the pattern (plan) of the Tabernacle, therefore Sir Edwin X. is within his rights in telling me, a stone carver, to work in the Gothic style or the Classic style? That's different, isn't it?] Now, after all this, where does ornament come in? Well, it naturally doesn't —in these days. How can it?

Planning you can do, and strictly reasonable, therefore noble, elevations, but ornament cannot be done to order. The early Renaissance architects did fairly well — but then they were able to employ carvers and decorators who hadn't been through the nineteenth century. That made a bit of difference! But it soon went to pieces, and if there's some fairly lively acanthus carving on St. Peter's, or St. Paul's — well, there's nothing like that on the new north front of the British Museum. There isn't. No, you can order bricks by the million, and concrete by the thousand tons, and you can *force* men to place them exactly where you wish. But you can't force half a square inch of good carving out of a man who doesn't care a damn whether it's there or not. If every now and then you can find a man who does care, employ him. But we can do without ornament — even cornices (if you want something to throw the rain off the top of your building — make something to throw the rain off, but don't pretend it's a Classic cornice). Let us leave it to the time when (if ever) we can again count on employing a set of workmen who are not quite degraded. Meanwhile, in addition to those men who find their job in the planning of big buildings, there is an opening for the little man who will take up again the job of the old-fashioned builder. Let him have his own yard and collect round him a trustworthy group of workmen. Let him build small houses and churches — anything he can get. Let him live on the job (like a mere artist, in fact), and, perhaps, he'll come into his own when 'big business' has burst itself.   ERIC GILL, O.S.D.

137 : TO 'THE ARCHITECTS' JOURNAL'
17TH. FEBRUARY, 1926

'The Superfluous Architect'

Sir: It will, of course, be impossible to reply to your many correspondents as their various points of view deserve.

I am grateful for the sympathy of Professor Abercrombie,

and I am pleased to note some measure of agreement with me in the letters of Mr. Howard Robertson and Mr. Rowland Pierce. No doubt Mr. Purchon 'only did it to annoy' when he compared my letter to 'the chatter of the 'eighties and 'nineties,' and I *was* annoyed, so he scores his point (I'm getting over it now). But, of course, it is not true. The protest being made to-day is different in kind from that made by Ruskin and Morris. For, on the one hand, we are much less blinded to-day by the glamour of the artistic product of the Middle Ages, and, on the other hand, we are much less scornful than they of the philosophic achievements of that time. The artistic product of the Middle Ages we now see to be comparable in kind to that of similar periods in India and China, and wherever religio-philosophic concepts of life have been widely accepted and acted upon (see, for instance, A. K. Coomaraswamy, introduction to catalogue of the Indian collections in the Boston Museum of Fine Arts). It is true that European Medieval art is Christian art —'the art of man redeemed' —and is, therefore, redolent of what, to Christians, seems a more reasonable philosophy —a truer view of man's place in the universe than that of the Hindus and Buddhists, but, artistically, the Middle-Age Europe is not the unique thing it seemed to our fathers. Artistically, we now only use it as an example because it is the handiest —everyone has some acquaintance with Medieval work, whereas comparatively few have any intimate acquaintance or sympathy with Indian or Chinese work or that of pre-Periclean Greece. The gibes of some of your correspondents are, therefore, ill-aimed. Artistically, the Gothic revival is played out, and we may be grateful to architects for that. If it had not been for the Pugins and Scotts and their following thousands we might not even yet be in the position to realize how foolish an experiment it was. No; we are not Gothic revivalists to-day, and I should have thought that would have been clear from my letter wherein the random list of (to me) admirable works named only one Gothic building. The power station in

Lots Road, Chelsea, is not a Gothic building in the architectural sense, and even that would obviously be better without its little embellishments – dull as ditch-water as they are.

For this reason I think I may pass lightly over the letter of Mr. Manning Robertson. He is old-fashioned. He has not followed the progress of criticism whereby it has become clear that ornamental additions cannot be done merely to order. The order must find some correspondence in the mind of the craftsman. If it does not, the result is a dead thing, and, later, a putrid thing. To suggest, as Mr. Robertson does, that I, a stone carver, wish to 'eschew every form of ornament' is, well, is it likely? No; I want stone carving. What I do not want is mechanical ornament. And as for not being able to design a prison satisfactorily without ornament –there, again, Mr. Robertson shows himself old-fashioned. Of course, it can be done. A jolly fine prison could be done without a scrap of ornamental business –what about Porchester Castle? But if the prison authority or even the architect (please note) chose to commission me to do a statue of St. Peter *ad Vincula* (shall we say?), and they kindly provided a niche, why I'd be only too glad of the job, and would be as willing as anything to do my best to do something fitting, both to the subject of the sculpture and to its architectural environment. If there were pillars I would carve the capitals, if they had any, and, if it came to that, I would carve the plain walls all over with histories of famous villains –showing how they all got 'copped' in the end.

In regard to Mr. William Harvey's letter. As immediately practical (i.e. 'first aid') politics there is hardly a word with which I disagree. What Mr. Harvey says about the intimate relations existing between the Medieval client and his builders is very much to the point. There was a similar intimacy between the Medieval king and his subjects. The English aristocracy succeeded eventually in destroying the popular monarchy and substituting 'Cabinet rule.' Similarly in building, the architect has been interposed between the client and the master builder. So also the Privy Council has been interposed between the Church and the people!

Whether this is right or wrong, good or bad, it is so. Some people may think the situation entirely contrary to the nature of man and his destiny — others, having no clear idea as to man's nature nor any conception of a destiny, may applaud it. But the fight between those who, in the words of Sir Josiah Stamp, think freedom better than sobriety and those who think sobriety better than freedom; between those who prefer wild flowers with swamps and occasional and excellent hot-houses and those who prefer all hot-houses, no swamps, and very rare and dilapidated wild flowers; between those who think man's soul is more important than his body and those who, doubting whether he has a soul or denying it outright, think his body the only thing to worry about, between those who think you can have it both ways, and those who know you can't, will not take place, I suppose, in the pages of *The Architects' Journal*.

But let us get back to the question of servility. That's the main difficulty. Admittedly this is a servile age. That is to say, it is an age in which the workman in the mass is servile, and we legislate to keep him so. The servile state is here and now, and it is a more intense slavery than that of Rome or Egypt because, whereas the slaves of antiquity (or even of the United States) were 'chained' in body, the English slave, though nominally free of his body (at present), is chained mentally. Modern industrialism, by its use of machinery and by the division and subdivision of labour, has achieved this. The ancients knew only the whip.

Never mind about this. Accept it if you will. Say 'machinery has come to stay.' Say 'you cannot put back the clock.' Say 'we cannot be ancient Britons.' But deny it in the face of all the modern world — well, who could? Mr. Purchon compares the British Museum with the Parthenon, and the comparison is apt. Both are the work of slaves. The only difference is that modern British slaves are bad stone carvers, but can still (at present) go on strike. The Athenian slaves could not go on strike, but they had not been degraded by a century of mechanical industrialism and were pretty good workmen.

Now, as I say, accept this servile state of ours if you will. That's not what I'm up against in *The Architects' Journal*. As Cardinal Manning said: 'All human conflict is ultimately theological,' and it is pretty clear that ultimately the differences between your correspondents and me are theological differences. I do not believe that man, *as such*, is a servile animal. I believe he has free will, and has, therefore, responsibility for his acts and for the willed effects of his acts (i.e. the effects which he intends). Also, I believe that he has responsibility for the intellectual quality of what his deeds effect. I understand the theological implications of such beliefs, and they are quite at variance with modern materialistic philosophy. I say never mind. *The Architects' Journal* is not the arena for a fight between rival theologies. But when it comes to aesthetic criticism and to the observation of the works of man it is a different matter, and I say you cannot have it both ways. You cannot have the full development of modern machinery and, its necessary concomitant, the degradation of the workman to the level of a mere tool, and at the same time have that quality of good carving and ornament which depends upon the existence of generations of men uncorrupted by a mechanical commercialism. Nor, even among architects, can you have that quality of architectural design (as in the Parthenon or in Chartres Cathedral) which depends upon the existence of a high level of culture permeating a whole people. Under modern conditions the architect of culture tends as much to be a hot-house plant, a lap-dog of the rich, as does the artist and craftsman like myself. But whereas I recognize the state of affairs, your correspondents do not seem to do so. They *will* go on trying to eat their pudding and have it. They *will* go on patting themselves on the back, and talking about the progress of architecture in Tennysonian style — 'on stepping stones . . . to higher things' — whereas anyone with half an eye can see that, short of scrapping this civilization, there's nothing to be done (as far as building is concerned) but build plain buildings — only using such carving and painting as can be got from responsible people — workmen as responsible for their carving as the architect is for his plan.

There is not *properly* any such thing as applied ornament in the modern sense. If you put a pattern on a priest's vestment it should not be to make it ornamental, but because the vestment is better so — because that particular pattern is appropriate to such a garment. If you make your pattern out of embroidered *ikthyosauri* it will be inappropriate ornament. The embroiderer's art is not ornamenting, but doing in embroidery what is *wanted*. So with all so-called ornament. It starts with necessities, appropriateness. Even the famous 'dog tooth' did not start as an architect's ornament (i.e. something applied to order), but was originally a carver's invention. As for 'full-size details,' there could not have been such things simply because there was no paper big enough. Granted that, as Mr. Howard Robertson might have said, the necessity of one age becomes the ornament of the next; but this is a tendency to be resisted, not wallowed in. I simply cannot understand (and surely a sculptor chap like me may be allowed to take architects thus into his confidence) why architects do not see the beauty, the intellectual delight, of plain walls, square block buildings like Queen Anne's Mansions (though the utilitarian has laid his hand on that and spoilt it), factory chimneys (without architectural cappings), railway viaducts, and so forth. (*Note.* — I said what I meant by the word utilitarian in my last letter — so won't repeat it.) And on the other hand, I simply can't understand how people can continue to be taken in by the ornament designed by architects and turned out by the employees of the contractor. The stuff's as different from what was done before Industrialism as Protestantism is different from Catholicism (and whether you like either or neither, you must admit they're different) — different and, yes, uglier.

Now, another point, because it's important. What about *effects*? I think Professor Abercrombie and others of your correspondents overrate the medieval builder's effort after effect. Features that seem to us to be primarily for effect were very often not so thought of by their makers; thus the great porch of Peterborough — to the modern eye it looks like a piece of pure architectural swank. But then we think in quite different terms. From Inigo Jones onwards we have *thought* in terms of effect. We don't realize that there might be another road. Thus: does the maker of bishop's mitres make them the way he does for effect? Not much! They're made that way traditionally, and the tradition is founded on the fact that the bishop's ceremonial hat must be something mighty fine and large. It signifies all sorts of official things (many of which are forgotten). So it is with such things as Peterborough porch. It's an attempt first of all to make a really grand entrance door — a front door, and the door has become a front! But they started with the *thing* — not with the effect of the thing. That's typical of the whole difference between us and them. And as I said before, it's only because it is close at hand that we take European Medieval examples. It's just the same all over the world.

I am obliged to Mr. Trystan Edwards. I think he's done the thing very well. I'm sorry about William Morris and the Forth Bridge, but, as I said above, his sort of Medievalism is nothing to do with us. It's very interesting, that quotation from Sir Benjamin Baker.[1] To like the arch form is a very innocent foible. Think how different it would have been if he'd said: 'the Corinthian capital is admittedly graceful, so we have put as many of them on our bridge as we could without

[1] 'Sir Benjamin Baker, replying to William Morris in 1889, said: "It would be a ludicrous error to suppose that Sir John Fowler and I had neglected to consider the design from the artistic point of view. An arched form is admittedly graceful, and we have approximated our bridge to that form as closely as we could without suggesting false construction and shams." '

suggesting . . . ' etc. As to Waterloo Bridge, what Mr. Edwards says is, fortunately for me, quite adequately answered by Mr. Howard Robertson (Oh, God! Oh, Montreal!).

In conclusion, though I apologize for the length of this letter, may I say that I think you will agree that few things are more important in practical life than an understanding between those concerned with the planning and erection of buildings and those concerned with the planning and execution of paintings, sculptures, furniture, and all the lesser arts which minister to life and crown it.

My contention is that, as some of your correspondents say, we've got to make the best of modern conditions —no crying over spilt milk —and that the best will be made when we all agree together to start with sheer reasonableness, continue with honesty, and let the end be what it may.   ERIC GILL

138 : TO HIS BROTHER EVAN

Capel-y-ffin, Abergavenny   25-2-1926

Dear Evan: Many thanks for your card of the 18th and *Times Lit. Supp.* (No, I have not read G. K. C's *Cobbett*). I had already seen this, it was very interesting, but of course very inadequate. I suppose the kind of people who write such things, being almost entirely ignorant of the real issues at stake, can do nothing else but run through the book looking for gossipy items. The phrase: 'the fierce intellectual strife of the celibate' left me wondering about the entire absence of any fierceness (or any reason therefor) in the strife of —shall we say —His Grace of Canterbury! I dare say you agree about this (you high church people don't seem to love your bishops) even if you disagree about other things.

Thank you very much dear brother for your welcome birthday greetings. It was jolly kind of you to remember. I am hoping you may manage a visit to the Black Mountains this summer. You will be very welcome. Then we can polish off

O

arrears of goryspondence. You are busy. So am I. Most of
my writing time is taken up with 'literary' efforts. *Blackfriars*,
Pax, & the architectural papers. Did you see the fight in the
Architectural Journal recently? —great sport. Love to you all —
your wife & children from me & my wife & children . . . Your
v. loving bro.   ERIC G. O.S.D.

139 : TO DESMOND CHUTE

Salies de Béarn, Basses-Pyrénées   5-5-1926

My dear Desmond: No doubt you are surprised to hear from
us from here —no doubt, but we are surprised to find ourselves here. Any way it is first of all an opportunity for writing
to you for it is a few days' holiday that I am having. The
immediate occasion is twofold — 1., I wanted to go to Paris
to see if I could fix up with some agent there for the sale of
prints & 2., Miss Bill, whom you know, is buying a small
property here at Salies and, as we intend to share it with her,
we thought it good to come and inspect with her before she
actually settled on it. So that's the explanation! We left
England last Friday night & spent Saturday in Paris & came on
here by the night train on Sunday. We go back to Paris on
Saturday & I shall spend a few days there before returning
home. I hope to do some drawing at an Académie there to
which I have an introduction. I think it will do me more good
than harm —don't you? (But since our departure the great
strike has started! What will be the end of that? Is it, as in
some respects it seems to be, a really determined effort on the
part of the strikers to get *control* —or is it merely a wage war?
How long will it last? Which side will the soldiery take? Is
there one single leader on either side who sees that a civilization is judged by its products & not by its social conditions?
Incidentally shall we get home again or shall we be stranded in
France?) Well, as to the property here, Miss Bill has decided
to buy and I think it is a just decision. It is a nice little villa

just out of the town with several acres of land (partly vine-yards). The house, about 100 years old, is quite a solid little place with 8 rooms and will hold all we need. We will tell you all about the scheme when we see you in England. [. . .] I do not at present regard it as involving departure from C-y-ff. It's a different sort of thing altogether. But it's too much to write about — considering that we shall be seeing you very soon. So I'll leave it at that. But you might give it a thought in relation to yourself! Salies de Béarn is, as you will see from the map, in the western foothills of the Pyrenees. It is a very nice little old town — still thriving on its ancient trades of salt distilling & sandal making — with a 'Spa' in the background or foreground according as you look at it. The country is gently rolling with trees & vines — more anon.

Now I must thank you for your long letter of criticism & appreciation of the *S. of S.* I am most grateful to you for it & delighted to know that, for the most part, you give it such enthusiastic approbation. I am very grateful too for the trouble you took to glean the opinions of others — most valuable.

(*Item*: Thank you very much for your birthday wishes.)

With regard to Fr. O'C's version of the Song: the history of this is that when Robt. Gibbings (Golden Cock! Press) first commissioned me to do the engravings I stipulated that the text shd. be the Douay version because I wanted to disarm the criticism that I was doing something outside & apart from Catholic authority to lend me countenance. Then, when it came to setting up, we found it imposs. to know how to divide the thing — who was speaking to whom etc. — without guid-ance. So I put them on to Fr. O'C, & he, tho. with some demur, took on the editing. Then we discovered that he was full of 'ideas' on the subject & landed ourselves in this 'new version'. Well, I think no harm & very much good has been done, in spite of some adverse critics. (Incidentally — much to my surprise & disappointment — Fr. —— comes out quite violently on the 'Enemy' side — saying it is an immoral book —

ought not to be published – a disgrace to my name . . . & so
on.)

Item: I'm glad you think the black & white of the engravings
is typographically right. I think myself that it is fairly successful. I don't object as you do to the mixture of type & engravings but I do think there are too many pictures for the amt. of
text.

Item: It surprises me that you like the picture 'at night on
my bed' so much. I thought it quite the worst. Equally I'm
surprised that you think 'the flight' is the worst. I agree, very
much, that the Solomon & the departing lovers in the 'Dancer'
picture are coarse & uninteresting. You are right – their place
in the picture is purely illustrational & it bored one to have
to include them. I am sorry. The dancer is good – it's a pity
about her belly – I tried hard to get at a decent convention
& spoilt it in the effort so had to leave it in that semi-natural-
istic state. Sorry again. From my point of view the best block
is 'I sleep but my heart is wakeful, the voice of my beloved
knocking.' & I think the final 'fawn on the mountains' is
passably good.

Item: Mary writes to say that the copy you sent to C-y-ff
for signature has arrived. I will sign & return as soon as I get
home. We will, if you will, discuss these matters at greater
length when you come to C-y-ff – especially 1) the 'miasma
of physicality which emanates' from the work . . . & 2) the
matter of *types* – of men & of women – of Him & of Her.
[. . .]

Item: Passion Book, I'll see that a copy is sent to you.

Item: Powys Mathers is a fat man who lives in Lincoln's Inn
Fields. I scarcely know him. *Red Wise* is very good & very
naughty – I think it probable that P-M is the same. I think the
times are hard – The right & proper Naughtiness of life, as
God made it, is classed by the police with mere filthiness. I
think it well to go ahead doing what seems good – however
naughty it be. On the other hand (sic) I have got the Bristol
job – a statue of the Good Shepherd for the *Congregational*

Chapel & an altar piece (7 feet by 3) for Rossall School —a crucifix in centre with St. John B. (beheading of) on one side & Baptism of O. L. on tother. These will take me most of the summer & autumn.

Item: Some of Robt. Gibbings' engravings are good but he hasn't weaned himself yet of a bad past. He himself is the dearest creature ever known.

Item: That engraving by C. —well, poor old C.! It was a mistake to put it out.

Item: I must also tell you about Rome. Oh! that was a magnificent business —sing high —sing low. Much love dear Desmond from me to you —   ERIC G. T.S.D.

I hope you are well

140 : TO THE REV. JOHN O'CONNOR

Capel-y-ffin   *15-11-1926*

Dear Fr. John: I hope you are quite well.

We are all well here.

I have much work —among other things an oak panel (7 feet × 3) for Rossall School —altar piece —war memorial —crucifixion & scenes from life of St. J-B. Item: *Id quod visum placet*, that small book, was published at the beginning of the month and is now sold out —indeed it was sold out before publication! I wish I had had a copy to send you.

N.B. The immediate cause of my writing to you is that Robert Gibbings is complaining to me that *Havelock Ellis* is complaining to him that Renan's translation of the S⟨ong⟩ of S⟨ongs⟩ & his stage arrangement of same is so nearly like yours as to suggest that his was the model. I recently saw Renan's book in a 2nd. hand catalogue (curiously enough it was Magrath's, of Manningham Lane!) & got it. Certainly the correspondence between the two versions (yours & Renan's) makes it seem that at least you were acquainted with Renan's & used it for what it was worth. If in fact you do know

Renan's book you will not need an ignoramus like me to tell you how 'bloody awful' it is in its preface —interesting, yes, but horribly annoying too. But if in fact you do not know it —well you ought to see it. It's really miraculously similar in its stage arrangement & stage directions to your version. (I can lend you my copy if you shd. wish.)

Anyway the point is what shall I say to R. G. for him to say to H-Ellis? I could easily invent a suitable reply but I thought I'd write to you first. Much love & hopes that you are *well*. Yrs affectly.   ERIC G. T.S.D.

Mary says 'give Fr. John my love' —

141 : TO THE REV. JOHN O'CONNOR

Capel-y-ffin   23-11-1926

Dear Fr. John: Thank you very much indeed. I will pass on what you say to the proper quarter. It shd. do the trick. I am very sorry you have been ill with 'Flu' —moi aussi. I got caught at Bristol & had to go to bed at Desmond's & have the awkward experience of making a frightful nuisance of myself in a strange house. However I only had 3 days in bed & Mrs. Chute was most awfully kind & good.[1]

Yes, I *shall* be coming to Bradford when I come north. I rejoice. It will be after Christmas tho'. For Christmas we are going to France! Fancy that . . . and I am taking several months' wood engraving to do. Joanna has already gone with Miss Bill (whom I think you do not know —our friend —my secretary —the lady who has bt. the little house in Salies-de-Béarn to which we are going) to get the place in order —make curtains, sew sheets, buy local crockery & furniture etc. They are having a good time in warm sunny weather (here it has rained without stopping for weeks & weeks!). It will be, I hope, a pleasant experience and, I hope, an opportunity for

[1] It was during E. G's. recovery here that Desmond Chute made the drawing opposite.

ERIC GILL

Drawing by Desmond Chute

uninterrupted *work*! (They have hired a small room in the town for me to work in.) I will write from there & let you know if dreams come true. [. . .]

As for books on Modern Art —well that's a corker. There is a quite good series (Italian and English text) published by 'Valori Plastici', publishers, Rome, on Picasso, Rousseau, Matisse etc. (@ 1/-) Of English books there is Frank Rutter's *Evolution in Painting* or some such title.[1] This is quite a good introduction & calculated to persuade the conventionally minded. But it is all wrong *philosophically*. Like Clive Bell (& Co) he regards emotion as the objective of the artist. 'Significant form' is for him (& for them) that form which is *emotionally* sans reproche. That is all very well but, as you know, it's *post hoc*. To *aim* at a certain emotion (however cultured) is to take an effect for the end. The real end is *being* —a being in itself right & good & therefore splendid (*splendor ordinis*) —but what shd. Frank Rutter know of this? Yours affectionately   ERIC G. T.S.D.

Mary sends her love & is writing to you.

142 : TO DESMOND CHUTE

Capel-y-ffin   *18-12-1926*

My dearest Desmond: May every Christmas joy be yours.

At last I am able to send you the ordination cards.[2]

I hope they will arrive before you leave Rome & I hope, even more, that you will like them & that they won't damage your reputation for good sense or sanctity. [. . .] I rejoice with you in your wanderings. [. . .]

No, I wrote to Maritain & sent him my last *Id Quod* but have as yet not heard from him either re *Id Quod* (!) or Cocteau. I *am* sorry I couldn't let you have 2 copies. I had a job to

---

[1] *Evolution in Modern Art* (1926).
[2] For Desmond Chute's subdiaconate.

make 'em go round & they didn't [. . .] Orders are still coming in. *Times Litt. Sup!* gives approving but feeble review this week.

I hope you will find Kessler. Give him my love.

Salies address: Villa des Palmiers

> Salies-de-Béarn
>
> B-P. (Basses Pyrénées).
>
> France (or whatever the Italians call her).

Mary & Betty & Gordian leave England next Wednesday (Dec. 22). Alas! Petra & I are too much pressed with work to go with them. We follow in January if poss.

I have to be in Manchester on Feb. 16 (to give a lecture)!

I have not yet got the wood panels for the Rossall job.

I'll remember about engravings.

LOVE & prayers Your affect^e. bro. in J. C.   ERIC G. T.S.D.

I enclose some snippets herewith

1, experiment with multiple tool
2, Good Shepherd (for D. Cleverdon)
3, Lovers (intaglio, wood)
    (These by way of Christmas Cards!)

143 : TO DESMOND CHUTE

Salies-de-Béarn   *11-3-1927*

My dearest Desmond: [. . .] Thank you very much for your letter of January. I'm very glad the ordination cards arrived safely & were approved. [. . .] Thank you also v. much for your letter of February & birthday greetings. We are indeed enjoying life here. The daily round is all I could wish & the occasional fine days are so superlatively fine. The villa is about 15 minutes walk from the centre of the town and as I've got a workroom down in town it's a nice little walking exercise for me. Mass at 8.0, Breakfast at the Café in the 'Place' (at which one or other of the girls join me), work till 12.30, Déjeuner 12.45. Work from 2.0. to 6.0. Evening

Prayers at the Church & Ben.ⁿ 6.15. Then home to supper —
reading & music till bed time 10.0. & that's that, & one day
follows another. I call it an earthly paradise. I'm getting on
with the *Troilus* blocks. But it's a long job. About sixty
different borders to do! as well as 5 full page pictures & some
initials.

Thank you for notes re engravings sent at Christmas. I'm
v. glad you liked the intaglio version of 'Div. Lovers'.

I've not yet heard from Maritain. I'm going to write again.
[. . .] Keep us informed as to your health. We are all well.
In fact it seems to do us good altogether —this place. Mary's
getting as fat as anything, & B. P. & J. are all flourishing.
[. . .]

By the bye. Yes, I did draw a chalice for Fr. O'C. But I
only did it from measurements he gave me himself. I never
saw the result. [. . .]

Laurie Cribb is at Capel-y-ffin working at the Rossall altar
job —cutting out the background. That'll be a summer job
for me. [. . .] Your brother   ERIC G. T.S.D.

P.S. I'm sorry I forgot to say anything about Manchester. I
think it was rather an important occasion. I was asked by the
University to lecture on the relation of sculpture to architecture & I took it as a good opportunity to work up a statement.
I think it was fairly successful —anyway the University is
going to print the lecture. I'll send you a copy. They said
they'd give me several copies. The *Manchester Guardian* gave
a very good report! (Thursday Feb. 17).

144 : TO MRS. WILLIAM ROTHENSTEIN

Villa des Palmiers, Salies-de-Béarn B.-P.   *4-4-1927*

Dear Mrs. Rothenstein: Thank you very much indeed for your
kind remembrance from Rome. I am very glad to have the
sacred leaves & your charitable thought. It is a fine chance for
Betty. Rome is full of wonders. Stᵃ Sabina has only one rival

in Rome & that is St. Clemente. Did you see his Church too?
Oh! most marvellously beautiful . . . I hope Betty will form
some holy acquaintance in the holy city & not find herself
swamped by the glory of its antiquities. My friend Desmond
Chute told me he was in touch with nice people on her
behalf —I wish you had met him there —he was there at
Christmas time. I hope William is now strong & well again —
and Billy too & that Rachel is also regaining full health —you
have had so much sorrow these last years.

We are all out here for a month or two. I am doing a lot
of wood engraving for a new edition of Chaucer's *Troilus*. It
is nice to work uninterruptedly in this Catholic town near the
mountains & it's very good for the girls & our small boy. We
return to England after Easter. I see Benn's book on E. G. is
out! I wish I were better pleased with John's introduction.
He's managed to get so many facts wrong & there are other
matters . . . Greetings to you all. Yours affectionately

                                             ERIC G. T.S.D.

1 4 5 : T O ' G . K . ' S W E E K L Y ', 4 J U N E 1 9 2 7

Sir: As one of those who was unable to be present at the
meeting at 'The Devereux' on March 25, may I beg for some
explanation of several of Fr. Vincent McNabb's principles? A
friend has sent me a copy of the pamphlet which was given
away at the meeting, and I have the report, which appears in
your issue of April 9. The phrase which puzzles me is 'most
economically consumed'. How are things economically consumed? It is easy enough to understand economic production,
but economic consumption is not so plain. What is 'economic
consumption'?

You can produce stone from a stone quarry, and you can,
if you are careful, produce it economically. But you cannot
produce stone in London because there are no London

quarries. So far it is clear, and if London wants stone (and stone is not an undesirable commodity, in spite of the presence of London clay), London must buy stone from the place where it is produced, and naturally London will buy from the place where it is most 'economically' produced. The same applies to many things —from Persian carpets to wine.

But the pamphlet says: 'Things should be produced where they can be most economically consumed'. Assuming that this means 'where they are most needed', we have to ask, 'How can they, unless they can be produced there?' Of course if you are thinking of things like corn and milk (though not only by such does man live), you can see a certain meaning behind the words. Clearly it is absurd for corn for English mouths to be grown only in Canada (or other foreign lands) when it can be produced in England of equally good quality. But then it is only by a certain trick of the markets that corn for English consumption is grown more cheaply in Canada.

The principle that 'things should be produced where they can be most economically produced' is not therefore rendered absurd. The absurdity lies in the fact that English corn lands, for one reason and another, cannot produce corn as cheaply as Canadian. Corn will grow in England, and will grow very well I am told. The fact that we do not grow enough to feed our population is in no way a proof that things should not be produced where they can be most economically produced. You might as well tell a farmer that because he needs his corn for his household therefore he must have his corn fields near his house, whether or no the land nearest his house be suitable for the crop. Surely he must choose for corn those fields upon which he can grow corn to the best advantage?

I don't profess to know anything about these things (and I write only for information), but I know my own trade, and it seems to me to be rather confusing to say 'things should be produced where they can be most economically consumed'. I should have thought that a better principle, and one having an obvious meaning, would be: things should be produced where they can be produced best. What does it matter where things are produced provided they are produced well? Our complaint against foreign corn is not that it is foreign, but that it is generally and obviously inferior. It is inferior because it is grown on 'mass production' lines and 'doctored' and 'treated' in all sorts of ways by unscrupulous people, whose only interest in the stuff is the price they can get for it. But our objection to foreign and inferior produce is, it seems to me, no excuse for denying a true principle, and it seems to me that it is, and must be, a true principle that things should be produced where they can be most economically produced (i.e., produced to the best advantage of the thing produced), and that the evils from which we suffer are not due to the following of that principle, but to the insubordination of the trader under whose evil domination the standard of quality is replaced by the standard of money value.

Another puzzling principle put forth in the pamphlet referred to is stated thus: 'To cease to live in the town, while continuing to live on the town, may be serving Mammon rather than God . . .' Of course the word 'may' makes the statement innocuous, but still one wonders what is meant. I knew a man who lived in Hammersmith and had two small children. In Ravenscourt Park the children played, in spite of notices warning them not to pick the flowers (quite reasonable warning, for if the flowers had been picked there would not have been any flowers). It seemed desirable to the father and mother of the said children to bring them up under more open conditions; they feared, in fact, that in Hammersmith their children would be produced where they would be very 'economically consumed' indeed. So they moved to 'the country', and the children gradually overcame their reluctance to plucking flowers![1]

We are told that the family is the important consideration. Supposing that Hammersmith conditions (or Glasgow conditions) are economically consumptive of children, why should

[1] Cf. *Autobiography*, p. 134; U.S.A. ed., pp. 134-5.

not parents, if they are able to do so, move into quarters where their children get a better chance?

Again, and quite apart from family considerations, why shouldn't a man work where he can work best? Suppose I do nothing else but make neckties for sale in Bond Street (and they might be very nice neckties—why not?), why should I not make the said neckties in Timbuctoo if I find Timbuctoo a good place for my necktie-making? Why should my conscience be disturbed by a pamphleteer who says I 'may' be serving Mammon? I take it unkindly of this pamphleteer, and, after all, what is this 'town' and 'country' business? Towns are all right. A good town is not inconceivable, and the whole notion of civilization is a town notion, hence the word. Because many towns are overgrown cesspools of commercial rottenness is no reason why we should abandon towns altogether and take up this high-brow attitude. As you yourself, Sir, have said: Only he who loves Pimlico has any right to pull Pimlico down, or words to that effect. Personally, I am all for living in the town and, as 'man does not live by bread alone', and as therefore all men cannot be bakers, it seems that we have got to envisage a very considerable number of people not engaged in agricultural pursuits. But we are told in the pamphlet that farmers should sell as little as possible; that they should farm principally for self-support. Well, well! Such people aren't farmers in any decent old sense of the word at all—they are 'self-supporters'. A tombstone maker doesn't only make tombstones for his wife and family; he doesn't even make his own tombstone (dearly as he would like to do so). He makes tombstones for all and sundry. He makes tombstones to sell! In the same way, there is a quite honest kind of man who produces corn, or milk, or roots (he knows better than I, the names of the things), and he produces them to sell! That man is called a farmer. He is even something of an artist at his job, and has been known to take considerable pride in the high quality of the goods he takes to market to sell. Is all this very wicked? Just because we hate the factory system (chiefly because it produces such very rotten goods), and don't want to see it applied to farming, we have no right to talk, as our pamphleteer talks, as though making things to sell was in any case rather beastly. Because specialization is, or can be, overdone, because labour is, or can be, too much subdivided is no reason for going back to a jack-of-all-trades condition, insisting on every clerk rolling his own lawn and every pamphleteer milking his own cow. In fact we have got to recover a state in which growing good food for sale is as honourable a trade as writing good books for sale, and in such a state it is unlikely, as all history goes to show, that the farmers will write books or the writers grow corn —nor will the Pope starve because farmers will not sell as little as possible.

The pamphlet finishes by saying that 'the family, not the individual, is the unit of the nation'. This is just rhetoric, surely, and, as a counterblast to all those law-makers who seek to destroy the Christian family, it is a very valuable slogan; but it cannot be strictly taken, for as the family is antecedent to the state, and has rights independently, so the individual soul comes before the family and has rights independently. Strictly, therefore, the unit of the nation is (as at the Communion Rail or in the Confessional) the individual soul. Or am I wrong?

ERIC GILL

P.S. You will understand that this letter is not in any way an attack on Fr. Vincent McNabb, whom I very greatly revere. It is simply in criticism of the unsigned pamphlet distributed at his meeting, and I apologize for my contentious tone.—E. G.

146 : TO DESMOND CHUTE

Capel-y-ffin

10-6-1927

My dear Desmond: Thank you very much for yours of Whit-sunday.

Yes, the awful day is past —a week to-day! Nought but a p.c. so far from Betty, from Lulworth Cove, saying they arrived there safely. [. . .] Betty was charming so was Teslin. I'm v. glad you liked the invitation card. (Yes, & T & C tailpiece. Was it v. tactless? The figures are not portraits of T & C — just any couple of lovers . . .) I'm glad to have Fr. John's letter re chalice. I will make design very shortly. Where are you going to have it made? Do you know an individual good workman in metal or are you going to a 'firm'? [. . .] I shd. like as designer to be in touch with executant for I wish to do as little as poss — merely a diagram in line translating Fr. John's diagrammatic *word*. [. . .] Much love from me & all. Your bro.   ERIC G. T.S.D.

V. kind letter & present to Betty from Mrs. Chute.

I'm v. glad you like the T. & C. borders and specially the Crucifix one. Chaucer gave me the chance. On the last page of the poem he invites the reader ('o, youngé freshé folkés, he or she') to remember 'Him, the whiche . . . upon a cross, our soulés for to beye, first starf . . . (i.e. died)' & to eschew 'of Jove, Apollo, of Mars, of swich rascaille.' . . .

I enclose a print (early proof) of one of the *Art & Love* pictures. I also enclose ½ doz. prints of your ordination card. I think you'd better not ask for any more. The block being in two pieces & having been printed from (with *damp* paper) nearly 75 times now refuses to print clean. I shall know in future that for intaglio printing the block must not be composite.   E. G.

1 4 7 : TO THE REV. JOHN O'CONNOR

Capel-y-ffin   *19-7-1927*

Dear Fr. John: Thank you for your letter of Saturday, with instructions about paten. I am still waiting to hear from Desmond.

With regard to the engraving, thank you for doing business on my behalf. I enclose a print to replace it, together with a/c therefor.

I am sorry there appears to be disagreement between Fr. Vincent & myself, but it is a long story with more in it than meets the eye — some of which I will uncover when we meet. I hope you will approve of my letter in this week's *G. K'S Weekly* (if they print it); if the movement is to be any good at all it must not alienate all those who look out of workshop windows. Much love

ERIC G. T.S.D.

148 : TO HIS BROTHER EVAN

Capel-y-ffin, Abergavenny   18-8-1927

Haven't forgot about *South Wind*. I've read it & enjoyed it frightfully much, great sport & v. well done.

Donald A. has read it — same verdict — tho., having a tooth-ache at the time, he said it nearly made him lose the faith . . . Mary Ethel is now reading it.

I shall be up North I hope towards end of next month — then will meet again.

ERIC G. T.S.D.

149 : TO DESMOND CHUTE

50a Glebe Place, S.W.3   18-9-1927

My dearest Desmond: [. . .] I look forward to seeing you next Sunday — meanwhile many thanks for note re *Art & Love* and your v. just criticism. Yes! in future marks of exclam. shall be confined by me to real exclams. and I will certainly try the under-statement stunt — not 'arf!

Yes! Of course I want you to do the introduction for the Cleverdon-Morison-Gibbings Gill engravings book. I can't imagine there's any hurry because I told them I couldn't do anything about it till next year. [. . .]

Item: I've not received an invitation to your wedding.[1] I'd like to have one to (as the Americans say) put in my filing cabinet. [. . .]

Love from

ERIC G. T.S.D.

[1] Desmond Chute's ordination to the priesthood (at Downside Abbey, Sept. 25th, 1927).

αβγδεζηθικλμν
οπρσστυφχψω

ποῦ μοι ἄπεπτας

top: GREEK ALPHABET

bottom: POSTCARD TO WALTER SHEWRING

[About this time I had been discussing Greek lettering with E. G., and he had drawn for me (in ink) a specimen alphabet in upper and lower case. The latter (reproduced opposite) was sent to me with one letter missing; this was supplied on the postcard following (also reproduced). There was no direct connection between this alphabet and the 'Perpetua Greek' type (designed in 1929 but never carried to quite its final stage). However, for purposes of comparison, I print a line in Perpetua Greek (the opening of a Greek version of *O mistress mine*):

που μοι απεπτασ' απεπτασ', εμον θαλος, 'Ηλιοδωρα;

The proof of Greek type here mentioned was in Mr. Van Krimpen's 'Antigone'. My visiting card, and Mr. Morison's, came from Emery Walker; E. G.'s was engraved by himself.]

London   *18-9-1927*

Many thanks for yours of 14th & proof of Greek type wh. I am glad to have. How about: [A¹] for ξ? I don't like your visiting card or S.M's any better than mine. Lettering much too fanciful and too [B¹]. It shd. be more [C¹], i.e. if there were such a form.   ERIC G.

50a Glebe Place, S.W.3   *23-9-1927*

My dearest Desmond: Thank you very much for your card from Downside & for making arrangements for my lodging (also thanks for introduction card for use with Fr. Russell). But, alas! I cannot come. Things have worked out so that I must take Gordian across to France that very day (25th). There are other children going back to Salies on the 26th. in charge of a grown up & we *must* take advantage of this. So

¹ See photograph opposite.

P

there. It cannot be helped. My absence will not delay your
wedding — but I particularly deplore not receiving Our own
Lord at your hands (kissing the said hands thereafter) on the
first occasion of your offering the holy sacrifice. May all go
well with you. I shall be with you. . . .

Anyway I shall see you in London. You will let me know
when you come up. I shall certainly be back from Paris by
Wed. morn. the 28th. if not before. Give my great love to
Fr. John & express to him my regret at not seeing him. I
shall see him on my journey North when I go to fix up the
Rossall panel. Should he be in London next week perhaps we
could meet.

Please also give my love to Walter S.

Yours, dearest Desmond, affectionately and on this occasion
with very fervent love —   ERIC G. T.S.D.

P.S. The Rossall panel is to be shown at the Goupil during
Oct. November — So I shan't be going North till after that. E. G.

152 : TO THE REV. DESMOND CHUTE

Capel-y-ffin   *25-3-1928*

My dearest Desmond: At last! . . . It's lucky we're more or
less completely confident of one another or we'd never get
over it. No letters even at Christmas . . . I was and we all
were most sorry to hear of Mrs. Chute's accident. It must
indeed have upset all your plans & hers. I hope she is really
quite well again & not suffering any permanent damage. And
we are dreadfully sorry *you* have been so knocked out again. I
trust you are really better & will soon be as right as ever or
more so. I was at Bristol for 2 hours last week — on my way
back from London (& other places) and Douglas C. showed me
your woful letter and then I got your card of March 13 saying
the same thing. I was very sorry indeed that you could not

undertake the 'prefatory essay' or whatever it's called. But now I hear again from Douglas saying that you have relented and I am v. glad. 's matter of fact it wd. have been v. difficult for him as he had more or less definitely announced your name in print. But I hope no ill results to your health will follow the effort – and I hope none to your priestly reputation . . . That wd. be an awful thing. But I don't really fear it. 'The nude in art' (damned cliché) is perfectly respectable *in se*, and none of my definitely love-making blocks will appear in the book. I hope the book will be decent. One gets fed up with the sight of any but the more recent engravings and a select few of the early ones. I hope you won't lay it on too thick about religion. In my mind a consciously religious attitude of mind in the artist & (definitely so called), 'religious' subjects become less & less necessary. It makes me quite 'all overish' to read old *Games* again & to remember how 'outward' it all was. I'm not complaining at or despising the past – I only mean it makes me shy & I'm hoping you won't dig it up too much. Just to keep you more or less up to date (what ho!) I'm sending herewith G.C.P. new list & also reprint from the *Month*. In Feb. I had to go to Manchester & lecture to the Cath. University Students – subject (because I wanted to get clearer in my own mind, not because I have any qualifications you understand) Art & Prudence. The lecture is to be printed 'uniform with *Id Quod*' by the G.C.P. I will send you a copy, but it won't be out yet a while. But briefly the notion is that man as artist is the *male* creature, collaborating with God in creating – a channel for God's creative-power – not a critic of nature nor an expositor of nature & not a propagandist. Though by accident he may be all these things & indeed cannot escape being – as when he is used (employed) by a customer (the Church p'raps) to paint or carve or even when he uses himself – but in this last case, let him beware of himself. On tother hand the man of prudence is man *female* – the bride of Christ – seeking her *happiness* & that is to be in the arms of her Lord. The object of prudence is happiness – that of art pleasure.

Happiness –ultimately heaven: pleasure –ultimately of the
mind & in *things*. & so on. . . .

Well well. My London sojourn is now over & I am back at
C-y-ff. I am much occupied at present picking up loose threads
& arrears of letters & accounts. Mary & I purpose visiting
Gordian v. shortly. It will do us good to have a jaunt. The
last six months have been very strenuous for us both & separa-
tion didn't make it easier. She has been heroically good keeping things going at C-y-ff in my absence & on my part I've had
a really strenuous job to (more or less) fill the Goupil in six
months. As to that, yes, the blooming show is an absurd
success –monstrous. Approbation galore & you know what
absurd things critics can say when they try and in the mundane
sphere: well, we look like clearing a thousand pounds –fancy
that! a lot of things have sold. For the big figure I carved in
that big lump of Hoptonwood which I had & never used at
Ditchling I'm getting £800 . . . Eric Kennington is buying it.[1]
(Rotten bad photos. of it in *Illust. London News* & in *Sphere*.
Notice in *Times* really very decent, also *M'chester Guardian* little
to complain of.) Anyway it's a success one way & another &
we can breathe freely for a bit & really pay our debts (some
£375 worth). But as I say we were going to see Gordian &
were going this week but now, and this brings me to a bit of
news, Mary has had suddenly to go off to Ditchling. Betty's
babe has arrived! Born on Friday night last. How can they
escape calling him (it's a boy) *Gabriel*? It's good news isnt it?
And me a grandfather, Mary a grandmother, the girls *aunts* &
Aunt Vi a great aunt –fancy that! Mary only went yesterday,
so, beyond telegraphic news, we have none. 'Mother & son
very well'. Consequence is that Mary will probably stay with
Betty till she's about again –so we shan't go to Salies, probably, till after Easter. Enough of myself –tho. there's lots
more to say –about future work, present work & what not.
I wd. indeed sympathize with you in your incapacity for
mobility –but also it's a fine job –just saying Mass, as you say –

[1] 'Mankind'; it was later acquired by the Tate Gallery.

well — in reparation . . . excellent. I *wish* we could get to Rapallo. [. . .]

Much love dear Desmond. I must stop. I am your ever loving friend & brother   ERIC G.

I wish I could tell you all about my London 6 months. It *was* a go! I enjoyed it v. much really & Glebe Place became quite a 'home from Home'. Mary & the girls visited me from time to time — seems like a dream to look back on. C-y-ff is v. heavenly — but . . . whether we stay here or not when P. gets married remains to be seen. V. difficult for Mary with only Joanna.

Fr. J.-B. Reeves is coming here tomorrow. Stayed a week end with Fr. O'C. when I went to Manchester. He was v. well & cheerful & full of sympathy.

153 : TO WILLIAM REID DICK

[On March 22nd, 1928, Mr. (now Sir William) Reid Dick had written: 'Dear Mr. Gill, Your work at the Goupil Gallery has given me great pleasure, and, if you have no objection, may I enter your name in the nomination book at the Royal Academy? Please let me know before I do so. Yours sincerely, W. Reid Dick.']

Capel-y-ffin   *26-3-1928*

Dear Mr. Reid Dick: Thank you for your letter of the 22nd. I am glad that you liked my work at the Goupil.

Your kind suggestion that you should enter my name for the Royal Academy places me in a difficulty, for I am strongly of the opinion that academic honours should only be sought by those having academic qualifications — and obviously I have none.

My art education consisted of evening classes at Chichester, where I took certificates in perspective drawing and geometry, and a three years' apprenticeship to an architect, from whom I learnt nothing but a certain amount about drains and how to draw full-sized details in sham Gothic. During this period I attended evening classes in lettering and picture-frame making.

As a sculptor I am clearly an outsider and I feel that my inclusion at the Royal Academy would be unnatural. You will understand that I do not imply any insensibility to the honour you suggest. I simply feel that I am in the position of a Labour M.P. who is asked if he would like to be nominated for an honorary D.C.L. He might say to himself, 'It is one thing to *receive* this honour but quite another to ask for it'. In brief: I should regard my acceptance by the R.A. as an honour conferred. I do not regard it as a thing for which I have any natural right to be nominated. Yours very sincerely,

ERIC GILL.

154 : TO GRAHAM CAREY

Capel-y-ffin　　　　　　　　　　　　　　　　　*31-3-1928*

Dear Mr. Carey: Herewith I enclose a small drawing for the panels of the bedstead. It is rough but I hope will serve to indicate possibly pleasant carvings. The drawing will, I think, explain itself; but I may say my idea is, 1. Mother and Baby, 2. Man and Woman, 3. Death. The idea of the first is obvious. Of the second I will only say that I have tried to convey something of the notion indicated in the story of Tobias and Sara.* In the third, the angel is as it were awakening the dead person. The foliage is, of course, decorative, but it would serve, I think, to act as a suggestion of the world in which we live.

I have been considering the matter of making the bed and have come to the conclusion that it would be much better for you to have it made in the U.S.A., and send me the panels for carving. I am not equipped here for making a thing requiring such expert joinery, nor do I know how to allow for the fixing of the mattress, and so on. I hope you will agree about this. It would also save you a lot of time, as you can get the bed made at once. Yours sincerely,　　　ERIC GILL

* i.e. a certain holy detachment

155 : TO DOUGLAS CLEVERDON

C-y-ff   *7-4-1928*

Dear Douglas: Our discussion on 'Mods' & 'Greats' makes me
think the article on Card. Mercier in this *Pax*[1] will interest you
(i.e. as one who took 'Greats') — especially p. 32 et seq.

But the whole thing is to the point. I'd be grateful if you'd
tell me how it strikes you — is it a fair summary of philosophical
tendencies — from your point of view? Yrs.   ERIC G.

p. 77[2] may also amuse you!

156 : TO DOUGLAS CLEVERDON

Capel-y-ffin   *30-5-1928*

Dear Douglas: [. . .] I have been re-reading Clive Bell this
a.m. Can you tell me what is meant (by him & others) by
'emotion', 'feel' & 'feeling'? Are we now agreed that from
your point of view the beautiful (i.e. the beautiful in *art*) is not
a matter of the *intelligence*? Yours,   ERIC GILL.

---

[1] *Cardinal Mercier and the Revival of Thomist Philosophy*, by Fr. Austin Barker, O.P.
(*Pax*, Spring 1928.) In the pages specially referred to the writer points out how
the fashionable philosophies of the day are in fact revivals of ancient errors —
'interesting hypotheses issuing from old tombs'. Thus the positions of Haldane
and Hegel are reducible to the position of Parmenides, those of Bergson and
William James and Schiller to that of Heraclitus; and both are countered
already by Aristotle and St. Thomas.

[2] Part of a book-review by E. G. himself. 'That life in this world has anything
to offer which may make it in itself worth living, that the misery and squalor
of the modern town, the grinding insufficiency and boredom of the modern
countryside, are not inevitable accompaniments of human existence — these
things do not seem to be even at the back of the author's mind.

For all we can gather from his book, life is a weary business to be got through,
and the only thing is to obey certain rules in the hope that the next life will be
better. We admit that there is much excuse for such a point of view, and we
should take it for granted as being the proper point of view for a non-Christian
sociologist. We regret that nothing else should emerge from the pages of a
writer who is both a Catholic and a priest.'

Capel-y-ffin   *10-6-1928*

Dearest Desmond: Herewith just to answer questions & to
convey much love . . . I trust you are well, well, *well*. V. many
thanks for yours of Palm Sunday. All right here. Frightfully
busy doing engravings for *Canty. Tales*. Yes, I can do engravings
on my own of course, but G.C.P. is the only *press* & I'm to give
them the *refusal* of other engraving.

Item: I'm now a salaried official of the Lanston Monotype
       Corpn. What ho! This means advice in 'type faces'.
       Salary v. handsome too. & I like typography don't you
       know.

Item: V. glad you like the 'self portrait' so much. No – there
       ain't not one single print. Cleverdon bought the lot. But
       you'll get one with your copy of *the book*.
       How goes the preface, or what not? I long to read it.

Item: G.C.P. is about to publish new book by self intituled
       Art & Prudence with two copper-plates by author. Hope
       you'll have one.
       We visited Gordian in April-May –but *couldn't* get to
Rapallo. I had to return to do a carving –Crucifix & B.V.M.
on tombstone for Fr. J. B. Reeves' Mother –*promised* for
May 18 so *had* to be done. Very much love from me & Mary
& all.   ERIC G.

Betty comes to-morrow for a week with babe. Petra &
Joanna return on Tuesday from week with Uncle Evan in
Liverpool.
       P. not married yet –still in hopes. Denis v. well & helping
me scorp *Canty. Tales* blks.
       Fr. Joseph[1] has been ordered to Switzerland & his Prior
agrees. So we are probably leaving . . . Further news later.

[1] E. G.'s chaplain at Capel.

Item: Am under contract with Goupil to have another sculp-
    ture show in March 1930! *Must* get studio in London
    again.
Item: Maillol exhibⁿ. at Goupil in October.
    Will you be there?   E.G.
  Have you seen *Order*, the new critical magazine?

158 : TO ROMNEY GREEN

Capel-y-ffin   *10-6-1928*

Dear Romney: I was very glad indeed to hear from you again —
we were both very glad and we both rejoice with you and
Bertha in your marriage —where and when was the happy
event? Also I am very glad to have the book of Sonnets.[1] I
like many of them very much —*especially* the one about coming
'to those green places once again' & of course the W. Closet
& love & death. (I think you miss the thing a bit in 'to a certain preacher' and the 'free woman' —seems to me they're
both coloured by a too exclusively *a posteriori* line of argument
—*a priori*'s the thing for poets . . .) And I'm very pleased that
the photos.* in *Artwork* pleased you. Yes, the exhibition was a
great success & as I sold all but three things I am now able to
pay all my debts & carry on for a bit. It really is a marvellous
feeling when you can look your banker boldly in the face —not
that I often enjoy that pleasure for he's 15 miles away at Abergavenny & I go there about once a year. The *New Statesman*,
yes, he was pretty foolish I remember. It's the curse of the
literary man, & the art of letters being paramount at the
moment they try & impose their literary business on painters
& sculptors & musicians. But I don't think it's quite right that
it's what the artist has 'seen or felt' either. The registration

---

* I'm v. glad you approved of the article also.
[1] Published as *Twenty-One Sonnets by J. S. N.* (Allen & Unwin, 1926).

of what one has seen or felt is simply one of the possible lines of artistic activity — not the very essence of the matter. It seems that the essence of the thing is very simple — art is concerned with *making* — just that; and a good artist is one who makes things well (a bad one makes them badly). What people like the *N. Statesman* johnny seem to miss is the work of art! They don't see *it*. They don't even ask themselves: *what* is it? I make a statue & they ask: what does it say? I reply: it doesn't say anything; it just *is* — it has being. You make a table in the same way. Possibly my statue & your table both render *service*. My statue may furnish a church or commemorate a bloody politician & your table may support a dinner or a writing pad, but in both cases, yours & mine, though the service to be rendered may be essential to the being (i.e. because a table that won't support things simply isn't a table) yet in neither case is it the mere doing that matters most. It is the thing made, the thing 'seen' & the thing as such delightful to the mind.

I wish we could meet again & talk of all these things. How we did enjoy that week at Christchurch. We often look back with love to that time. I hope Bertha is quite well & you too. We are all well. You know Betty (our eldest) was married last year & is now mother of a son? Well, it is so. Are you ever in London? I am sometimes — Are you to be seen at Percy St.? Much love from us both   ERIC G.

159 : TO ROMNEY GREEN

Capel-y-ffin   *11-7-1928*

Dear Romney: Many thanks for yours of the 8th. Alas no! I shall not be in London this week end. I'm fixed up in Wales for the present. We must await another chance for meeting —— & talking. Re definition of 'artist': I forget exactly what I said. If I said 'a man who makes things well' I would add: 'i.e. as well as he can or knows how'. Then if he makes bad things he's simply a bad artist but it may still remain true that he made them as well as he could. (e.g. the maker of the Q. Victoria Memorial must in charity be supposed to have done his best.) Plato's theory is right enough but does not go *all* the way. The word 'type' suggests one thing which is typical of many things. No doubt this is an important department of 'art' — the discovery of the *type*, the weeding out of the accidental & extraneous so that, as in a Hindu sculpture of a tree, all trees are resumed. But this job is only one department & not I think the *most* important — it is one of the arts but not the highest or most specifically artistic art so to say. The art which is art specifically & at its highest is that of pure creation — *de novo, ad hoc* & *ex nihilo*. This is God's art & not man's. But man, in the second degree, by virtue of 'free will' can create (not out of nothing but, *de novo* & *ad hoc,* out of what God has made). Thus he makes not types but *uniques* — things that represent nothing but themselves & of which there is & cannot be another example in the whole Universe of created beings.

No, I haven't seen your pamphlet. I want to. Tell Mairet to send me one. I must wait until I have had a talk with P. A. M. before doing anything. I am not yet clear as to what he's up to. Love from us both to you both   ERIC G.

160 : TO GRAHAM CAREY

Capel-y-ffin   21-9-1928

Dear Mr. Carey: Thank you for your letter of Sept. 5th. and for the money order enclosed. I am very glad to hear that the two little carvings arrived safely and that in spite of various things you are pleased with them on the whole. I do very well understand your partial disappointment. I am very sorry they were not more completely successful. Apart from the wet wood, it was a difficult job. To make, in so small a space, a composition which shd. illustrate the B & P story was, for *me*, too much. I fell back on your sketches. I liked them & I like the carvings —but I do think they lack a bold & monumental & architectonic quality. I *hope* for better success with the bed panels. I have now got the wood for these & shall shortly begin the carving. At the present moment however things are enormously complicated by the fact that we are packing up & about to move from Wales to a place near London! I am over-whelmed with affairs in consequence. You will forgive me if you do not hear from me for a few months. I expect we shall be settled, & at work more or less normally, again by the end of October. Meanwhile it is prayers we need! It is as bad as all that! Yours very sincerely   ERIC GILL

I enclose receipted bill.

I am pleased to hear that you liked the rough proofs you came across. I am wondering what they were.   E. G.

161 : TO THE REV. DESMOND CHUTE

Capel-y-ffin, Abergavenny   *8-10-1928*

The new address is: PIGOTTS
                        North Dean, H. Wycombe . . .

My dearest Desmond: Let this be the last letter I shall write from Capel-y-ffin. The furniture removers are even now in the house and having finished packing & all such activity I am free for a few minutes for contemplation. Thank you for your (I write with a windowsill for desk) letter of Michaelmas and for the pretty card therewith —Thank you also for your blessings on the new home —blessings having, I take it, a priestly operativeness as well as a friend and brother's. The new home is like this 'ere: —Proceed to H. Wy. by train or on foot and take the Speen road northwards therefrom. Pro-ceed thus for $3\frac{1}{2}$ miles* until you reach the hamlet of *North Dean*, in the parish of Hughenden, then ask —and you will be

* There's a motorbus (5d to N. Dean)

told to go back a hundred yards or so and take a lane going northwards from the road you have just come. Said lane goes steeply uphill, beside some beechwoods, for about 500 yards. Arrived at the top you proceed along the level for another 200 yards and find yourself at a clearing in the 'forest' of about 18 acres in midst whereof is a courtyard of buildings with red tiled roofs (with XXX pattern in new tiles): this is Pigotts and consists of a courtyard surrounded by erstwhile farm buildings — viz: —two large barns, stables, etc & a farm house and two cottages thus: — [1]

A —Cottage for Petra and Denis T.
B —   ,,   for Laurie Cribb and family
C —   ,,   for E. G. & Co.
D —Barn for E. G.'s workshop
FFF open sheds for future workshop
* Future chapel — (may yours be the 1st. Mass therein).

Such is Pigotts and a magnificent place it is, and all for £1750, including 1 acre orchard & 16 acres grass. (Note by selling statue of 'Mankind' I was enabled to put down £500 & borrow the remainder from Bank as an overdraft! If this isn't providential —what, oh, what is?)

Oct. 10. I was not able to finish this on the 8th. and yesterday all the morning I was feverishly correcting the proofs of that *Preface* to Cleverdon's book of *Engravings*! That Preface! Well, I wonder whether, when you see what I have written, you won't think that it would have been better to have gone blind and written it yourself. Excuses: I wrote it at full speed because Cleverdon wanted it as soon as possible as the book, on which he has laid out large sums of money, simply *must* be published soon or he will be broke. Surely *you* will forgive the faults due to haste —bad construction and arrangement — hasty assertiveness & dogmatism —bad paragraphing —faulty sentiments in theology and philosophy. One thing I think you will approve of and that is the part at the end which Walter S. has translated into *Latin* for me. You may not approve of the

---

[1] A plan drawn here, with letters explained in the following lines.

matter (tho. why you shouldn't I don't know —it's only a childish catalogue of *things* that as a *maker of things*, I delight in —) but I think the *manner* is noble and decent.

You will not misunderstand and think that when I say I love my Julia's leg I am implying that I take no account of her mind or that loving the creature I am denying the Creator. It is simply that I wrote the thing to accompany a book of pictures —my pictures —pictures of a certain kind of objectivity. I wished therefore to expose what kind of objects I love *in life* so that it might be clearer to the critic why I make that kind of objets *d'art*. But you will let me know what you think when you've read it. I wish I had more time & I wish I could have read it over with you or some other discerning critic —then it would have been possible to get it more fool-proof. As it is I only hope I have not uttered too many palpable heresies or let Holy Church down too badly. Pray that it may not be so I beseech you.

I am very sorry indeed about your eyes. Your mother told me —I called on her with Joanna when I was last in Bristol and she received us very kindly —I hope they will soon improve. It must be a terrible privation for you —of all people. But you are blessed with good ears and madness comes to the deaf more than to the blind —not that —I trust —you are going blind —it's not as bad as that is it? As for *my* ears —they're nothing to worry about. Dr. N. N. pumped them out and I've no complaints now. The left one is a bit weak that's all. The other is near-as-no-matter perfect.

I dare say D. Cl. wont mind if you sneak that portrait. But I don't know. He bought every bally print except 5, and those I gave to the family & Fr. O'Connor. [. . .]

As soon as I get to Pigotts and can get at the engravings stock I will see if I have got a Crucifix —'*sic enim Deus*' you call it — out of the *Art & Love* set (that's the one I call 'Bread of these stones' —I suppose it's the one you mean). If I have one left I'll send it to you. Or I may be able to get one from the Goupil. By the same token . . . Have you received notice of the fact that at the Goupil at this moment there is a show on of my engravings? and also a show of Maillol's things! Very honourable concatenation of circumstances – what?[1] The Maillol lead torso is very grand & big & bulgy. I enclose *Times* cutting which Mary had sent to her. *Please return same.* I am very much gratified by Marriott's remarks on my things. (Charles Marriott is the *Times* art critic) I say *please return* 'cause Mary collects them! (indeed – believe me – it's she who subscribes to the bally agency – not me – apart from Marriott I don't think there's a single art critic worth reading – I mean in the daily or weekly press.) The Maillol show was chiefly or in the first place organized to advertize the Kessler-Maillol Vergil-English edition & set of the Maillol engravings therefrom are part of the show. And Douglas C. is taking advantage of the concurrent exhib^n. of my engravings to advertise his book – he has a sample copy (without preface of course) on view at the Gallery. So it's rather amusing that 2 sculptors shd. be having exhibition at same place and time largely in order to advertise books of their *engravings*!

Talking of Marriott: Did I tell you that as a result of my sculpture show in March last *Jon^n.* *Cape* is bringing out book of my sculps. – with preface by Joseph Thorp and 'critical monography' by C. Marriott . . . This is just about to appear. The Thorp preface is not too bad [. . .] and the C. M. part is truly admirable and most kind and generous.* The 40 collotypes are on the whole very good – leastways the proofs I saw seemed to me so. Did you see my do in the *Dublin*? In case you did I send herewith an ERRATA slip! (Reason for *un*reason is too bloody to let pass.)

Alas! that *Dublin* article is already out of date – and I get more and more painfully aware of the fact that I ought not to

---

* considering that he's not R.C. & depends solely on his own decency of mind.

[1] On E. G.'s relations with Maillol see pp. 26-30 here and *Autobiography*, pp. 179-82; U.S.A. ed., pp. 185-8.

be writing at all — not sufficient philosophical training. It's painful — every week I get the thing clearer in my mind and last week's writing seems mostly tosh — or if not mostly, still, enough to damn it. I'm just reading Maritain's *Three Reformers*. *Very* good it seems to me — specially the Luther and the Rousseau — the Descartes is rather beyond my small philosophical powers, though I think I get its drift sufficiently to see that 'Angelism' is a very pretty trick of the Devil's. Having recently read Rousseau's unexpurgated *Confessions* I am able to get the hang of Maritain's essay pretty clearly.

By the bye I said on 1st. p. of this that we are packing — well, now it's all done. The house is empty. Petra has gone on to light fires etc. Mary & I & Joanna & Gordian go by road, with chickens, dogs & cats, to-morrow. We hope to arrive by evening. So this is positively our last day in the Vale of Ewyas!

Well, we have had a wonderful four years and well worth the expense (it *has* cost a bit one way and another). We shall remember . . . oh, too much to say.

I am glad you are about to hear confessions. [. . .] Next Saturday evening we all hope to go to confess at H. Wycombe — a poor little 'Gothic' Church but much better than many. I don't know the priest yet. I'm v. interested to hear about W. B. Yeats. I met him, only once, at W. R.'s. I think you'll like him. I believe he's a jolly fine mind at bottom — or at top. And I am glad your Don Marcellino's 'resilience' is such as you mention. Oh that we may all meet in heaven. This tight-rope of an earthly life . . . Well, good bye now. I look forward to your visit next year. By then we shall, I hope, be all in order to receive visitors . . . for the next six months we shall be all upside down — repairs and alterations to be done everywhere. But my hat: when you see my barns you'll sit up and take a bit of notice. Much love dear Desmond from your brother in St. Dominic. & love from Mary (she says so).   ERIC G.

162 : TO DOUGLAS CLEVERDON

C-y-ff   *9-10-1928*

Dear Douglas: Proof of preface received from Ingham yesterday & returned to him to-day with corrections. I have done
what I could, in the midst of a universe in which there appears
to be neither being nor becoming, to improve it. I can only
hope that the circumstances of its writing (last moment, speed,
what not) may excuse its many faults of construction and
arrangement. I hope there may be discovered a thread, of
hemp if not of silver, by which the weary reader may guide
himself through its labyrinth. I have added about 14 lines
before the Latin (jolly fine the Latin looks) to disarm certain
criticism — I hope this is allowable — & I have made several new
'paragraphs' — some of the pages looked too unrelieved altogether: Let me hear from you. Yrs.   ERIC G.

Mrs. Marchant tells me you were at Goupil last Thursday.
     We leave to-morrow morning — & hope to be at Pigotts
to-morrow night. PIGOTTS, North Dean, High Wycombe.

163 : TO GRAHAM CAREY

Pigotts, North Dean, High Wycombe   *2-12-1928*

Dear Mr. Carey: Thank you for your letter of Nov. 18.
     Yes, I am glad that the Professor of Fine Arts at Harvard is
so pleased with the little carvings. It is well! (I don't think
I know anyone called McCloggin — oh — yes! of course — you
mean MacLagan — Eric MacLagan who is head & boss of the
South Kensington Museum in London. I am glad he has been
in your neighbourhood. He is that rare mixture of very fine
culture, much learning and extreme goodness & charm — with
a face like the mad-hatter's.)
     I am interested in what you say about *your* work. I have not
the least objection to your using any design of mine that you

Q

fancy, nor have I any objection to your selling or otherwise disposing of the finished work. Please consider yourself quite free to do whatever you wish in the matter.

I am at present doing some big but unimportant sculptures on a building in London —architectural fal-lals merely but a valuable experience. We are working against time —horrible clanging & noise & mess all round —revolting contrast between our (there are 5 sculptors on the job) attempts at 'love-making' and the attitude of mind of the 1000 'hands' around us. The building is good and plain —iron with plain stone facing —we are quite out of place. Yours sincerely   ERIC GILL

164 : TO DOUGLAS CLEVERDON

Pigotts   29-12-1928

Dear Douglas: Very many thanks for the *Pillow Book*.[1] We are delighted to have this. I look forward to the reading of it. The introduction is most interesting (but I think Waley tempers the wind to our shornness a bit). When shall we see you again? How goes the *Engravings* book? [...] Love from us all.   ERIC G.

165 : TO 'THE OBSERVER', 3 FEB. 1929

'Art and Prudence'

Sir: In your issue of January 20 you have done me the honour of reviewing my little book, *Art and Prudence*, in very kind terms. For the interest of the matter, may I take up one point?

I said 'Prudence is doing good to oneself; art is doing good to things'. Your reviewer asks how the artist can be said to do good to things. The saying is, I think, both sound and simple. Thus, we say: 'Aeroplanes have been greatly im-

[1] *The Pillow Book of Sei Shonagon*, translated by Arthur Waley.

proved' —i.e., aeroplane designers and builders have improved them, i.e., done good to them. So in all the arts and in any individual case the whole job of the artist is that of one who goes about doing good. Suppose a rough lump of stone, destined in my mind to be, let us say, a Venus — how knock it about so as to improve it, make it more Venus? And, having knocked a semblance of the goddess into it, how improve it still more? Shall I polish it? . . . How, in fact, shall I do it good, or do good to it? —Yours faithfully, ERIC GILL
High Wycombe.

P.S. Your reviewer implies that I think that the wood-engraver does good to the tree from which his block is cut. Of course, this is not so. For the engraver the tree is accidental; he starts with the idea in his mind and he takes a wood block as being best for its embodiment. It is the engraving to which he attempts to do good. Doing good to trees is the art of arbori-culture.

166 : TO HIS MOTHER

Pigotts *25-5-1929*

My dearest Mother: We are indeed grieved to hear the sad news you give us. Your letter came yesterday morning. Mary Ethel was in London seeing Petra off to Ditchling where she, Petra, has gone for the week end and to bring little Stephen back to stay with us while Betty is at Plumpton for her confinement. Mary Ethel also went to the Flower Show at Chelsea as the man who does our garden (I scarcely like to say 'our gardener' though it would be accurate enough) was going and he was very anxious that 'Madam' should see some things of interest which he wished her to see — quite the proper thing — all the duchesses do it. So there you see it — Petra going to Ditchling on account of a new baby coming and Mary Ethel discussing flowers with the gardener and in far away New Guinea dear Cecil & Nonie mourning their lost child. We've got to see life whole —none knows that better than you who have borne so many and borne so much in life —a new baby in Sussex, and a new baby in Heaven —and flowers blooming and dying all the time and everywhere. In any individual case life is either too tragic or absurdly lovely and successful, but the whole thing is neither tragedy nor comedy . . . We can only say 'Thy will be done' and endeavour to mean what we say and rejoice. Alas, this sort of talk is small comfort to those who grieve the loss of a child— unbearable loss, unbearable memory —one can only be thankful in knowing that the poignancy must pass. I hope you will soon stop 'doing over much' and will have a rest. I wish indeed that you could come and have a few days rest here. Would it not be possible for you and father to come between Sunday and Sunday? When exactly do you expect Romney to arrive? We send you and dear Father much love. I am your ever loving son

ERIC

167 : TO THE REV. DESMOND CHUTE

Pigotts   *2-8-1929*

My dearest Desmond: At last we are in touch again. I was very glad indeed to get your letter & to know you are in England again. Of course we shall love to have you here, for the Assumption, with Fr. Gray. So that's a fixture. But now — alas —I'm just off to West Wittering. My mother has been ill and Mary went down yesterday to look after my father while my mother went to Chichester for an operation. Mary rung up this evening saying result of the operation is that 'there is not much hope'. So I'm going at once. I don't know anything more. I will write again in a few days. I *hope* I'll be able to come to Bristol. Rather distraught at the moment so forgive my shortness.

Much love dear Desmond —don't overdo it now —keep quiet. My love to Mrs. Chute —your dear brother   E. P. J. G.

168 : TO THE REV. DESMOND CHUTE

West Wittering   *7-8-1929*

My dear mother died yesterday morning. R.I.P. The funeral
is to-morrow at Brighton. Mary & I hope to return to Pigotts
on Friday. Much love from us both.   ERIC G.

169 : TO HERBERT READ

Pigotts   *19-10-1929*

Dear Mr. Read: Thank you for your letter received this
morning. I am very interested in your proposal.[1] I should like
to come to lunch with you and Mr. Goldsmith and Mr. Lam-
bert. I shall not be able to do so next week. Will one day the
week after be possible? Please fix a day.

I was very interested to read your article in the *Listener* a
few weeks ago. Of course I agree with most of what you say,
but I think there is something in the nature of a fundamental
disagreement in connection with your use of the word
'*emotion*'. It seems to me that your view is that of the consumer rather than that of the artist, the maker of things. I
don't believe the working artist really desires to 'communicate
his exceptional vision' to his fellow men or that that is really
his function, tho' I quite understand it may appear like that.
It seem to me perfectly certain that the artist's function is
simply maker of things — ships, shoes, sealing wax etc — to
paintings sculptures etc. Perhaps we can talk about this when
we meet. I am glad to hear about Bedford's tour.

Yes! we are getting on well with the building. And I am
now working in my big studio — you must come and see.
Yours sincerely,   ERIC GILL

[1] 'This was the first approach to E. G. to do the sculpture for the new Broadcasting House. H. R.'

170 : TO 'THE TIMES', 6 NOV. 1929

Pylons on the Downs

Sir: May I add a word in support of Sir Reginald Blomfield's letter in your issue of November 1? I write not only as an artist but as a Sussex man —born and bred —to whom love of the South Downs is as natural as it is enthusiastic. Anyone who has seen the aqueducts striding, almost galloping, across the Roman Campagna must have been struck by the inexorable majesty of them, and the need of Rome for water is analogous to the modern world's need for power. In France I have seen these great electric standards striding across the country — delayed by nothing, hindered by nothing. In England, in Buckinghamshire, on a small scale the same thing may be seen. Are we to suppose that beauty is only to be found in certain recognized 'styles' of architecture? Is the Forth Bridge ugly because it is not built of stone? Is the Tower Bridge beautiful because the citizens of London, remembering the proximity of the Tower, saw fit to clothe its iron work in machine-made imitation Gothic? Such an attachment to 'Nature', which goes with a refusal to see beauty in engineering, while making use of engineering and making money by it, is fundamentally senti- mental and romantic and hypocritical. Let the modern world abandon such an attachment, or let it abandon its use of electric power. Yours, &c.,   ERIC GILL

Pigotts, North Dean, High Wycombe

171 : TO WILLIAM ROTHENSTEIN

Pigotts   *8-12-1929*

Dear Rothenstein: I was very gratified to hear from the Goupil that the 'East Wind' had been bought by the Tate Gallery. And I am very much obliged to you for your interest & kind energy in the matter. Thank you very much.

I wish it were possible for me to come in and see you more frequently. I am overwhelmed with work at present & it is very difficult to get things done. I am doing an heraldic carving at Jesus Coll. Cambridge just now. We, Joseph Cribb and I, have been on it since the beginning of November. I have been seeing a little of the Cornfords & that has been good. But out of doors on a scaffold this time of year is not too pleasant. I hope you are well. I look forward to seeing John some time & his wife. Yrs. ever   ERIC G.

172 : TO GRAHAM CAREY

Pigotts   *2-1-1930*

Dear Mr. Carey: At last I have finished the panels for your bed.[1] I am sending them off in one box, and hope they will reach you safely.

I also hope that you will be pleased with them altho' it will be very evident to you that I am a very inexpert wood carver.

The oak is genuine antique stuff that I got from a dealer before we left Wales.

Of course the panels explain themselves, and I hope the expression and so forth will seem to you appropriate to each subject. I am sorry the child's face is not very satisfactory, and I am not very pleased with that of the young man in the centre panel. Personally I am pleased with the figures of the mother, and of the young woman in the middle, and I do not think the dead man is altogether a failure. [. . .]

I can only add that I am very grateful to you for your patience in waiting so long. The delay has been caused chiefly by work for the Golden Cockerel Press and various architectural carvings. [. . .] Yours sincerely,   ERIC GILL

[1] These panels are reproduced on the last page of *It All Goes Together* (Devin-Adair, New York, 1944).

173 : TO G. T. FRIEND

Pigotts   *16-1-1930*

Dear Friend: Yours to hand.

As to the question: which side was Christ wounded?:—
The question has not I believe ever been decided. I made
enquiries on my own account some years ago and was informed
that there was no certainty in the matter. I understand there
is no decisive text in the Gospels. I was told:—that in ancient
times the wound was usually shown on His *right* side but
during the last several hundred years, i.e. since the growth of
devotion to the Sacred Heart, the tendency has been for
artists to place the wound under the heart on His *left* side.

As to the rib question. I think there is no doubt (a) the
wound should be clearly between the ribs or (b) below the
bottom rib. If the spear were pointed up from below it wd.
easily pierce the heart although entering the body below the
bottom rib.

Tradition has it (and *n.b.* tradition is more authoritative
than surmise) that the wound was given by the Centurion.
But, as you say, it does not really matter. The only essential
is that it shd. be towards one *side* or the other. Yours sincerely,

ERIC GILL

174 : TO HIS BROTHER EVAN

Pigotts   *13-2-1930*

My dear Evan: Thank you very much for returning my MS.
and for your letter. [. . .]

Thank you for sending the 'form of Service'. I was very
interested in it though I must say I do not fully appreciate that
imitation 'Common Prayer' style.[1] And the whole thing

[1] *The Form and Order of the Consecration of the Cathedral Church of Christ in
Liverpool* (1924). It includes the rubric: '*Then shall the cathedral organist*, H. Goss
Custard, *make music.*'

seems to me a good example of what M. Julien Benda calls the Great Betrayal. You ought to read his book. I haven't read anything for ever so long, more to the point. The English version is called *The Great Betrayal* and is published by Routledge. [. . .] Yours,   ERIC

175 : TO G. K. CHESTERTON

Pigotts   *26-3-1930*

Dear Mr. Chesterton: The *Studio* sent me the number with your review of my book in it. I am most gratified & honoured by what you have written & thank you very much. Of course we really are agreed about the 'representation' business. My trouble is that, being only an amateur writer & writing only at odd times, I have never been able to sit down & deal adequately with the whole business. Consequently I have only dealt with those things by which I have been stung & therefore give an impression of one-eyedness. You remember the Sailor in *The Four Men* who, on the last night of the journey, sang a song about the wicked moneymakers & an old country man got up and said, at the end, 'we must all get on, maister' to which the sailor replied: 'yes, but I give you to understand that they overdo it in the towns' (or words to that effect). Well, I find that remark most useful and in this case, with reference to 'representation' in art, I might say 'Yes, master, but they overdo it in the art schools' or pr'aps it is n't that they overdo the anatomical exactitude business so much as underdo the other thing. I had a little fling on this same subject in the current (March) *Architectural Review*. I wd. much like to know how that one strikes you.

Again, thank you v. much for your review. Yours affectly.

                                                          ERIC G.

176 : TO A. D. KNOX

[Among E. G.'s neighbours at North Dean was A. D. Knox (d. 1943), the distinguished classical scholar who edited the Mimes of Herodes. He sometimes wrote epigrams on his acquaintance, and sent E. G. the following lines:

> A rancorous hate and envy fills
> My soul at sight of daffodils.
> May I not wander dressed as they,
> A green and yellow popinjay?
> There's nothing vexes so my heart
> As Nature when she conquers art.
> This is the testament of Eric Gill,
> Residing on the top of Pigotts Hill.

E. G. rejoined appropriately.]

Pigotts   *2-5-1930*

TO A. Δ. K.

> I thank you for your pretty song;
> 'Tis pity that its thought is wrong.
> For Nature never conquers Art;
> 'Tis man who oft neglects his part.
> Nature in blind obedience moves;
> Man's works are prompted by his loves.
> And thus on Nature Art improvement proves;
> Save when in temples men go selling doves.

> Such rancour then as fills my mind
> Is of a somewhat different kind —
> 'Tis not that Nature is too good
> But that men spurn their heavenly food
> And, both in 'Corner House' and cottage,
> Barter their souls for mess of pottage.
> My ground is really quite like Peter's rocks,
> So you must hit more, harder, bloodier, Knox.

E. G.

177 : TO GORDON MACFARLANE

Pigotts   *23-10-1930*

I am much better. They brought me home yesterday. I am however to do next to nothing for a while. Touching that matter of the theology of 'The Natural Man': I can think of nothing better to illustrate my meaning to you, an architect and a father, than that Psalm *Nisi Dominus* — Unless the Lord build the house they labour in vain that build it — and every verse of the Psalm has, in addition to its literal meaning, that significance. You as architect are a builder of the Lord's houses, as a father you are a father of the Lord's children — happy if your quiver be full of such — and it is no use getting up early and expecting to escape. There is no escape. We are *His* people.   E. G.

178 : TO MISS PRISCILLA JOHNSTON

Pigotts   *29-10-1930*

Dear Priscilla: I've just read your *Narrow World* and hope it won't come amiss if I write and tell you that I like it very much — in fact I was absolutely enthralled by it. I think it was most wise of you to write about *school* seeing it was a world you had only just left — how much better than writing of a world you had only just entered. And I was so intrigued to know what a modern girls' school was like. I must say it's pretty fairly incredible — but I take your word for it. What strikes me is (a) the extraordinary laxity in real discipline — at least that's the impression I get — i.e. mental discipline and, even more, (b) the apparently complete absence of any kind of real religion — there is only apparently a sentimental (no harm in sentiment, I don't mean that sentiment is bad — not at all) & emotional attachment to hymns & cards and the thrills of seasonal celebrations. And (a) & (b) are very much connected. There doesn't seem to be the least awareness of God as in & behind & above every thing. I doubt if the word God occurs in the book. You'll understand this is not a criticism of the book but simply an expression of surprise at the nature of the thing described in the book. It seems so completely secular and merely ethical & girl guide ethical at that. Is it really true? I think the book is very melodramatic —but I like melodrama. How I wanted to screw the villain's elegant neck —how I suffered with poor Joyce —how I rejoiced at her amendment & success in the lacrosse match at the end. But still it is a bit overdone when you look at it seriously. I mean Joyce is *too* weakminded for a girl of her sort. After all she's 'a jolly good sort' & her home life & horse riding & what not do imply a less completely lead-astrayable girl. I'm surprised you didn't get her into much more serious trouble still — letting her go about in bed & elsewhere with that Nita of hateful memory. Then Nita is *too* wicked if she was really as attractive as you affirm or she's *too* attractive if she was really as wicked. Then Alix —she's too uniformly *good*. But then who can blame you? —surely the most difficult job on earth is to write convincingly of & make attractive a really good schoolgirl. Look how Dickens went to pieces with his good girls! But in spite of and to some extent because of its melo-dramatic quality I do think the book is good. The psychology, especially in one or two special places, seems to me admirable (i.e. in so far as I know anything about the psyches of school girls) and generally speaking the analogy between the 'Narrow' world & the so-called wider world of adult life is very well done. Moreover the way you managed to hold the scales evenly & not get bitter & disgruntled about a world which in many ways is more damn silly than merely narrow is, well, very noble of you. Give my love to your most dear father[1] & remember me kindly to your mother & sisters —Yrs. sincerely

ERIC GILL

Please forgive such small & illegible writing —it's done in bed —after 'fluenza.

[1] Edward Johnston.

179 : TO DR. G. G. COULTON

Pigotts   *1-1-1931*

My dear Dr. Coulton: I think you honour me very greatly by sending me the galley of your preface but I am too highly honoured for I am no scholar of any sort and know as near as no matter nothing about the matters involved nor do I see any newspapers, either religious or secular or ecclesiastical, so I am even ignorant of what happened at Liverpool. 'The Catholic Church proceeds confidently in her doctrine of God' and she is the only body known to me which does so. That's all I ask of her or ever did ask. From that confident procession all other important things proceed — personal sanctity, social & political order and, as a certain theologian said, 'even the arts and crafts' are affected. Then you say or ask: What about Honorius the third or Eugenius the fifth? Moreover I myself possess a document (at least I think I've still got it) of Bp. Challoner's in which he most indignantly repudiates the notion of Papal Infallibility as an impious fable. And so on. Well, it seems to me that historical research is very much like trying to shoot the sq. root of 2 with a gun (Wells' phrase) — it doesn't touch the spot — there isn't a spot to touch. It only leads to horrid wrangling & misunderstanding. Moreover the best Catholics or, if you like, the best Christians are not historians any more than the best philosophers are gardeners or mechanical engineers. History seems to *me* a sort of highly interesting hobby. But now I'm being inadvertently rude to you and I didn't mean to be at all. I only mean that, though one knows there must be true history or false, the discovery of which is which is, compared with the knowledge and love of God, unimportant. I'm trying as much as possible in all that I write (and think) to avoid the historical basis — it's beyond my competence, anyway, to judge the value of documentary evidence. I remember at all hours the Preacher's words in Ecclesiasticus (ch. 38, vv. 25-39) where, speaking of the craftsman, he says that tho. without him a city is not built yet he shall not go up & down therein nor sit where judgment is given, i.e. he should keep out of politics and suchlike. (I regret my ignorance of this in former years!) So, tho' I like nothing more than metaphysical arguments and, at the other end of the pole, arguments as to how to use chisels, I'm no use to you in your job. I am most sorry. I send the galley back herewith; without notes so that you can choose another fourth man. I really thank you very much indeed for thinking of me. I look forward to seeing you again when next I come to Cambridge and I do wish you could come and see us here — this is a jolly fine place, this is. I hope you are well after your holiday & will have a very happy new year. Please remember me kindly to Mrs. Coulton. I am yrs. affectionately

ERIC GILL

P.S. On second thoughts and on rereading the galley, I've marked in pencil a few places which strike me as unnecessarily rude or unintelligible. I take it you share my dislike of the R.P.A. style.

E. G.

180 : TO DR. G. G. COULTON

[This answers a letter of Dr. Coulton's from which I make two extracts:

'I thought we agreed long ago that there were to be no M^r·s or D^r·s between us: if I put one in inadvertently when I wrote from Caux please forgive me . . . Your letter I think it must have been which stimulated one of the strangest & most realistic dreams I have ever had last night. I think we must have been in Mexico, somewhere at least where religion is bitterly persecuted. There was some sort of public call & a question whether there was anyone ready to die for his faith. A Roman Catholic priest at once came forward, dressed in that black costume that hides the whole face, e.g. the *Misericordia* costume in Italy. I have a sort of feeling that if I had seen his face it would have been Father Reeves — the Dominican who heckled me at Cambridge last year. Anyhow he came forward at once & went up somewhere; & then practically without an interval (you remember the wonderful scene-shifting of a dream) he was back again in his black *Misericordia* on the left of a regular stage which was crowded with niggers, singing negro spirituals & beating time with their umbrellas on their hats. The enthusiasm of the crowd behind me was in measure with theirs: the whole atmosphere was one of magnificent triumph for Theism as against Atheism. He said nothing & didn't move & the dream left me wondering whether he felt he had scored a victory for the faith or whether he was distressed at finding himself involved in a non-authorised religious manifestation . . .']

Pigotts   *24-1-1931*

Dear Coulton: I am very sorry to hear you have been ill. I hope you are quite well again. Thank you indeed for your letter. (No, the 'Dr.' was a slip on my part — take it as an abbreviated form of endearment). I am most interested in your astonishing dream. Fr. J-B. Reeves would be much flattered. Do you know of a Belgian historian called Kurth? He says somewhere in his book on *The Church at the Turning Points of History* the modern priest is 'more ready for martyr-dom than the apostolate'. I think you would agree. I look forward to seeing you here and at Cambridge if I get a chance of coming. Yours affectionately,   ERIC G.

181 : TO HIS BROTHER CECIL

Pigotts   ⟨1931⟩

My dear Cecil: That truly beautiful soup licker, spoon, dagger, paper knife & what not[1] arrived safely & very nearly sound (only a small tip broken — but what trust in Providence you do display in your packing!). I am, we are, they are, he & she are absolutely thrilled by it. It is simply superb both in design & workmanship. Thank you very much indeed. Would that I could write an adequate letter of thanks or indeed of any sort. But no, at present I'm so pressed with work that I not

[1] From New Guinea.

only mustn't but can't. So I will only say we are all well & we hope you are. Joanna is expecting a babe & hoping for a daughter at Christmas. The printing work is going strongly & the B.B.C. Sculpture job is in hand – also other works. The book on *Clothes* is just out. I am sending Romney a copy. He will doubtless pass it on. I must stop – it seems very churlish but you will forgive. Every blessing be yours & much love from us all & hopes that you are quite well again & strong & at work & enjoying life & love. From your bro.   ERIC G.

182 : TO THE REV. DESMOND CHUTE

Pigotts   15-2-1931

My dearest Desmond: Thank you very much for your letter of Jan 29. It is indeed bad news. We are much concerned & distressed. I will say 'novenas be blowed' and continue praying.

Meanwhile I am glad you have the consolations of music and that reminds me: I've got that B.B.C. job and am even now in the thick of making designs. There is a huge group, ten feet high, representing Prospero & Ariel and these panels – (a) Ariel, supported by angels learning celestial music, (b) Ariel between wisdom & gaiety (c) Ariel piping to the children. The panels are about 6 feet long by 4 high. The big statue goes in a niche about 20 feet up. & the panels about 13 feet up. The building is commendably plain & machine made in appearance as in fact.

This job will occupy all 1931 and as it is well paid we are in luck. [. . .] Betty's baby – Helen Elizabeth – was born a month ago. All well. Her eldest, Stephen, has been staying here & has just gone home again – a very bright lad he is.

Hilary is down with pleurisy & pneumonia – but is better – out of danger they say.

Joseph is working here on a monument job for me at

present; he is well. [. . .] I am about to begin engravings for G.C. Press *Four Gospels*. The *Clothes* book has gone to Press (Cambridge Univ^y. Press). René H & Joanna are very happy and contented & comfortable.

René is busy printing a book on *Typography*.

We all send you our love and condolences and will continue our prayers. Your loving bro. in S.D.   ERIC G.

Enclosed prints are illustrations to *Clothes*

There are 10 altogether.

183 : TO GRAHAM CAREY

Pigotts   15-2-1931

Dear Carey: Many thanks for your letter of Jan 21. I would have replied sooner but have been very much rushed lately doing designs for some sculptures on the new British Broadcasting Corporation's building in London.

Thank you very much, I am quite well again & my fortnight in hospital was in fact a nice holiday and a week at the seaside was a delightful novelty.

I am very glad you liked the bedstead when at last you saw it. I'm sorry about the spelling mistake but, as you say, you can easily put that right and also the scale of the carved pattern.

I am interested to hear that you came on that silver alms dish. I made a very rough pencil drawing and it was carried out in the first place by a young man in the metal work dept. of the Ryl. Coll. of Art at S. Kensington. He did it v. nicely but without any real understanding. Then someone else made a copy and apart from criticising this while the work was in progress I did nothing – did not even see it finished. The thing was done at the instigation of the London Goldsmiths' Company. But, as you perceive, things can't be done like that. And those attempts to bolster up Industrialism by collaboration between 'artists' & manufacturers are all bosh. I am interested in your

R

plaque à jour & will enclose a design on spec. with this. I hope you will like it & find it workable. The arrangement you suggest is v. generous. I look forward to seeing the result. I hope you will visit us again before long. Yours sincerely

ERIC G.

Did I thank you for your solution of spider & fly problem? V. good & painstaking but lacking just that flick of perfection which the true solution has.

184 : TO 'THE ARCHITECTS' JOURNAL' 4TH MARCH, 1931

Sir: Mr. A. J. Penty's article on 'Engineers and Aesthetics' in your issue for February 18 is obviously of great importance at the present time. Doubtless a lot of nonsense is talked and written, by me and others, about the beauty of engineering and the unimportance of architects, and therefore we can only be grateful when our slips are shown up. I have said a lot about the Forth Bridge as an example of 'functional beauty' and about ships, and now I am informed (or, rather, I was informed in 1926) that the curved cantilevers of the bridge were made thus for 'elegance,' and that the funnels of liners are raked for the same reason.

But, Sir, my proverbial withers take a lot more than that to wring them, I do assure you. When I learn that a Buckingham-shire cottage was pulled down in order to supply real old red bricks for the 'Tudor' smoking-room of the 'Berengaria,' I am more inclined to say, 'Some architect hath done this,' than to blame the engineers; and when I was told about the curved cantilevers, and heard the profound words, 'compressional members,' I could only say, 'Well, I never knew they *were* curved.' For the beauty of the bridge and of the liner is quite independent of such trifling as imitation arches, sloping funnels or Tudor bricks — such things mar rather than make their beauty.

Indeed, the whole trouble lies in that dope word, 'aesthetics.' The respectable Annandale says it means 'the theory of the fine arts; the science . . . of the beautiful; the doctrines of taste,' and no one can complain of that. But, getting down to it, why, we may ask, are things called beautiful? People find that kind of question annoying, I know; but if your contributors are going to make their arguments hang on the word, we must at least know what they mean by it. I know what I mean, and it is this: beautiful things are those which please when seen —and, of course, I mean mentally seen, and therefore pleasing to the mind. I don't mean anything else at all.

But obviously there are all sorts of mental pleasures, and therefore all sorts of beauties. One sort of thing is more naturally the product of our industrial system of manufacture than another. Steel and concrete building is the natural product of industrialism, as stone building was naturally the product of other times. Writing was the natural product of the Middle Ages as printing is of today. Fur is the natural clothing of the Esquimaux as cotton is of the Hindus, and to say that some of these things are beautiful and others not is pure art-nonsense.

Anything is beautiful if it be made in such a way as to give pleasure to the mind which perceives it, and the question as to what should or should not give pleasure to the mind is no more and no less difficult than the question as to what should or should not give annoyance. I am annoyed, and so, Sir, doubtless are you, by any manifestation of diabolism (grand word for deceit), and so sham funnels annoy me. I should also be annoyed by those curved cantilevers if I took them seriously enough. As it is, I regard them as pretty harmless foibles — but I'd rather have them straight as in the bridge at Quebec. And it still remains true that 'if you look after goodness and truth, beauty will take care of itself,' provided that your notions of those divine attributes are respectable and you do not 'kid' yourself.

The thing called 'functional beauty' is the beauty of bones

and beetles and plain railway girders and plain precipices. There are other beauties. There is the beauty of the west window of Chartres and the beauty of, say, Persian carpets. There is also the beauty of holiness. Our age would be quite good at the production of the first kind, and even of the last, if it would give its mind to it and forget about aesthetics.

ERIC GILL

185 : TO 'ARCHITECTURAL DESIGN & CONSTRUCTION', OCTOBER, 1931

Sir: I am grateful for the gracious review of *Clothes* in your current issue. But may I point out that there is some misunderstanding involved in your reviewer's remarks about Puritanism and architecture? He complains that my plea for plain architecture savours of the Puritanism I condemn. But, as I said at length in the book, our present method of manufacture and building (which we call industrialism) is the product of Puritanism and so the proper architecture of industrialism is plain architecture just as the proper clothes of the Puritan are plain clothes. Yours faithfully,   ERIC GILL

186 : TO THE REV. DESMOND CHUTE

Pigotts   *8-10-1931*

My dearest Desmond: So she is gone — praise to God & thanks — joy submerges sorrow. A good life and a long life (as earthly length is measured) is matter for rejoicing. The work leaves the workshop — seventy years in the making — may the Customer be pleased with it. A poor simile but better than one implying that there is no Jerusalem to be adorned. I dare say that you will feel your mother's going very poignantly, there were many bonds between you and, considering the difference of view and interest, her patience and generosity, in the presence of what, to her, must have been your strange enthusiasms, were great & very tender. If you need consolation, may we help to console. If you weep we weep with you; if you rejoice we rejoice. Your loving brother in St. Dominic.　　　　　　　　　　　　　　ERIC G.

187 : TO THE REV. DESMOND CHUTE

Pigotts　　　　　　　　　　　　　　*22-11-1931*

My dearest Desmond: Herewith sketches for gravestones. I hope you will approve. They are very rough. [. . .]

As to the figure of *Christ*: I hope you'll approve the robed & crowned version. I'd rather *carve* the naked figure but it seems to me: 1, Christ the King is what is wanted to-day — more than Christ the victim. 2, the risen Christ is more the thing for a Christian's grave than the dying or the dead Christ. But I'll bow to your wishes in this matter.

I hope all is well with you. Have you seen the *Song of Songs* book[1] at Cleverdon's? Pity about the poor printing of the engravings. Much love from your bro.　　　　　　　E. G.

P.S. Gilbert Spencer is coming this p.m. with his wife (Ursula, née Bradshaw) with ref. to tombstone for *her* father.

188 : TO DAVID JONES

Pigotts　　　　　　　　　　　　　*on Good Friday, 1932*

my dear & my dear david, I hope you will be having a very hap⟨p⟩y Easter and gaudium de veritate.
I am very sorry to hear that you were not well enough to go to Caldey after all. I am very sorry. We are all well here except me, and I am only tired. I hope perhaps I shall see you

---

[1] The Cranach Press edition (Latin text, 1931), not the Golden Cockerel (English text, 1925).

next week and in any case on Tuesday evening of *April the 5th*
at the Aquinas Soc[y].

It is a lovely day here. Denis & René Bill — Ansted are
levelling the new tennis court. We have just come back from
Wycombe where we went to 'make' the Stations and to adore
the true Cross. René H. is out giving his young wife a lesson
in motor driving. Mary is just bringing in tea. I am trying
some new pens. I am sorry I am making such a mess. I must
now begin some designs for tombstones.

I am coming back to London on Tuesday next (the 29th) to
go on with the B B C job. Now I must stop this therefore
with much love from your bro. in ✠.   E. G.

Please give our love and Easter greetings to your dear parents.
We hope they are well.

[Photographed as frontispiece]

189 : TO 'THE TIMES LITERARY
SUPPLEMENT', 26 MAY, 1932

Sir: In the second volume of Sir William Rothenstein's often
entertaining memoirs[1] it is stated (p. 201) that 'for Gill
modelling was a cardinal sin'.

On page 280 (footnote) reference is made to a small work
of mine in coloured plaster — an image of the Madonna and
Child. The original of this image was modelled in clay. A
copy, in bronze, was purchased by the Johannesburg Art
Gallery, Sir William himself possesses a copy, and many
others are in private ownership.

I have never said or thought that modelling was sinful or
even silly. On the contrary, I have frequently said and written
that carving and modelling are two arts, each having its own
proper good qualities — as is obvious.

This matter is of much importance to artists and critics,

[1] *Men and Memories: Recollections of William Rothenstein, 1900-1922* (1932).

and it is important that the public should not be misled. I shall be grateful if you will allow it to be recorded that I do not hold, and have never held, the opinion often before and now again attributed to me.

Again, on page 189 of Sir William's book it is stated that I taught stone-carving under the late Professor Lethaby at the Regent-street School of Arts and Crafts. For the sake of historical accuracy I think it should be recorded that I never taught at that school; nor have I taught stone-carving anywhere but in my own workshops.   ERIC GILL

Pigotts, North Dean, High Wycombe.

190 : TO HIS BROTHER EVAN

Capel-y-ffin, Abergavenny   *28-5-1932*

My dear Evan: Here is chq. $\frac{s}{7}$/6. I'd have sent it before (long ago) but I've been thinking I'd send a P.O. & I've kept forgetting (except when I was not near a post office). Many thanks for seeing about the book.

Also I've been hoping to be able to write to you & Maillie to say thank you very much for your most kind remembrance of my birthday. But pressure of work has been v. great all this winter & I've had to put all private letters aside. (haven't yet written to Romney or Cecil for Christmas!) Also I had bronchitis & 'flu & lost a lot of time over them. Now I've come down here with Mary & Gordian for a week's rest & so I'm able to write to mere friends & relations . . . We did pity you all when you had the mumps. Poor, poor, things. I trust that is all a thing of the past. As for us. We are all well at present. Renà & Joanna & their Michael are coming down to-morrow & we all return together at end of next week. Then I'll be hard put to it to get statue of 'The Sower' done in time for King's visit to B.B.C. in mid. of July. All this winter I've been doing the three panels on the outside of the building. Bad weather, bad stone, & bad health. But they're done at last. Item: I'm coming to speak at the architects' conference at Manchester on June 16. The meeting is in the morning. Could I spend the *previous* night with you? Don't hesitate to say 'no' if it's not convenient. I'd like to v. much if I may. I must return home in the afternoon. Can't afford time to stay longer. Again thank you & Maillie very much for remembrance. My love —our love to you both. More news must wait till, as I hope, we meet. Your bro.   ERIC

We drove over to Dormansland & saw Father last Sunday. It's a very comfortable & excellent place & the other inhabitants are most kind & good to him & v. nice people too. Haven't seen Max lately. We hope you are all quite well & work flourishing. God! What a mess the bloody financiers are in — As I said to the manager of 'my' bank when he asked me what my prospects were for 1932: 'that depends on you chaps —it's your bloody mess, not mine'. To which he laughed & said it was so!

191 : TO HIS NEPHEW PETER GILL

Capel-y-ffin, St. Augustine's Day[1]   *1932*

My dear Peter: I hope you are quite well. Thank you and Michael & Susan very much indeed for your letters on my birthday. Love from uncle   ERIC
I am having a rest here—as you see.

[*Photograph opposite*]

192 : TO DR. COOMARASWAMY

Pigotts   *26-6-1932*

My dear Coomaraswamy: I hope you have got the bookplates safely by this time & that they are to your liking. I wish you had a better one.

I received your *Introduction to the Art of E. Asia.* I had

[1] St. Augustine of Canterbury, May 28th.

Capel-y-ffin, St Augustine's Day 1932

My dear Peter. . I hope you are quite
well. Thank you and Michael & Susan
very much indeed for your letters on
my birthday. Love from uncle Eric
I am having a rest here — as you see.

LETTER TO PETER GILL

already got a copy (sent to me, I think, by the Museum) & had just finished reading it when the post brought the inscribed copy from you. I think it is absolutely first class. Just splendid, excellent, good —words fail me. I want at least half a dozen more copies. Can you tell the publishers to send them —with bill. I need not say I am terrifically 'bucked' & flattered by your various references to my writings (especially by your quoting of me in the text). But, apart from that, I think it's the best thing in a small way that's been done in the way of elucidation & illumination. I suppose you're right in what you say on p. 13 about Eckhart & others being unorthodox and about the identification of knower & known being *heretical* in European religion —I doubt it. Of course there has been all along in Europe a great insistence on the value & reality of individual experience & responsibility. But does it amount to a condemnation as heretical of doctrines which lay more stress on identification & submergence —unity of Soul & God etc.? I think I could put up a good show of quite respectable orthodox people (John of the Cross, Denis, St. Thos. Aq. etc.) who have written & taught the identification doctrine. My reading isn't half as wide as yours but I think that generally (if not absolutely always) writings and teachings condemned as heretical have been condemned rather on account of some implicit or explicit *denial* than on account of any thing affirmed. Nevertheless I suppose, and I get the supposition largely from you, that in India there is a more general appreciation of 'the unitive life', of the identification of lover & beloved, than there is or ever has been among our, as it appears, more active & fussy & inventive people. Hence our obsession with morals. Hence the police.

I hope you are quite well —you and yours. I wish I could come to see you in Boston. I wish you could come to see us here. We are all well. We have 5 & nearly 7 grandchildren now! All our three daughters are married —one to a farmer in Sussex, one to a painter & engraver & one to a printer. The two latter live & work here.

I enclose for your acceptance a few rough prints of a set of engravings I did last year for a *Song of Songs* printed by Kessler at Weimar (but he printed the engravings exceedingly badly). I hope you'll approve of them. I also enclose a pamphlet which I hope you'll approve of and a type specimen from our press here. Yours very sincerely   ERIC GILL

Dont forget to send me the half doz. copies of your pamphlet if they're available.

193 : TO DOUGLAS CLEVERDON

(In train to Cambridge)   *16-7-1932*

Many thanks for yours. Will write on my return home next week. Got to go to C. to carve a crocodile . . .[1] What shd. we know of reptiles who only reptiles know? Love to all. E. G.

194 : TO HIS BROTHER CECIL

Capel-y-ffin   *29-8-1932*

My dear Cecil & Nonie: I've been wanting to write to you for about a year and a half — perhaps longer. It's not been possible in the rush of work which has overwhelmed me during that time to deal with letters to relations or friends. However I'm having a few days holiday at Capel and letters to you & Romney are no longer going to be delayed. [. . .] Meanwhile work at Pigotts goes on strong. I am still entirely occupied with the carvings on the B.B.C. building in London. I was working all the winter on the panels over the doors on the outside of the building. Now they are done and I am about to begin the statue, representing a man 'Broadcasting', to stand in the entrance hall. Comic thought, when you consider the quality of B.B.C. semination, to compare it with the efforts of a simple countryman sowing corn! However it's

[1] For the Mond Laboratory, in brick.

their idea, not mine. Mine not to reason why . . . mine simply, to carve a good image of a broadcaster. After that there's a big (11 foot high) group, representing 'Prospero & Ariel', to go in a niche over the main entrance. Comic thought again —the B.B.C. kidding itself that it may be likened to a sort of wise old prince putting the world to rights & its bally apparatus likened to a sort of heavenly sprite! I will try & send you photos when the work is done. Pray for its success. René Hague is going strong with the printing. He's just starting an edition of *Hamlet* for an American publisher. Lucky to get the job in these mad times. It will take him at least the rest of this year & a bit more. I'm to do 5 engravings for it & initial letters. We published our first book last Christmas (just before Christmas) —a book on Typography — sub-title:—*Printing & Piety, an essay on life & works in the England of 1931*. We printed 500 & have sold over 400 so it's not too bad. *Clothes* is about to be translated into German! What ho. Times are very bad in England —in Europe & America & everywhere. Do you notice anything in Papua? Seems to me very doubtful whether we'll pull through without catastrophe. Are the bankers clever enough? They don't look like it. Mary is writing to Nonie. I do send you my love. I do indeed. *Orate pro invicem.* When shall we meet again? Your bro.   ERIC

195 : TO 'THE NEW STATESMAN AND NATION', 8TH OCT., 1932

The 'Times' Coat of Arms

Sir: I am honoured by your reference to me in your issue of October 1st.[1] I hasten to inform you, however, that I was

[1] 'It is a pity, we think, that it was not decided to cut a new coat-of-arms to accompany appropriately the new Roman title; the present coat is a very depraved piece of work, but no worse than the simpering lion and disgusted unicorn, both of obviously vegetable origin, which are to take its place. Why did not the *Times* ask Mr. Eric Gill to give it a coat-of-arms?'

approached by the responsible authority with a view to my engraving a new coat of arms to accompany the new Roman title of the *Times* and I decided it was not my job. May I explain briefly?

1. When you consider the nature of modern life, modern religion, politics, arts and manufactures it is clear that the mediaeval business of shields and emblems has no proper place. Such things have degenerated into either family or institutional snobbery or into sentimentality and blindness to the real state of things. The display of a coat of arms (or even a crest) to-day proclaims a romantic or a snob.

2. But because I don't want to be a prig, even in the cause of reason, I am quite willing to undertake the carving or engraving of heraldic devices, as a job and to order. Here a fresh set of difficulties arises. You cannot make a good pair of boots for a committee. The only thing you can make well when you are up against a group of varying minds is something measurable, something patient of statement in defined terms. How can you state or define the expression of a lion's nose? And it is just such things which make the difference between the living and the dead.

The success of an engraving depends upon the sensibility and good sense of the artist and upon his freedom (i.e., responsibility). When the artist is in the position to deal with a personal customer there is fair give and take. The needs of the one and the knowledge and sensibility of the other are more or less amicably combined. But when the customer is not a person and when, in addition, this impersonal customer wants something which the artist thinks rather silly and out of date, then the job had better be turned down.

In the case of the *Times* coat of arms there were too many people to be pleased and not enough reason for pleasing them.

But I do want it to be clear that the blame, if any, is mine, not theirs; they did ask me and I refused.   ERIC GILL

High Wycombe

Piggotts. 16.12.32.

I am most sorry I wasn't well
enough to come to London on
Wednesday. It wd. have been
fine to have met you and Mary.
I am better now. The cold on the
scaffold last week did me in. I all
swole up! Much love to you and all. I hope your
visit was pleasant. Eric.

POSTCARD TO EVAN GILL

196 : TO HIS BROTHER EVAN

Pigotts   *16-12-1932*

I am most sorry I wasn't well enough to come to London on Wednesday. It wd. have been fine to have met you and Max. I am better now. The cold on the scaffold last week did me in. I all swole up! Much love to you and all. I hope your visit was pleasant.   ERIC

[Photograph opposite]

197 : TO 'THE LONDON & NORTH EASTERN RAILWAY MAGAZINE', JANUARY, 1933

On the Flying Scotsman

'Well, did you get your ride on the Engine?'

'Rather!'

'What was it like?'

'Marvellous, simply marvellous — a jolly sight more marvellous than you'd expect and yet in some ways quite the opposite.'

I got to King's Cross about 9.30 (wasn't going to risk being late) and, after a cup of tea and a sandwich, I ventured into the Guard's van of the train, at which the guard, looking very spruce, had just arrived with bag and flags and what not, and said: 'I say, good morning, look here, it's like this; I've got this engine pass to Grantham.' 'Oh, have you?' 'Yes, and, I say, can I leave my bag in here till I come off the engine?' No objection to that, so I stepped back on to the platform and there I saw Mr. Sparke, the District Locomotive Superintendent, and a friend of his. Mr. Sparke had very kindly come to introduce me to Mr. Young of Newcastle, the driver of the engine, and his friend kindly presented me with a nice clean swab to wipe my hands on from time to time. (Forgot all about it afterwards, but kept it as a memento!) The engine,

No. 2582 of Newcastle, then backed in and I was introduced to Mr. Young — very grand and important and an object of curiosity to the group of enthusiasts on the platform (I mean me, not Mr. Young).

I was born beside the railway at Brighton, and I spent most of my childhood examining and drawing locomotives, and what surprised me now was, first, how little things had changed in fundamentals since I was a child 35 years ago and, second, how simple in idea the mechanism of steam engines still is. A detail that struck me immediately was that the throttle lever on the L.N.E.R. engine was worked by pulling it upwards towards you, whereas on the engines of my Brighton childhood it was worked by a lever at right angles to the axis of the boiler.

The remaining few minutes were spent in explanations of the brake apparatus, steam pressure required — the names of this and that and then someone called up from outside: 'right you are' and I gathered that it must be exactly 10.0. The engine was driven from the right hand side, so I was given the piano-stool or perch on the left side, with one foot on a pail (a quite ordinary household-looking pail) and the other dangling. Up to this time the fireman had been doing various odd jobs about the place. He now shut (if you can call it shutting, for it only about half covered the gap) the iron door between engine and tender, and Mr. Young, having made a suitable response to the man outside who had shouted 'right you are,' pulled up the handle (both hands to the job and not too much at a time — a mouthful, so to say, for a start, to let her feel the weight) and, well, we simply started forward. It's as simple as that. I mean it *looks* as simple as that.

And, immediately, the fireman started shovelling coal. I shouted some apology to him for taking his seat. I could not hear his reply. It was probably to say that he had no time for seats. He shovelled in about 6 shovelsful; then, after a few seconds pause, another half dozen — a few seconds pause and then six or more shovels and so on practically without stopping the whole time. What strikes you about this, even more than the colossal labour of the thing and the great skill with which he distributes the coal in the fire and his unerring aim in throwing a pretty big shovelful of coal through a not very large opening, what strikes you is the extraordinary primitive nature of the job. You stand in a space about as big as a hearthrug spread out longways to the fire and you take a shovelful of coal out of a hole at one end and throw it through a hole in the other end – spilling a bit every time. You go on doing this for hours. Your attention must be as great as your skill and strength. You must watch the pressure gauges and you must watch the state of the fire at the same time. And your only relaxations are when, on entering tunnels or passing stations, you give a tug at the whistle handle and when, on a signal from the driver, you let down the water scoop to take up water from the trough between the rails (which occurs every hundred miles or so). And talking of primitive things, look at the whistle handle! It is a round ring on the end of a wire (there is one on each side of the cab). It dangles down about a foot from the roof. When the train is travelling fast you have to make a bit of a grab for it as it is never in the same place for two seconds together. On receiving a nod of acquiescence from Mr. Young, I pulled the handle myself as we approached Peterborough, and again as we went, at reduced speed, through the station itself. (My first pull was but a timid little shriek, but my second was, it seemed to me, a long bold blast.)

But don't imagine I'm complaining or sneering about this primitiveness. It's no more primitive or less venerable than sawing with a hand saw or ploughing with a horse plough. I only think that it's surprising how these primitive methods persist. Here we were on an engine of the most powerful kind in the world, attached to one of the most famous of all travelling hotels – the string of coaches called The Flying Scotsman – with its Cocktail Bar and Beauty Parlours, its dining saloons, decorated in more or less credible imitation of the salons of 18th century France, its waiters and guards and attendants of all sorts, its ventilation and heating apparatus as efficient as those of the Strand Palace Hotel, and here we were carrying on as if we were pulling a string of coal trucks.

All the luxury and culture of the world depends ultimately upon the efforts of the labourer. This fact has often been described in books. It has often been the subject of cartoons and pictures — the sweating labourer groaning beneath the weight of all the arts and sciences, the pomps and prides of the world — but here it was in plain daily life.

And what made it even more obvious was the complete absence of connection with the train behind us. The train was there — you could see it if you looked out when going round a bend — but that was all. And just as the passenger very seldom thinks about the men on the engine, so we thought nothing at all about the passengers. They were simply part of the load. Indeed there may not have been any passengers — we weren't aware of any.

And the absence of connection between engine and train was emphasized by the entirely different physical sensations which engine travelling gives you. The noise is different — you never for a moment cease to hear, and to feel, the effort of the pistons. The shriek of the whistle splits your ears, a hundred other noises drown any attempt at conversation.

Though the engine is well sprung, there is a feeling of hard contact on the rails all the time — something like riding on an enormously heavy solid-tyred bicycle. And that rhythmic tune which you hear when travelling in the train, the rhythm of the wheels as they go over the joins in the metals (iddy UMty . . . iddy UMty . . . &c.) is entirely absent. There is simply a continuous iddyiddyiddy . . . there is no sensation of travelling *in* a train — you are travelling *on* an engine. You are on top of an extremely heavy sort of cart horse which is discharging its terrific pent-up energy by the innumerable outbursts of its breath.

And continuously the fireman works, and continuously the

driver, one hand on the throttle lever, the other ready near the brake handle (a handle no bigger than that of a bicycle and yet controlling power sufficient to pull up a train weighing 500 tons) keeps watch on the line ahead for a possible adverse signal. If the signals are down they go straight ahead, slowing down only for the sharper curves and the bigger railway junctions. You place absolute trust in the organization of the line and you know practically every yard of it by sight. You dash roaring into the small black hole of a tunnel (the impression you get is that it's a marvel you don't miss it sometimes) and when you're in you can see nothing at all. Does that make you slow up? Not at all —not by a ½ m.p.h. The signal was down; there *can't* be anything in the way and it's the same at night. I came back on the engine from Grantham in the evening, simply to find out what they *can* see. You can see nothing but the signals —you know your whereabouts simply by memory. And as for the signals: it's surprising how little the green lights show up compared with the red. It seemed to me that they went more by the absence of a red light (in the expected place) than by the presence of a green one. You can see the red miles away but the green only when you're almost on it. And if it seemed a foolhardy proceeding to rush head-long into tunnels in the day time, how much more foolhardy did it seem at night to career along at 80 miles an hour in a black world with nothing to help you but your memory of the road and a lot of flickering lights —lights often almost obliterated by smoke and rain. And here's another primitive thing: You can generally see nothing at all through the glass windows of the cab at night because the reflections of the firelight make it impossible. To see the road, to see the signals, you must put your head out at the side —weather or no. The narrow glass screen prevents your eyes from being filled with smoke and cinders, but, well, it seems a garden of Eden sort of arrangement all the same.

And they don't even fill the tender with coal of the required size. Sometimes a big lump gets wedged into the opening and

S

has to be slowly broken up with a pickaxe before it can be dislodged — what about that? Well, I call it jolly fine; but it's jolly rum too, when you think of all the electric gadgets and labour-saving contrivances which the modern housewife thinks herself a martyr if she don't get.

Up the long bank before Grantham — yes, and, you notice the ups and downs when you're on the engine. They are both visible and hearable. You hear the engine's struggle (there's no 'changing down' when it starts 'labouring'). You feel it too, and, looking straight ahead, and not only sideways like the millionaire in the train behind, you see the horizon of the bank before you. It *looks* like a hill. And when you run over the brow you *see* the run down and you hear and feel the engine's change of breath, you hear and feel the more easy thrust of the pistons.

And, on the return journey, going down into London in the dark (on No. 2750 with Mr. Guttridge and Mr. Rayner, a London engine and London men) with steam shut off and fire nearly out — just enough fire to get home with — we were pulled up by an adverse signal. Good that was too. Nothing visible in the blackness but the red lights over our heads. Silence — during which the fireman told me that Mr. Guttridge had driven the King 28 times. Suddenly one of the red lights turned green — sort of magical. 'Right ho,' said the fireman.

198 : TO WALTER SHEWRING

[I REGRET I have only this portion left of an argument on aesthetics which continued through several letters. It concerned the relations of the artist's intellectual idea with its material embodiment. I thought then that E. G. overstressed the autonomy of the idea and underrated the possibilities of change and development between conception and execution. I remember suggesting that Prospero and Ariel had 'developed theologically' in the process of work upon them, and giving a number of instances from literature where a writer's first conception had been changed for better or worse by extraneous influences—as when Dr. Johnson visibly spoiled a good notion by translating it from monosyllables into polysyllables, or when Keats wrote a better line after being told that he gave a false accent to 'Uranus'. It seems to me now that E. G. may have stated his thesis somewhat too simply, but that I blundered badly in failing to recognize the continued primacy of the mind. If an artist chooses, rightly or wrongly, to embody his second thoughts instead of his first, it is still on the mind that the embodiment depends.]

Pigotts   *28-3-1933*

My dear Walter: I've read your letter (really it's a substantial essay on the subject) with most great interest. I'm sending it back herewith because I think you ought to use it —it would need v. little altering to make a printable article.* I wouldn't mind if you were to keep it as it is, in the form of a personal letter, & print it with mine to you, if you think mine well enough written, as a joint contribution to the subject. There is at least this to be said for my little note: that it provoked your carefully documented essay. Even if all I said be non-sense —at least it was the instigation.

Meanwhile I can do nothing but await our next meeting & discussion of these high matters. All you say, or at least, roughly speaking, most of it, seems to me true enough & yet & yet . . . it doesn't seem to me to touch the heart of the matter —the fact, the mere bloody fact that you & you alone, you, in the depth of your own soul, are the responsible maker, controller, responsible agent, creator in the first degree (or at least the second), maker (ΠΟΙΗΣΙΣ has something to do with it), maker of your own poems, and that your spirit, mind, imagination (what's the word?) is the former *of* things & the poem is not formed *by* things. Allow every sort of extraneous instigation & spur, the advice & criticism of your-self & friends, the existence of abstract ideas, the presence of visible created nature, time & place & occasion, fashion &

* of course if you've got a copy, I shd. be v. glad to keep it.

convention, & still it remains that in the genuine article, the thing, form & content are inseparable. I allow, most of what you write is true, if you will allow this one small, central, burning point. I don't ask you to deny anything that you really affirm —I only ask you to join with me in affirming this central fact of the formative imagination and in affirming that, whatever else may happen in the process of 'making' things, this thing is the one essentially important thing. Yours affectionately

ERIC G.

199 : TO G. K. CHESTERTON

In train   25-5-1933

Dear Chesterton: First of all this is to say that I am very sorry not to have been able to come to your meeting at Wycombe last week. I'm sorry in any case but, as you sent such a kind message on the occasion of your absence from *my* little do, I do at least return the compliment. I was (& still am) away doing a carving on the L.M.S. hotel at Morecambe Bay! (Incidentally: it is what is technically called a 'holy picture' — but the L.M.S. don't know that.) I regret also that no one else of our family was able to be at the meeting either. (My wife & one of my sons-in-law, & our car, were up at Morecambe with me. . . .)

Second: I'm disturbed in mind about next Tuesday's affair ('Mock trials'). I've never attended one of these things & wonder what happens. Do I leave it all to you & just answer your questions to the best of my ability? am I expected to be entertaining? am I supposed to collaborate in any way with my co-defendants? Do we meet beforehand & hear from you the lines of your prosecution? As to collaboration with co-defendants I'm troubled by the fact that I'm not v. friendly with Rothenstein. As prosecutor you must *not* assume that I agree with his views or like his books or drawings. In fact it wd. be a good line for you to take that artists are a danger to mankind because they, like doctors, don't agree among themselves & therefore cause confusion & you can bring your victims forward as examples. Anyway if you can spare time to send me half a line before Tuesday I'll be most grateful. (I'm sorry for this jerky scrawl.) Yrs. affectly.   ERIC G.

2 0 0 : T O ‘ T H E   F R I E N D ’ ,   1 4 T H   J U L Y ,
1 9 3 3

Sir: With reference to the letter of Sidney Trenaman in your issue of July 7: by the word Art we do not mean ‘the interpretation *of* Art’; we call that business ‘art criticism.’ Perhaps Mr. Trenaman means to distinguish Art which is of its nature interpretative from that which is original creation, *i.e.*, between the works which ‘hold a mirror up to nature’ and those which are themselves *part* of nature. It is clear that the characteristic works of post-Renaissance painters and sculptors are of the interpretative kind, while the works of the European and Indian middle ages and those of China, Mexico, Egypt and all ‘primitive’ and ‘savage’ peoples are of the other kind. They are ‘natural’ objects in the sense that they are the natural product of the kind of being that man is —a creature that needs things for use, who delights in making what he needs and who can only with difficulty be prevented from making things in such a way as that they please him when made.

No one denies that man needs things, but, confronted by his tendency to dote on material to the exclusion of spiritual values, many people look askance (to say the least) at man's delight in making (they hold it virtuous in the workman if he concern himself solely with the service of his fellows and eschew the pleasure of making —the actual delight in the doing of the work as such). Still more people are to be found who, confronted by his tendency to dote on things made to the exclusion of things ‘not made with hands,’ his tendency to idolatry in fact, and to the worship of his own works and of the works of God in 'nature,' to worship 'stocks and stones,' look askance and even condemn outright the whole business of 'Art' — lock, stock and barrel.

It is here that Friends and Catholics fall foul of one another. The Catholic Church takes man in general, savage and civilised, rich and poor, learned and simple, with all his gifts and appetites, his needs, his delight in doing and making, his delight in things made. She omits nothing, refuses nothing. She condemns nothing but ill will — *i.e.*, the privation of *good* will, the will to love God. She needs (*i.e.*, men need) places of meeting (churches). Let them be as men delight to make them and let them be delightful when made. 'The beautiful thing is that which, being seen, pleases' and, as 'the Preacher' says, 'a man shall have joy in his labour and this is his portion.'

When your correspondent suggests (in common with many other critics) that the Arts (music, drama, painting, architecture), being 'charged with great spiritual power,' are employed by the Church as 'means of grace,' he is not so much wrong in fact as by implication. It is a fact that the carvings of Amiens and Chartres are a sort of 'Bible in Stone,' but it is not true that to be a Bible is the sole *raison d'être* of such carvings. Men will make things, whether pots or paintings, whatever ecclesiastics may say or do. Where the Church shows and has always shown her common sense (wisdom, if you prefer the word, Sir) is in taking advantage of men's aptitudes, using them for her own purposes, curbing them (if possible) of what is irrelevant to salvation, glorifying God by them, giving back to God what he himself gave to men.

It seems to me, Sir, that your correspondent places us artists (what is an artist but a responsible workman — in contrast with a factory hand, who is responsible for nothing but for doing what he is told?) on too high a pedestal. Like a Friend he may well be led by an 'Inner Light,' but so also may a Hottentot chief and a mediaeval saint. All men are subject or, at least, liable to illumination. We make no special claim to the mantle of the prophet or to any chariot of fire.

It is not for me to say where or how the practice of the Society of Friends is wrong. I prefer to think that, as far as it goes, the Society is right. I prefer to think that, in the midst of a world somewhat drunk with its own exuberance, the Society of Friends is like a religious order, a company of persons specially called or specially talented for the cultivation of a special experience of God, an experience otherwise wanting. In this respect the Society of Friends is like those lay orders (the 3rd Orders of St. Dominic and St. Francis, the Brothers of St. Vincent de Paul, etc.) which, by a certain asceticism and devotion to good works, act as a leaven in the great lump of more or less careless humanity —a humanity not always culpably careless, a carelessness not always culpable; for God is worshipped in laughter as well as in tears, in works as well as in faith, in music-hall songs as well as in silent prayer, in every kind of light and not only an inner one. —I am, Sir, yours faithfully,   ERIC GILL

2 0 1 : TO ROMNEY GREEN

Pigotts   30-9-1933

Dear Romney: Thank you very much for your letter. I do hope it may be possible to meet some time in London, but time is very short at present as I have so many things on hand. Meanwhile I think the difference between us is very difficult to remove. I do not in the least understand what the word Beauty signifies for you, when you say the most comfortable chair is never the most beautiful and when you imply that the sheep is not as beautiful as the tiger or the cockroach as beautiful as the viper. Yours   ERIC G.

202 : TO THE REV. JOHN O'CONNOR

Pigotts   *1-10-1933*

Dear Father John: I returned from Manchester last Tuesday.
If next time you are there you shd. see the carving I hope
you'll approve.

Here is the list of ancient nations for the Jerusalem Museum
carvings: (as given me by the architect)

> Canaan
> Israel
> Philistia
> Assyria — Babylonia
> Egypt
> Persia
> Greece — Macedonia
> Rome
> Byzantium — Crusades
> Islam

I had sup. with Desmond on Thursday last and I am meeting
him at Bristol on Wednesday next. I am going there to finish
the carving on the gravestone of Mrs. Chute. Then I'm going
to Capel-y-ffin for three days & then back here. Desmond
seemed very well indeed. You seemed very well when I was
at Bradford. I was very glad.

I am very well —all are well here and work is in plenty.

Yours ever affectly.   ERIC G.

203 : TO GRAHAM CAREY

Capel-y-ffin   *7-10-1933*

Dear Carey: Here are solutions to your puzzles. Many thanks
for writing. I was glad to hear again from you & you say many
kind things about my *Beauty* book.[1] As for Herbert Read: he

---
[1] *Beauty Looks After Herself* (1933).

is a nice man & has a v. wide knowledge of ancient & modern art and an appreciation of the latter possessed by few. But I do think he's greatly in error in important matters of philosophy & religion so that while he is to be trusted in his appreciations of ancient works he is only to be trusted in his appreciation of those modern works which he can regard as 'pure' art – i.e. art without thesis – pure form . . . I shd. think you'll find his *Form in Mod. Poetry* rather disappointing & inconclusive. I shall be v. glad indeed to see & read your book. I'll look forward to it. I'm terribly busy at present but hope to be less so in a few months. Forgive this short note. Yours　　ERIC G.

204 : TO GRAHAM CAREY

Pigotts　　　　　　　　　　　　　　　　　　*17-11-1933*

Dear Carey: I am most sorry I haven't answered yours of Oct 11 before now. I have been and still am overwhelmed with work. I'm a subscriber to your *Liturgical Arts Magazine* and appreciate the efforts of your Society (though I regret the preponderance in it, as it seems to me, of the architect's point of view, and the apparent lack of appreciation of the fact – I think it's a fact – that, for the present, the *ornate* is out of place, quite completely out of place, in places of religious worship. Ornate churches *presuppose* an ornate world – a machine world is of its nature a plain world – possibly a very good world in some ways but not a world in which personal artistry or ornament are natural products). I can't undertake to write an article on Sculpture at present. I'm booked up till next June at least. I'm sorry. I hope for the time when I shall be less rushed with work.

I shall be pleased to meet your friend J. H. Benson if he comes to England. I shall be most interested to see a photo. of your crucifix when it is finished. In the stage of which you sent a photograph it has great possibilities. There is a wooden crucifix in the Louvre to which it has remarkable resemblance. (French 13th. cent. I think).

Forgive this brief reply to yours.

I'm in a bit of a turmoil at present — rather too much on hand. Yours

ERIC G.

205 : TO 'THE MONOTYPE RECORDER'
AUTUMN 1933

Dear Sir: I am very much honoured by the many references to me in your special number on Type Faces and particularly by that on page 30.

If you will allow it, however, I should like one correction to be made.

It is not true that I have started a 'private press' with Mr. René Hague. It would be strictly correct to say that we have started a printing business: the style of the firm being 'Hague and Gill, Printers'.

It is, of course, difficult to define the term 'private press', but it seems clear to me that the real distinction between such a press and others is not in the typographical quality of the work it does or in the typographical enthusiasm of its proprietors, but simply in the fact that a 'private' press prints solely what it chooses to print, whereas a 'public' press prints what its customers demand of it.

Doubtless the circumstances of a private press enable it to pay more attention to questions of typography, aesthetic and otherwise, while the public printer is very often at the mercy of his customers, especially in these days wherein the press is run more as a purely business affair, that is to say an affair having only financial success as a test.

On the other hand it is obvious that private presses suffer from their very freedom, and in many cases have been conspicuous for the worst kind of self-conscious artistic eccentricity, while the public press in spite of its financial obsession

—the tyranny of auditors and shareholders —often achieves a good reasonable commonplace and therefore pleasant standard of excellence.

It remains clear that much useful experimental work has been done by the private presses and that many business houses have not failed to take advantage of the fact.

I think it would be good if we could all agree that the distinction between private and public is what the words themselves suggest, and has nothing whatever to do with the use of machinery, whether hand-driven or otherwise, or with questions of the artistic quality of the product. Yours faithfully, ERIC GILL

206 : TO ROMNEY GREEN

P & O, SS. 'Rajputana', in the Mediterranean
nearing Port Said   *20-3-1934*

My dear Romney: I'd no time to answer your letter of Jan 12 & 19 before leaving home so I brought it with me. I'm on way to Jerusalem to do a three months carving job on the new Archaeological Museum there (I always said: the future of sculpture is the museum —it is becoming the present.) First of all: thank you for your letters & apologies for not replying sooner.

Item: You said: do adventurous things. I said (quoting J. M. Barrie) to die is a great adventure —meaning that suicide might be a good thing to do according to your scheme & wondering if you wd. agree. To *hazard* your life is *another* adventure but not *that* one.

My objection to your scheme is that it is both too vague & too emotional (& therefore shy-making) i.e. it doesn't offer enough pabulum either for intellect or will. When I say the object of man's life is happiness, I expect you to ask: what do you mean by happiness? And that leads to the necessity for coming to agreement as to the nature of man —his powers, potentialities, origin & destiny. And so the argument wd. go on & on. You put forward your 3 sentences as tho. they were immediately understandable & acceptable. But p'raps you expect *me* to ask questions too, e.g. What do you mean by 'wonderful', 'beautiful' & 'adventurous'? I have nothing but the vaguest idea what those words mean to you.

Further, all your three sentences imply different kinds of *doing*. Am I to take it that *doing* is superior to *being* in your mind? I don't say you'd be wrong, I only ask.

Item: I'm not much impressed by your schoolgirls. I mean, schoolgirls! Well of course there's all sorts & doubtless all are darlings, but I don't see that their witness is very impressive. It's like Buchmanism — nothing wrong with it (or very little) but a thing that naturally fires the young emotion.

Item: You ask: what word would I use instead of 'beautiful' if I wanted to say that one chair, not necessarily stronger or more comfortable, is nevertheless more beautiful than another 'as it often is'? It's just that 'as it often is' which gets me down. I simply don't see what you mean.

And when you say 'stronger or more comfortable' you don't nearly exhaust the functional necessities of a good chair. E.g. there are such things as a baby's high chair, a deck chair, a dining room chair, a bishop's chair etc. A good baby's chair is not merely stronger or more comfortable in some abstract sense of 'strong' or 'comfortable' but strong as related to the *baby's* use of it, comfortable according to what is proper to a *baby's* comfort. So with a bishop's chair. Who or what is a bishop that we shd. talk of strength & comfort in relation to his chair? Then, further, not only is a baby's chair a chair for a baby but it is also so & so's baby's chair and is a chair in such & such a house. It is the function of a chair to satisfy all these requirements — and more besides. The chair-maker who has got thus far can, that is my contention, stop talking about beauty & the beautiful. He's a chair-maker, not an aesthete.

So with your vases. In my view there's no such thing as just *vase*, 'just like that', as Geo. Robey wd. say. There is this or that vase, and vases for this or that purpose in this or that place & time. The curve you sent a drawing of is a thing on paper and must be judged as such. It is not a vase; it is only, by *convention*, a drawing of one. A nice curve, yes truly — but what curve is *not* nice? You ask: how do I account for 'the fact' that a vase with a parabolic arc for profile 'is more beautiful' (*is*), though not more 'efficient', than one with a circular arc? I don't account for it because I don't believe it is a 'fact'. I think you'll have to say that I'm deficient in a sense of beauty in your use of the word.

'The beautiful is that which being seen pleases.' And what in fact does please when seen? I think those things please which are *good*, i.e. satisfying to us as moral beings, i.e. beings desiring what is good for us (hence the necessity of knowing our origins and destiny) & I think those things please which are *true*, i.e. satisfying to us as intelligent beings, i.e. beings knowing what's what, i.e. beings to whom the truth is connatural. So I think beauty proceeds from the good & the true & is neither one nor the other but compounded of both and there's no need to talk about it — look after g. & t., & b. will take care of itself.

If you say that man is well occupied who does adventurous things, makes beautiful things & understands wonderful things — of course I agree. He is indeed. But when you say that those three things constitute the object of human existence, I don't agree because it's not good enough & not true enough (I speak loosely, for of course there are not really any degrees of good & true).

Item : My book is in the press. I'll see that you get a copy — $\frac{s}{2}$/6. Bodley Head XX Century Library. What a blessing to be outside the edition de luxe business for once! Much love to you both. I hope to be back home in June; meanwhile my address is: c/o Austen S^t. B. Harrison, P.O. Box 585, Jerusalem. Yours, ERIC G.

Couvent des Dominicains, Jerusalem   *5-4-1934*

Dear Carey: We arrived here a fortnight ago but I've had no opportunity until now of writing to say that I have read the typescript of the 1st. part of your book. I think it is a most noble effort, most excellent, most useful & jolly good altogether — really first class & A 1.

I hope to see the second half soon. When & where are you publishing it? I don't find it at all dull — most exciting in fact. When you come to applications! then the trouble will begin. Do you, you don't say in your letter, want the t-script back? If so, send a card to above address & I'll send it at once. I've very few & they are v. small criticisms: —

I'm not happy about p. 11 of your t-st (I'll write t-s for type-script in future) i.e. top paragraph. I think its a pity to mention such things, at that stage, as 'abstract & geometric principles' & 'individuality'. It seems to me that they confuse the idea of formal cause. I see it like this:

Final   cause   the *defined* purpose of thing to be made
Material   ,,   material (this is easy)
Efficient   ,,   tools, will & skill of maker (also easy)
Formal   ,,   the thing as seen in the mind and/or imagination
                of the maker before he begins the work.

You see (and say) the customer may define the purpose; but it is the workman who *sees* (either immediately, or after a process of sketching, trial & error, etc) the thing as a *thing*. Geometrical principles & his individuality of course are bound up in the result. But I think it is a pity to mention them at the beginning. I think it's best to let it be clear that (e.g.) if a man says: I want a road from Boston to Cambridge & it's to be Macadamized & it's to be done in no time by forced labour — up to that point there is no road at all. But directly the order or suggestion is made to a workman (engineer or contractor or mere 'artist') a *thing* comes into existence — in the mind of the workman. The thing takes *form*. It doesn't matter what sort of thing it is (ships, shoes, sealing wax, cabbages . . .) The thing in the mind is bound to be geometric & bound to have the impress of the workman's individuality —yes; but I think your statement seems to confine the thing a bit too much in 'artistic' terms. You say: '. . . certain principles . . . which may be combined . . . to give the table individuality'. My point is that the formal cause is *necessary* —it's not a case of principles which *may* combine. You can't *have* a thing without a formal cause and I don't think it matters about individuality at this early stage of your argument. You lay down (Fi) table, (M) wood, (E) machine. I come along and *envisage* a machine-made wooden table —but it may be a facsimile of a hundred others. Of course if *I* envisage it it will be impressed with *my* individuality —but the necessity is that I *envisage* it. Or am I wrong? [. . .]

I am getting on with the work here (10 small relief carvings on the new Rockefeller museum!). The weather is not yet too hot. It is an astonishing place. Words fail me. I can't begin to describe it. There is a mad balance (preserved by Brit. Govt.) between ancient & utter loveliness & mod. bestial commercial enterprise —in fact they cancel out.* There is also a mad confusion of religions, all worshipping & scrapping at same shrines. I expect to be here till end of June.

I've just sent off the galley proofs of *my* book on art! I expect it will be published in a month or so.

Item: a young man (looking like a Greek portrait) called Rob.ᵗ Amendola came to see me yesterday. Said he was from Boston, Mass. Was going back to U.S.A. to wage war on mod. ecclesiastical art. Said he was something to do with Liturgical Arts Soc.ʸ. I told him, I hope, some home truths. He said I was an 'ecclesiastical artist'. I said I was not. I said I was an engraver & stone carver who did things when asked (which was v. rarely) for churches. . . .

* i.e. between the two you may say there is no real Jerusalem at all.

I agree, I wish I could get to cutting steel. I want to cut punches.

That Persian relief you sent photo. of was fine.

I hope you're very well & your family.

I have good news of mine —and a new grandchild (the 8th.)

Yours ever   ERIC G

208 : TO GEORGE HORSFIELD

Austrian Hospice, Jerusalem   *Sunday 27-5-1934*

Dear Horsfield: It's Sunday again & this time at Jerusalem — marvellous to remember last Sunday at Jerash & impossible to say how good that 'week-end' was & exciting & interesting & beautiful —graced by your goodness & hospitality & that of Mrs. Horsfield —altogether wonderful. I can only merely say thank you very much.

I wish we could have had or could have more talk about church & faith & what not. I'm upset, or, shall I say, scratched, by one or two of your remarks —little pebbles not too well rounded —thrown at me. Lack of charity, lack of humility, arrogance (sorry for this scribble —fingers won't keep steady in the heat) & so forth. What worries me, gnaws at me, is that it's not argument to drag those things in so soon —argument is stoppered at the start. I'm reminded of similar occasions —years ago, for I've quite given up saying a word now-a-days when I meet them —with my 3 high church brothers. (One a missionary, biggish bug, in New Guinea, one a parson in N. Wales, one on a milling business in Liverpool). Whenever I started what I thought was arguing with them I saw a sort of more-in-sorrow-than-in-anger look come over them & I knew it was useless —I shd. only be accused of uncharitableness or arrogance (& the same has happened with other Anglican friends). There is no doubt it's true —can anyone claim to be free from such things? —but it seems to me that these moral judgements ought not to be dragged in at all. (It's as if, two people boxing, one kept on saying to his opponent: 'don't lose your temper', or 'that blow was not given in kindness'. Of course boxers do gibe at one another but it's not boxing & it spoils boxing). So we don't get any further, either morally or intellectually. The questions of right & wrong don't get touched. You sail off on a high horse of moral superiority & leave me grovelling in the mud of my sinfulness. You say I'm not humble. How can I not agree? Meanwhile the point of view I want to share with you is not shared, the things I want to say are not said. I am left miserable. I think we ought, as between more or less reasonable & friendly people, to assume charity & humility & freedom from prejudice (why, e.g., *assume* that I 'imbibed all the prejudices' of English Catholics when I was received into the Church?). However I'm only saying these things because you left me so jolly unsatisfied, in the lurch, and because it seems so unsatisfactory that discussions between your people & ours shd. always be thus frittered away in recrimination.

Forgive me for dragging all this up —please. I can't tell you how much I enjoyed staying with you. Yours　　ERIC G

Lunch at Amman & prowled on the 'Acropolis' with Dr. Keams.

Tea at Jericho & as fast as I drank it, it came out through the pores.

209 : TO ROMNEY GREEN

Pigotts　　　　　　　　　　　　　　　　　*9-8-1934*

My dear Romney: [. . .] I am sending you a little book (written 1926, so not quite up to date) which will, I hope, show you that the 'id quod visum placet' is not so

T

inadequate an idea as you suppose. (Please return when done with.)⋆

I return your notes. I was much interested in reading them. I still don't understand how you can say that you can have an efficient dining table which is not a beautiful one —unless you reduce the word efficient to a purely engineering meaning. & as to some yachts being more efficient & less beautiful —that seems to reduce the word beautiful to a purely physical meaning —as one might say such and such a chord in music is ugly *because it jars on my ear* & I don't like jarring noises. Any way I don't believe in *bothering* about beauty. I still hold that: look after the good & the true & beauty will take care of itself. (I'm having a controversy with Penty on this. Vide his article in *Criterion* for April & my reply in the September number)[1] Love to you both   ERIC G

N.B. The above isn't a definition of *Beauty* but a statement of

⋆*Id   quod   visum   placet*

i.e.: —
That *thing* which   being *seen*   *pleases*

i.e.:—
the thing *itself*   by the *mind*   gives *satisfaction*
& not that of   via the senses   to the rational being
which it reminds   i.e. not that   (soul, mind). rational,
us etc.   which merely   but not necessarily as a
                    tickles the sense   result of discursive rea-
                    of sight but that   soning. The satisfaction
                    which satisfies   may be intuitive or im-
                    the mind when   mediate, nevertheless it
                    it is seen (or   is the *mind* which is
                    heard etc.)   satisfied.

[1] Actually the October number.; Letter 216 here.

fact viz: the beautiful thing is that which being seen pleases.
Beauty itself consists in due proportion etc.

in short: *splendor formae* (S.t Thomas Aq.)

i.e. the radiance, shining out, clarity of *Being* — . . . etc.

E. G.

210 : TO HERBERT READ

In train   *20-8-1934*

My dear Herbert Read: I got a cutting of your *Spectator* review
of my little *Art* book & I am very much gratified & not a little
relieved by the serious way you take me — the friendly way —
the kind way. I am writing to thank you for these things. I
shd. do so in any case. But of course I'm disturbed by the
adverse parts of your criticism & I'm the more disturbed because it seems to me there's a sort of perversity in what you
say. I know the book is a hasty, cheap little effort — a mere
pamphlet — and it's much too short & sketchy. But you forgive
that — you don't mention it — you understand that that's the
only sort of book a person like me can write — so I needn't
apologise & I don't have to complain of lack of sympathy.
My complaint is that your review is more a repartee than
a criticism. (1) That business of *anonymity* for instance :
It seems perverse to me to pretend that there's no conspicuous difference between our situation to-day (& ever since
about 1500) in the fine arts & that of mediaeval Europe or India
or China etc. — that there is no greater contrast between
the painter of pictures & the factory 'hand' (i.e. as persons
known by name) than there was between sculptors & masons
in 12th Century Chartres, e.g. As a poet yourself you must
know (just as, as a sculptor, *I* know) that the essence of my
contention was not the absence of a signature but the absence
of isolation — So that whereas an 'Epstein', it is fondly hoped,
could not be a Harry Moore, a medieval Tom might easily be

a Dick or a Harry —In fact it was actually more necessary for Tom, Dick or Harry to *sign* their works than it is for Epstein or Harry Moore. In my book I allowed the reader to think I attached great importance to the absence of actual signature. I am sorry. If every single medieval carving were signed & not a single modern one, it wd. still be true that medieval art is 'anonymous' & modern art isn't —just because, as you say yourself, the medieval art was impersonal & hieratic & abstract & the modern (i.e. from Raphael to Augustus John) is not. (2) I'm sorry if I lead the reader to think that my complaint against machine industry (industrialism) is that it has 'destroyed the personal quality in mod. art.' I hoped I had made it clear that my complaint against machine industry was that it destroyed the personal quality in the modern workman. (vide: reply to A. J. Penty in *Criterion* —next issue, September) (3) I can't think why you think I wasn't taking that child seriously enough who said 'first I think & then I draw my think'. That child is the corner stone of my aesthetic (vide also p. 77 of my book). (4) Nor have I ever been able to understand why you, & other critics, are so keen to keep the common word 'art' for such exclusively exalted usage, nor why you are not revolted by the idea that the ability to think in plastic images is 'not a normal faculty'. Your idea of the artist as an abnormal man is what revolts me & I thought my book was about that. But in your review you imply that the idea will be new to me! My view is that art is making ($\therefore$ ability to make, $\therefore$ ability to *imagine* the thing to be made . . .) a non-thinking workman is not a work*man* but a creature 'reduced to a subhuman condition of intellectual irresponsibility' —that's p'raps why in mod. language he's no longer a work*man* but a 'work*er*.' I wish we could frequently meet & discuss.

I hope you are well. Yours   ERIC G

I'm sorry for this scrawl —my only chance of writing to you at present.

211 : TO HERBERT READ

Pigotts　　　　　　　　　　　　　　　　*27-8-1934*

My dear Read: Thank you very much for your letter of the 23rd. I do thank you. And I do agree that most of our differences are matters of terminology. Of course, I agree: our philosophy must retain 'the uniqueness of the individual'. (That's the chief original contribution of Christianity to the world, is it not?) But, and I'm certain we really agree about this, the man who says: 'my portrait painting is primarily valuable as self expression & incidentally as a portrait' is in a worse position than he who says: 'my painting is primarily this or that & incidentally self expression.' —as you say there shd. be ' no need to worry about the personality of the workman'. (It's like this don't you think: before the altar rail each person is a unique soul but, in the town, one is a blacksmith, one the banker, one this, one that . . . & the artist who insists on his unique soul is asking the public to get the wrong side of the altar rail.)

The other part of your letter is more difficult to reply to briefly. It amounts to this: I want to keep the word 'art' down to the level of ordinary making & I want to exalt the workman to the high level of the imaginative maker. (I agree that in all ages many workmen have been largely unimaginative, but I think medieval conditions or say pre-industrial conditions made it possible for most men to develop at least a small degree of imagination whereas *our* conditions do the opposite & make 'imaginative making' more & more the sphere of special peculiar, 'abnormal' men.) I don't think *in our language* the word 'art' means only 'imaginative making'. There are too many words like 'artful' & 'artificial'. And as a matter of politics (& it's a fearfully political business writing a book or giving a lecture) I'd rather encourage a grave digger to think himself an 'artist'* than encourage a picture painter to think himself 'abnormal' —even abnormally imaginative —because I don't think it *is* abnormal to possess the rudiments of the power of 'imaginative making' in spite of the tendency of industrialism to deprive the factory hand & the clerk of any opportunity of exercising that power. I think it is precisely Christianity which supports that view and I would do all in my power to make a rebellion against everything which militates against it. I *will* come & see you when I get a chance. Yours

ERIC G

* i.e. a responsible workman (& potentially an imaginative one). Would it not be possible to use the word *poet* more precisely to designate man as '*imaginative* maker'? Then I shd. say every man is potentially an artist & every artist potentially a poet.

212 : TO MISS HALL[1]

Pigotts, High Wycombe, England   *27-8-1934*

Dear Miss Hall: I have received your letter of a few weeks ago. I am most interested by all you say in it. I wish I had the time to answer fully. I'm terribly busy at present & long letters are an impossibility. You must forgive a short reply therefore. Moreover the problems you raise are not such as can easily be dealt with. The whole trouble of our civilization is involved —its godlessness & its false gods & its consequent economic muddle & injustice, & its consequent ugliness & disorder. The only real advice I can give (at this great distance of miles away) is that you, by 'prayer & fasting', perfect your mind — by reading, writing, talking, loving, thinking, probing, criticising —referring all things to their sources . . . Thus, in spite of all the misery which you must necessarily suffer, you will have an interior peace of mind. (There's only one source

[1] Librarian of the Catholic Library, Johannesburg.

of all *good* things. If your criticism & probing lead you to any
other source —well, you will know where you are . . .) In this
welter of to-day the most & the best we can hope for is peace
of *mind*.

Your problem: —

How is it that if industrialism is bad we can get benefits from
its products? e.g. Medici prints, gramophone records, etc.

Answer: The essential badness of industrialism is its effect
on *men & women*, e.g. 'it reduces them (in Fr. Martin D'Arcy's
phrase) to a subhuman condition of intellectual irresponsibility.' It makes marriage & the home & children more &
more difficult. It makes profit-making more urgent than
enthusiasm for quality of production, etc. But it doesn't
follow that *all* industrial products are bad *things*. Simply
because the method of production entails subhuman development of men & women the product is not therefore a bad product. A machine-made nail is not necessarily a bad *nail*. So a
photograph of a picture isn't necessarily a bad *photograph*, etc.
But it is a bad civilisation which makes men & women more
& more dependent upon such things —so that their creative
powers are more & more atrophied & they become dependent
upon specialists —and the 'artist' becomes more & more a
peculiar person, etc . . . [. . .]

N.B. It's not machines in themselves that are bad —it's their
use & control almost exclusively by 'business' people rather
than by those who design or use them. Our trouble is not
primarily the *existence* of machines but their ownership and
control by persons whose one concern is profits. Don't be
misled by their own account of themselves . . . etc . . . Yours
sincerely,   ERIC GILL

Please forgive my hasty scribble.
P.S. It occurs to me that I ought to add that while it's true
that machine-products aren't necessarily bad things, *they aren't
necessarily good either*. This is obvious —still, it must be said.
A profit-making system (i.e. a system primarily concerned with

profits, of which profits are the test of success) inevitably produces many bad things because its control is in the sole hands
of business men & for them a good thing is simply what will
sell.   And the standard of criticism in the buyer becomes
lower & lower as he becomes more & more intellectually irresponsible. (Hence all the efforts of things like the B.B.C. to
elevate the public taste! and, e.g., the efforts of people like
Carnegie to give back in the form of libraries what they have
taken away by the industrial degradation of the workers.) E. G.

213 : TO ROMNEY GREEN

In train   *30-8-1934*

Dear Romney: Thank you for yours of Aug. 24. If you take
that *non poss^{s.}* line about theology & metaphysics the argument
is settled & p'raps it's a good thing. Like the old women in
the slum we're arguing from different premises.* So I hereby
give up arguing & will be content with the feminine tactics of
mere assertion. [I agree with you entirely that 'a beautiful
boat might turn out to be the most efficient' – in fact I see no
'might' about it. The only difference between my practice &
yours being that I should, in boat building as in sculpture (for
making an image of, e.g. St. Dominic, can be thought of as
making something to do something) I should confine my attention to the efficiency & leave dear old beauty to jolly well take
care of itself or be taken care of by the aesthetes. That *is* my
practice. Whether I achieve 'beauty', I don't know or care.]
So I hereby assert that I see no difference of *beauty* between the
two bows & sterns you sketched. I just simply don't. I can
see that their *efficiency* would be different – one boat wd. be
faster than the other & the other more stable in a sea. But

* i.e. you saying that science comes before metaphysics & I
the opposite – that metaphysics is anterior to physics – ∴
philosophy & religion before science & sociology.

that's nothing to do with beauty —or, rather, it doesn't make one more beautiful than the other —to *me*. We'll just have to leave it at that. It's an impasse. I'm a political writer you're a poet. I think beauty's bad politics —thundering bad. If I wanted a statue or a steam engine I'd leave out all beauty talk. I'd say, just as exactly as I could, what I wanted & leave the artist (stone-carver or mechanician) to get on with it. Yours

ERIC G

214 : TO HIS BROTHER CECIL

[Cecil Gill had been an Anglican clergyman (for some years a missionary in New Guinea); he now announced his conversion to Catholicism.]

Pigotts   *10-9-1934*

My dear bro. Cecil: In the midst of death we are in life and your letter made me think so too. I hardly can say how glad I am, now that you have made the final decision by sending in your resignation. All these years we've been hoping . . . and of course praying. Now at last . . . It's as much a case of 'calloo callay' as 'thanks be to God'. (For, as the theologians agree; there is no valid distinction between the sacred & the profane.) I'm hoping to see you this week. Of course we will help all we can —don't know what that amounts to yet — heavy extra difficulties & expenses now being put upon us by darling Betty's bereavement — So, till then, *Saïd* —Your loving bro.

ERIC

215 : TO HERBERT READ

Pigotts   *16-9-1934*

Dear Read: Thank you for yours of 30th. Aug. and for quote from Schuhl. Very useful & apposite. Yes, I agree, best to use common speech generally, and that's what I kidded myself I was doing, but I quite see that it's a bit of a 'kid' —I mean that

I was more or less assuming that the primary dictionary meaning of the word 'art' could be taken as the meaning of the word in common speech. E.g. *Shorter Oxford Dic'*. (& that dic. does profess to be a dic. of mod. english as spoken) says Art: I Skill. 1. Skill . . . 2. Human skill . . . 3 Learning . . . 4 Application of skill to subjects of taste . . . esp. in mod. use: perfection of workmanship . . . as an object in itself . . . 6 Skill applied to the arts of imitation . . . II anything wherein skill may be attained — sing. an art, pl. the arts. etc. Nevertheless I admit that if you gently breathe the word 'art', 'just like that', it is quite commonly, in m-class circles anyway & probably also in up. class and lower class also, taken to refer to 1. painting & 2. the other arts practised by the gentry. I think most people think the title 'M.A.' is verbally archaic & that to talk of the 'art' of cooking is slightly facetious.

All the same I don't think in common speech the word 'art' means primarily or exclusively '*imaginative* making'. I don't think ordinary people feel any mental discomfort in hearing a person who copies pictures in the Nat. Gall$^{y.}$ called an artist. (I don't for a moment think that they assume that such 'artists' put anything original into their copies. They'd think it a breach of contract to do so, and very regrettable if unavoidable.)

In your *Spectator* review of my book you said, and it seemed to me a v. extraordinary thing to say, that it wd. not be right to dignify by the name of art the making (by hand) of standard bricks, and that there might be 'even more "art" ' in tending a machine for making bricks. I'll admit that machine minding is or may be an art. ('Can you make this machine go?' is a phrase which implies that the workman has an image of the thing 'going' — it really *is* a kind of art work. It's as tho. the machine were a dancer whose 'going' were a pleasure to watch — & it jolly well is so on cold mornings when one's blasted Austin won't start) (the garage man is no mean artist). What I don't admit is that *brick making* is not an art however low.

So, all things considered, & you know one could write pages & pages about the use of words, I think myself justified in my use of the word 'art' & in thinking that, on the whole, your use of the word is too exclusive. Yours   ERIC G.

216 : TO 'THE CRITERION'
OCTOBER 1934

Beauty does not Look after Herself

Sir: I am honoured by Mr. Penty's attack on me (*Criterion*, April, 1934) and shall be honoured if you will allow me to answer it.

I am not disturbed by the charge of inconsistency. Apparent inconsistency is unavoidable—and, I might say, proverbial. If I say 'too many cooks spoil the broth' and then hasten to add 'but many hands make light work' I may appear more inconsistent than I am. If I say 'look before you leap' and then 'he that hesitates is lost' Mr. Penty will be confused, but the discerning will understand. So one may deplore the lack of sensibility in the parish clergy and their readiness to assume that modern painting is the work of either imbeciles or charlatans and yet still believe that aesthetic education is no part of the curriculum of seminaries. 'The public must be educated' said the leaders of the arts and crafts movement, meaning educated in aesthetics; I say rather that the public should be educated in faith and morals. I do not expect Mr. Penty to agree, but to me it is clear that commercialism, dishonesty, avarice, self-will and self-esteem, conceit, vanity, love of luxury and ostentation on the one hand (i.e. moral failings) and stupidity, blindness, and every kind of silliness on the other (i.e. intellectual failings) are more damaging to civilization and culture and therefore to art (i.e. the making of things — for art is not merely the making of paintings and sculptures and buildings) than any lack of art-school training or *ad hoc* cultural education.

Mr. Penty does not like the idea that beauty proceeds from truth and goodness. He admits the possibility that 'in the final consummation morals and aesthetics may be one' (though he does not explain why the word morals should be taken as equivalent to the two words truth and goodness), but meanwhile he clings to 'taste' and 'aesthetic perception' and 'a keen sense of line and colour' (curious indeterminate words upon which art critics, as initiates of a mystery, depend for their livings) and will not see that tables and chairs and buildings and carriages are not primarily objects of aesthetic satisfaction.

One of our troubles is the confusion of mind in which we fail to distinguish one art from another. There is the art of living. Of this art the saints, both canonized and otherwise, are the exponents (and, we must remember, the saint is not a special kind of man, but every man is a special kind of saint). There is the art of cooking and that of building. There is the art of husbandry and that of singing (and, again we must remember, 'the artist is not a special kind of man, but every man is a special kind of artist'). But when we say that beauty proceeds from truth and goodness we mean that beauty proceeds from good sense and good will. We do not mean that the good carpenter never beats his wife any more than that the bad carpenter always does (though we agree with Mr. Penty that, *in the long run*, a really good carpenter is sure to be a decent sort of man —I mean you can't do work suitable for human use if you are an inhuman sort of person). We mean that to make a good table you must first of all have a good idea of a table in your head; you must know precisely what a table is; you must know the truth about tables and your mind must be such that you can see a vision of the table before you make it and your vision must be conformed to the truth of table-making.

But, obviously, such good sense is not enough. You must also have goodwill. That is to say you must strongly desire the table you have imagined and your will must be equable and firm and persistent. You must not allow yourself to be put off by this trifle or that — by this irrelevance or the other.

Good sense, strong will, surely these are obvious necessities (though not so obvious, alas, to Mr. Penty). And the enemies of good sense and strong will, are they not all the common enemies of truth and goodness? If our minds are nurtured in falsehood and our lives in hatred and selfishness is it likely that we shall bring good sense and good will into our workshops?

Mr. Penty says we are familiar with 'the spectacle of people single-hearted in their devotion to goodness and truth, yet without a scrap of taste or aesthetic perception'. But in saying that he is only making confusion. For in the finity of human powers few men and women can claim to have devotion to all possible applications of the true and the good, and a man devoted to religion, to visiting the fatherless and the widows in their tribulation, may perhaps have neither time nor inclination to visit the gothic cathedrals or the National Gallery. All the same, the builders and the painters must also be devoted to the true and the good or they will be bad builders and bad painters.

Mr. Penty says aesthetics cannot be explained in the terms of morals. I did not say they could. I said aesthetics were to be explained in terms of the mind. I said that the faculties of the mind are the intelligence and the will and that therefore, the object of the intelligence being the truth and that of the will being the good, aesthetics were to be explained in terms of truth and goodness. Mr. Penty's identification of truth and goodness with morals alone leads him unto his morass. Ugly churches do certainly imply a bad civilization and beautiful banks would certainly imply a good one (though it is perhaps difficult to conceive of the trade of money-lending leading to anything but grandiosity), but we need not judge the Christians of to-day by the church architecture of to-day any more than we need judge the shopkeepers of to-day by the architects of to-day. We must be just a little bit careful. The matter is not so simple. A saint must buy bread; it is not necessarily his fault if the only bread available be a Viennese bun. The usurer must have a shelter; it is not always his merit if the only

building available be a disused temple. We must return again
and again to the first principles. Whatever job we are confronted by, we must first ask ourselves *what* is it; we must find
out the *truth* of the matter. We must then consider *why* it is;
whether it be worth while, very desirable, a *good* thing, an
object of love. Taste, aesthetics, the styles of architecture!
These things can be discovered afterwards by the critics. Let
the workman stick to his job and use his intelligence and his
good will.

Perhaps Mr. Penty's chief difficulty is in the matter of
industrialism and perhaps that is because he is an architect.
Architects more than other people suffer from the difficulty
of adjusting their minds to the facts of modern commerce and
manufacture. 'Beauty looks after herself' is a saying more
difficult for architects than for other people to swallow. They
are in a special sense trained and paid to look after 'beauty'.
If beauty is going to look after herself their trade is largely
gone. The builder and the engineer can build; you only call
in the architect because, after three centuries of commercial
rule, you do not expect either builder or engineer to have any
ideas but those of profit and utilitarianism. The architect is
beauty's professional custodian. Hence all his business of
Gothic and Classic, styles and orders of architecture and all the
paraphernalia of office draughtsmanship and museum study.
The march of commerce and applied science has passed him by
and left him in a blind alley or, rather, left him with nothing
but the appearances of things.

I am not saying that the architect is not concerned with
plans and construction; I am only saying that those things are
not his *raison d'être* —either historically or in fact to-day.
Hence his indignation when you say beauty looks after herself.
Beauty! why it's his stock in trade; it's his speciality; the one
thing he's quite sure he knows about and the one thing he's
really proud of. So Mr. Penty thinks I'm an iconoclast moved
by 'colossal folly' and he cannot understand how a person who
sees the inhumanity of industrialism can yet see beauty in the

characteristic products of machinery as well as in the characteristic products of modern painters and sculptors.

I am afraid this cannot be helped. You cannot make a man
see by writing a book. But at least you can tell him a few
home truths. Architecture is a social art. Buildings are not
built in the architect's office but on the job. They are not
built by draughtsmen but by the contractor and his 'hands'.
Whether Mr. Penty likes it or not, buildings to-day are not
built by men but by mechanics and machines. And they are
not made of 'natural' materials but, more and more, of manu-
factured or artificial materials — iron and steel, reinforced concrete, artificial stone and glass. Mr. Penty may not like all
these things — that won't stop them being used. Mr. Penty
may prefer a horse and trap — that won't make it easy for him
to get one or safe to drive it on a road made for motor cars
and surrounded by them.

Now Mr. Penty's difficulty is this: Industrialism is a bad
thing; how can it produce good works? It is the same difficulty
as that posed by the moralist when he asks how an immoral
painter can paint good portraits. Mr. Penty is very scornful of
the moralist; why can he not see that his own question is a
similar one? What do we mean when we say Industrialism is
a bad thing? We mean that it is bad for *men*. It reduces the
workman to a subhuman condition of intellectual irresponsibility. It deprives him of what had hitherto been his pride,
his responsibility as a craftsman, a man skilled in handiwork,
and it deprives him of his responsibility as a citizen, a man
dealing independently (or in accordance with the regulations
of his guild) with his own customers — the servant not of an
impersonal Joint Stock company but of the persons for whom
he actually makes his goods. And so on — I am not writing a
book or I would say much more.* I say Industrialism deprives
the workman of these things and that these things are necessary

---

* See on this subject my little book *Art*, Twentieth Century
Library, John Lane, 2s. 6d.

to men; for men are rational souls and not mere 'hands', mere units in a factory.

For these reasons and many others Industrialism is a bad thing for men and the plethora of cheap manufactures is no compensation for the loss of the workman's responsibility. But it does not follow that all machines and all machine-made things are bad things. A locomotive, a motor car, properly designed (i.e. designed in accordance with the nature of such things and not designed in imitation of horse-drawn carriages), a telephone, a typewriter, a fountain pen, plain linen, plain brick or concrete buildings, iron bridges — all such things, when properly designed, are good things, and as they are pleasing when seen, we may rightly call them beautiful. Men are sacrificed but the goods are goods. They are a different kind of goods, but goods none the less, and while we continue the industrial system we may as well have the best it can do rather than imitations of pre-industrial things. Industrialism means the reduction of workmen to a subhuman condition but subhuman things are not bad things in themselves. A beehive is not a bad thing, an insect is an admirable mechanism, bones and beetles are constructed purely in accordance with function and are beautiful to behold. The inspiration of Industrialism is also a functional inspiration. Both Mr. Penty and I may regret the institution, but neither of us can stay its course and it seems certain that it will reach its term the quicker the less we camouflage it.

I am sorry Mr. Penty introduced the personal business. I must needs answer him. In the matter of lettering he says my work is based upon the inscription on Trajan's column. He is quite wrong. (He ought to go and look at that inscription — there is a cast in the V. and A. Museum). It is true that as a student I was taught to study Roman inscriptions, but as soon as I got down to doing real inscriptions for real tombstones I saw the folly of going back to old models. I told my apprentices, and I've said it in books and lectures countless times, that we have to take the lettering of our own time and, if necessary, improve it by rationality and good workmanship. My inscriptions are no more like the Trajan than Caslon's type is.

Mr. Penty says my sculpture is 'inspired by the Primitives' and some are 'even archaic'! The implication is that I am working in a primitive style on purpose —because I like it. The facts are quite otherwise. *I work the only way I can.* If I like primitive sculptures more than, shall I say, late Greek or modern Royal Academy sculptures, it is simply because they seem to me more in harmony with the nature of man and religion and the nature of stone carving —they are more reasonable and better done; their attention to truth and goodness more obvious and complete. But that I have ever worked deliberately in a primitive or archaic manner is not true; I took to carving after ten years as a letter cutter and, having no 'art school' training and having never drawn from 'the life' in my life, my carvings were inevitably of the kind Mr. Penty calls 'even archaic'. Some people think I ought never to have done them; other people said 'no, go on; it's time we broke away from the superstitions of the art school'. People bought my stones and ordered more —naturally I went on.

I am not going to follow Mr. Penty into the question of the goodness or badness of reinforced concrete as a building material or as a method of building. It may be as bad as he says it is, or it may be as good as it is said to be by other people of equal intelligence and even wider experience. I do not set myself up as an expert in the technical question and obviously it is for us a new material and a new method and one not yet fully tried out. But I cannot see why it should not be experimented with, especially as the results of contemporary experiment already show many grand and pleasing works (e.g. the new bridge at Cologne, the church at Le Raincy and the Horticultural Hall, Westminster. I may mention also, as Mr. Penty so much admires the design, that Mr. Edward Maufe's Guildford Cathedral is to have a reinforced concrete vault similar to that of his new church at

u

Hanwell). Mr. Penty's attitude is very priggish and it is simply silly to say that the modern use of concrete is nothing but the result of a cement manufacturer's ramp.

Another excellent reason for the use of concrete for building is its obvious suitability to the industrialization of labour. The reinforced concrete building is the Industrialist building *par excellence*. Let us get on with the experiment; meanwhile I am not hindered from saying on all possible occasions that Industrialism, whatever the grandeur of its products, is ultimately incompatible with the nature of men. It will come to its end not because its products offend the old-fashioned architect but because it offends humanity.

But, good or bad, concrete is not the only material even in an industrial world. I have done carvings in concrete and am willing to do as many more as I am asked for. But stone whether natural or artificial, and wood and all kinds of metal are also available. I do not carve in stone for aesthetic or sentimental reasons but simply because that is the material to hand or the material ordered by my customers. (Mr Penty asks if I do not think concrete is 'an inartistic material' What a question, what a phrase! He might as well ask if I don't think iron inartistic, or glass, or putty.)

Then Mr. Penty goes on to talk about a 'cult of ugliness' I shall not follow him into this discussion either. The beautiful, the ugly! The beautiful is that which being seen pleases the ugly that which displeases. Mr. Penty is displeased by such and such; therefore, without more ado, he calls it ugly It is precisely this kind of deadlock that compels us to go back to rational principles — to principles of good sense and good will — in order to discover the grounds of pleasure and the nature of the act of seeing. For when a man's mind is disordered his pleasure or displeasure are of no importance in an argument. Let the art-critics have their little game. We workmen, are too busy making things that are wanted as well as we are able to bother about whether what we make is beautiful or ugly.

Mr. Penty yearns for a revival of art patronage. But every man who spends money on things made by men is a patron of art. Again, it is precisely the artificial division of human works into art and not art which compels us to return to first principles. Let the so-called patrons of art continue to buy paintings and sculptures at absurd prices and let us forget about them.

I must leave the matter thus. Mr. Penty and I live in quite different worlds. His letter is, to me, nothing but 'art non-sense'. The arts, he says, are in peril! What nonsense this is. The arts are never in peril. If one art languishes another flourishes. If old fashioned drawing-board-Gothic architects are being discarded so much the better. There are more rational people to take their place. I don't believe in his high art nonsense about the architect being a prophet. The archi-tect is simply the ruler of workmen —and he would be a useful member of society if he would build buildings as they are required and use whatever materials are available to the best of his intelligence and ability without bothering about either the past or the future or the critics. (And the same applies to sculptors and all makers of images.) Yours faithfully,

ERIC GILL

Jerusalem, 10th May, 1934.

217 : TO 'THE CATHOLIC HERALD'
3RD NOVEMBER, 1934

Proletarian Art

Sir: As one of the exhibitors at the exhibition of pictures arranged by the society called the Artists' International, held in London recently, you will perhaps allow me to comment upon the remarks of your contributor G. M. Godden.

I visited the exhibition rather expecting to find many 'anti-God' paintings, as I had been told I should do, but in half an hour's walk round I could see none. All I saw were various works depicting the hardships of the proletariat, the brutality of the police, the display of armed forces against street orators, starving children, and slum conditions generally. There were also a few works in the vein of Van Gogh's famous 'Yellow Chair,' that is to say, works depicting simple workmen and scenes of working life.

It was not a big exhibition. It was not held in a fashionable quarter. It might be described as a pathetic affair compared with the exhibitions of what your contributor doubtless calls 'Art' in fashionable West End galleries and art dealers' shops.

As for the bookstall which so much impressed Miss Godden, it was not exclusively reserved for Marxian propaganda, for I saw, prominently displayed, Upton Sinclair's *Mammon Art*, a book written at least ten years ago and nothing to do with Russia.

Suppose it to be true that the Artists' International is primarily concerned to propagate Communism; even so, there was nothing in the terms under which we exhibited which made it obligatory. And there was nothing to hinder any Catholic artist from showing that he could stand up for social justice as well as any Marxian.

So much for that aspect of the affair. But I am less concerned to defend the exhibition than to defend the principle governing it. Your contributor says that the exhibition was 'neither British nor international nor primarily concerned with art.' Further on she says that the Union was not created 'to promote good art but as a section of the army of propagandists.' Further, she quotes Lenin's saying that 'art must serve propaganda,' and, describing a discussion which took place at the exhibition, she says: 'Speakers denounced the present English social system and the Sedition Bill — subjects familiar to Communist speakers but unexpected in a course of addresses connected with an exhibition of art.'

Now what, may I ask, is this extraordinary thing called art if it is not propaganda or at the service of propaganda? What are the sculptures on the medieval cathedrals and in modern churches but propaganda? What are the effigies of eminent politicians in Westminster Abbey and Parliament Square if they are not propaganda for the values and politics upheld by famous statesmen? What is the Royal Academy exhibition but propaganda for the bourgeois culture of modern England; just as Van Gogh's 'Yellow Chair' is propaganda for the values of simple people and simple things?

Art which is not propaganda is simply aesthetics and is consequently entirely the affair of cultured connoisseurs. It is a studio affair, nothing to do with the common life of men and women, a means of 'escape.' Art in the studio becomes simply 'self-expression,' and that becomes simply self-worship. Charity, the love of God and your neighbour, which, here below, every work of man must exhibit, is lost. If you say art is nothing to do with propaganda, you are saying that it has nothing to do with religion —that it is simply a psychological dope, a sort of cultured drug traffic. I, at any rate, have no use for it. For me, all art is propaganda; and it is high time that modern art became propaganda for social justice instead of propaganda for the flatulent and decadent ideals of bourgeois Capitalism.

Every artist must be a preacher, a missionary. But it does not follow that he should make up his own sermons. What is wanted is precisely what Lenin said, with this difference: that, as Catholics, we are serving not the propaganda of Marxian materialism but the propaganda of the Kingdom of God and his justice. —Yours, etc.,   ERIC GILL

Pigotts, High Wycombe, October 28.

Tarnside   *7-11-1934*

Dearest Denis*: I'm glad to hear from Mary this morn that
Blundell's want you to visit them. This is merely to say what's
much in my mind on that subject, viz:—

There is on one hand (i.e. in schools as we know them):

> *Book   education* —therefore thoughts, words, ideas. read-
> ing *about* it, writing *about* it, learning
> *about* it, and *exams* about it. (*mental*
> discipline, *intellectual discipline*)

& on the other:

> *Games education* —therefore actions, physical develop-
> ment, combative enthusiasm, loyalty
> development —the 'team' spirit. Per-
> sonal prowess, pride in oneself —self
> respect . . . (in fact *moral* discipline,
> discipline of the *will*.)

But on *neither* hand is there any education in *things*!

There is no *poetic experience* —

Intellect is trained almost entirely by books.

Will is trained almost entirely by games.

N.B. *I'm* not starting a complaint about this. Many others
before me have complained. and I don't know if anything
can be done about it.

But that is the core of Mr. Gorton's difficulty. We live in
a world of *things*. Making things is a large part of man's life —
any man's, & certainly the majority of men are *operatives* of
one kind or another. And yet there's no education in things —
no education in poetic experience. We grasp an idea, a con-

---

* Item. V. many thanks for *T. & T.* Your cartoon is
excellent. My only complaint is that I think 'Justice' might
have come to life a little tiny bit & had a v. slight but v.
legible sneer on her face.

cept, an abstraction, a representation, i.e. we train our *intellects*. We grasp balls & bats & one another's ankles (tackle low, Smith minor!). i.e. we train our *wills*. But we grasp no *thing*. No thing *as such* and for itself, no *being* – only thoughts *about* things, only actions in *relation* to things. Poet, poiesis, *maker* – grasper of *things*, reality as knowable by *experience* of it. Art, artistry (from cats' meat to cathedrals) is all a matter of poetry, grasping reality, grasping things.

But can it be done in schools? V. doubtful, what? V. difficult – damn art & art schools as we know them. It's not *that* we want. What we want is an education which is not, on one hand, entirely bookish and, on the other, entirely games – we want the *thing*. But do middle class parents want *things*? Not a bit. Does Mr. Gorton want to set up a peculiar school for peculiar parents?   Love from   E. G.

Love to darling Petra & Judith & Prudence & Adam.

2 1 9 : TO 'THE NEW ENGLISH WEEKLY'
15TH NOVEMBER, 1934

[AMONG obituary letters on A. R. Orage.]

Nearly thirty years ago we met – Fabians both. We worked together on the Fabian arts group – vague efforts to deprive Fabianism of its webbed feet – vain efforts. I wrote occasionally for the *New Age* – arts and crafts stuff. We had intimate friends in common, common enthusiasms, common appetites for earth and heaven. Then we drifted apart – he to Fontaine-bleau, I to Rome. We did not meet again until his return from America in 1932, sadder and wiser both of us, perhaps. At any rate, we both saw that 'a starving man needs food, not instruction' – that the state of the modern world is not so much due to crime as to folly, though, truly, a folly almost criminal – that the immediate enemy is not so much ill will, deliberate wickedness, as extraordinary stupidity, a gross and ridiculous ineptitude in our system of finance —that religion and piety cannot possibly have effect and bear fruit, material or spiritual, while a poverty as unnecessary as' it is unholy condemns millions to misery, and a financial system as anti-quated as it is ridiculous compels the rest of us to an insane war-provoking commercialism.

As editor of the *New English Weekly* Orage had the dove and serpent mixture to perfection. The policy he had to promote is no sectarian fancy. You haven't to be a Roman Catholic in order to support it any more than you have to be a Plymouth Brother, an atheist or a Jew. It is a policy of mere intelligi-bility and intelligence. It subserves human life; it does not determine its goal. The control of credit, as the present Pope has said, is the control of 'the very lifeblood of the people.' For this reason every supporter was welcome, whatever his faith or unfaith —provided he had faith in human reason. Roman jostled humanitarian and 'blue domer.' Engineers, journalists, poets and parsons met for a common purpose and lion lay down with lamb.

There was no 'art nonsense' about Orage, nothing puritan or prudish, nothing precious or eccentric —above all, nothing of the 'crank.' He was therefore the best possible person to promote an idea, a thing, which all its enemies said was cranky. And, behind his urbanity, and supporting it —behind his great intelligence, and maintaining it, was a rich humanity —his hatred of fraud and cruelty, his loathing of the downright indecency of the existing commercial world.

I do not know what gift or what grace he received at Fontainebleau. It is certain that his deep appetite for religion was there, in some manner, satisfied.

220 : TO 'THE CATHOLIC HERALD'
24TH NOVEMBER, 1934

Art as Propaganda

Sir: Your correspondent L. M. Parker questions my assertion that 'art which is not propaganda is simply aesthetics.' But, of course, I did not mean to imply that propagandist art made no aesthetic appeal; I meant simply that works which rely solely on aesthetic appeal (i.e. works of art which have no meaning) are merely a studio affair and, as such, are divorced from the common life of men and women.

It is true that industrialism kills the workman's sense of beauty, but he will not recover that sense if the idea becomes prevalent that 'art' has nothing to do with anything else. The subject matter is what normal people buy works of art for primarily. The state of affairs wherein the ordinary workman has no intellectual responsibility and, therefore, no responsibility for either beauty or meaning, is one in which the studio artist (i.e., the one kind of workman who is outside the factory system) is inevitably obsessed by aesthetics; for, confronted by fifty competing religions and complete chaos among philosophers (and you cannot expect him to continue the F. G. Watts prophet-and-seer business — he has that much sense) pure aesthetics is the only decent thing left to him.

This brings me to Mr. Perceval's trouble. He asserts that the sole criterion by which works of art of all times and nations can be judged is *shape* — that the one common feature which makes it possible to compare certain works of China, India, Egypt or medieval Europe with the works of say Michelangelo and Henry Moore is shape. My contention is that this is only true from the studio point of view, and that it is not true from the point of view of the human being as such; that from the point of view of human beings *meaning* is a more primary and more important criterion; and that it is as inevitable as it is right and proper that the ordinary person should dislike works of art whose meanings revolt him.

If it happens that you are confronted by a work whose meaning escapes you and which is, therefore, as far as you are concerned, meaningless, you are, of course, compelled to regard it merely as a shape, and like it or dislike it accordingly. But, actually, human nature being what it is, such works are exceedingly rare. Human nature is the same in all times and places and it has hitherto been impossible and is even now extremely difficult for artists to rid themselves of their humanity; moreover, that they should do so is the last thing the customer wants or will pay for —unless he is that rare bird, the rich connoisseur. —Yours, etc.,   ERIC GILL

High Wycombe, November 18.

2 2 1 : TO 'THE CATHOLIC HERALD' 1ST DECEMBER, 1934

Money and Morals

Sir: I am honoured by Fr. John-Baptist Reeves's criticism of my book *Money and Morals*, and, though a lot of what he says is rather over my head and, therefore, runs like water off a duck's back and, so to say, cuts no ice, I will do my best to reply.

I think Fr. John-Baptist agrees with me fundamentally, and even if I did not think so before, I know it after reading his article in your issue of November 10 (not the one in which he attacks me, but the one in which he attacks that which I am chiefly concerned to attack, the Industrial System and all its vain-glory), but there seem to be matters in which we are not agreed, although I suspect that his argument is a little bit forced and perverse.

With my thesis that 'under existing economic conditions the practice of Christian morals is for most people exceedingly difficult, if not quite impossible,' Fr. John-Baptist does not seem to quarrel; it is indeed obviously true. But with my argument that 'Just as Christian faith requires, as a necessary preamble, a certain natural integrity of reason, so Christian morals presuppose a certain natural moral integrity,' he seems to disagree and I think his disagreement is largely misunderstanding, a misunderstanding doubtless due to my bad presentation of my case.

My argument amounts to little more than this: that (as the Church teaches) a starving man cannot be condemned for taking bread from him who has plenty — that is to say theft is not always stealing; and that, therefore, if the natural requirements of physical life are withheld our judgment of people must be different from what it would be if they were prosperous.

So far it is easy, and so far we have staved off widespread theft by means of the 'dole'; but we have only just staved it off and may not much longer be able to do so. Moreover, we have not granted the 'dole' on account of either justice or charity, but simply because we are afraid of bloody revolution.

But when it comes to other and more subtle matters it is not so easy. The industrial system does not only involve unemployment; it also involves the reduction of the majority of men to 'a sub-human condition of intellectual irresponsibility'; it involves the destruction of the family; it makes it necessary that all things made shall be regarded simply as merchandise, not made for *use* but made for *sale*; it involves a world-wide competition for markets; it almost certainly involves us in war, and war the more horrible as it becomes more mechanically waged.

Now Fr. John-Baptist seems to think that I accuse the Catholic clergy of being largely to blame for the institution of industrialism. But it is not so. I did not blame anyone. I know perfectly well how difficult it is for people to think differently from the way in which they have been brought up; and the clergy, like everyone else, have been brought up to revere Great Britain as the workshop of the world, to admire the conveniences which industrialism showers upon us, and it is not for me to accuse anyone of sin. I state a complaint rather than an accusation. I complain because I do not find, or find very rarely, any realisation among Catholics, clergy or laity, that the industrial system is inimical to Christianity — that it destroys the family, that it degrades men to the level of mere tools, that, as Fr. John-Baptist himself says, it makes 'cunning men fat, and drives . . . skilled craftsmen back to the land to dig their own graves.'

Naturally it makes you angry to hear people urged to have large families when you know, as well as you know that two and two make four, that the children will probably have to starve and, if they live, they will have to live the sub-human lives of factory-hands, with the cheering thought that they will end up as cannon-fodder.

This is not in the least to say that 'birth-control' is right and proper or that the clergy do wrong to preach against contraception; it is simply to register the complaint that the clergy rarely preach against avarice and rarely seem to realise that man has intelligence as well as will and that, therefore, there is something just a little bit wrong with industrialism.

It seems to me (and I am fully aware that I may be wrong) that the only possible argument which could be used to support our pastors in their silence as to the evils of industrialism, or in their praises of its benefits, would be that Christians have always been and must always be a 'little flock,' that Christian virtue has always been and must always be heroic virtue; and that 'a man can be a very good Catholic in a factory,' simply because factory-life makes it more difficult.

I know this argument is used by some, and it would in many ways be a great relief if it were promulgated officially —we should then know where we are.

But this does not seem to be the line of thought encouraged by papal encyclicals. The Pope, like our Lord Himself, seems to have compassion on the multitude. The Church does not seem to demand heroic virtue from all. She seems to say that people should be helped and not hindered.

I did not say, and I did not imply, that before a man can have faith he must be trained in philosophy. I did not say or imply that before a man can be good he must have houses and lands. I only said that the Christian faith is not the faith of idiots, and that, therefore, a certain natural sanity must exist among men if they are to be converted. And I only said that as Christians are *men* (man is matter and spirit, both real and both good), they need food, clothing, and shelter, and that in the absence of such things few people will either care for salvation or listen to preachers.

You may reply, Sir, that nobody is starving, nobody is naked (Good Lord! we do make sure of that), and nobody is allowed to sleep out. But in the South Wales coalfields there are thousands of men who are too weak to dig in their gardens because they have been underfed for years. All over England there are millions of people clothed like rats (and starving rats at that —mangy.). And as for houses, do the clergy not care a bit what Birmingham is like so long as the Church has gothic tracery? But no, of course, they care. I know they care. I know they are full of compassion for the multitude. I only want it to be clear, I only want it to be notorious, that the Church is as much the enemy of injustice as she is the friend of righteousness. I want to see it denied and, more than that, I want to see it disproved that the Church is afraid to speak because she has too much money invested in the industrial system. And if my complaint seems to be chiefly against the clergy, it is only because they alone have authority to teach. — Yours, etc.,   ERIC GILL

P.S. I say nothing about 'Nature and Grace.' Of course, I accept, without demur, what the Church teaches about that and/or them.

Pigotts, High Wycombe, November 18.

Art and Authority

Sir: Undeserved praise is harder to bear than undeserved blame, and so I am moved to point out that the reference to me in your issue of November 16 is very misleading. The article in the *Studio*, from which you quote a sentence, is almost completely mad. The author praises the authorities at Westminster Cathedral for allowing the sculptor of the Stations a free hand. He praises the sculptor for (as he imagines) not allowing 'edification . . . to interfere with sovereign art.' He says 'each group is dominated by the sculptor's search for balance and design.' He praises the Roman Catholics of England, saying that they are 'the least English of the English,' for their freedom from the 'national prejudice against the freedom of art.'

It seems ungracious to protest, but what nonsense and, having regard to the author's nationality, what double Dutch all this is. Edification was, of course, the paramount concern of the Westminster authorities and the sculptor's preliminary drawings were criticised in detail by them from that point of view. His search for 'balance and design' was always a search for that balance and design which would most harmoniously convey the meaning of each Station. It is absurd to say that English Catholics show their unEnglishness by their freedom from the 'national prejudice against the freedom of art' because the precise opposite is the truth. The Catholic Church, and therefore English Catholics, almost alone in a mad world, uphold the right and proper principle that the artist is a servant and must subordinate his ideas to those of the spiritual authority.

The Catholic artist is only free in the sense that he is free to run on rails. He has not got to invent a religion for himself as the non-Catholic artist must —and that is why the modern non-Catholic artist, being an intelligent person, has given up the prophet and seer business and confines himself exclusively to aesthetic experiments.

Suppose, for charity's sake, that the Dutch author is right in his contention that the Westminster Stations have 'significant form.' Even so, it remains true that that form is subordinate to, dependent upon, and expressive of, each Station's *religious* significance.

I beg, Sir, to be allowed to state publicly that I repudiate the notion that the artist as artist is not subject to religious authority.   ERIC GILL.

2 2 3 : T O ' T H E   C A T H O L I C   H E R A L D ' 1 9 T H   J A N U A R Y ,   1 9 3 5

Proletarian Art

Sir: Your correspondent ' P A S M O I ' in the *Catholic Herald*, January 1 2, invites me to solve his puzzle. He says 'Repositories supply crucifixes which function (as propaganda) just as well' as those made by 'an artist' and so he wonders why he should prefer the latter.

But it is precisely his 'just as well' that I deny. A 'repository' crucifix may be better than one of mine or it may be worse. I deny that their propaganda efficiency can be equal. If there is the least difference between them, there *must* be difference in their effects.

Either a thing is in line with man's last end or it is not. 'He that is not with me is against me . . .' If man cannot live without bread, then inferior bread is better than none. If the rubrics specify the crucifix as a necessity then an inferior crucifix is better than none. But better bread nourishes the body better than inferior bread and a better crucifix nourishes the soul better than an inferior one. What is it to be a propagandist but to have a cause at heart and to work always in line with that cause and never against it or in forgetfulness of it? You can't add colour to a crucifix or alter its shape in the smallest particular without making it a better crucifix or a worse one, more in line with the cause or less, better propaganda or worse. And, if you give up the struggle, you may end up with a crucifix which is actually bad propaganda.

Your correspondent talks about my 'art.' But I deny that there is any such thing except in relation to the job in hand — e.g. the art of making crucifixes. There is no such thing as beauty by itself unless you mean a purely physical thing (as when you say: rice pudding is beautiful — it agrees with me; or the 'Golden Section' is beautiful — it satisfies my sense of proportion), and even then it is doubtful, because man is not a purely physical being and is never moved by purely physical considerations.

So, I repeat, let us give up talking about 'art' and beauty — let us leave such things to the repositories and the art critics and if you don't think my crucifixes are better *crucifixes*, for God's sake don't buy them. —Yours, etc., ERIC GILL

Pigotts, High Wycombe, January 13.

224 : TO THE REV. JOHN O'CONNOR

Pigotts
28-1-1935

Dear Father John: Thank you for your letter of the 25th. [. . .]

I enjoyed my brief visit to you more than tellable. [. . .] I send herewith *Sun-bathing Review*[1] of which the Editor came and interviewed me. I detest *Nudism* [. . .] but I saw no reason for refusing to speak and so endeavoured to push across what seemed to me the truth. He has dished up my remarks as an article and stuck in quotations from *Clothes*. It's a bit of a jumble but I don't see any serious errors. Now I get the

[1] Winter 1934-5.

enclosed from our dear Fr Vincent.[1] I have told him in reply
that I am very sorry to have given him offence but wish I knew
how. Also that it seems somewhat uncharitable to assume that
I am *wilfully* perverse and not simply mistaken in my opinions.
Also that it is nothing to do with '*Art*'. Please, of your
charity, advise me. Have I said anything heretical or impru-
dent? If so, what?   E. G.

225 : TO THE REV. JOHN O'CONNOR

Pigotts   *31-1-1935*

Thank you very much for yours of 30th. Drawing of Madonna
next week sans fail. I rejoice like anything to have your
assurance as to orthodoxy, decency & general o.k.ness of the
S.-B Review 'article'. Love from Mary & all.   E. G.

226 : TO GRAHAM CAREY

Pigotts   *26-2-1935*

Dear Carey: I was overwhelmed when I received the *American
Review* this month and found your review of my book in it.
I do think you have honoured me too much but, apart from
that, your article is an admirable essay on the subject and a
very valuable contribution to the controversy. Thank you
very much for it.

Curiously enough, a few days before the *A.R.* came I had
sent off to them a lecture on 'Sculpture and machine made
buildings'. I hope they will accept it and I hope it won't be
thought to let you down – i.e. not up to the high standard you
claim for me.

[1] For reasons that seem to me sufficient, I have kept intact in this correspondence some allusions to Father Vincent McNabb which reveal disagreement on
certain matters. I must add that throughout his life E. G. continued to venerate
Father Vincent as one of the holiest men of our time.

X

I believe I did send you the solution of your three caps problem. I liked it very much. In case I did not send my effort I enclose copy herewith.

Now about the Exhibition you wrote about.

Of course I have no personal objection to your scheme.

On the contrary I think it is most noble of you to do it. But my trouble is that I am simply overwhelmed with work and simply can't do anything about it myself. The best I can do is to hand your letter to my agent in London and ask her to communicate with you and fix things up if possible.

David Jones is not here now but I know Denis Tegetmeier will be glad to send things.

The Glastonbury Madonna you ask about is quite a small thing —about 2'. 6".

I am very glad you like it. It is in a niche over the door of the R.C. Church at Glastonbury. I did it in 1928.

I am very glad you have met Dr. Coomaraswamy. It is many years since I have seen him —about 24! He is I think the most downright lucid man I know, and is doing a very fine work. He sent me recently a Broadcast speech of his on art. Wonderfully good. Did you *hear* it?

Yes, I saw the *Pencil Points* and *Art* articles. They are both pretty fatuous I think and the *P.P.* article was* illustrated with some bad early drawings. Yours ever.   ERIC G.

* I know the old boy who wrote it. Nice ⟨sort⟩ of man — but 1870 trying to be 1930 —mutton dressing as lamb.

227 : TO THE REV. JOHN O'CONNOR

Pigotts   28-2-1935

Dear Fr. John: That's just the trouble —I *can't* stick to the picture. Of course I can do the statue[1] with face looking straight forward, but what I *know* I can't do is a face like the picture —i.e. a *portrait* of the man. It's not my kind of job.

[1] Of St. John Bosco.

I am sorry because I don't even know whom to recommend to you instead. Epstein is the greatest portrait sculptor of our time, but, apart from expense, I doubt if he'd have much sympathy for the job. But he's the right *kind* of sculptor for the job. I can copy a face on paper if the sitter is in front of me, but I can't do portrait *statues* from pictures. I can't do that *kind* of thing. It wants, *needs*, a different kind of imagination from mine. For your own sake you must get someone else. I shd. only make a hash of it & disappoint you.

We can discuss the matter when you come next week. I've got to go to S. Wales to-morrow until Monday night (to see the builder re Capel-y-ffin repairs etc.) & I've got to go and lecture at Blundell's school, Tiverton, on March 8. But I shall be here in between.

NAPHILL 42 when you get near. (Toll call) Yours ever affectly. ERIC G.

This sounds awfully brusque —it's only because I'm in a rush & tear on account of having to go off first thing in morn. E. G.

228 : TO 'ST. ANDREW'S (CROYDON) PARISH MAGAZINE', FEBRUARY 1935

[THIS description of E. G.'s carving at St. Andrew's church hall was sent to the parish magazine at the vicar's request.]

St. Andrew

The carving shows St. Andrew pulling at the net. He was a fisherman. Our Lord said to him 'I will make you a fisher of men,' so in the net are the men he is catching with his preaching. One man and two women —partly because there are in fact more women than men in England and partly because all creation is female to God.

Our Lord himself sits at the tiller of the ship, because he is guide, counsellor and friend. He is holding the end of the sail, because he does not only steer the ship but controls it in every way. St. Andrew is pulling very hard because it is a very difficult 'catch.' Our Lord is quite calm all the time.

The ship is the Church, it is very strong but not very fast.

St. Andrew is wearing a vest and kilt. Our Lord is wearing a sort of alb like a priest, the human fishes are naked because they are quite humble when they are caught.

The 'P' on the bow of the ship is 'P' for Peter —because it is Peter's barque. The carving is made of Portland stone.

It is not meant to be very much like 'nature,' because it is a *symbolic* carving and in carving of this kind the important things are, first, what it *means* and, second, that like a poem or piece of music, the different parts of it should rhyme together nicely.   ERIC GILL

229 : TO THE 'ARCHITECT & BUILDING NEWS', 5 APRIL, 1935

Sir: I am honoured by the note in your issue of March 22 with reference to my lecture to the West Yorkshire Society of Architects on the subject of Sculpture on Machine-made Buildings. May I briefly reply?

My argument is this:

Architecture is more than simply building, but it springs from building and cannot healthily be separated from it. The necessities of building are the material of good architecture. If new methods of building arise, then a new architecture inevitably follows —sooner or later. The industrial revolution has produced new methods of building and a new architecture is obviously evolving in consequence. The evolution is very slow; architects cling to pre-industrial styles and habits; steel and concrete are still cased in Greek and Roman shells; pillars and cornices are still thought desirable —and so on. But these things, this play acting, is passing away. The constructional engineering which is the reality of modern building is gradually emerging. The best architects ('best' because they admit and welcome the realities) now see clearly that architecture is more than building, not because it denies building or hides it or camouflages it, but because it affirms it and glorifies it.

So much for architecture; where does sculpture come in? Where did it ever come in? Sculpture is more than the self-expression of individual workmen, but it is, in the nature of things, dependent upon the faculty of self-expression – it is not patient of exact exposition in measured drawings. To get good sculpture you must have likely workmen bursting with sculptural enthusiasm. The only places in which to find such workmen to-day are the studios, and in such places workmen (we call them 'artists') are divorced from the life of building. The studio workman has inevitably become more and more divorced from the scaffold, and the men on the scaffold become more and more a sort of tools (willing or unwilling according as pay is good or bad) in the hands of the contractor. These things are so – no use denying it or crying over the spilt milk, and we must make the best of it, and the best is to recognise the incompatibility of hand-made sculptures with machine-made buildings. Let us have grand machine-made plain buildings in our streets and grand hand-made sculptures in our parks and museums. There is no justification for sculpture on modern buildings because the two things belong to radically different worlds, spring from different wombs, are produced by processes inimical to one another, and the architect who drags in sculpture, to make a focus point here or there, or out of reverence for past tradition, is only confessing his architectural weakness and timidity, and he cannot get away with it by saying that such sculpture is justified 'by its quality as sculpture and its placing where it can be seen and enjoyed.' The architect is not a 'welfare worker' kindly providing jobs for artists and entertainment for the passer-by.

So much being agreed, I hope, I went on to argue that in spite of all the foregoing there did remain the place of 'furniture sculpture,' i.e., sculpture required by the owner of the building rather than applied by the architect. You are perfectly right in holding that this is a very small place and getting smaller. You are also right in all you say about 'outworn, half-romantic badges, symbols and insignia.' I say two things in reply: (1) However small the place of 'furniture sculpture' may be, it will always remain, because it will always be true that some things are said better in image than in words, and some things cannot be said in any other way; and (2) one of the chief objects of my lecture was to point out the fatuity of 'outworn, half-romantic symbols,' and to urge that exactly as architecture must return to its basis in building-construction, so sculpture must return to its basis in *meaning*. Just because architects still play about with 'outworn, half-romantic' styles, and sculptors still fool about with 'outworn, half-romantic symbols' is no reason why they should continue to do so, and a return to rationality is the solution in both cases.

Looking at the matter from the point of view of the architect, there is no need whatever for sculpture on modern buildings. Looking at it from the point of view of the building operative there is no possibility of it. From these two points of view sculpture is an entirely irrelevant addition. But the *owner* of the building *may need it*, very seldom perhaps, and perhaps very foolishly. Let us therefore abandon the use of sculpture except as needed by the owner, and let us criticise this need very closely. Above all let us criticise the meaning of the image or symbol demanded. I spoke sarcastically about the image of Prudence on the Prudential and St. Pancras for the L.M.S. Such things are obvious nonsense. I agree that in general there is very little that the owners of modern buildings have to say that cannot be said adequately in plain block letters. And just as in lettering I have endeavoured to get away from mediaeval romanticism and 'Trajan Column' snobbery, so in sculpture I wish to return to the firm basis of necessity. If there is no necessity for sculpture I am very happy to do without it.

What are the *needs* of the case? That is the question, and it is a question that must be answered properly, by the architects no less than the sculptors, and by the owners no less than the architects.   ERIC GILL

230 : TO 'THE PUBLISHERS' CIRCULAR'
6 APRIL, 1935

Mr. Pat V. Daley asks me 'Who is a Typographical Artist?' I may disregard, as more flattering than accurate, his remarks about my reputation as an engraver and type designer, but I must deny that I am, or that I desire to be, in relation to my customers or clients, in the position of a dictator. He who pays . . . calls the tune, and I am as much subject to that law as anyone else. The only advantage I enjoy is an excess of work. This is an advantage, because, if a customer comes to me and says 'Please draw me a fat cherub on a cloud,' instead of doing as asked, as I should do if I had no other work, I am able to say, 'I can't do fat cherubs, you must go somewhere else.' In other words, having an excess of work, I can choose what seems more within my powers and let other things go. And, not using any machinery, or employing an army of assistants, I am more easily able to maintain this position than are those who are confronted by the twin horrors of high overheads and big wage bills. But I dictate to no one.

Mr. Daley describes very clearly the modern position as between publisher (i.e., customer) and printer. According to Mr. Daley the publisher has the ideas and the printer merely the executive ability — or if the printer has ideas he is not in the position to give effect to them. If, therefore, we are right in saying, as the dictionary says, that art is skill in making (human skill, therefore deliberate skill, for power to deliberate is the mark of the human being), it is clear that in so far as the printer is deprived of all deliberative power he is not an artist. And it is also clear that in so far as the publisher, or someone in his office, has power to give effect to his deliberations he is an artist. (Just as is a musician who only writes a score or an architect who only walks about and directs the operatives.)

In practice the printer is not entirely deprived of responsibility, nor is the publisher wholly and solely responsible. But the printer may well complain that a large part of his proper responsibility has been taken from him and that the publisher takes too much on himself. Before you can judge, you must note the causes of these things. Good or bad is not the point, but the *fact* is clear; we have got more and more into the thing called 'commercialism.' That means the rule of those who supply money. That means that the chief reward of industry is the reward to the seller and chiefly to the seller of money, the investor. That means that, if you want to reduce costs (and in competition with others you *must* do so), it is the cost of *production* which bears the brunt. That means division and subdivision of labour, machinery, rationalisation, etc. That means 'overheads' for the producer. That means his constant obsession is getting orders. That means that he becomes business man first and printer second. In the end that means that his opinions as a printer become degraded, and highbrow publishers, educated at Universities and browsing in libraries, get to know more, or think they do, than the printer as to what's what in typography. A very bad business it seems to me, but quite inevitable in a commercial world. (Exactly the same thing happened in architecture. Compare architect and contractor, and printers and building operatives.)

Who is the typographical artist? Well, if Mr. Daley's description is correct, the publisher seems to be. Of course, he delegates a certain amount of artistic responsibility to various people. Perhaps he keeps a 'lay-out' man. Perhaps he employs me to design a jacket. Perhaps he even gives a little responsibility to the printer. But, as things are, he regards the printer chiefly as the proprietor of a printing outfit and doesn't think of him as anything but a man of business; just as the architect doesn't think of the contractor as anything but a man of business. And, of course, many publishers, like many architects, are themselves only business men camouflaged.

If Mr. Daley doesn't like this state of affairs he must join in with those who want to supplant business rule, the rule of the investor, the bourgeois state, by something else. What? But that's not the subject of his letter.

There is one error in Mr. Daley's article. My 'Joanna' type was not designed to facilitate machine punch cutting. Not at all. Machines can do practically anything. The question isn't what they *can* but what they *should*. It is clear that machine products are best when they are plain. Machine-made ornament is nauseating. Assuming that the serif is not an ornamental but a useful addition to letters (especially in book faces), the Joanna is an attempt to design a book face free from all fancy business. It might easily be better. I only claim that it is on the right lines for machine production.

No, it is not economic status that makes a man an artist. The test is simply and solely responsibility. In so far as a man is responsible, thus far he is an artist — the artist is the responsible workman. In our commercial industrialism it is generally true to say that the only responsible workman, the only artist is a gentleman in an office, and as the said gentleman is generally very little acquainted with the physical making of things (he is only a designer), it generally follows that he is responsible for a lot of rubbish. Books, like buildings, are not merely ideas; they are things made of material. Therefore it is better when the designer and the maker are one person or a group working together in harmony, a group bound by craft enthusiasms and not, as in our commercial world, bound only by a cash nexus.

The man who 'licks a thing into shape' is the artist, yes,

precisely. But in the book trade to-day the man who does that, who has the real responsibility for doing that, who can be praised or blamed for the result, is very often not the printer.   ERIC GILL

231 : TO HIS BROTHER CECIL

Geneva   *15-4-1935*

Am here till to-morrow. Arrive Victoria 3.30 p m on Wednesday. Very difficult business this job. Very big – & no one knows what they want me to do. They think I'm a prophet & seer & at same time don't believe in my prophecies. I'm distressed by your position. We must help as required. We must meet soon. Can you possibly manage a night at Pigotts? I'm v. rushed with work at present. This Geneva journey has rather cut into things. Love to all.   ERIC G.

232 · TO 'THE ENGINEER', 3RD MAY, 1935
Social Credit and Demechanisation

Sir: By a remarkable coincidence, the letters of Mr. Charles R. King and 'New Briton' in your issue of April 19th deal with the two rival solutions for the financial difficulty of to-day.

Mr. King advises demechanisation or restriction of machinery in order to keep people in work, in order to give them earning power, in order to give them purchasing power, in order that trade may revive, for without consumers production of plenty is useless. 'New Briton' draws attention to Major Douglas' scheme of Social Credit, that is, the direct financing of consumers so that increase of mechanisation shall not lead to loss of purchasing power. One says, machinery is throwing people out of work, therefore destroying purchasing power, therefore cutting its own throat; so let us cut down the use of machinery. The other says, machinery is throwing people out of work, that is, making their labour unnecessary — what a blessing! Let us remedy the loss of purchasing power by giving people money to buy things with. For if *without* machinery ten men can make ten pairs of boots in ten days, and *with* machinery one man can make ten pairs in the same time, then obviously the sensible thing to do is to arrange things so that each of the ten men gets one pair of boots out of the ten while only working one-tenth of the time. That is, abandon the notion that you can only earn ten days' pay by doing ten days' work (a notion long ago abandoned by the *owners* of machinery), *i.e.*, distribute purchasing power according to the social value of the product rather than according to time worked.

Which scheme is the better? Which is the more practicable? Is either of them? Is not mechanisation a sort of disease which must run its course — a disease which could not have attacked us had it not been for the breakdown of the agricultural system, the dispossession of the peasantry, the consequent growth of a hungry proletariat, concurring with the rise of commerce, the growth of the money power, and the reduction of all things to quantitative terms. For in spite of the blessings of industrialism (*e.g.*, button-pushing instead of hard sweat; machine-minding instead of craftsmanship, and degraded craftsmanship at that; countless conveniences and services for everyone such as were formerly unknown even to kings and princes), we must never forget its origins. As Mr. King points out, machinery was not introduced for altruistic reasons. The whole point of machinery is that it enables its owners to make things more quickly and with less labour, and therefore to sell them with greater profit. The chauffeur loves his car, but that is not why his master bought it. The engineer loves machines, as we all do, but that is not why manufacturers buy them.

On the other hand, Social Credit means loss of power and profits to financiers. Is it likely that financiers will be beaten, when we consider that the rest of us after several hundred years of commercialism are ourselves profiteers, big or small? We all regard industry simply as the production of merchandise, things made for profit, and chiefly the profit of investors. It is not only bankers who have 'the money mind,' every little man who has a small business or small investments is in the same boat.

Mr. King quotes instances of the restriction of machinery in the seventeenth and eighteenth centuries; but that sort of thing cannot be done now. It is too late. The thing has grown too big. No modern prince has sufficient power. Politicians wear the 'cap and bells,' but the financiers call the tune.

Moreover, the habit of mind of the craftsman is now destroyed. Few factory hands have any more desire to return to pre-industrial methods than their masters. On the whole, therefore, Social Credit seems the more likely solution; it assumes the continuance and even the increase of mechanisation, and makes no attempt to eradicate commercialism.

Suppose, for the sake of argument, the bankers were beaten. Then we shall be confronted by the problem of leisure. We must look this matter in the face squarely. People talk about machinery releasing the world from drudgery and leaving us free for 'higher things.' What are these 'higher things'? I know what the highbrow educated people say, but what do you plain rational engineers say? Do you, like them, kid yourselves that millions of factory hands when they become men of leisure, supported not on the dole, but on an adequate dividend, are going in for the arts and crafts and writing poetry? And as to those arts and crafts, you know as well as I do that the best arts and crafts are those done for use and not for art. If all useful things are made by machinery, there will only be the 'Art' left. Is it conceivable that Art, pure Art, Art divorced from any notion of utility or service, will occupy and satisfy and make happy the majority of ordinary men and women? I do not believe it. I think Art is only endurable when it is allied to service.

So there goes Social Credit! And the restriction upon machinery is impossible. What, then, is the remedy? I do not believe there is one, the disease must run its course. This civilisation, like all others, must come to its term. And why not? Then we shall begin again—a new cycle: chaos, order, achievement, decay, disease, death. This view is only pessimistic if you think this life is all. I do not.

Forgive my intrusion into your paper, but the time is past when artists could live in Chelsea and not notice Birmingham, or when engineers could remain oblivious to the problems of the artist. For the artist is essentially the responsible workman, the normal man, the maker of things. And the abnormality of our time in which the artist is a peculiar person, an aesthete, a sort of lap dog, whose highest ambition is to have his works put in museums, and the majority of workmen have been reduced to a sub-human condition of intellectual irresponsibility, is a thing which concerns engineers as much as stone carvers like me.   ERIC GILL

High Wycombe, April 25th.

233 : TO I. J. PITMAN

7-5-1935

Dear Mr. Pitman: Herewith I am sending you the article on Lettering and Phonography to which Mr. Tegetmeier referred when you saw him the other day. I hope you will see from it the point of the cartoon of which you saw a photograph.[1]

The point is that up to the present shorthand or phonography has appealed to very few people except those who had professional reasons for writing quickly, therefore phonography has been associated in people's minds with mere time saving, and those who practice it have thought of it merely as

---

[1] A painting by Denis Tegetmeier in five panels depicting a Roman stonecutter, a mediaeval scribe, Wynkyn de Worde, a commercial advertiser, and a schoolmistress teaching phonography. Cf. the last chapter of the second and third editions of *Typography*.

a means to a living. On the other hand, typographers and pedants have made such a fuss about the beauty of 'lettering' and the venerableness of printed books that no one has realized how ridiculous spelling has become, and what a clumsy method of communication 'lettering' is.

It may be a forlorn hope but at least it seems worth while to me, the idea, viz. that phonography is much more than a mere time saver, it is in fact a logical and sane method of communication having the inestimable advantage of a real time-correspondence between speech and writing —I mean, think how marvellous it would be if everyone could write and everyone could read shorthand, and especially if shorthand were redeemed from its merely utilitarian aspect so that the phonographic word took on for us the nobility of the lettered print. Yours sincerely,   ERIC GILL

P.S. I also enclose prospectus of a school run by my daughter, from which you will see that they propose to make phonography an ordinary subject.

2 3 4 : TO PHILIP HENDERSON

Pigotts   *13-5-1935*

Dear Henderson: After you had gone yesterday I looked up your review[1] in *New Britain* and this is only to say that my memory was correct; it is extremely good —very good indeed. Of course I might quarrel with you a bit over the last paragraph. For instance, walls cased with stone and filled with rubble sounds bad but actually the thing called rubble, when properly mixed, is the same as what we call nowadays concrete,* and the stone casing was like a sort of tube into which the concrete was poured, with this difference, that the casing

* except that they had no Portland Cement!

[1] Of *Art* (XXth Century Library).

was bonded in. All the same of course it is true there was lots of bad work done in those days, but my point was and is that if bad work was done it was the fault of those who did it, and not of their system. As for routine work, it still remains true that routine work was not characteristic of the early middle ages; it only became so in the 14th and 15th centuries, by which time the rising commerce and commercial frame of mind was pervading everything. We must talk about this next time we meet. I do not really think the productive system of the middle ages was charming, I think simply that it was commonplace and normal whereas ours is extraordinary and monstrous. Yours sincerely,   ERIC GILL

2 3 5 : TO PHILIP HENDERSON

Pigotts   *29-5-1935*

Dear Henderson: Many thanks for your letter of the 28th May. For various reasons I hold that the present industrial system is abnormal, however admirable its products may be, but as it seems clear that nobody wishes to destroy the industrial system then I agree, as I have said, all pre-industrial ideas must be scrapped. I incline to agree also that Communism is the only solution politically, but I think a re-arrangement or reform of our monetary system would ease the situation and is necessary in any case. I suspect in Russia they are pretty much tied to the banks when it comes to borrowing money — what are Russian 7% Bonds? Yours sincerely,   ERIC GILL

2 3 6 : TO ANTHONY EDEN

                                              27-6-1935

Dear Mr. Eden: I have now got hold of what seems to me an overwhelmingly good idea for the sculpture at Geneva, and

I wish to give you a preliminary description of it so that you may be prepared, and I hope sympathetic, when I produce the drawings, which I shall do in a few weeks' time.

To start with, the League exists to promote co-operation among the nations and to that end it is necessarily opposed to the piling up of armaments and the continuance of war; especially in view of the fact that war among industrialised nations does not mean more or less human hand to hand fighting with the attendant glories of human prowess, but a more and more disgusting, filthy and obscene destruction of humanity.

At the back of all this there is, to my mind, the fact of the rule of financiers and men of commerce exploiting racial animosities.

Now it seems to me that instead of doing a sculpture of the nations co-operating (Mons. Avenol's boat and rowers), it would hit the nail more on the head if we did a grand sculpture showing the thing itself which the League of Nations is out to preserve, namely, Man.

Imagine the centre panel 28ft. long and 7ft. high, practically entirely filled with a naked figure of a man reclining (rather as in the picture of the 'Creation of Adam' by Michael Angelo) a vast and grand figure of Man with hand outstretched and the tip of his finger touching the tip of the finger of God which is coming down from above, and in fine letters on the background, in Latin because it is a universal statement and not specially an English one, the words, 'AD IMAGINEM DEI CREAVIT ILLUM'. Because *that* is the point, Man was created in the image of God and it is *that* image which is being defaced and befouled. And then underneath, because it is an English gift, the words from G. M. Hopkins' poem:[1]—

[1] It will be seen that the opening here is a departure from Hopkins' text. I do not know whether E. G. quoted from memory or made a deliberate change to meet the exigencies of space in the design as then conceived. The same wording appears in his first working drawings. But it was later changed to the true text, 'Thou mastering me/God', and this was cut in the final work.

GOD MASTERING ME —
GIVER OF BREATH AND BREAD
WORLD'S STRAND, SWAY OF THE SEA
LORD OF LIVING AND DEAD —
OVER AGAIN I FEEL THY FINGER
AND FIND THEE.

The left-hand panel would contain figures of animals, trees, etc. moving as though drawn by an invisible Shepherd towards the centre panel. And underneath would be inscribed, 'CONSTITUISTI EUM SUPER OPERA MANUUM TUARUM', because the created world is God's gift to Man, and it is that gift which we are defacing and befouling also.

In the right-hand panel there would be represented Man's gifts to God, and obviously these gifts should be ourselves — the Cloud of Witness —and I would carve a group of children, again moving towards the centre panel as though drawn by the invisible Shepherd. And underneath would be inscribed, 'NOS AUTEM POPULUS EJUS ET OVES PASCUAE EJUS'.

The point of my writing all this is to win your sympathy for the idea because, especially in the case of the centre panel, it will require a pretty good effort of imagination and courage to accept the idea of so vast a man covering so large a space, and therefore I shall need all your kind assistance to put the idea across. I think some people might think that just the figure of a man is insufficient, but I am sure that if that figure were grand enough in composition and attitude, and if people would be patient and let the idea sink into them, they would see that it is the right one. It is Man who is in danger, it is Man who must be saved. And I think the crowds of people walking up and down the foyer lobbying one another would be moved by the thought, and would perhaps find it a support in their efforts when they enter the Council Chamber through those doors.

I pray to God you won't turn this idea down. I shall be anxious to hear from you. Yours sincerely,   ERIC GILL

Y

Pigotts   *10-7-1935*

Dear Mr. Eden: Thank you for your letter of July 4th. I was
very glad to hear that the scheme outlined in my letter of
June 27 attracted you. I have now made preliminary drawings
on the lines suggested and am sending them herewith. They
speak, I hope, for themselves, but there are a few things to
be noted: —

In my letter of June 27 I described the arrangement of the
panels thus: — MAN in centre and animal creation on left hand
and 'cloud of witness' on the right. I was then thinking of the
MAN as facing towards the left with *right* arm outstretched.
But when I got to drawing I found that this involved his finger
touching the finger of God's *left* hand. I think this would have
been bad. So I reversed the whole thing — MAN in centre
facing towards right; 'Witness' panel behind him on left and
animal panel on right. (Incidentally this makes an important
variation on the Sistine Chapel picture — in that picture Eve
and her children are something God has, so to say, up His
sleeve. In my vision it is the *return* offering which is emphasized.)

As well as the $\frac{1}{2}''$ scale drawings of the separate panels I am
sending you a $\frac{1}{50}$ drawing showing the whole façade of the
foyer. From this you will be able to judge how the three
panels go together and how big they are in relation to the
pillars, etc. and doors. The little bits of 'foliage' on the right
and left hand bottom corners of the centre panel are put in
to carry the scale of the side panels through. But to make the
big figure of the man 'go' with the small figures of the animals
and children is chiefly a carving matter. I mean that if all the
three panels have the same kind and quality of relief they will
all go together, just as a long line will go with a short line
provided that it is the same kind of line and not merely a
magnification of it. [. . .]

Re the *right* hand panel: the animals are nondescript, i.e.

they are *all* the animals and not a few particular ones; the same applies to the tree and foliage.

Re the *left* hand panel: the diagonal line of the group of figures (left bottom to right top) has a double intention: (a) it is the movement ↗ towards the imagined figure of God and (b) the diagonal division of the panel balances with the line of the MAN's right arm in the centre panel.

I shall of course be glad to explain anything which seems obscure but I hope the general notion is obvious and commends itself and I hope you like the drawings and that the other people concerned will also approve.   Yours sincerely,

ERIC GILL

P.S. I should add that the clouds, lightning and water suggested on the background of the right-hand panel are put in to indicate the inanimate forces of 'nature'. I think I might also put in a toothed wheel in a low relief, for machinery is also a gift *to* man, rather than a gift *from* him. And I would like to add that I particularly wish the head of the MAN to go out of the top of the centre panel; for I don't want the panel to be simply a picture frame into which the figure of a man is neatly fitted, but I want it to be really the universe itself into which man does not really completely fit. . . .

P.S. 12.7.35.
And another point might be mentioned!
The inscript. AD IMAGINEM DEI . . . etc.
You will note that this is slightly more tactful to our atheistic friends [. . .] than if we had put Et creavit Deus hominem ad imaginem Suam because in the latter case God is mentioned as subject of sentence — but in the other case 'HE' might be anyone & God might be thought of simply as an exemplar cause — a fiction of the imagination! [. . .] E. G.

238 : TO DR. COOMARASWAMY

Pigotts   *9-8-1935*

Dear Ananda: Thank you for your letter of Aug. 1st. It is very
kind of you to send two more copies of *Medieval Aesthetics*.*
This week I asked the *Catholic Herald* to send you a copy of
the issue of Aug. 3rd which contains a little article written in
review of a recent production by Michael Sadler and Wm.
Rothenstein about West African Sculptures, etc. It is only a
small thing but I hope you will approve of it.**

I have recently begun a new book for Faber and Faber with
the same title as the article, and the article is, as it were, a
forerunner.

Your story about the clergyman (Friday D.V. Saturday in
any case) is a more serious version of — 'the ship will sail on
Friday weather permitting, on Saturday whether or no'! Yes,
I do indeed approve of Christian name appellations. Yours
ever,   ERIC G.

* I am most grateful. I heard from the Coll. Art people
that they had no more reprints. So I ordered a copy of the
Art Bulletin —but it's jolly expensive! It must be a very 'posh'
magazine.

** But, it has just occurred to me! There are a lot of rude
remarks about museums & museum keepers in the article. I
know there are other things to be said about museums, but I
rely on you to forgive me for my one-sidedness.   E. G.

239 : TO 'THE SUN-BATHING REVIEW'
SUMMER, 1935

Sir: I do not think you will do good to the cause you have at
heart by assuming that the Catholic opposition to it is mere
prejudice and prudery. The Catholic Church is not likely to
disappear in the near future. It would be better politics,

therefore, to 'make friends with your enemy quickly'; for such articles as that appearing in your Spring issue under the name of C. E. M. Joad will do your reputation definite harm in responsible quarters.

Mr. Joad is a professional philosopher, and philosophers are supposed, by the nature of their profession, to be superior to the cheaper and more infantile prejudices and ignorances. Therefore the lapses in his article are the more surprising. He makes fun of the Papal 'edicts' regarding bare arms and knees in churches, and contrasts this narrow-mindedness with the enlightened behaviour of the Russians 'lying in hundreds in the hot sunlight on the banks of the Dnieper at Kiev without a stitch of clothing.' I pass over Mr. Joad's playful dalliance with the story that the Pope has a large holding of shares in a Milanese textile firm and that the depression in the clothing trade is the real cause of the Papal displeasure, but we ought not to pass over the *suggestio falsi* and *suppressio veri* contained in his implication that what is appropriate for the river bank is appropriate for attendance at public worship. This is too absurd. If only Mr. Joad had some slight knowledge of what public worship means he would not think church going comparable to sun bathing. Church going, in the Catholic sense, is not the same as what they call 'church parade' at Brighton. To go to church in order to display your charms (and that involves competition with all the other charmers) is to miss the point of going to church.

And why all this talk about *women*? Men are doubtless physically attractive. If men took to personal display, either by exposure of their arms and legs or by pretty clothes, there would be the same protest on the part of the clergy. It's not half so much to do with 'female beauty' as Mr. Joad imagines, only it so happens that at the present time it is the women who are the peacocks.

I do not suppose that Mr. Joad is one of those who would abolish clothes altogether. I think it probable that he agrees with me and most people that clothes have their proper use and occasion. He probably enjoys the sight of fine robes and dresses as much as any one and he would agree that his enjoyment is not wholly irrational. The questions, therefore, are: What clothes are good clothes and what clothes are suitable for such and such occasions?

Suitable place and occasion being granted, no clothes at all are suitable for sun bathing and swimming and posing in art schools. Shorts and sleeveless singlets are suitable for walking and running, rowing and riding and all sorts of public games. What clothes or robes are appropriate to the theatre, the law court or the church? It is a pity that women regard the theatre as a showing-off place, and I think there is some connection between this behaviour and the general frivolity of modern plays. The playwright caters for an audience that doesn't much care, and few women care very seriously. But the playwright is under the thumb of the box office, so what can he do? The church is another kind of theatre; and there, at any rate, 'the play's the thing'; and the audience being themselves *participants in the action* must behave accordingly. In such a place personal display, whether male or female, is an unmitigated nuisance. Suppose some or many priests are prudes. Well, they are not the only ones; prudishness is more typically the vice of the protestant puritan. And in any case it is not primarily or fundamentally a matter of prudishness, but of reasonableness. It is as unreasonable to make church-going an occasion for personal display as it would be to make sun bathing an excuse for exhibitionism.

Mr. Joad confesses to great ignorance as to the nature of decency. I don't want to enlighten him; I only invite him to 'return to philosophy.' In his recent book with that title he laments the decay of intellect. His remarks about the Church in your Spring issue are a lamentable example of that decay.

I am much honoured by Professor Flugel's remarks in reply to me.[1] I will only say now that it seems to me a pity that he

_____
[1] 'Clothes and Man Naked.' Winter, No. 8.

should confuse the issue about the word 'natural.' When I say 'clothes are natural to man' I mean simply that it is as natural to man to make and put on clothes as it is natural to him to make and live in houses and to make and use tools. Clothes are not natural in the sense that they grow on man without his conscious effort; they require his intelligent contrivance. But I hold that it is natural to man to use his intelligence. I think that is clear and obvious. I hold that clothes are primarily for dignity and adornment and secondarily for convenience and modesty (and modesty is a kind of convenience). These facts are overlaid in our time by all sorts of foolishness, and foolishness is the devil. Whether we say that we are naturally naked, but put on clothes for good reasons; or whether we say clothes are natural to us and we have good reasons for taking them off on occasion doesn't much matter on the face of it. But it does matter philosophically; for it is really a confusion —it is a case of using a word in two senses without saying so. In the first case the word natural means simply that which happens without the intervention of mind; in the second it means that which man, being a rational animal in his very being, does by wilful choice —*such action being in accordance with his nature*, and man's nature is defined and determined by his end or destiny. Thus in the first sense I might say: a railway locomotive is 'born' without rails; therefore it is 'naturally' railless. In the second sense I might say: it is in accordance with the nature of a railway locomotive to run on rails, therefore rails are 'natural' to railway locomotives.

You know I am entirely with you in saying that nakedness 'is deliciously and healthily refreshing.' And I say it is delightful and healthy to go out of doors and walk in the sun and wind. It remains true that men naturally build houses and temples (and banks and town halls too) and would be poorer and sillier without them. Modern clothes, especially men's, are degraded and stuffy garments. Modern villadom is as bad. 'Nudism' is an inevitable reaction exactly as 'functionalism' in building is. Both reactions should provoke us to a healthy renaissance of rationality and spirituality. Yours faithfully, Pigotts.   ERIC GILL

240 : TO 'THE LISTENER', 16TH AUGUST, 1935

I am, of course, much honoured by Mr. Herbert Read's review of my book, *Beauty Looks After Herself*, in your issue of August 2. Will you allow me, however, to reply to a few points raised?

In the first place, I see no reason why it should be assumed that I am the sort of prig who is intolerant of Sèvres porcelain; nor do I see why anything which pleases anybody should be called 'perfectly useless'. I think, and I have said it often in other words in my book, that a pendant on the neck is as useful and possibly more so than a trouser button. Again, why should Mr. Read assume, without asking me, that I 'would not like' Joan Miró's painting? This dodge of putting your opponent in the dock is a horrid one. As a matter of fact, as far as one can see from a smudgy little half-tone, I should think the 'Femme Assise' is a very delightful picture. Perhaps it is not the greatest art —its scope is too narrow. It is the art of the jeweller, not that of the architect; lyrical, not epic; but the greater includes the less.

But Mr. Read's chief quarrel with me is a matter of logic and psychology. Here I am at a disadvantage in debate; for I know little of logic and less of psychology. Nevertheless I think I can explain my position and rebut your reviewer's charges. When I use the word 'sense' as identical with 'knowledge', I do no more than use the words as they are commonly understood. We call a man 'a sensible fellow' meaning that he has good sense, commonsense, a good working *knowledge* of things; that he is a *knowing* person, not an idiot; that he can be relied on as a rational being. I am well aware that the word 'sense' has another usage. We talk of the five senses and we have the derived word 'sensibility'. But even in this use the word 'sense' is not divorced from intellectual connotations; for what we call the five senses are simply the five doors to knowledge and, as the philosophers say, nothing is in the intellect but what comes to it through the senses. If the senses are not means to knowledge then we are a lower animal than we think.

But, worst of all, Mr. Read quarrels with me because I identify the beautiful with the rational, the beautiful thing with the reasonable thing. He would have it that the sense by which we appreciate the beautiful 'is not a rational mode of apprehension at all, it is a direct intuition'. Is intuition therefore irrational? Is it not the mind which is pleased? Why identify intuition with the non-rational? Is this not as great a logical slip as any of which I am accused? And when, later on, Mr. Read says that only they who are blessed with an 'ear' 'can hope to have good judgment of music', what on earth does the word 'judgment' mean if judging be not, *par excellence*, the act of the mind and therefore a rational act? Mr. Read wishes to maintain that appreciation of the beautiful is by a non-rational mode and at the same time he calls the result 'judgment'. I think he should find a less compromising word.

I, however, am untouched; for, to me, the thing we call intuition is precisely the highest act of rationality. I suspect that Mr. Read is confusing the word 'rational' with the word 'ratiocinative', forgetting or not noticing that I have said in several places in the book in question that though the artist need not reason (*i.e.* ratiocinate), the work of art is not therefore unreasonable (*i.e.* irrational or non-rational).

As for St. Thomas Aquinas' dictum, it is not beauty itself but beautiful *things* which the philosopher says are pleasing when seen. And if we are going to appeal to St. Thomas and 'leave it at that', why not read the context? Here it is: 'Beauty relates to the cognoscitive faculty; for beautiful things are those which please when seen . . . and sense is a sort of reason'. (*Pulchrum autem respicit vim cognoscitivam : pulchra enim dicuntur quae visa placent . . . et sensus ratio quaedam est*'. *Summ. Theol.*, I, Q5, A4.) Taking the dictum in its context, it is clear that St. Thomas associates the sense of sight with the faculty of knowing. I am indeed quite agreeable to leave it at that.   ERIC GILL

High Wycombe.

241 : TO THE REV. DESMOND CHUTE

Pigotts   31-8-1935

My dear Desmond: [. . .] Talking about the *Catholic Herald*, [. . .] I hope you approved of that article entitled 'Necessity of Belief'. Which reminds me, I do not suppose I told you that I have been commissioned by Faber & Faber to write a book with that same title and more or less on the theme of that article. The MS has to be delivered by December. I am now about half way through it (80,000 words). It is a very big job for me who has never really written anything before but pamphlets. Also it is very difficult as the subject is one which really calls for authority to expound. [. . .]

At present the shop is very busy. We are doing some carving on some flats near Baker Street. The Geneva work has not yet been decided about, but unless the League comes completely to an end there seems to be good hope that the work will proceed, as my designs have been accepted by the British Authorities concerned, and are now only awaiting the official confirmation of the Architect and Co. at Geneva, and I am told that it is not likely they will refuse anything which H.M.'s Government approves. But this Abyssinia business has, I suppose, put all such things out of their minds and I do not expect to hear any more about it yet awhile. Apart from that I am still doing engravings for the Aldine Bible. I am just

EricG. 24.12.'29

Fr. Desmond Chute

FATHER DESMOND CHUTE

Drawing by E.G.

about to begin those for volume three. Did you see the other volumes? The type was set here by René, but the actual printing was done at Dent's press, Letchworth, as the numbers required are too great for us to cope with. That is why the printing itself is nothing to write home about.

If I can think of any more news I will add it as a postscript. Yours ever,   ERIC G.

Alas alas no time —have got to dash to London & don't want to delay this longer. Much love dear Desmond.

242 : TO RICHARD DE LA MARE

17-10-1935

Dear de la Mare: Thank you for your letter of Oct. 15th. It is difficult to do what you ask, but I quite see that it is desirable. Perhaps you will be able to make something up out of this letter.

In the first place, I have always taken the title of the book to be 'The Necessity *of* Belief' not '*for*' as you write it. Do you attach any importance to this? Your title suggests that belief supplies a long felt need. The other version suggests rather that there is something about belief which intrinsically necessitates it, whether people feel the need or not. As a matter of fact, the book will deal with both these sides of the matter. I am about halfway through at present, and so far have dealt with the matter from the point of view of my title. But the second half is to deal with the matter from the other point of view. That is to say, that so far I have been dealing with the various convergences which seem to make belief not only possible but necessary, logically and philosophically and humanly.

As you know, I cannot claim to be a philosopher. My reading is only that of a quite ordinary person who is interested but not learned. The importance of the book, if it should have any, will, in fact, depend upon this position. I do not say such and such is what philosophers have thought and theologians have taught. I say rather, such and such is what human beings of all sorts think.

I remember once discussing the difference between the High Church Anglican position and the R.C. position, and my friend, when I asked him what authority he admitted, said: 'We admit the authority of the first five General Councils, that is up to the Council of Chalcedon', (or words to that effect; anyway he mentioned Chalcedon). And I replied: 'But look here, I cannot be a learned man and read up the General Councils. I may be dead before tomorrow and I have got to be saved before then. You cannot maintain that salvation depends upon knowing about the General Councils'. Well, it is the same in this other matter. It would be absurd to maintain that belief depends upon being learned. There must be ordinary grounds upon which ordinary people can stand, and this seems to me analogous to the relations we find ourselves in today in the matter of the Arts and Politics. Take Politics for instance, we are confronted by a mass of complicated treaties, conventions, etc., which only people in the diplomatic service can be expected to understand. Is it impossible therefore for ordinary people to know what is right and wrong in the dispute between Italy and Abyssinia? Are there no principles which rule men's minds? Or must we be blown to and fro by lying newspapers? And take the Arts. Is art a mystery as Mr. Herbert Read and Co. make out — a thing which ordinary people cannot be expected to understand without special training or special genius? Is it not rather the fact that 'the artist is not a special kind of man, but every man is a special kind of artist'? Should it not be possible for a bricklayer to know a good piece of bricklaying — whether a plain wall or an Elizabethan chimney? And should it not be possible for a man who uses paints and brushes, a man not an automaton, to understand a painting, whether it be a plain wall, a shop sign or a reredos? Does not the reredos signify something which concerns the beggar who prays before it at least as much as the aesthete who admires it?

So at all costs it must be made clear that this book is not addressed to experts. But I think two criticisms must be disarmed:

A.   There must be no suggestion that I am writing down to the level of the unlearned. I am not doing so because I am on the low level to start with.

B.   There must be no suggestion that the learned are therefore of no account, on the contrary.

If it can possibly be stated, the point is this, that the book is, as it were, a conversation between me and myself, in which I endeavour to arrive at the grounds of belief such as they seem to me to be. It therefore has the nature of a confession or an autobiography,* but I do not think this should be stated. I only mention it for your information because I think that when you see the manuscript you will see that that is the nature of the book. Yours ever,   ERIC GILL

* or an 'autopsychography' could such a word be coined.

2 4 3 : T O   P H I L L I P S   T E M P L E

Pigotts   *26-11-1935*

Dear Mr. Temple: I am much interested by your letter of the 10th. Thank you very much for what you say in praise of my article in the *Colosseum* in June 1934. I may say that the subject was dealt with more fully in a book which appeared later in the same year entitled *Money and Morals* published by Faber and Faber in London. But this, I regret to say, is now out of print.

I do not see any objection to your plan except the objections you yourself mention, namely that at the present time the clergy are very shy of offending their subscribers. The same difficulty exists in England. There is a story going round that the present Archbishop of Birmingham mentioned the matter to the Pope himself, saying that the preaching of *Quad°. anno* alienated the more prosperous Catholics, and that the Pope replied: 'they may be prosperous, but they are not Catholics if they are offended.'

While I agree that your plan would be extremely good if you could get anyone to apply it, I think the first step really is to hammer away at the fundamental question of social justice, and above all things, to point out that the thing called 'class war' is not a product of gratuitous malice, but is the inevitable result of the dispossession of the peasantry and the creation of the proletariat. It is not a question of upper classes or lower classes; it is entirely a question of the division of the population into a class which has economical power and resources, and another class which has nothing but its power to labour.

Leo XIII said: 'As many as possible should be encouraged to become owners', but our industrialism does exactly the opposite. Yours sincerely,   ERIC GILL

244 : TO 'THE CATHOLIC HERALD'
20 DECEMBER, 1935

The Chinese Exhibition

Sir: Whatever may be said about the beauty and historic interest of the things at the Chinese exhibition, and however much art critics and the general public may, in a manner of speaking, rave about them, there is room, plenty of room for at least one jarring note.

What is the difference between this kind of exhibition and the Free Libraries, 'Open Spaces,' Children's Playgrounds, Tate Galleries, etc., which our millionaires provide to balance, as it were, their depredations?

First of all, not to mince matters, they dispossess the peasantry, and, in effect, rob the poor by keeping their wages down to the lowest possible level, and then, having made

enormous fortunes, they seek to put the matter right, assuage
their consciences, and what not, by giving us these Free
Libraries, Italian, Dutch, French and now Chinese Exhibitions.
And look at the way the dealers are all scrambling round like
vultures in the hope of coming in on the boom! And what
politics are we to suspect in the background? Is it Chinese
silver, or what?

And then, forgetting all these considerations, there remains
the fact that these glass cases contain things that are *holy* and
that we are asked to treat the gods as curiosities. (It is rather
like trying to 'hear Mass' on the wireless or by gramophone
records.) Better stay at home and play with the children.

England, Europe, the whole world, is sacrificed to money-
making and turned into a Cannes for their tinned meats and
a dump for their scrap-iron. Why should we walk into
Burlington House and say: Thank you very much for letting
us see these beautiful, beautiful things. 'Too sweet'; 'Too,
too exquisite'; and 'Isn't it wonderful what an interest the
people take in art?' The only appropriate reply is unprintable
except in dots.   ERIC GILL

245 : TO GRAHAM CAREY

Pigotts   *16-1-1936*

Dear Carey [...] Yes, it is true that Fr. O'Connor of
Bradford has recently build a round church, (actually it is
octagonal, but it comes to the same thing in practice.) The
Altar is right in the middle, and the result, as you may guess,
is very remarkable. The sacrifice is offered not only for the
people, but by them and in the midst of them. But, no, I
was not his architectural adviser, though I did talk to him
about it from time to time during the building. Actually it
is not a very notable piece of building. [...]

I am most interested to hear of your dining with Dr.

Coomaraswamy. I wish I could meet him again; it must be twenty years or more since I saw him. I do not know anybody with so clear a head as he. [. . .] Yours ever,   ERIC G.

246 : TO GRAHAM CAREY

Pigotts   *28-2-1936*

Dear Carey: Thank you very much for your letter of the 15th. I will reserve the puzzle with this for a leisure moment (hour, day or what not, as the case may be). This is just to reply to your question about coins. Yes, I have several times done designs for the Mint people but they have never actually used any, though I may claim one or two suggestions of mine were not altogether useless. So far as I know the drawings have never been reproduced; they are the property of the Mint and I have only got here rough sketches and some discarded designs. Anyway I do not think you will find much of interest as I did these a long time ago* and I don't suppose they are very much good.

I have not yet heard anything about new stamps and coinage, but of course they will soon be on the job. I suppose if you wrote to His Majesty's Mint they would not mind, in fact the Deputy Master of the Mint, Colonel Sir Robert Johnson, K.B.E., was very kind to me, and if you wrote to him (supposing you really want to pursue the matter that far) I am sure he would reply in a friendly manner. (The address is: The Royal Mint, London E.)

I do not think there is much prospect of another book on my sculpture at the present time. I have not got good photographs of everything, and I really think it is much more important to get certain ideas across and let sculpture happen, than that individual works should be set up to be admired. I know you agree about this. Yours ever,   ERIC G.

* pre war I think or just after.

2 4 7 : TO HIS BROTHER EVAN

Pigotts   *11-3-1936*

Dear Evan: [...] With regard to a possible lecture at
Liverpool, of course I am reluctant to refuse you as I suppose
I could fit it in when I come to Manchester, but I do find this
lecturing business very difficult and very absorbent of time
and energy. [...]

As you say about the winter number of the *Monotype
Recorder* — Wow! But as you like to have the details correct I
may say that Douglas Cleverdon's shop-sign was not the first
public exhibition of that style of lettering, for we painted
letters in that style at Capel-y-ffin saying 'This way to the
Church', and so forth. And these were done some time before
the Bristol sign. Yours ever,   ERIC

2 4 8 : TO GRAHAM CAREY

Pigotts   *3-4-1936*

Dear Carey: Thank you very much for your letter of the 21st
and for the coin, which has great merits, and is in any case
infinitely better (i.e. as belonging to an entirely different
world) than the usual thing. But it seems to me probable that
what we have now in the way of stamps and coinage, etc. is
the sort of thing we deserve. The chief fault I find with your
coin is illegibility, not so much of the lettering as of the
picture or symbolic scene or whatever you call it. It seems to
me the symbolism is too diffuse. I shall be very interested to
see your essay on the subject.

I like your problem and will give my attention to it at the
earliest moment. Yours ever,   ERIC G.

P.S. The book I told you of[1] was published yesterday. I hope
you will approve of it. I am thankful to say I had it 'vetted'
by a Dominican, so it is free from the worst errors I hope.

           [1] *The Necessity of Belief.*

Z

249 : TO GRAHAM CAREY

Pigotts, High Wycombe   5-5-1936

Dear Carey: Thank you very much for your letter of April
23rd. I have asked Faber's to send you a copy of my book.
I greatly hope you will like it and forgive its breathlessness.
You see Faber's more or less ordered me to write it and I
could only do it in a manner of speaking by doing it. I just
began at the beginning and wandered on to the end and did
not separate it into chapters or even paragraphs until afterwards. The consequence is some parts are much worse than
others.

Yes, I did miss the beautiful simplicity of the rowing
problem.

I am getting the *Christian Front* every month. I have written
them a letter which I hope will not go amiss.[1] Your articles
are very very good. Yours ever,   ERIC G.

250 : TO P. W. SINGLETON

25-5-1936

Dear Mick: Re your letter of the 22nd. I cannot reply at
length but I agree with all that you said. It seems to me that
in this discussion we have to avoid,

   (a) The suggestion that we think machinery in itself is bad.
       This would be absurd.
   (b) We are not endeavouring to promote an Arts and Crafts
       movement.

On the other side we are definitely opposed to that use of
machinery which deprives the workman of his human rights
as a responsible being. Expressed positively — we demand that
all work shall be such that it is possible for the worker to
regard it as a 'sacrifice of praise'.

[1] Letter 252.

The control of machinery and the initiative for its introduction shall be the worker's and not the salesman's.

The alternative to the present system therefore is simply a Society in which there are no proletarians; as Leo XIII said, 'as many as possible should be encouraged to become owners'. In a non-proletarian society the use of machinery is to lighten labour not to displace it. Its introduction shall be for the good of the work, not for the increase of profits (except *per accidens*). Yours ever,   E. G.

251 : TO 'THE TABLET', 13TH JUNE, 1936

Jews and Arabs in Palestine

Sir: In the matter of Palestine it is obvious that much is to be said on both sides, but it seems to me that misleading arguments should not be used. For instance, in your issue of June 6 your correspondent says (page 720) that the general trend of Arab arguments 'is hysterical, being based on a clamour to be saved from losing their land to the Jews —a matter which is and always has been in the hands of those Arab landowners who chose to sell.' This is misleading because it implies equality as between buyer and seller. It is a fact that the Arabs are desperately poor, whereas the Jews have been able to call upon world-wide financial support. Moreover, it is a common and pitiful phenomenon —the giving of money for a poor man's little plot of land, although the price be a fair one according to market standards. The possession of money is not equivalent to the possession of land. Compare the similar phenomenon in our own country when the common lands were enclosed. The former owners were compensated in money, but our whole civilization was changed from that of a peasantry to that of a commercial community. In brief, it is not sufficient to say that if the Arabs have sold their land, at any rate they have had the money.

You refer to 'the long-demanded' Tel-Aviv port. What does this signify but the conversion of Palestine into a modern industrial, exporting country? Many people, especially many Jews, wish for this conversion, and the new Jerusalem, like the new Tel-Aviv, is evidence of this wish. In the same spirit you say (page 720) the Arabs have made nothing of Palestine, and that 'it is said that not a single tree was planted between the departure of the last Crusader and the arrival of the British in 1917,' and I know that it is true that in the Jewish settlements they have made ten blades of grass grow where one grew before. I know this sounds on the one hand very bad and on the other very good, and of course it seems ridiculous not to make the most of one's land, but I do think you are missing something out. The thriftlessness of the Arabs is not only the product of bad character, nor is the quantitive enthusiasm of the new settlers the product of unmixed virtues.

Doubtless it may be said that a short stay in Palestine has prejudiced me, and I admit that it seems to me frightful that a peasant country should be turned into an industrial one —as though the existing industrialism were not already enough for the world, but at least let us avoid arguments based merely upon quantity. Yours faithfully,   ERIC GILL

June 8, 1936.

252 : TO 'THE CHRISTIAN FRONT'
JULY, 1936

In your March number there is an article by Fr. Gleason, s.j., on 'The Quest for Security' which is prefaced by an editorial note saying that 'spiritual and intellectual reform must precede the economic reform.' Please will you allow me to comment on this as I think it reveals and leads to misunderstanding and similar statements are often no more than an incitement to or an excuse for inaction.

If you say that it is useless to reform the money system until men have changed their minds about robbery and cheating, justice and injustice, you are forgetting that it is, in human affairs, precisely the effort to make physical changes which most surely awakens the mind and elicits spiritual reform. Can we have the monetary reform or the destruction of the financial tyranny which is now corrupting our society without a change in intellectual and spiritual things? Of course it is impossible — the one implies the other. But in our space-time condition things are not done in text-book order and things react on one another. In your effort to get a political or physical reform effected you will inevitably find yourself up against the mentality and spirituality of your opponents and will as inevitably be bound to 'convert' them before they will act. None the less you may well start by urging the politics rather than the conversion. 'Seek first the Kingdom of God and his justice' — yes, and that kingdom and that justice are not only to be stated in spiritual and intellectual terms. The best way to convert people from a habit of robbery may easily be the making of robbery illegal, for in your effort to get such laws enacted you will have to convince the electorate or legislature that your proposed law is just. Therefore I find myself somewhat irritated by your editorial note; for it gives a handle to the do-nothings and putters-off and those whose great possessions incline them to turn away more or less joyfully. Yours faithfully,   ERIC GILL

Pigotts, High Wycombe, England.

2 5 3 : TO 'THE CATHOLIC HERALD'
3RD JULY, 1936

CATHOLIC ACTION AND INDUSTRIALISM

An Analysis of the Right to Private Property

Sir: May I support the protest of Fr. Ceolfrid Heron in your issue of June 26? The pathetic attempts of Catholics to find

reasons for their adhesion to industrialism are based upon a
false idea of property and of the natural human right to it, and
this false idea of property is the consequence of a forgetfulness
(natural enough in our degraded world) of the two-fold
nature of human personality. Man is matter and spirit and the
mind of man is both intellectual and moral. The right to
property follows from man's material necessities and his intellectual nature. The right to property is not primarily a
moral right, a right due to man on account of his freewill but
is, so to say, an intellectual right, a right due on account of
his intelligence. The right of ownership does not derive from
men's need to *use* things but from his need to *make* things.

As a moral being, purely as such, man has no right of private
ownership. On the contrary, as Pope Leo XIII said:

> 'Man must not hold external things for private but for
> common, so that he may freely give to others in their
> necessities.' (*Rerum Nov.* § 19)

and St. Thomas Aquinas:

> 'With regard to external things, a man ought to possess
> them not as his own but as common, and always be ready
> to put them at the disposal of others who are in need'
> (*Summ. Theol.* II-II, 62, 2).

It is to man as workman, as an intelligent being who must
manipulate things in order to make them serviceable, that
private ownership is both necessary and a natural right. Only
when there is full control of the means of production can there
be proper and suitable manipulation. Unless I own the fields
I cannot exercise my skill and intelligence upon the land. (It
is for this reason that ownership is better than tenancy and
that, in the case of a tenant, the terms of tenancy must be as
nearly as possible equivalent to ownership). Unless I own the
stone and my tools I cannot properly exercise my skill and
intelligence as a stone carver. Unless I own the mine,
individually or jointly with my fellow miners, I cannot or we
cannot properly control the job of mining. It is this necessity

of manipulation which gives the right of private property in the means of production. As Maritain says:

> 'The exercise of art or work (whether it be that of a craftsman or a manual labourer) is the formal reason of individual appropriation . . . In the case of the bee there is no *reason* in operation; neither is there any individual ownership . . . the notion of person must be included in any complete theory of property.' (*Freedom in the Modern World*, App. I, 3 and 4).

These things being clear, we may now see clearly their application to our special problem of capitalist industrialism; and it is now obvious that, as things are, the ground upon which we claim and that upon which alone we can claim private property has been destroyed. The factory hand, like the bee, can make no claim to private ownership and the big machine industries of manufacture and transport are no longer in any true sense private enterprises; they are (as their directors boast) public services. Hence the moral force of communism. The workers see the facts which we so culpably endeavour to hide: what are public services should be publicly owned for the profit of all. The only reason for private ownership, the intellectual operation of the workman (by which he imprints on matter the mark of a rational being) having been destroyed by our development of machine industry, there remains no christian, no rational objection to communal ownership.

The conclusion emerges and is obvious. We cannot demand private property in the means of production unless we are prepared to abandon industrialism. If we are *not* so prepared then we must prepare ourselves for communal ownership. Capitalist organisation implicitly and Communist organisation explicitly lead to public ownership for private use. This is the exact opposite of christian organisation. In a christian society there is private ownership for the sake of common use. In our society we have reduced all manufacture and transport (except the lap-dog fine arts) to the level of impersonal and therefore subhuman enterprises (as Fr. D'Arcy says: 'We have reduced the workman to a subhuman condition of intellectual irresponsibility') and in our abominable selfishness we endeavour to maintain private ownership in the use of things. And then we say that private property is a principle of christianity, and by means of Catholic Action seek to perpetuate the crucifixion of the workers, saying to them: Have patience, 'be you warmed and fed.' They will not much longer endure it.   ERIC GILL

254 : TO 'THE TABLET', 11TH JULY, 1936

Jews and Arabs in Palestine

Sir: I do not doubt that the facts are as stated by your correspondent Israel Cohen (June 27th). (I disregard the somewhat romantic letter of 'Witness.') I have, as who has not, great admiration for the Jewish land settlements in the valley of Jezreel, and for the young settlers. Nevertheless, I have been in Palestine, and I have seen what is happening at Jerusalem and Tel Aviv. Your correspondent admits, and even boasts of, the great increase of export trade. Whatever may be said in admiration of the settlers, there remains the fact that a great commercial and industrial movement is being fostered by the Jews and their financial backers, with the result that Palestine is becoming an industrial country on English lines, and the Mohammedan and Arab culture is being destroyed.

And another fact remains: Whether we judge that justice be on the side of the Arabs or on that of the Jews, the physical power resides with the British Government, and we may be sure that that power will be used on behalf of whatever policy seems best to suit British foreign policy. Whether our financial

obligations to the Jews compel us to support Zionism or our
fear of a widespread rising of the Mohammedan world against
us compels us to side with the Arabs is beyond the prognostica-
tion of one whose only concern in this dispute is to expose the
fact that at the present moment Palestine is being 'modern-
ised' and corrupted by European commercialism and vulgarity.
Yours faithfully,   ERIC GILL

255 : TO STANLEY MORISON

[THIS is the only surviving letter from a long correspondence of
special interest; the rest were destroyed in the raids on London.
I take the text from a slightly imperfect typewritten copy preserved
among E. G's papers; with it was the preceding letter from Mr.
Morison, from which I quote a relevant passage.

'When the Anarchists took over the biggest cinema in Barcelona
and found there was a contract with a certain famous tenor who
filled the house, they pointed out to him that he was receiving
something like three hundred times more than the weekly wages
of the charwoman who swept up the cigarette ends from beneath
the seats of the patrons who provided the reservoir from which the
salaries were paid. The charwoman was paid 15 pesetas a week
(about 16/8) and nowadays the stalls accommodate each evening
half a dozen Anarchists whose revolvers cover the tenor while he is
singing — (also for 15 pesetas a week.) Now, this tenor's responsibility is for his song. I do not doubt that with the revolvers pointing
towards him he sings better than he ever sang in his life. Thus, the
Anarchists enforce what they regard as social justice — that is their
idea of human responsibility. It is their duty to secure social
equality, and this is what they are 'making' — to use your favourite
word. Now the one common bond between you and the tenor, i.e.
distinguished persons, and those who have no capacities which leave
them distinct, is the physical one, the desire for food, shelter and
women etc. Because all these in themselves are more immediate and
urgent to the greatest number of mankind, the style of the optional
things to be made is of correspondingly less importance today.
And I say that social justice is the 'thing' which, as members of a

given geographical constituency, we each have to feel and to take responsibility for. I do not see, therefore, how you advance social justice now by drawing attention to the 'right' making of chairs and tables, as chairs and tables.']

16-9-1936

Dear Morison: I imagine all decent people are ultimately anarchists — certainly all Christians must be. The only problem is how to bridge the intermediate stage.

It seems to me common sense to suppose that the ultimate anarchy to which Christianity leads is not to be achieved here below. Nevertheless, a Christian politic should always be one which leads in the heavenly direction, looks to anarchy as its guiding star.

Meanwhile I agree with you that patience is all-important. Surely in this connection, verse 2 of the 4th. chapter of 2nd. Timothy, and all that follows is to the point. And I do think that one does exhibit patience by arguing, in season and out of season, that while we live in an industrial machine-using world we must make the *best* of it and not the worst, and that this best, as regards things made, means such things as GILL SANS (begging your pardon), the new Daily Express building (except the sculpture inside), plain furniture and utensils etc. As regards politics, I entirely agree with you ⟨about⟩ the transference of ownership of the means of production to the workers.

I do not know what theological argument of mine you refer to. If you mean the one about the metaphysical basis for the human right of property, I can only say that this was St. Thomas's ⟨as much as⟩ it was mine. For the rest, I agree with St. Basil: All saving ⟨is⟩ robbery, i.e. the retention of superfluity and the refusal to distribute it, is robbery.

I agree of course that I have not yet made sufficiently close analysis of the principle of human responsibility. I shall do my best in the few years remaining. It is something however to bring the notion to the surface. Maybe the job of analysing it belongs properly to someone wiser than I. But of course I cannot submit to your definition of 'Artist' — 'A man who earns his living by doing what he likes doing,' unless you include in the word, doctors, lawyers, many priests, many soldiers, yourself and all those many hundreds of still remaining bricklayers, carpenters, masons who regard their jobs as their vocations. If you do include all these, then of course I agree with you. But I should prefer to say not that the artist earns his living by doing what he likes doing but by doing what it is his vocation to do — he acts according to his nature (Aristotelian sense of the word), not according to his whim. Moreover I think it is somewhat unfair or at least undiscerning of you to regard me primarily from the point of view of the French Gallery and the art critics rather than from the point of view of Fetter Lane, and that of the weary widows who want tombstones and of the architects who sometimes, for quite good reasons, want stone carvings on their buildings. A man is what he tries to be and intends to be rather than what foolish people advertise him as being.

I like your amusing story about the tenor at Barcelona but here again like the art critics you overdo what you call, or rather imply as, my 'distinguished' personality. The most that can be said of me in that respect is that I am not such a fool as not to spoil the Egyptians while they are in the 'stable'.* Nor am I so blind to what we both call social justice as to be blind to the fact that all the surplus I can earn** I hold in trust, first of all for the good of my children and my children's children and after that for the good of the community. Catch me spending it at Monte Carlo (or anywhere analogous) and I will ask your forgiveness but not your approval.

P.S. Have you read Mounier's *De la Propriété Capitaliste à la Propriété Humaine*? It deals with, very decently, some aspects of these problems.

* dictated 'saddle' — but 'stable' is too good to erase.
** or shall I say 'collect'?

So you see we really agree entirely. I only ask that you cease to regard me as a West End artist, and to believe that my efforts to reach the truth about human work and property do not prevent me from taking a practical line in relation to the present situation. And in that matter I value your judgment exceedingly. Yours,

E. G.

256 : TO 'THE TIMES', 22ND. SEPTEMBER, 1936

New Postage Stamps

Sir: As one who has had much to do with engraving and letter-ing and with the reproduction of both and also with the design of articles for machine production, I should like, if you will allow me, to record my opinion that the new postage stamps of King Edward VIII are exceedingly good both in themselves as postage stamps and in relation to current methods of facture. A pictorial device to be used by the million cannot properly be produced except by the most extensive and inten-sive use of machinery. Such methods are in their nature impersonal, and those who employ them are well advised to eschew the fanciful and the ornamental, however natural and even inevitable such things were in a pre-machine economy. On the contrary, a strict attention to the real needs of the case and to the conditions of industrialism and the moral courage to accept the resulting plainness and simplicity are much to be commended.

Therefore I regret the opinion expressed by Mr. Frank Pick in your issue of September 16, for, as it seems to me, the new postage stamps are eminently an improvement on previous issues and mark a bold step in the right direction. The photo-graph is obviously a good photograph and its reproduction is an admirable example of mechanical expertise. The lettering,

though not actually as good as plain lettering can be, is the
right kind. The little Victorian crown fulfils its object of
marking the fact that the stamp has Governmental authority.
There is no unnecessary and consequently meaningless ornament. The only reasonable criticisms (apart from those which
involve an adverse verdict upon our whole industrialism) are
that it would have been possible, by a different lighting of the
head of the King, to have avoided the gradated background
(reminiscent of academic portrait painting) and the consequent
outlining of the right-hand letters; it would have been possible
to draw a better crown (one less obscure in its detail), and it
would have been possible to design a better A and E. Above
all, it is a pity that the head of the King is cut off at the neck
in the manner of a sculptured relief (with a sham shadow
underneath the cut), thus destroying the integrity of the
design. But these criticisms are all concerned with matters of
secondary importance and should do nothing to prevent us
from tendering to the Post Office the congratulations it deserves for releasing us from the banalities of imitation hand-
engravings and stupid ornamentation. Yours faithfully,

ERIC GILL

Pigotts, High Wycombe.

257 : TO THE 'NEW ENGLISH WEEKLY'
8TH. OCTOBER, 1936

Balancing the Books

Sir: I hope you'll pardon me intruding. My husband said
write to the Editor and that's why I'm making so bold. It's
like this. My man is porter at the Bank. It's Lloyds Bank and
one evening he went to one of these meetings about abolishing
poverty and he came home and told me that the gentlemen had
said banks made money out of nothing so it might just as well
be give away to anyone. I said to him like 'don't talk so wet,'

if you'll excuse me, and he said 'struth' if you'll excuse me. So I said why dont you mention it one day at the bank to one of the young gentlemen and so he did it to-day and the young gentleman laughed at him and said if we lend you money we haven't got, not but what they ever ave leant my man any, he said how do you think we would be able to balance our books he said. I dont know anything about balancing books so I said to my man whats he mean. So my man said he means if they hand you out money then they put it down against you in the book, and if they ad said they ad leant you money which they ad not got they couldnt of taken it out of anywhere and so they wouldnt of been able to put it down what theyd taken it out of and so what they calls double entry, which means you must put down where you get it from as well as who you lend it to my man says, wouldnt work. So I said well thats that and your poverty gents must be wrong but my man says hes not that satisfied because he says he knows for a fact funny stuff does go on in rich curcles and he wouldnt put it parst them. So then he says why not arsk someone who knows about it and asnt got nothing to ide. So then as I do charring Sir in the office next to yours and ad some words with your charlady one evening while we was putting out the dustbins and so I knew about you and how you know all about money curcles, I said to my man what about Mrs. Pennyfeathers editor in Cursitor Street and he said righto and so Im writing this and hopes Im not intruding and please tell me what shall I tell my man about balancing the double entry if its not troubling. I remain yours obedient,   THE CHARAADY NEXT DOOR

[This letter had no immediate response. E. G. wrote again on the point (Oct. 29th), this time under his own name, and the Editor of the *N.E.W.* offered a guinea for the best answer received. There was then a fairly brisk correspondence, which may be consulted in the succeeding issues of the *N.E.W.* The charlady added a short note on Nov. 12.]

Sir: As Mr. Harold Speed rightly observes (October 5), Greek civilisation was a slave civilisation and Greek architecture a slave architecture. What he has not noticed is the difference between B.C. and A.D.: for, strange as it may seem, the birth of Christ has made a change in men's views and the prestige of slave cultures has suffered an irreparable wound. In spite of the modern return to slavery (for industrialism, by reducing the workman to a subhuman condition of intellectual irresponsibility, means a return to servile labour), men can never be as they were before: they can never take slavery for granted; there is always an atmosphere of rebellion and discontent.

In these circumstances, therefore, we view industrialism, in spite of its manifestations of power —manifestations which, indeed, chiefly exhibit a materialist allegiance, —not as a fine thing productive of holy works but as a degradation, a retrogression. We admire its achievements, but we see them for what they are: the product of a world subservient to the profit motive in trading, the power motive in politics, comfort and convenience in domestic affairs, and a world which looks with enthusiasm to the time when, all necessary work being done by machinery, we shall be released for 'higher things' in leisure time — a world in which, work having ceased to be holy, men can look only to leisure for the spiritual satisfaction which necessary work normally supplies.

It is much too late, therefore, to drag up the Greeks (a nation of slave masters, a nation of homosexuals), and we must view industrialism through Christian eyes. Any other view is ostrich-like in its unrealism. And it is unrealist to write, as Mr. Harold Speed writes, saying 'art is a way of life (the beautiful way) that should govern all we do and make, not to say think.' In what way is such government possible to the millions of workers in factories? Such talk, if it have any reference to them at all, only applies to them when they are not working. But postage stamps are not a product of leisure time; they are a product of the factory and are, therefore, a slave product. Pre-Christian slavery was able to be proud of its culture; we can work up no such pride, and, that is the point of all this correspondence, we must be content with the unvarnished product of the machine, rejoicing in its starkness even as we rejoice in the beauty of the machines themselves. For the rest, there is no other work worth doing but the re-affirmation of the holy poverty which Christians, no less than anti-Christians, have betrayed. —Yours, &c.,   ERIC GILL

Pigotts, High Wycombe, October 7.

259 : TO MISS NAOMI WALFORD

[AN English newspaper had reported that Michael Angelo's nudes in the Sistine Chapel were to be draped at the Pope's command. Miss Walford wrote to E. G. enclosing a copy of the report and asking for his comments.]

13-11-1936

Dear Miss Walford: I am much interested by your letter and by the cutting enclosed: you did not say what paper it is from. However, I am glad to be able to reassure you, for in today's *Catholic Herald* (November 13th, 110 Fleet Street) there is an article on page 15 dealing with the restoration of the Sistine Frescoes, in which the following sentence occurs: 'Professor Biagio Biagetti who, as director of the Vatican pictures and restorations . . . as might be expected, has denied that the Pope has given him any such order'.

Had I not seen this statement I should have accepted your cutting as stating the truth for, as you know, prudish fashions are rampant from time to time, and there is always a great tendency on the part of those who are in charge of public morals to be over zealous.

In this case, as you will now see, there is no need for alarm with reference to Michael Angelo's paintings (unless, of course, the *Catholic Herald* is wrong and your paper is right, though I imagine the *C.H.* is more likely to have the official truth), but I should like to say just one thing. It is this: that I think you take a much too solemn line with regard to what are nowadays called 'works of art'. Speaking as a sculptor (artist) I maintain that if a man buys from me a statue and does not like the shape of any part of it he is quite at liberty to remove that part or alter it or do anything he jolly well pleases. All this talk about the sanctity of the work of artists, as though it could be claimed that artists were directly inspired by the Holy Ghost, is, I think, flat nonsense. A work of art of any sort is as much the product of a civilization as of an individual and, is, therefore, a product of the collaboration of both workers and their customers. The artist is not a God kindly handing out his infallible works. And one other thing: Churches and banks, etc. are not museums in which things are kept as curiosities or as objects simply of interest to visitors. If, for instance, the Bank of England came to the conclusion that Mr. Charles Wheeler's sculptures were unsuitable, they have every right to remove or alter them — just as much right in fact as a man has to alter the throttle valves (or whatever they are called) in his motor car, whatever Mr. Morris, Lord Nuffield or whatever he is called, may say. Personally, as you know I think, I am in favour of a much less prudish attitude towards human nakedness, but that doesn't stop me from recognising that people who buy things can do what they like with them. Yours sincerely,   E. G.

260 : TO 'THE LISTENER' 2ND. DECEMBER, 1936

Prospero or Abraham?

With reference to the letter from Miss Rosemary Godden in your issue of November 18, I should like to explain that the statue called 'Abraham and Isaac' now on view at the French

Gallery is not the same as the Prospero and Ariel at Broadcasting House, though it was done originally as a model for the Prospero and Ariel. In the course of carving it I came to the conclusion that the proportions of the figures to one another were not appropriate to the subject, so I abandoned it. Later on I realised that what I had begun as Prospero and Ariel was really either St. Joseph and the Infant Jesus, or Abraham and Isaac, and so I went on with the carving with this idea. If anybody chooses to compare the two groups he will see that the sizes of the figures in relation to one another are quite different and that whereas in the Prospero and Ariel the relation is that of magician to fairy (*i.e.*, the figure of Prospero is monstrous and that of Ariel much smaller than any natural child could be in relation to a parent), in the Abraham and Isaac the proportions of the figures are those of father and son.

Apart from all this it remains true that a statue of Prospero and Ariel is not a portrait group. There is no Mr. Prospero now living, and so it is true that such a group must be taken in a spiritual manner. In my view the figures at Broadcasting House are as much God the Father and God the Son as they are Shakespeare's characters, and so it is quite appropriate that the group at the French Gallery should be either Joseph and Jesus or Abraham and Isaac, for all these things are different views of the same thing.   ERIC GILL

High Wycombe.

261 : TO GRAHAM CAREY

Rapallo   *22-12-1936*

We send you best wishes for Christmas. We are here for a few weeks. I am getting rid of cong^n of lungs. It is lovely here & warm & sunny. I hope you are well. I have still not answered your long last letter. I understand about the qualms you have regarding my use of words not considered 'nice' — can't be helped. It wasn't that I was trying to kill two birds with one stone or to throw two stones at two birds at one go! It was simply that (as I think) a certain kind of bird can, to-day, *our* day, only be got at by throwing a net from which *nothing* escapes. There is no such thing as impropriety when it comes to saving souls —such souls, our souls, the souls of our fellow men, brothers, sisters, lovers. Yrs.   ERIC G.

262 : TO THE RÉV. DESMOND CHUTE

Paris —Hôtel de l'Europe, Rue S. Séverin   *2-1-1937*

My dearest Desmond: We arrived here an hour ago and I have had a good wash & am now resting. We had a good journey and by divine providence we had one of those queer half carriages all to ourselves all the way from Genoa (you know, a compartment with one seat on one side only —v. comic) which was a comfort and we got wine & orange & sandwich at Turin, coffee at Modane and again at a place (whose name I never discovered) about 7.30 a.m. & déjeuner between Sens and Paris. So the journey passed and we slept in between-whiles, and then in the very middle of the journey, in the dark about 3.0 a.m. I suddenly bethought me:

NB {
O Lord! *I never packed the things in the drawer in the table!* There's a black portfolio thing full of letters to be answered as soon as I get back! And there's a *Diary* & there's some of this nice writing paper, only *white*. I can't remember anything else. I am most sorry to have been so careless & forgetful. Could you kindly make a parcel of the things and send, recommandé, *to Pigotts*. I enclose some *lire* for postage. I hope enough. I am sorry to give you this trouble, but the *letters* at least are important & the *Diary*.
}

Well, we'll write again when we get home. Words fail me at present, when I think of the gorgeous time you and Kathleen gave us. Much love from us both to you both & a cheerio to John —Yours   ERIC G.

P.S. I do appreciate what you said re priests only being re-
( ) quired to be *spiritual* men & not leaders of society & cap-
tains of cricket clubs & platform socialists.

And I do think that the converse is true — that until the
priests of (e.g.) England are known as spiritual men, i.e.
unworldly men, i.e. men who, without being prigs or
puritans or manichees, are *against* the world, the devil
and all his pomps etc. (including our materialist scientific
prowess — cars & radio & what not) *until then*: there is no
hope of a real Church in England.   E. G.

(2) (1) *A just price* is a labour price (i.e. price reckoned in
terms of labour costs), ∴ a worker's price (i.e. the idea
of price as got at from the worker's end of the biz.)
(2) *A bargain price* is the result of *salesmen* v. *consumers* (It is
not generally the result of haggle between *maker* and
consumer)* Hence it is true that we do not want *fixed
prices* in the sense that is meant by Monopolies and
Trusts (*i.e. price fixed by salesmen*). What we want is just
price, i.e. price fixed by *Maker*. What?   E. G.

* This is the bargain price you favour and rightly so — because if prices are to be *fixed* the salesman is the *last* man to do
the fixing.

263 : TO DR. CHARLES BURNS

Pigotts   *14-1-1937*

Dear Charles: I was very sorry not to have a talk on the 5th.
That boring tea-party did us in. I am much gratified to receive
Auden's message. I will send back to-day or to-morrow the
parcel of books you lent me. The Lawrence introduction[1] is
a very valuable thing, and I am keeping a copy of the paragraphs

[1] D. H. Lawrence, introduction to *Memoirs of the Foreign Legion*, by *M. M.*
(1924).

relative to war and peace. The meeting with Alick West and Herbert Read was interesting though neither of the other speakers really prepared a proper paper, and consequently they seemed to me rather vague. I understand a report is being published by the people who got up the meeting: I will send you one if it turns up. Yes, there are many things to discuss in this matter. I think to put it briefly my position is that 'art' means normally 'making' and therefore all things made by human beings are works of art, and therefore, normally, artists are in harness to the community, their function being to supply what is needed. There is the thing called play (recreation) and here below this is not the chief occasion of human work. The conditions of our material existence are such that men play in order to return refreshed to work. They do not work in order to play. But under the conditions of our industrialism we have so far destroyed man's pleasure in work and reduced the workman to the state of a mere instrument in the hands of profit-seeking employers that we have reversed the normal state of affairs so that now it has come to be true to say that men don't play to work, but work to play; for leisure time is the only thing to be looked forward to. And so the 'artist' has come to be regarded simply as the minister to leisure, the entertainer, the playboy, and to a large extent the lapdog. But more anon. Yours,   ERIC G.

P.S. I know my position sounds puritanical and over-strict, but in a world gone wrong, as I think it has done in this matter, reformers must always appear puritanical.

264 : TO GRAHAM CAREY

Pigotts   *21-1-1937*

Dear Carey: [. . .] I am overwhelmed by the sentiments of respect and affection which you express. I am also much touched by what you say about Fr. D'Arcy & Gilson. D'Arcy

I know well & love much; I did not know that M. Gilson was so much as aware of my humble existence! I am much honoured. If only I can get really well again (at present I'm in a rather weak & uncertain condition – tired, cough, a little bit of heart trouble etc.) I will endeavour to 'foot the bill', 'come up to scratch' and generally try to 'keep the ball rolling', if you see what I mean.

Your friend Langdon Warner has sent me his admirable book on Jap^e sculpture.[1] It is most kind of him – a noble gift. [. . .] Yours affe^ly.　　　　　　　ERIC G.

265 : TO THE REV. DESMOND CHUTE

Pigotts　　　　　　　　　　　*Sunday 24-1-1937*

Dear Desmond: Herewith I enclose letter from Bernard Wall
in case he has not written to you, and also review of *Eyeglass* ~~in~~ *less*
Gaza.⋆ I've had no decent chance of going on with a letter to you until to-day. I'm v. sorry to have been so long before writing to say the impossible viz: That Mary's & my loving gratitude to you for the fine time, the high old time, the heavenly time and the comfortable & comforting time we had at Villa S. Raffaele knows no bounds. It will not d.v. be our last visit. We are fully determined to come again before long. Do you think it would be possible to do what I suggested about Palestine? Suppose we came to Rapallo – put in a few days there and then, with you, took boat to Haifa. Don't you think it could be worked – the hot weather would be grand and the Holy Land remains holy. You must think this out. It would be jolly fine. Well we got home safely and I did my lecture job –

---

[1] *The Craft of the Japanese Sculptor* (1936).

⋆ a good error on the secretary's part!

but I must tell you, when we got to Paris we met my pal
Eldred Hitchcock and he, having business friends in the touring
line of biz., just because I mentioned that if I had a few days
I would go to *Le Mans*, went and borrowed a whacking great
car and on the Sunday afternoon we set out from Paris and via
Chartres where we had tea (but it was dark, so we saw little),
arrived at Le Mans about 8.0 p.m. We stayed at the Hl. de
Paris, same as where Mrs. Simpson (alias the Countess of
Cork!) stayed on her flight thro. France—saw her name in the
visitors' book. It was a bit of a joke, for none of us having
been there before and it being black night we didn't know
whereabouts in the town we were, and so when after supper
E. H. and I went for a stroll round to find the Cathedral, as to
which you had told me such marvellous things, we simply
couldn't find it! It was between 11 and 12 so there weren't
people about and all we found was a pretty dull sort of
modernish town with one solid looking romanesque church
dimly visible behind high railings at one side of a big open
space, with big residential sort of palace on one side and we
supposed that must be your marvellous church. It was
drizzling with rain, so we crept back to the hotel, tails between
legs, saying: well it's got to be a dam fine church inside if it's
going to come up to schedule. Altogether we began to think
I must have been mistaken in thinking you said *Le Mans* —perhaps we'd come to the wrong place. So we went to bed and
waited for daylight. Well, well, when the day came we had
an early breakfast and asked in the bureau: where's the cathedral? They fished out a map of the town and at one glance I saw
the truth. We weren't in the city at all! We were in the
middle of the modern town right outside the old city; the
church we saw was about a mile from the cathedral and in
proportion as shown below![1]

    When I saw that great apse & church on the plan I saw that
we had indeed come to see a great church. So we went there
straight. You don't need me to tell you in words about it. I

[1] Plan drawn below.

couldn't begin anyway. I can only say thank you for telling
me to go. The blue of Chartres — the red of Le Mans. The
solid weight of the 11 & 12 century, the incredible lightness
& grace of the 13th. What silly words for heavenly things.
Well we did a spot of thanking God for giving such powers to
men, at least I did, and truly it made me cry & laugh all
together. So we had coffee & brandy in a café (how fine it
went down on top of such nervewracking sights!) and left
about 1.o. We visited Chartres again on the way back to
Paris —just before dark. We went into the cathedral just in
time to see the blue of heaven (but they'd lit a few electric
beastly lights —I found a switch just near the west door and
was bold and impudent enough —no vergers being visible —to
jolly well turn all the lights of the nave out! It was grand, the
church nearly dark and only light coming through the W.
windows and the windows of the apse . . . then I turned them
on again & we hastily departed.) So we returned to Paris via
Maintenon & Versailles and the grand avenues. Have you ever
done that —driven into Paris by road from the west? What
magnificence of roads and trees! What puny sordidness the
approach to London is by comparison! After dinner we de-
posited Mary at our hotel & E. H. & I went to a dance place
called *the Sphinx* which would be exactly like 'a pub in Paradise' if it were not for original sin . . . & so to bed & up & off
by the 8.20 train, arriving in London at 4.o & discovering that
the lecture was at 2.30! Awful discovery —but had telephoned
from Dover beforehand and persuaded them to postpone it to
4.30. The bulk of the audience had done me the honour to
wait! So all ended well, but it was an awful moment at Dover
(1.30) when I found that the time was 2.30 & not 5.o as I had
thought —lucky we telephoned —which I only did because I
wanted to know *where* the lecture was, not *when*. Well, well,
some week-end. And it took a week to recover. I'm in the
thick of it now and more or less normally back at work. The
Geneva job is well in hand and I'm finishing a portrait of Baron
Anatole von Hügel (brother) which is to go on the wall of the

museum at Cambridge. [. . .] Now good-bye dear Desmond with much love from me and Mary & all of us and love to Kathleen too from your brother in St. Dominic   ERIC G.

All well here and the children blooming like a Perkins rambler *in lateribus*. . . .

266 : TO DR. COOMARASWAMY

Pigotts   *1-2-1937*

Dear Ananda: Thank you very much indeed for sending me the typescripts of the radio talks you are giving. I think they are absolutely 'the goods'. It is rather a joke, it almost seems as though you and I and Carey were a kind of secret society founded to 'put across' a certain point of view. The way we bag things from one another is, in a manner of speaking, jolly fine. It really is a wonderful phenomenon that with 3,000 miles between us we should be moved, as we seem to be, to say the same things, though I am not alone in thinking that you say them better than anyone else in the whole round world. It is also fun to think that we shall most certainly win in the end, though, as Belloc says, 'Truth will prevail a bit, but not in our time'. Shortly I will be sending you a book of essays we are printing here. Yours,   ERIC G.

267 : TO A. TYDEMAN

2-2-1937

Dear Tydeman: I am coming to see you on Thursday morning at 11 o'clock as arranged by telephone yesterday. I should like to say one or two things before I do so because I might be too nervous to say them on the spot.

From my point of view the whole idea of a picture stamp is essentially unreasonable.

The essential things in a postage stamp are the statement that the thing is a stamp (the words 'postage', etc.), the denomination, and some sign indicating that the thing has official origin (the King's head, a crown, etc). It seems to me that to use a pictorial subject is simply pandering to sentimentality and the appetite of collectors for anything curious. But if, for reasons unknown to me, it is decided to use a pictorial subject then I think it is desirable that the situation be faced quite frankly and that a really good photograph (i.e. good for the purpose) of the subject chosen be made and the necessary information (the word 'postage', the denomination, the crown) be frankly imposed upon the photograph and no attempt made to combine the two things, because they are essentially incompatible. In effect we should be saying, here is a pretty picture of, e.g., Windsor Castle, which we are going to use for a postage stamp: to show that we are so using it we have surcharged it with the necessary wording and numerals. I can imagine a perfectly decent postage stamp being thus made, even though I should regret that it seemed desirable to anyone to use a small picture of Windsor Castle for such a purpose.

From this you will see that what I am really opposed to is any attempt to combine a photograph of such and such with ornamental border, etc.

I don't suppose that H.M. Government is prepared to take my advice in this matter, but I should like you to know what I think, because there is no point whatever in my assisting you except on lines in harmony with my opinions. I will try and bring with me on Thursday a sort of sample of what I mean.

One thing more: I think it would be extremely undesirable to have both a view of Windsor (or whatever it is) and a photograph of the King's head. It is difficult to imagine anything worse than a combination of ornamental border, view of Windsor and photograph of King.

Is there any reason why England should not set the pace in these matters? Why should there not be one rational Post Office in the world? Why must we all follow one another sheepishly in these outrageous sentimentalities? Yours sincerely,   ERIC GILL

268 : TO GRAHAM CAREY

Pigotts   *15-2-1937*

Dear Graham: (Yes, indeed, let us address one another as Christians): I have received your letter of February 4th and am somewhat overwhelmed by the generous suggestions you make. [. . .]

Of course I agree with all you say about the hippopotamus and have often had to argue in favour of the beast as you have yourself. Thank you very much for the print. She is indeed beautiful, as well as grand.

I understand all you say about the sculptures. The statue of St. Joan has been sold. I don't think the Abraham and Isaac would have done for you. Its proper place is a church niche or at any rate a niche somewhere for I see no reason why such things should only be in churches, but it is not a thing for private possession. I am glad to know that you like the black Deposition: in my opinion it is the best thing I have done. So now I know your views and will bear them in mind and as soon as I get a chance will put something in hand. It won't be this year I am afraid as I shan't get the Geneva work done till next Spring anyway, if then. (And I may say in parenthesis, because it is a joke to put it in brackets, that I have just been and gone and fallen down and broken a rib, so all work is delayed for some weeks — more discomfort than pain, except when I sneeze).

Just incidentally, I should be interested to know which engravings struck you as 'obviously too hastily executed'.

Doubtless there are many such, but I should like to know which you consider obviously so.

I hope the *Catholic Worker* will accept that article. I understand about *Free America*, but I didn't realise that the Distributist movement had so much better chances in America than here. I shall be pleased to write something for them later on. Just at the moment I am too full up with work in hand, but I quite see the kind of thing they want. The pay offered is quite satisfactory.

I have just finished reading *Light in August* by William Faulkner —all about Alabama and the Mississippi country. Have you read it? It gives a truly frightful picture of the madness involved in the negro question. Yours,   ERIC G.

I'll be writing shortly to tell you also about the plans we're making for a sea trip!   E. G.

269 : TO GRAHAM CAREY

Pigotts   20-2-1937

Dear Graham: [. . .] I have now read your Fogg lecture.[1] It seems to me entirely admirable and a most valuable document. I hope you will distribute a large number of copies. There seems to be nobody in England (unless you think I fill the bill) who is doing the same work that you and Coomaraswamy are doing on your side. [. . .] Yours,   ERIC GILL

270 : TO DR. CHARLES BURNS

[FRAGMENT of a letter; date about February 1937.]

[. . .] I quite understand the difficulty: I really do, but Lor' bless my soul, can't these blokes see that it is no use talking about pure art with war, pestilence and famine going on all

[1] *The Majority Report on Art* (John Stevens Pamphlet, 1937).

around, or about to do so? It will be time enough to worry about the place of the Beethovens, Shakespeares and Dostoievskys when Tom, Dick and Harry and you and me have established the Kingdom of God and His justice, if ever. Let us agree that I am a Martha and that Mary has chosen the better part: but the five thousand have got to be fed, and the halt and the maim dealt with. Yours,   ERIC GILL

271 : TO DR. CHARLES BURNS

Pigotts   *1-3-1937*

Dear Charles: Thank you for your letter. I am sorry you have had the 'flu: I hope you are quite well again. My rib is nearly healed. I have got to go to Dublin next Monday and I pray to God it will be a good crossing and that my strapping stands the strain.

What you really want is a lecture and I think one ought to be written on the subject you mention. In fact I have more or less done it and it will be printed in the forthcoming book called *Work and Property*, of which I enclose prospectus herewith. I am sorry you think I appear too intolerant, narrow, etc. I try to avoid this, but the risk must be taken. There are plenty of apologists for the 'fine arts' already and what these people never realise is that the thing called fine art is the flower, and that the flower is fed from the roots as well as from the sun. Moreover, there is no need to be sorry about the fine arts. There was plenty of what we call 'high spot beauty' in those times wherein artists and fine art were never spoken of. You didn't have to have art schools and royal academies to produce Chartres or Ajanta, or, if it comes to that, Homer and Chaucer. I do not despise these things, I only say that to get them healthy you must have the whole plant strong and well and that, surely it is obvious, is not the state of affairs to-day, for at present the common arts are reduced to factory production and high spot arts are going off the top in psychological miasmas, as you know as well as anyone.

So I am not worrying even if people think I despise the fine arts. They can take care of themselves, they don't want any special nursing. What we have got to do is to redeem the common man.

No, our visit to Italy was politically unhelpful. Rapallo is so quiet and cosmopolitan that we hardly saw anything of Fascism. It is a pity about — — — —, but people like him only see things from the superior vantage point of the upper class looker-on. I shall have to wait until Maritain's book[1] is translated: I cannot read French well enough, but I hear from all sides that it is very much to the point and the best he has written. Love to all. Yours,   ERIC G.

purely (?) Useful Underground drains
purely (?) Useless Lyric Poetry, Picasso, etc.
but in between: the whole show of human makings & there's no hard dividing line. For even drain pipes are made so that you can't say they are n't human works & even poems have a kind of utility — as solace or what not.   E. G.

272 : TO THE 'CATHOLIC WORKER' (U.S.A.)
4 MARCH 1937

Dear Mr. Curran: Thank you for your letter. I cannot write at length now about this machine problem. I should like to say simply that fundamentally the problem of the machine is one which should be dealt with by those who actually use machines.

At present, as you know, the responsibility for using or not using machines is entirely that of men of business whose interests are, of course, simply in buying and selling and not

[1] *Humanisme intégral.*

in making, and therefore, in a broad way it may be said that the first thing to be done (first in the sense of most important) is for the workers to recapture the control of industry. This, of course, is the Communist idea, but, unfortunately the Communists couple with this their very crude materialist philosophy and their equally crude idolatry of the machine. For the rest, it should be obvious that some things are better made by machines than by hand. For instance, it would be ridiculous to make typewriters except by mass production, otherwise they would be absolutely prohibitive in price, and the whole point of a typewriter is to save money and time. But again it should be obvious that the whole idea of saving time and money, to such an extent as we have developed it, is a product of our quite mad and unholy commercial competitive rush.

Then again, such things as water-mills and windmills, which save human labour (grinding corn, sawing wood, etc.), are obviously proper instruments, and this brings us to the point of distinguishing between those machines which simply save human muscular labour and those which displace human creative skill.

I might use a watermill to saw stone, but it would be quite another thing for me to introduce into my workshop a letter-cutting machine. In the former case I am using a common-sense contrivance to do a job as well as it can be done; in the second case I use a contrivance which inevitably reduces the quality of the work and has no advantage but that of turning out the work more quickly and cheaply. Obviously what we want is a world in which the quality of work done rather than its cheapness is the ruling consideration. We shall never get this world all the time we are ruled by men of business. We might get it if the world were ruled by the workers, but only if they themselves were led and inspired by religion. Yours,

ERIC GILL

Pigotts, High Wycombe, England.

273 : TO MGR. JOHN O'CONNOR[1]

Pigotts, High Wycombe   15-3-1937

Dear Fr. John: I was very pleased to see, in the current number of *Parthenon*, article and photographs of the new Church; (I was also pleased to see that the statue of St. J. B. does not look so bad).

I hope all goes well and that the arrangement of the new Church is winning general approval. It seems to me that what you said, as quoted in the article, is the whole law and the prophets on the subject of liturgical revival. I am at present completely one-eyed about it. I see no hope whatever of any such revival until the Mass is brought away from the mystery mongering of obscure sanctuaries separated from the people by rows of clergy and stuff. I don't believe a single atom of good will be done by teaching people the Chant or talking about vestments or Church images until what you have done at the Church of the Holy Martyrs is done everywhere.

I do hope you are well. I wish we lived next door. Life is so full of works of all kinds, I get no chance to write.

I heard from Frances C. last week. She wants me to design a Crucifix for G. K.'s grave, and I am also designing a medal to commemorate him at Notre Dame University, U.S.A. Otherwise my chief job at the moment is to get on with the Geneva affair. Unfortunately, a month ago I went and broke a rib, which has put me back some weeks, but I am nearly well now and hope to start carving again in a few days.

Having had a touch of congestion of lungs last Autumn I was advised to have a few weeks in the sun, so Mary and I went out to Rapallo and stayed with Desmond for a month. We did enjoy ourselves, although the sun was not very conspicuous. Desmond seemed pretty well and full of intellectual beans. We all send you our love, indeed we do. Yours ever, ERIC G.

[1] In 1937 Father O'Connor became a Privy Chamberlain to Pius XI, and hence Monsignore; but for E. G. he remained 'Father John'.

274 : TO GRAHAM CAREY

Pigotts   *16-3-1937*

Dear Graham: [. . .] Mary & I are going to Palestine in May
for a month or so! [. . .] You know I was there 3 years ago
& ever since I have longed to return. [. . .] Unfortunately
I can't get away till May. I've got 2 lecture engagements
(Ap. 28 & May 5) which prevent me. I am afraid it'll be frightfully hot in Jerusalem in May-June. It can't be helped. We'll
be staying, part of the time at least, with the Gov.ᵗ architect —
Austen Harrison —for whom I did the carving job when I was
there in 1934. Anyway we'll have the sea voyage to & from
& that alone shd. set me properly up in health again. (But,
what d'you think?, as tho. I'd not been delayed long enough
last autumn —a month ago, just when I was getting nicely back
to work, I went & fell off a low scaffold in the workshop & fell
on a baulk of timber & broke a rib! (didn't half hurt too!).
So that's another month gone —except for drawing & writing
work. I haven't started carving again yet —but hope to do so
this week. It's v. nearly well.)

I hope *you* are well & I hope all goes well with you. Yrs.
ERIC G.

275 : TO HIS BROTHER EVAN

Pigotts   *7-5-1937*

Dear Evan: Thank you very much for your letter and for the
magnificent telegram, but I did not get one of Max's design —
pity.¹ I am glad if you are pleased about the new stamps.² I
can't write much now but, you know, really the responsibility
for the design is more the Post Office's than mine. I only drew

¹ The form of 'Greetings telegram' designed by his brother Macdonald Gill.
² The first issue of King George VI stamps, put on sale for the first time on
May 10th, 1937. E. G. was responsible for the frame design and the lettering of
the nine values from ½d. to 6d. The King's head was the work of Edmund
Dulac.

the stuff as instructed. Certainly I will send you a letter on
Monday with the new issues on the envelope. Many thanks for
postal order: it was kind of you to think of it. I didn't take
any note of your telephonic efforts but I expect you are correct. Love to all. We leave on Monday next. Yours, ERIC G.

forgive haste

2 7 6 : TO GRAHAM CAREY

23-6-1937

Thank you very much for your letters of C. Christi & Ascension. We leave for England on the 2 8 – due in *Liverpool* July 1 2.
We have had a truly wonderful holyday & I am now I think
quite well & ready for the work which awaits my return. We
did *not forget your requests at the Holy Sepulchre & other Holy
Places.* I'm v. glad you like the new stamps – they are of
course just a compromise between my wishes & those of the
authorities. I look forward to seeing your Harvard lectures.
I will write again on my return home. Love from   ERIC G.

2 7 7 : TO GRAHAM CAREY

Mid-day 7-7-1937
*S.S. 'Sagaing', Sailing i.e. steaming along coast of Spain, expecting
to arrive at Gibraltar this evening*

My dear Graham! This is simply to say that our Palestine
interlude is now coming to a close [. . .] It would be impossible to tell you everything about it. We have had a marvellous time in many ways. We went by train to Trieste &
stayed one pleasant night there & then on an Italian boat to
Haifa – arriving on May 1 7 – We then went straight on to
Jerusalem (via Jenin & Nablus) where we stayed with Austen
Harrison (item: I hope you've got the photos. by now. A. H.
told me he had given instructions for them to be sent) all the

time except for four days during which A. H. & I flew to
Cairo! & a week spent at the Austrian Hospice in the old city.
A. H. lives on the S. side of the city in a very beautiful house
with fine arab vaults to all the rooms. (Item: I am much gone
on the arab vaulting system – an alternative solution, to the
medieval European one, of the problem of cross vaults. Instead of the pointed arch they use ellipses. They make *the
diagonals first*, & always semicircular, but not necessarily
crossing at right angles, thus:–

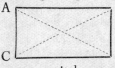 Dotted lines are semicircular, so AB &
AC will be ellipses. It's a jolly fine
system giving very strong vaults & is, as
you see, as flexible as the Gothic –
moreover it harmonizes with the round headed window . . .
if that's a comfort to you! (I think it rather is to me.), and
it's much more suave and restful to the eye & naturally never
developed into a complication of groining.) Jerusalem was
much the same as three years ago. No visible effects of the
recent Arab strike but the longer we stayed the more audible
became the underground murmurings of discontent. We
went to lunch several times at the High Commissioner's but
naturally he, H.E., did not divulge state secrets. One thing
transpired: viz. he has commissioned me to design a new
Arab type for poss. use at the Gov.t Printing Works! I have
also done a new Hebrew type for use at the Hebrew press
about to be started in Jerusalem. And while I was there I did
several inscriptions for various people and, strange to say, did
a 'broadcast' for the Palestine B'casting Service with the title
'Art in England, as it seems to me', (the first time I've ever
spoke into the m'phone – not so difficult or alarming as I'd
imagined) in which I took the opportunity to rub in the
connections between art, whether 'fine' or otherwise, and
our commercial industrialism, ending up with the theme
adumbrated on the post-card I sent you from Marseilles (I hope
you get it) – about the drunken bus driver. [. . .]
 Well, apart from these few small jobs, we did nothing at

Jerusalem except enjoy it. Our friend Harrison was most kind and took us round a good lot in car — down to Jericho quite a lot, bathed in Dead Sea (very delightful & amusing) several times, miles away from any other living thing except a scrubby sort of bushes. The heat was terrific (to my English senses) but the prevailing thirst was grand. We also went to Jaffa, Tel-Aviv, Bethlehem, Hebron, Beersheba & Gaza on other occasions and, as I said above, A. H. & I went to Cairo. That was a very interesting & exciting few days. I enjoyed the air plane flight very much — marvellous, wonderful, lovely, flying over the sea & over Port Said & the Delta. What an astoundingly different kind of landscape from that of Buckinghamshire! Cairo itself is a corrupt & bad old city (I should think) & very hot & enervating. But there are things there which for sheer splendidness & holiness cannot be surpassed. For instance the mosque of Sultan Hassan & that of el Haz'r. But as a city it is just nothing compared with Jerusalem — a city of mud bricks, noise, buses & trams & cosmopolitanism superimposed on the eastern city of the bazaars; whereas Jerusalem is a city of stone & as there are no streets wide enough for wheeled traffic (except a few hundred yards by the Jaffa gate & the Bab Siti Miriam) there is no noise save that of human voices & footsteps &, inside the walls, there is a complete absence (except in the cheap factory stuff & tinned foods which they sell in their little shops — or in some of them) of our filthy western life & none of its filthy apparatus. And, in the midst, the Holy Sepulchre (which, whatever one may say about the silly squabbles of the rival caretakers, Catholic, Greek & Copt etc., is a palpably holy place) and, occupying all one corner, the Haram el Sheraf (called by us 'the Temple Area'), than which nothing, nothing, nothing could be lovelier, holier, more dignified, more humane or more grand. Thank God I got a permit from the Grand Mufti to go in and out every day ('cept Fridays, when it is reserved for Moslems exclusively & jealously). I did a few drawings sitting on the roof of a house in the via Dolorosa. Which, whatever the

JERUSALEM

Drawing by E.G.

valuelessness of the drawings, was a fine way of staying put &
thus really soaking up the scene.

Well, well, this is all absurdly inadequate to convey to you
(a) my overwhelming love for Jerusalem & for Palestine —oh
my dear Graham you can't believe how lovely they are, and
(b) my very deep and inexpressible gratitude to you for your
part in our privilege.

Now we are nearing Gibraltar & next week we'll be back
in England & I shall be, I expect, up to my ears in arrears of
work. (Item: I'm really most awfully well now & can't see
how I can possibly get ill again for years . . .) I only hope I'll
find that things have been going well in my absence. Yours

ERIC G.

I did go and see the great Pyramid! and went up & into its
middle! Nought but exclamation marks will convey to you
its amazing & marvellous mad grandeur! Did you like the
Pyramids? Not half!

Item: (5.0 p.m.), just passed 2 Brit. cruisers, patrolling the
Spanish coast!

278 : TO 'THE CATHOLIC HERALD'
21 JULY, 1937

Sir: It is, of course, impossible for me to reply in detail to all
the many letters you have received in reply to mine in your
issue of May 14th. Moreover it is unnecessary to do so for, if
I may say so without offence, very few of your correspondents
have really taken up the point of my letter. I think I cannot do
better than briefly restate it.

This is an industrially organized society (it seems unnecessary to define industrialism, but briefly it means machine and
mass production of the necessaries of life and many of the
luxuries). Assuming that no-one wishes to abolish industrialism or that it is impossible to do so, the only question is:
What is the best form of ownership? It is clear that individual

ownership is not possible: at present we have collective ownership by the shareholders with the inevitable consequence of production for profit. On many grounds this state of affairs is offensive to Christian morals. But some form of collective ownership is necessary; no other meets the case. I therefore see no alternative but collective ownership by the workers for the sake of justice to them and production for use.

How this can be brought about is a matter for politicians to decide. Whether violence is necessary is not my immediate concern, nor am I concerned to discuss whether or no collective ownership by the workers necessarily involves its advocates in alliance with Moscow.

The alternatives seem to me quite clear —either abandon industrialism, or proceed to collective ownership by the workers. Individual persons may be prepared to do the former, but I have never seen it stated, either in Papal Encyclicals or elsewhere, that the Catholic Church is committed to this line of thought. Yours faithfully,   ERIC GILL

279 : TO MGR. JOHN O'CONNOR

Pigotts   *4-9-1937*

Dear Fr. John: Thank you very much for your letter of the 2nd. I am most awfully glad to hear that your cruise has done you good. I should like to see A. M. Wong in the flesh: such photographs as I have seen indicate extraordinary fineness.

About the statue: I kid myself that I am going to have it ready for you by next Spring, and with your approval I propose to exhibit it at the R.A. before sending it to Bradford. You see it is like this: having been elected to that august body I am under the obligation of exhibiting once in three years, and I am most anxious not to do something just for exhibition purposes or anything of a merely West End garden statue kind, but something that somebody wants. So do you agree?

Thank you for the photograph. Great minds evidently think alike, as usual: I had already saved one out of our *Daily Mirror*. The throw of the head and neck are extremely good. Jealous Joanna said she stuck out too much behind, but I think it is only shorts. Whether I will ever do a statue is another story. Besides, it is a bronze not a stone — the sort of thing that Derwent Wood would have done to perfection. [. . .] Yours,   ERIC G.

280 : TO DR. CHARLES BURNS

Pigotts   *15-10-1937*

Dear Charles: Thanks for yours and 10/-. Glad you got back safely. The Saturday evening talk was most useful: it was a pity the — was such an M.D. As to co-partnership, well, bad as it is and may be that workers should be encouraged to become as much profit-seekers as the other shareholders and indeed to become shareholders themselves, nevertheless it is clear surely that co-partnership is at least a step in the right direction, i.e. in the direction of recognising that the workers are partners and not merely bits of the machinery. I don't like co-partnership because I don't like the company of capitalists. I would rather turn the latter out completely, buy them out, blow them out, liquidate them, but until that can be done I am not going to take an intransigent line and refuse all substitutes. Yours,   ERIC G.

281 : TO 'BLACKFRIARS', NOVEMBER 1937

Sir: Fr. Ceolfrid Heron's very valuable and appreciative article in the August *Blackfriars* on my book *Work and Property*, invites a short comment. Misunderstanding seems to arise from my advocacy of 'collective ownership' by the 'workers'.

It is thought that such advocacy is out of line with adverse criticism of industrialism and the 'leisure state'. People ask: how can you be in favour of collectivism and of a return to responsible workmanship at the same time? How can you believe in distributed property and also acquiesce in industrialism? The answer is easy. I believe in workers' ownership of the means of production and distribution. I believe in the village blacksmith (still one or two left) owning his own workshop and tools. I believe in the farmer owning his own farm and implements.

But what about the Great Western Railway? That also is an affair of workmen. Is it a bad thing? Is it immoral? Does the Pope refuse to go by train? And what about all the other industrial enterprises? I may not like the kind of world they imply. I may be able to show that it is all wrong and leading to war and disaster — cheap amusements and conveniences, vulgarity on every hand, not to mention the corruption of family life, the destruction of human culture and an increasing madness of international rivalry. But what of it? Does any theologian of importance condemn railway trains or telephones or tinned food? Does any theologian condemn the factory system, as such, or say anything against the wage system? As far as my information goes theologians ask for no more than good trade unionists do —higher wages, shorter hours, better canteens, insurance against ill-health and unemployment and possibly a share of the profits large enough to enable employees to buy a bit of property (if there's any for sale).

Very well then, I take it that no one wants the G.W.R. to be abolished. The question is: who shall own it? At present it is the legal possession of the shareholders. We all know what they're like. You read the finance pages of the daily papers. I say I believe in workers' ownership. Why should such a belief only apply to blacksmiths' shops, artists' studios and solicitors' offices? If it is good for me to own my workshop, why isn't it good for railway men to own a railway? And if I say these things, why should I be accused of going

back on my vocation to teach in and out of season that the ownership and control of any enterprise is rightly that of those who have the responsibility of doing the work and making a good job of it? A porter cannot own a platform, a guard cannot own a railway carriage, a driver cannot own a locomotive – that's obvious. But they can collectively own the railway – that's obvious too. And as in our existing society the ownership of railways and such things is that of those whose only title is that they have lent money and whose only concern is the profit on what they've lent, it seems somewhat clearer than daylight that it is time we made a bit of a change. Who wants to make a change – a change in the direction of workers' ownership? The workers do – and very rightly and properly. And their demand is entirely in line with what I've always said – that the man who does the work ought to be responsible for it and that there can be no responsibility where there is no ownership. And as I pointed out in *Work and Property*, enlarging on the theme of Prof. Maritain in his *Freedom in the Modern World*, 'the formal reason of individual appropriation is the exercise of art or work' and 'the notion of *person* must be included in any complete theory of property'. In our society we already have collective ownership – that of the shareholders. This is an impersonal ownership. The shareholder in relation to his holding is not a person; he is a receiver of dividends, if any. But porters and guards and engine drivers and foremen and clerks and managers are persons and they are personally responsible for the jobs they do. It is obvious that they ought to be the owners and controllers and that it is the shareholders who should be subordinate and powerless. If a man lends me money, I treat him as such, thank him politely and keep out of his way. I don't give him control of my job.*
I trust, Sir, that all this is clear and that it will not again be thrown up against me that I have done anything but carry my 'teaching' to its logical conclusion.

One thing more: May I say that I am sorry if, as one reviewer put it, I seem 'to have been particularly unfortunate in the clergy of (my) acquaintance'. The reverse is the truth. But I must admit that I share the opinion common among the masses who are 'lost to the church' that the clergy show some reluctance to condemn Capitalism —production for profit, production for the sake of dividends. Yours faithfully,

ERIC GILL

Pigotts, High Wycombe ⟨16 Aug. 1937⟩.

P.S. It should be added, to avoid unnecessary correspondence, that when I say that the farmer, the craftsman, should own his own land, workshop, etc., I do not refer to that quasi absolute ownership which goes today by the name of 'freehold'. Ownership means control, personal control, but, definitely, control for good not evil, not for private aggrandisement but in the interests of society and the common good —in the interest of the individual also, but of the individual as a member of society; 'A man should not regard his material possessions as his own but as common to all . . .' Absolute ownership, implying a right to destroy or misuse or leave unused what is necessary to the good of others, is an evil myth. Therefore the ownership I mean is a tenancy, hereditary if desired, granted by responsible authority, enjoying the support and defence of public opinion and law, but implying specified duties and obligations as much as rights and carrying with it no opportunity for the exploitation of other people.

E. G.

* See appendix to *Religion & Culture* on Fecundity of Money (Maritain), pp. 61-2.

282 : TO GRAHAM CAREY

Pigotts   ⟨*Christmas 1937*⟩

Dear Graham: Just a short letter to say I hope you are well and having a very happy Christmas. All well here and the work going pretty strong. Still full up with the job for Geneva. Am now packing up the first portion, seventeen stones. Am also doing a Statue of B.V.M. (Annunciation) for Fr. O'Connor at Bradford & Sts T. More & J. Fisher for a school at Newcastle-u^r-Lyme. Also writing & lecturing too much but what would you? This peace & war business sucks everyone into the jaws. I hope you also are busy. Did you meet Donald Attwater during his visit to U.S.A.? I hoped he would have a chance to visit Boston & you. How is Coomaraswamy & how is his book on medieval aesthetic getting on? [. . .]

You never sent *Thoughts & Things*. Is it out? I don't see how you can do Plato's trick with Beauty or Goodness as subject because the trick is a *truth* trick in its nature. I am most awfully glad you liked *Work & Property*. I'm now working up notes to do one on ownership! All well so far with health — & am not yet financially wrecked. I *will* let you know if serious difficulty arises. Yours affectionately   ERIC G.

Forgive so short a note. Just at present it cannot be helped. Come again to England before the end of the world. You'll have to hurry!

·

2 8 3 : TO THE REV. DESMOND CHUTE

Pigotts   *29-12-1937*

My dearest Desmond: We were very glad to get your even so short letter and your lovely Madonnas and we thank you very much. It is so imposs. to realize that a whole year has passed since the glorious time we had with you at R'o. A lot of doings have been done — every day, with us as with you, has its pint and a half trying to squeeze down into a pint pot. The sooner it's over the sooner to sleep . . . and yet on the whole life is worth living even for its own sake and as you know and as I know, I am one in a thousand for blessings flung upon me. It doesn't get easier though and the noise and rush and inanity of the life of our civilization get plainly and rapidly worse. However this place is, in spite of the beastly little cars & the telephone, still an oasis in which the little children, for all their yearning after aeroplanes & motor-cars & cinemas & other gadgets, can and do grow up sweet and good, and they do. Petra's four are truly lovely & Joanna's two too. Michael Hague, aged 6, is now revelling in a new small bicycle – you ought to see his real joy in it and on it. 'Oh I am glad, I am glad' he shouts as he rushes round. He went for a ride on the real highroad with René the other day – he on his tiny bike and René behind on his. It reminded you of the eighteen-nineties in Battersea Park when bikes first came in and you & I or our fathers & mothers went on them for joy! And Petra's young Adam has got an aeroplane with real red & green electric lights. It's attached by a sling to the ceiling and flies round and round in the dark room amidst shrieks of delight. But still the cows give milk and the garden vegetables, and pigs squawk and breed. And still the noise of hammer & chisel on good stone resounds in the shops. [. . .] The Geneva job is getting on. The central portion is now all but finished and most of the 17 stones, all but three, of which it is comp., are packed up. I expect it will all go off in a week or two and then when it's fixed up we, I & A. F., will go to Geneva to finish it off – a bit of touching up is sure to be required. How far is Geneva from Rapallo? Is it, so to say, getatable from R'o.? Geneva to Chambéry & Modane must be fairly easy and thence to Genoa is direct – so why not me come to spend a day or so with you? Tell me if you can face the thought. It does look like an opportunity. Let me know also, if you can without more strain, what sort of a price, 3rd class, is it from G. to R. and what sort of a time it takes. Well, it would be grand if we could manage that; then we could get up to date again in our reminiscences & prophetic utterances. It *wd*. be grand. Otherwise it's nigh imposs. to keep informed. I spend far too much time writing as it is. Why the devil I do it I don't know. Every blessed day I spend from nine to about 11.0 or 11.30 doing correspondence & if I get 4 hours carving done before dark I'm lucky. I'm doing a B.M.V. (of the Annunciation) for Fr. O'C at present in between bouts with the L. of N. It's to be in Red Mansfield stone — about 4.0 high to stand on that beastly round pedestal on the side of his sanctuary. So far I've only done the bath stone model. We're also doing a SS. Thos. More & John Fisher for a school at N' Castle-under-Lyme — full size in Portland for £150 — absolutely starvation price. Anthony F. is doing most of the work on them. So there.

Dear Desmond I'm truly sorry to hear you've been so un- well all the year. And are you now all alone with the 'natives'? Do they properly look after you? I do hope I'll be able to come and see for myself. [. . .] We all send you our love, we do indeed. Mary and Betty (she's here — came yesterday — for a few days with her 3 eldest) have gone to a wedding in London to-day. Yours —   ERIC G.

Have got to go to Ditchling to talk to P.P.U. meeting next month! Walter sends his love. He is well but for remains of a blue sapphire in neck. Fr. V. White O.P. said m-night mass here.

284 : TO MGR. JOHN O'CONNOR

Pigotts   *29-12-1937*

Dear Father John: I was so glad to get your letter yesterday and to gather from it that you are well, as well as cheerful. I am most grateful for your loving appreciation.

We are certainly having a fairly sticky time with Boggling Bourgeoisie, but by tactfully taking no notice and carrying on regardlessly, we shall probably last out without excommunication.

I will send a line to Ditchling to find out if they have any copies of M⟨istress⟩ of V⟨ision⟩.[1] [. . .]

We are just packing up the first portion of the stuff for Geneva, I should have liked you to have seen it. The rest is to be finished by August, and I shall be crammed up with work until then. [. . .]

285 : TO 'THE DAILY TELEGRAPH &
MORNING POST', 3 JAN., 1938

Sir: I have no knowledge by which to judge the authenticity of the four little pictures recently purchased for the National Gallery and ascribed to Giorgione, but if you will allow me I should like to make a protest against the suggestion that if a thing is by someone called Giorgione it is worth £3,500, but if on inquiry it turns out to be by George Jones it is not worth more than any other pretty thing.

I know that such an opinion is contrary to that of the whole commercial world. But what then? Things are not really more costly because they are rare, and though we are at the mercy of merchants for our supply of bread, surely we need not succumb to such madness when it comes to custard?

I would like to see all names removed from the catalogue of the National Gallery, and to allow Mr. Kenneth Clark and his advisers to choose what they like, as we have, I suppose, chosen him and them. — Yours faithfully   ERIC GILL

Pigotts, High Wycombe, Dec. 31. (1937)

[1] Francis Thompson's poem edited by Father O'Connor.

2 8 6 : T O   D R .   C H A R L E S   B U R N S

Pigotts   *1-2-1938*

Dear Charles: Thank you for yours of the 25th. and for the article,[1] which I will read at once. I am sure I shall find it most interesting.*

I have just got a thing from Coomaraswamy which seems to me to be as near as no matter the last word on the same subject. It is about 2 ft. square, so rather difficult to send on, but you must read it.[2]

Of course I should be very glad if you can bring Herrick for a visit, I do not wonder he is hopeless about things. It is like the Captain said in the shipwreck when he went to tell the passengers the ship was sinking. He said 'Our help is in the name of the Lord', to which the old lady passenger replied 'Oh Captain, is it as bad as that?' Well, it is.

Yes, we will be here off and on, but I shall have to go to Geneva towards the end of this month, and shall very likely be away about 10 days. We are all well.

Betty is about to marry again. She has an idea it would be nice to be married in the chapel here, so I am getting the legal business in order in the hope that the parish priest will give his permission. For this purpose I have to get 20 signatures of householders. Would you kindly sign the enclosed and send it on to *Tom as soon as possible*? Love to all. Yours ERIC G.

* P.S. I've read the 'psycho' paper.

I dare say (i.e. I shd'nt be surprised) a good lot of it is actually true.

I think a lot of it is pretty nonsensical —I doubt his ability as a mere critic of 'art work'. But the chief thing that emerges from such papers is the evidence they give of the unusual (&

[1] W. R. D. Fairbairn, *Prolegomena to a Psychology of Art* (in *British Journal of Medical Psychology*).

[2] *The Nature of Buddhist Art*, a preface to *The Wall-Paintings of India, Central Asia and Ceylon* (Boston, 1938). Reprinted in *Figures of Speech or Figures of Thought* (Luzac, 1946).

as *I* shd. say abnormal) state of affairs in our world. Having removed (at least as far as the awareness of psychoanalysts goes) all *real* teleology & the whole caboodle of ordered government (divine & human) the whole show is reduced to that of a squirming maggot under a microscope — what's he up to now? What's he squirm like that for?

Upset an ant hill & remove most or all memory of the ant hill from the 'minds' of the ants and then, after a generation or two, psychoanalyse the ants.

I, on the other hand, in my Olympian wisdom, view all 'art work' as I do house building or knitting. The psycho stuff fits in but is subordinated. I ask: what is it? (the artist), what's it for? (the percipient), what's it made of (the art work), how's it done? (the technique). The things in brackets being the categories named by your Mr. Fairbairn. And emotions are *post* hoc & not *propter hoc* — i.e. consequents not causes.   E. G.

287 : TO MGR. JOHN O'CONNOR

Pigotts   *28-2-1938*

Dear Father John: [. . .] I am sending herewith an article[1] for your criticism and hope you will approve of it. I should be very grateful if you will tell me where it is in error.

The occasion of this was a request from Blundell's School at Tiverton to help them with their chapel. The head master said to me 'Would the altar look better a few feet away from the East wall?', and I said to him 'It doesn't matter where it would look better, the question is where it would *be* better, and where it would be better, you will come to see that it looks better,' and so on. Arising out of this, I had to go to Blundell's and give the boys a lecture on 'Christian Altars', of which this paper is the substance. Yours   ERIC G.

[1] 'Mass for the Masses', reprinted in *Sacred and Secular*.

2 8 8 : T O T H E R E V . D E S M O N D C H U T E

Geneva   *3-3-1938*

Arrived yesterday. Have a few days work here. I will write
again saying what day I'll come to you. It will be next week
sometime. Love   E. G.

2 8 9 : T O ' I R E L A N D T O - D A Y '

[THIS letter, written on March 16th, 1938, was addressed to *Ireland
To-day* in reply to an article on *Collectivism and Workers' Ownership*
by Prof. James Hogan, published in the March number together
with E. G's *Is there a Papal Social Programme!* But with that number
Ireland To-day ceased publication, and the letter was communicated
to *Blackfriars*, where it appeared in the *Extracts and Comments* of
May 1938.]

Sir: I am gratified by the inclusion of my article in the same
issue as Professor Hogan's and honoured by his criticism of
my views. I agree with practically every word he says and,
had he not mentioned my name, should have no occasion to
write.

But as he has referred to me I must say this: What I have
written on the subject of workers' ownership as on other
matters must be taken more as a challenge to opponents than
as definite statements. I have neither knowledge nor ability
to deal adequately with such a complicated subject. It is
sufficient from my point of view if I can provoke discussion.
The times are desperate. We are in danger of succumbing to
mere inertia. But there is this to note: there is a certain
method in my madness. When I say or imply that 'modern
civilization is absolutely committed to the present system of
mechanized industrial production' I am not saying what *I* think
but what on all sides I am continually told. Very good, I say,
suppose it is so, let it be granted, what then? Such and such
logically follows. If I can show the logical consequences, and

CC

if those consequences are or seem horrible or inhuman or un-
christian then my opponents take note of the challenge.
That's what I want them to do. Professor Hogan says I 'leave
out of account (i.e., in my demand for workers' ownership)
the numerous small-scale industrial enterprises' even in England. Naturally I do; and so people come forward, as Professor
Hogan does, and rub the point in, and as a consequence the
trend towards industrial amalgamation is seen in a critical
light. Professor Hogan says that I say that the present trend is
inevitable. I don't say so. It's the other people who say so.
I only attempt to show them the consequences. 'Nobody
wants to go back to pre-industrial methods of production.'
That's what they tell me. All right then. If men agree to
work in that way, however evil I personally think it to be,
however destructive of all humane things, however inevitably
leading to the philosophy of the Leisure State, well, it's not
for me to say they mustn't. All I can do is to fight for a just
politics and the first necessity is workers' ownership of the
means of production. That is Christian politics. If we oppose
that politics we shall lose the workers for ever and we shall
deserve to do so.

Professor Hogan says I fail to make the distinction between
state-collectivism and workers' ownership. But I am not
concerned with state collectivism. I am concerned to demand
workers' ownership —for the sake of the work, for the sake
of the workers. Doubtless there are industries which are, in
their nature, best owned and run by the 'state.' Of course it
is so. What I am up against is the present prevalence of
industries owned by absentee shareholders and run simply for
the sake of profit to them —i.e. dividends. Because I confine
myself largely to that issue, it doesn't follow that I oppose
people who want something else as well. And of course I
agree that 'in the absence of wide-spread private property
workers' groups cannot exist . . .' But we must define what
we mean by 'private.' We must make it clear that it is for
the common good and not for individual aggrandisement that the

claim to property is made; and that the word 'private' does not imply an *absolute* ownership, but a *personal* trusteeship confirmed by law (what's wrong with law?); for, as Gide says in his *History of Economic Doctrines*, English law, in common with the traditions of European law as a whole, recognizes no absolute ownership of the land except that of the Crown.

So I hope it will be agreed that my method is a good complement to Professor Hogan's and a good way of provoking our pastors and masters to sit up and take notice.   ERIC GILL

290 : TO MGR. JOHN O'CONNOR

Pigotts   *6-5-1938*

Dear Fr. John: Thank you for your letter of the 3rd. We have just finished copying your 'Liturgy', I am very sorry we have been so long. I return herewith your original and hope very much that they will be pleased with it at Downside. [. . .]

I have just come back from Tiverton. The boys are working heroically on their chapel, and although it has not been feasible to put the altar in the middle, they have cleared a lot of pews out of the East end and have put the altar right in the centre of the cleared space. They are now making a new altar from my designs.

It is really a remarkable business because I have, I think, made it clear that it is not an architectural reform but a liturgical one. Yours   ERIC G.

291 : TO DR. COOMARASWAMY

[E. G. had sent Dr. Coomaraswamy a copy of his lecture on *Work and Culture*, given to the Royal Society of Arts on April 27th, 1938 and printed in the *Journal* of the Society for June 17th, 1938. It was reprinted in *Sacred and Secular*, where the sentence referred to below (p. 745 in the *Journal*) occurs on p. 87. In its first form it reads:

'Religious cultivation is the cultivation of the whole race of men with a view to eternal beatitude or temporal happiness.'

Dr. Coomaraswamy replied: 'Many thanks for your excellent lecture . . . My only criticism would be: p. 745, line 8, for "or" read "and". Is not religion to enable us to make the best of *both* worlds? The "or" implies an alternative. Would anyone who does not sin (all sin being "against nature") *not* have temporal happiness?— I feel sure that "barbarous" cultures are degraded. Most of the "savage" societies on which anthropologists base their studies *are* decadent; but even in these one can recognize that the decadence was *of* something high. I've been reading Lévy-Bruhl on primitive mentality recently, and am much impressed that apart from the accidental "superstitiousness" of the African tribes mostly cited, the "primitive mentality" is fundamentally that of Christianity and Hinduism: a realistic (in the technical philosophical sense) mentality. I feel in other words that Lévy-Bruhl is describing a mentality that is *essentially* ours, but *accidentally* perverted.']

Pigotts   *8-7-1938*

Dear Ananda: Thank you very much for your letter of the 29th. I am very glad indeed that you approve of the lecture. I entirely agree with your criticism about page 745 line 8. I felt the difficulty myself at the time and that is why I said what I did in the next paragraph. I propose to re-write the sentence you refer to by transposing the words as follows:—

'. . . with a view to temporal happiness and eternal beatitude.'

I think that will meet the case.

I am very glad you agree about 'savage' societies. I did not take a very dogmatic line in the lecture because I wanted the people to accept my reasoning rather than my assertions. With best wishes, Yours   ERIC G.

'Will someone tell us whether all this Nationalisation . . . is consonant with Catholic teaching about private property . . .?' asked the Bishop of Pella last week. I imagine there is a catch somewhere; for, otherwise, it is difficult to understand why it should be necessary for a Bishop to ask for information on 'Catholic teaching' in a paper run by and for laymen.

It is not for me to reply, but perhaps, without offence, I may make a few comments, and first I should like to draw attention to the fact that, as stated in Gide's *History of Economic Doctrines* (page 559) English Law, in common with the traditions of European Law as a whole, recognises no absolute ownership of the land except that of the Crown.

This is fact, however submerged by common ideas of 'freehold,' and not theory. Private property in land is not an absolute ownership but a tenancy secured and supported by the Crown, and this fact is not an example of royal tyranny but is based on the underlying truth that it would be clearly absurd if private owners could claim such absolute rights over property as to enable them to flout the common good. The notion of 'the Common Good' is the ultimate basis of public law (Note: the word tenant only means 'holder' —a person who holds property. A private owner is a holder of property direct from the Crown; a person who holds land from such a private owner is properly speaking a sub-tenant and so on.)

Second: We may consider the case of 'Treasure Trove' and ask ourselves in what way the discovery of coal and oil differs from the discovery of buried gold coins, and then ask what is the justice of the Crown's claim to treasure trove and whether it would not have been equally possible and just if coal and oil, etc., had been included as treasure?

Third: It should be pointed out that it is not quite in order to class the London Transport Board and the B.B.C. as public authorities without qualification. Both of these organisations, and others of the same sort, are only semi-public; they are amalgamations of private and public bodies, and private and public capital, and, as I understand, the profits are divided.

Fourth: It is not quite fair to say 'it is all a matter whether it is good business or not . . .' Doubtless, in our commercial world, that aspect is very much to the front in the speeches of both promoters and opponents of the bill; moreover unless the promoters can show reason for claiming that the public will be economically better off, they would have small chance of getting their bill through.

None the less, the main idea of the bill, as, in my innocence, it seems to me, is that only in this way can the bitter struggle of the miners and mine owners be obviated and the common good advanced.

Here you have the buried treasure called coal. It is a substance of importance and use to every man, woman and child in the nation and to our neighbours abroad as well. Its getting is both an arduous and a dangerous job. The quality and quantity of the product are not due to man's inventiveness or energy (you have to work hard to get it and be clever in your methods, but good coal is either there or not there, in big amounts or small ones).

It seems obvious to many, and at least arguable to many more, that coal mining is therefore, in the nature of things, a public job and coalmines public property. And whether or no we decide, for the good of the work and the good of the worker, to work the mines by letting them to syndicates of workers or capitalists or both, it may still seem obvious that the ownership of the mines themselves is rightly that of the whole people and therefore of the Crown as representing and personifying the whole people.

Fifth: Every honourable man is in one sense a public servant, but in another sense he is, equally honourably, a person seeking his private advantage. All property is in one sense public property, but in another sense some forms of property are naturally private and personal.

In my humble and quite unauthoritative opinion, all forms of hidden treasure are in the nature of things public property, and coal mining and all such collective works (railways, roads, posts and telegraphs), when the work is a service to persons in general rather than to individuals, might more justly and no less efficiently be run for public rather than private profit. Is all this consonant with Catholic teaching? I repeat: it is not for me to say. Rather would I respectfully ask the Bishop to point out where it is not.   ERIC GILL

293 : TO EOGHAN BUCKLEY

Pigotts   *28-7-1938*

Dear Buckley: [. . .] I think there is no doubt that were the 'minimum status wages' plan followed out or if the Pope's teaching of the family wage were insisted upon, it would wreck the capitalist-industrialist system. As things are, what with competition etc. it is obviously quite impossible for big business to pay sufficient wages to enable employees to buy property. Perhaps the Pope knows this and it is his scheme for destroying the system. Let us assume that. Yours sincerely,
                                                            ERIC GILL

294 : TO GRAHAM CAREY

Pigotts   *15-9-1938*

Dear Graham: Thank you very much for your letter of the 9th July. Rush of work has prevented my replying before and now I have got yours of the 12th August, which shames me more than ever.

I have been finishing the sculptures at Geneva and now at last they are done and I have just got back from Switzerland.

The first part was fixed in March and now the two side panels have been put up. The people there seem satisfied, but I have had no official intimation except that they have paid and now I am actually solvent for the first time in eleven years, which makes me anxious to know how I stand with you. I have tons of work in hand, so cannot immediately promise to undertake anything, but should like to know what your present views are.

I have got some carving to do on a Hospital at Coventry and later some more on Rugby Technical College as well as some other small jobs, including a Madonna and Child on a Nurses' Hostel in Essex and four engravings for a book of Donne's poems. I have just finished two engravings for *Travels of Jean de Brebeuf*, the Jesuit Missionary among the Indians in the sixteenth century. I enclose a print of one —I am sorry I have none of the other. So you see, though I cannot do anything very much for you at present, I could put something in hand if you have any definite ideas on the subject. Please let me know.

I am very glad indeed you so highly approve of the R.S.A. Lecture. I think there are several noticeable faults in it, e.g. the 'or' in line 8 page 745 should be 'and' as A. K. C. has pointed out. I hope to re-publish this lecture with revisions in the next book of essays, but don't know when that will be, so I should be very glad if you could do it in the U.S.A. as a John Stevens pamphlet or however you like. I don't think this would interfere with subsequent publication in a book here.

Surprising to relate, the R.S.A. were very amiable about this Lecture and awarded me a Silver Medal and one hundred copies! of their journal with full report.

I hope you approved of *Mass for the Masses*. Strangely enough no sooner was that essay published than I got a job to build a real Church with a central altar and all. It is at Gorleston-on-Sea near Yarmouth. We are just beginning building —I will send photographs as soon as there are any. It is an interesting plan with crossed arches to make an octagonal central space. I should like to tell you more about this but must wait. The Church will be very plain and small —no ornaments except perhaps a figure of St. Peter on the outside and a large Crucifix hanging over the altar. One good thing about this job is that being built in a country place, there is no need to have recourse to mechanical town methods. It will be just a plain building done by bricklayers and carpenters, though I suppose the Rector will insist on central heating and electric light. I don't mind if he does —if you build a good house for a man and he insists on putting in the telephone, that is his affair. [. . .]

About that tombstone in memory of E. G. aged 54 — don't worry. This was only a joke. I was asked to do a specimen tombstone so I did one for myself —it may come in useful some day and the age can be altered. The only reason why I chose 54 was that it seemed a very good age to die at.

I do hope your Harvard Lectures will be a success. I look forward to reading them. Blessings on the good work. Give my love to A. K. C. if you see him —blessed man.

Thank you, Yes, all the family are well — at present the grandchildren are all at the seaside. I send herewith a new pamphlet which I hope you will approve of —text, type and pictures. The type is a new one, only used hitherto for a reprint of *The Sentimental Journey* published by the New York Limited Editions Club. [. . .] Alas, the printing works here are forced into machine production. There is no escape if you want to do ordinary work for ordinary people and not merely expensive curiosities for connoisseurs.

When are you coming to England again? I hope it will be soon.

I never replied to your letter of the 13th January —I didn't, did I? Anyway I do now and thank you very much for *Thoughts and Things*; it is very good indeed. Your aphorisms about B.G. and T. seem to me very good and useful. B. is the desirability of T. Yes, and your quotation from Augustine is

the real goods —I will use it for all it's worth, I mean as much
as I can, but I think it must be made clear that 'utendum non
fruendum' does not mean that the useful is not also enjoyable
and to be enjoyed, but simply that 'here below' its category
is the useful, i.e. we enjoy the useful rather than use the
enjoyable.

In reply to yours of the 12th August, the little gravestone
in the catalogue is not for sale, but the Alphabet Stone is —or
rather a replica is. The one shown in the catalogue is already
sold to a compatriot of yours called Grady, but I can do you
one if you like. Mr. Grady paid £20 for his. Yours affectionately,   ERIC G.

295 : TO GERARD IRVINE

Pigotts   *5-10-1938*

Dear Irvine: [. . .] Yes, the events of the last few weeks are
certainly extremely puzzling, especially if you attempt a judgment on the basis of a study of modern politics. Such a study
is beyond me and therefore, without making any judgment of
those people who decide otherwise, I take the short-cut line
saying that I do not believe conditions of war-making to-day
are such as to make a just war possible. You will find some
very valuable comments on this matter in *Blackfriars* for this
month —pages 755-770.

The individual conscience must be the decisive factor in
any case and the same applies in lesser matters such as land
work and Red Cross work. My own opinion for what it is
worth is that land work is certainly allowable to anybody and
nursing also, but those who think that they can get out of their
difficulty by joining the R.A.M.C. had better beware, because
unless they are qualified doctors they are liable as soldiers to
be transferred to any other Regiment willy-nilly. Yours
           ERIC GILL

296 : TO DR. COOMARASWAMY

Pigotts   *13-10-1938*

Dear Ananda: Thank you very much for the *Art Bulletin* No. 20[1] and thank you for sending two copies. It is excellent and most useful. I cannot say more.* Yours affectionately,

ERIC G.

* I mean that it is too good for praise from me. Perhaps after we're dead people will wake up, & see that you're right. My God! how frightfully wrong *they* are.   E. G.

297 : TO HIS BROTHER EVAN

Pigotts   *29-11-1938*

Dear Evan: Words fail me when I try to find the right ones to thank you for what you have done about the engravings. It is the most marvellous job of work — infinitely better than I could ever have done myself . . . Well, I must give up trying to thank you and only say that what you have done is only what I wanted and now I feel satisfied because as far as it could be done the whole of my engraving output is catalogued and in order. It is not for me to say whether it is worth it, although other people seem to think so, but I, like you, like to have things tidy, so all is well. I will go through all your notes and queries and write again — this will take a little time, so I will leave it for the next few days. Absolutely o'erwhelm'd with wk.

(A) The difference in weight of paper does not matter a bit.

(B) I am sorry you had trouble with the *writing up*. Your corrections are not noticeable.

(C) Blind printing is simply printing without any ink — Nos. D.23 and 24 are wrongly called blind printing. I do not

[1] Containing *Mediaeval Aesthetic*, Part II.

know what they ought to have been called instead, but the point about them is this that they were very shallow wood cuts — so shallow that the ink from the roller touches the background, but this was done purposely so that you get a faint kind of modelling on the figure.

I do not know who *The Lancashire Players* were — some people Pepler got hold of. The title *Hampshire Hog* was, I think, the name of a public house in the lane in Hammersmith called Hampshire Hog Lane. I think the pub has gone. Anyway, Pepler started a Club and Workshops there and one of them was a bakery and so they called it the *Hampshire Hog Bakery*.

More anon. Yours   ERIC

I enclose the ex libris oddments with love — 1st instal.t

What price the Philatelic Cong.s Stamps?

298 : TO GRAHAM CAREY

Pigotts   *1-1-1939*

Dear Graham: At last I'm able to begin an answer to your letters of Sept. 29, Oct. 26 & 31, and also to thank you very much for sending me *College Art Magazine* with your last article in it. This seems to me most excellent, the very goods, and I am most glad to have it. I've got to give a lecture on Feb. 4 to the Ryl. Institution in London (a sort of posh scientific Society, formed 1750? Farraday, Ld Rutherford etc. past presidents & so on) and I shall take the liberty of quoting from your lecture. Some of your definitions are splendid and clear. (My lecture is called: 'Sacred & Secular in Modern Industry.' I'll send you copy in due course if published.) It's one of a series of four — general title 'Art & Industry' — other three by other people, Lord Gorell, Sir Thomas Barlow (manufacturer), Frank Pick (London Transport Board etc.) — and casting about for a really conclusive line to take, it, as the result of the last twenty years experience, has come to be clear that the bottom-rock thing is the *unholiness* of our Industrialism. I think that that is the line we must all now advance to. We've spent untold energy proving the general beastliness, vulgarity, inefficiency, anti-socialness, ugliness of the Industrial capitalist commercial world —and they go smiling on, thinking us a lot of 'arts & crafts wallahs' who have a sentimental attachment to the handmade and a snobbish dislike of 'business'. Now we've got to show them that the ultimate ground of our objection is something quite different from what they suppose. We've got to show them that it's not beauty, as they understand it, which we accuse them of destroying (though they do destroy it) but holiness in man & in all his works. This is the last ditch. It's the most difficult to deal with. That's why I'm glad it's a scientific society that's invited the lecture —because it will be appropriate to write the matter out in a straight matter of fact way —no frills, rhetoric, sentiment. Prayers are called for. (Anyway they have the decency to pay a fee of £10.10.0, so you do get a chance to put time into the preparation and really work at it.)

Item: I am quite well. I hope you are.

Item: with shame for not sending it before, I send herewith a 'life' drawing. I hope you will find it a good one. I wish I could do more drawing from boys & men. Strange how one's natural male inclination to see & draw women, makes one, spurs one on to seize opportunities for drawing the girls of one's acquaintance & to neglect the boys —tho. I'm sure one's men friends wouldn't refuse. I really must put it to them, before it's too late. I really truly must.

Item: I will do you an alphabet at the earliest moment —I'll cut it myself of course. I hope I'll be able to let you have this in a few weeks time or a month. At present I'm struggling to finish a Madonna & Child for a niche over the door of a Nurses' Hostel in Essex —got to be finished this month (January).

Item: there's simply tons of work on hand —nothing v. big at present, but shortly I've got to do a reredos for one of the side chapels in W'minster Cathedral – crucifix, St John Fisher St Thos. More & angels –about nine feet high. And, *mirabile dictu*, there's a possibility that I may be doing mosaics over the choir!

Item: As you know, I got proofs of the R.S.A. lecture from John Stevens and returned them with corrections. I am v. proud that they should publish it.

Item: I hope your lettering book is going on well. I told you, didn't I?, how grateful I am for your sending me Prof. Adler's book on *St Thomas & the Gentiles*. It is really a splendid contribution. And I told you, didn't I?, that I quite approved of your putting in subheadings in my R.S.A. lecture. I altered the placing of one or two that's all. I look forward to seeing the finished copy.*

Item: Apart from your lecture, I did think there was a lot of art nonsense in that College Art Assoc^n. quarterly. I don't think those nuns have got out of the rut yet. But I am most touched & grateful to think that they agree with my writings.

Item: the new church at Gorleston-on-Sea, Yarmouth, Norfolk, is now actually being built. They started just before Christmas. I will send you news when there is any and photos. if possible. God alone knows if it will be a 'success'. Anyway it's free, I think, from architectooralooralism and it's free, apart from electric lighting (which I can't refuse to instal) & heating (which, again, I can't resist –tho. I think its a shocking waste of money), apart from these it's free from industrial products. Just bricklayers', tilers' & carpenters' work. The only thing about it to write home about is the fact that it will have a central altar. Everything springs from that –the plan grows from that & the outside is simply the result of the inside. I bet you anything you like it will be jolly decent & a holy house, but whether it will 'go down' with the people, the clergy & the architects remains to be seen. We're carving St Peter in low relief in the brickwork over the main porch. Holy Water

*(I enclose a *Cross & Plough*, hoping you'll approve.)

Stoups, piscina, font, & altars will be made here —also a big crucifix to hang in centre over the altar. Item: I'd like to see the photos. of the church you wrote about at *Monongahela Valley*. *Our* church is supposed to be finished by the end of May, 1939. If you can have an article on it in the quarterly, I shd. be v. glad. But we must wait to see what sort of a job it turns out. (Now I must stop for a bit — & go to Benediction in our chapel! 6.0 & bell just ringing. It's a marvellous marvel that the Bp. has allowed us this privilege. It's also pretty marvellous that the said Bp. (Northampton) is so friendly & affectionate to us. I think the children beat him.) Because although I *know* it will be good in some ways (& those not the least important) I think it quite likely that it will be gawky & amateurish. (If ever we get another church to do, we shall have learnt a lot from this one . . .) and it is certain to be judged by all sorts of false canons. No one will believe that we designed the job from the altar outwards & trusted to luck after that. [. . .] Now I'll stop, reserving a separate sheet for remarks re the carved fireplace. With love from me & greetings from my Mary & best wishes for blessings on you in 1939 — Yours   ERIC G.

299 : TO HERBERT FURST

Pigotts   23-2-1939

Dear Furst: Sorry I did not realise you were the Editor of *Apollo*. Thank you very much for your letter. I think we understand one another now, but (forgive me if I put it like this) I think, like many people, you take rather a prim line — a sort of artistic-moral-theology line, for, as you indicate, it is really only a matter of extra work and not at all a matter of misuse of the medium. If you have *good reason* for raised lettering, then raised lettering is a good thing to do ; and if there be a good reason for black line engraving then that is a good thing too. And in conjunction with letter press, it seems clear that there *is* a good reason, namely that the letter press surface and the engraving surface are of the same nature and therefore give the printer a straightforward homogeneous job — in fact the engraving is a part of the typography.

Incidentally, I think if you were to examine the line of the engraving you refer to, you would see that it is not all like penline, because the two sides of the line vary according to the intention of the engraver, whereas the two sides of a pen-line (I mean a square-edged pen) are parallel and the peculiar quality of penmanship is due to that.

With kind regards, Yours sincerely,   ERIC GILL

300 : TO GRAHAM CAREY

Pigotts   *11-4-1939*

Dear Graham: Thank you very much indeed for your letter of the 20th March. I am very sorry not to have replied before, but I have been having a pretty bad time during the last fort-night, having been called upon to sit on the Selection and Hanging Committee of the Royal Academy Exhibition. A book could be written about this, but I must not start. It has been nearly a whole time job and even now is not quite finished.

I am awfully glad you liked the drawing of the girl and that it was what you wanted. I shall debit your account ten pounds for this and hope that is not too much.

Gorleston Church is getting on well and will be finished next month. I will send you photographs and write the short account, as promised. I will also send you the *Glasgow Observer* with a picture in it. [. . .]

I will do the alphabet first — I hope to get to this quite soon now and certainly before the summer is out to send you a design for the fireplace. I wish I was not quite so busy, although it is a good thing to have plenty to do. I will add the text from Virgil on to the alphabet stone.

When you can send them, I shall be very glad to see the photographs of St. Paulinus' Church.

I am very glad Gorton called on you — I like him very much. I am torn in half about his lecture scheme — I should much like to come to the U.S.A. for many reasons, but do not see how I can spare the time yet awhile and it would take two or three months at least.

The Future

I am overwhelmed by the generosity of your suggestions about the future. I really do not know what to say in reply except that I share with you your feeling that a breakdown, if any, is more likely to occur here before it does in the U.S.A. The thought of migration is, of course, very unwelcome, for though I can imagine ourselves perfectly happy anywhere, the mere physical business of uprooting is a kind of nightmare. We are so much dug in to this place now, and what with daughters and sons-in-law and their children and dependents in the workshops, it is almost unthinkable, and the worst of it is that if one were to do it at all, it would be better to do it while the going is good and not leave it until the general rush starts. My own nature is such as to make no preparation and take what comes, knowing that we only get what we deserve, so I cannot say much more at present, but I shall think about it, of course, and if things begin to look definitely worse or if a good scheme occurs to me, I will write again at once. Dear Graham, it really is extremely kind of you to think such thoughts. Yours   ERIC G.

PS. You'll be interested to hear that a large statue of mine,[1] belonging to the Tate Gallery, London, has been lent to the *New York World Fair* and is even now on its way there.

[1] 'Mankind.'

DD

301 : TO 'THE TABLET' 27 MAY, 1939

Sir: I cannot answer for Mr. Travers or Mr. Watkin, but as one of the pamphleteers[1] referred to by Colonel Trappes-Lomax (*The Tablet*, May 20th), may I say this in reply to his question: should pacifists be grateful to the airmen who drive enemy bombers from their homes? It is a good old question, reminiscent of the traps laid for C.O.s by the tribunals of 1916-18, and I am not clever enough to answer it directly. I can only reply like this: Col. Trappes-Lomax and most of our fellow-countrymen regard the British Isles and the British Empire as positively achieved goods and as earnests of even greater to come. He and they think these goods are appropriately defended by the methods of modern warfare. They think of the defence of our type of so-called civilization as a good end and of modern war as a Christian means. I, on the contrary, doubt the former and deny the latter. Col. Trappes-Lomax and most of our fellow-countrymen regard such doubts as indecent and such a denial as execrable. I understand, and even sympathize with him and them, and am willing to accept the consequence, namely that in his and their view we pacifists are the scum of the earth and should be treated as such. Does he think we are so mean as to wish to escape this? Scum should be exterminated or, if it would be any good, heavily punished. Really, sir, we do see this. We do appreciate that Col. Trappes-Lomax and most of our fellow-countrymen must necessarily think us hateful people. I don't think we really blame them or wish them any ill, and we are prepared to accept whatever treatment they choose to mete out to us. May God help us all. Yours faithfully,   ERIC GILL

[1] Authors of *Pax* pamphlets. E. G.'s was *And Who Wants Peace?* included in *It All Goes Together*, pp. 178-88.

Pigotts   *20-6-1939*

Dear Desmond: As I said in my note written in the car, I am
most grateful for your letter. I will now begin an answer to
the points you mention about the Altar etc. But first of all I
am very glad to hear that you are having good times in various
places. The weather seems to have broken again, but perhaps
only for a day or two. I am very glad indeed to hear that the
stones in the cemetery are weathering well and that you are
still so pleased with them. I wish I could get a chance to see
them again. [. . .]

I hope you will get to Norwich and therefore Gorleston.
G. is about three miles along the coast south of Great Yarmouth. Any one will tell you where the new Catholic Church
is —it is pretty conspicuous and as it was opened last Wednesday with a great flourish, the whole town is aware of its
existence. I very much hope you will like this building,
although there are many things we would do differently next
time —for instance, the east, south and north windows are too
big and too low and the panes of glass too big; the red-tiled
steps of the Altars are not satisfactory; the little Crucifix over
the main Altar is not really a Christian work though it says the
right word, I think; the Crucifix (Anthony F's) over the Lady
Chapel Altar is a failure and will be replaced by another. I
hope you like Denis' paintings and the big Crucifix, also
Anthony Foster's carving on the porch, and I hope you will
like the big crossed arches. [. . .]

At the opening on Wednesday a certain Canon Squirrell of
Norwich preached a wholly admirable sermon on the subject
of the Altar —Calvary —and the importance and indeed the
sine qua nonness of a return to this realization, especially to-day
when the Church '*has lost the masses*', and apart from being a
really quite hard-headed discourse, it was full of piety and
sweetness. And then at the luncheon party afterwards, at
which about thirty of the local clergy were present, the Bishop

made a speech in which he said he endorsed every word of Canon Squirrell's sermon and proceeded to rub it in a bit more, so that without any doubt this candle has been very well and truly lit. Much gratified also by obviously sincere approval and congratulations from many of the clergy, especially the younger ones to whom I spoke. But, of course, it is one thing to supply the bones —it is another to make them live —so we must not crow too soon. Any way, it is undoubtedly a great triumph to have established —at least in this Diocese — the notion that it is the right thing to do and apostolical to place the Altar in the middle of the Church and that it represents Calvary in the middle of the world. [. . .] Yes, indeed, that is an excellent remark: *God makes use of everything* . . . I will write separately about that matter.

I am awfully glad you met Brother Cecil —I am so sorry that my visit to Cardiff on the 2nd July will not find you there. Much love, Yours   E. G.

303 : TO THE REV. DESMOND CHUTE

Pigotts   20-7-1939

Dear Desmond: [. . .] Thank you very much for your post-card of the Round Church . . . Isn't it ridiculous to see the Altar put in the side aisle, though I dare say they had side Altars as well as the central one.

I hope you had a nice time at Ditchling.

Thank you again for your letter of the 12th. I can't write fully *now* in reply, but I must say that it seems to me ——'s criticism of your letter to me and the quotation is pretty good bilge. I agree it is absurd to make the absolute bow to the relative in that way. [. . .] Did you know that in London Art Galleries you cannot sell drawings of nude men and that for three reasons: —

(a) Because men are so modest.

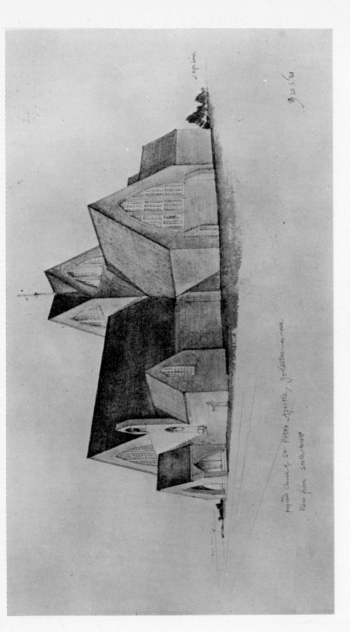

GORLESTON CHURCH

Drawing by E.G.

(b) Because ordinary men only want pictures of girls.

[(c) Because both sellers and buyers are suspected of perverse
    intentions.

I hope to goodness you managed to get to Gorleston, but
your silence seems to imply that you failed.

I am very glad you liked the Madonna at St. Cuthbert's.
The St. John Bosco is a joint work of mine and Anthony
Foster — pretty good in some ways but a bit queer. He, A. F.,
has done a very fine Ascending Christ, life-size, for an Anglican
Church in London. Much love, Yours   E. G.

304 : TO THE REV. DESMOND CHUTE

Pigotts   *28-7-1939*

Dear Desmond: Thank you very much for your letter and for
returning the typescript. I hope you will get this at Bradford-
on-Avon — please remember me to R. K. — it is chiefly to say
that although I am going to Cambridge on Monday and that the
job will last several weeks, I am not likely to be there all the
time, [. . .] so let me know precisely when you will be passing
through London and either I can come there from here or make
a dash from Cambridge. (My address in Cambridge will be
c/o St. John's College). [. . .]

GORLESTON — I am very glad indeed you like the Church as
far as it goes and especially glad to know you approve of Denis'
painting — I will tell him and I know he will be glad.

DITCHLING — Good. I am glad that you thought the bread
was coming back. [. . .]

CAMBRIDGE. — I will go to the FitzWilliam and see the Etty
and Picasso, but No, of course the ordinary man's view of the
matter (begging his pardon and by no means disdaining to be
one of the gang) is only just above low-water level.

I shall await the London date. Yours dear dear Desmond
                                                      E. G.

305 : TO 'THE EXAMINER' (U.S.A.)
AUTUMN 1939

I knew that our defence[1] was in good hands so, being far away,
I left it to them. But now that Mr. Richardson has replied,
perhaps you will allow me to add a brief comment. This argument, like so many others in this world, is one in which neither
side accepts the other's premises and, what is worse, there is
not only an antagonism of minds but also one of wills. We do
not want to believe or to think what Mr. Richardson believes
or thinks (God forbid!) and he is equally determined the other
way. If he wanted to find reasons for coming in on our side,
I am sure he is plenty clever enough, and I suppose if we were
as anxious as he is to keep Rembrandt and Brahms on their
pedestals, we also are clever enough for the job. The trouble
is our wills are differently set and so argument is indecisive;
for the matter is not, like an arithmetic sum, such that we can
prove him wrong or ourselves right; the most we can do and,
in such circumstances, the only valuable thing is, by more and
more careful writing and talking (and here we are thankful to
such as Mr. Richardson; for he shows us where we are careless
and unconvincing), to confirm the good will of those who are
already with us; to help the doubting, so that they come on to
our side and are not alienated; and point out to our enemies
wherein they are definitely in error.

And there is certainly one point in Mr. Richardson's reply
where he is mistaken. He says (p. 276): That the writers of
the Stevens pamphlets are moved by an *idée fixe, viz.*: 'the
superiority of certain types of art to certain other types'. This
is simply not true and woefully misleading. For even if we do
come to conclude that certain types of art are better than
others (supposing, if we may! that both we and our opponents
have the same notion of *good*, and therefore of *better* and *best*),

[1] See 'Art, Reality, and Romanticism' in the Summer, 1939 *Examiner*, containing criticisms by Messrs. Graham Carey and Ananda K. Coomaraswamy and
Miss Ade de Bethune of a review by Mr. E. P. Richardson of certain pamphlets
by them and Mr. Gill. (Note by the Editor of *The Examiner*.)

that is not what moves us in our efforts; that is, at most, only one of the conclusions. We do not start there; none of us does; none of us did. Indeed I think it probable that most people who are now of our way of thinking started where Mr. Richardson is and have only, by slow degrees and after much pain, arrived where they now are. For what moves us is something much deeper and more primary than an aesthetic emotion. It is something to which aesthetic emotion is only a more or less useful handmaid. The thing which moves us is a notion, conception, intuition as to the real nature of man —his nature and therefore his destiny and meaning. Briefly and, if it be possible, avoiding controversial terms, we hold that man is a responsible creature and all that that implies —and it seems to imply an immense lot. Free will, knowledge, hope, and love are all implicit in such a creature. A primacy of the spirit is implied, and, conversely, a subordination of the world, the flesh, and the devil. It is a matter of religion. I need not enlarge on this, but the point is that *that* is where we start, *that* is what moves us. Our 'artistic' opinions are conclusions not motives.

Now the notion of man we hold is, obviously, no peculiar invention of our own. It is, on the contrary, a common notion throughout human history. It flourished like the green bay tree in medieval India and medieval Europe. It is more or less explicit in all times and places. But it is a notion which is not always effective in society or in government. It is particularly ineffective in the industrial society of today. Persons who, like Mr. Richardson and the rich young man in the Gospel, have 'great possessions' —in this case great possessions in Rembrandt and Brahms —will nearly always 'turn away sorrowful' from our argument. It cannot be helped —except by themselves. It is a matter of the will. Meanwhile at least let it be clear that the first thing is our conception of man's nature and not aesthetic snobbery. Then, if our conception of man be accepted, we can proceed to discover how far man, thus understood, is helped or hindered by this society or that, what

kind of work results in these circumstances or those, and what
value, social or otherwise, should be placed on them. Then
perhaps we shall discover the pilgrims went to Canterbury not
to do 'something completely useless and purposeless' (p. 281)
but more useful than anything else and to better purpose. And
possibly we shall discover that, remarkable as they are and
almost heartbreaking in the poignancy of their effects upon us,
the great works of our 'masters', old or new, are, after all,
more pathetic and tragic in their quality than either holy or
salutary, and that, however deep and terrible, they are essentially barren. God knows. But let us not allow the argument
to descend to the level of art criticism. It is *man* we are talking
about —man in his millions and not only man in his studios,
drawing rooms, and art galleries —and how to contrive that he
shall again see himself as child of God —and heir also.   I am,
Sir, Yours faithfully,   ERIC GILL

High Wycombe, England.

306 : TO MGR. JOHN O'CONNOR

Pigotts   *6-9-1939*

Dear Fr. John: Thank you very much for sending back the
drawing. I will make a new design as soon as possible.

I note what you say about re-colouring of the Stations of
the Cross and we will deal with this when the time comes.
Originally they were painted in tempera, i.e. colour tempered
with egg, but they can be done in oil, as you suggest. Instead
of knotting, we used white of egg, which has the same effect.
'Knotting' is simply the name of the shellac mixture which
house painters use to cover knots in wood with before painting, because knots, being end grain, suck up the paint more
than the rest of the plank, hence the name.

I hope you will live in peace in Bradford. Yours affectionately,   ERIC G.

Pigotts   *18-9-1939*

Dear Mr. Thomas: Your letter has been forwarded to me by the Secretary of PAX. It is, of course, impossible for any one to coerce any one else's conscience in these matters.

The hierarchy in this country has apparently decided that England's, or shall we say the British cause in this war is a just one and they are apparently satisfied that the means employed in warfare to-day are just. On the other hand, Cardinal McRory, speaking in Ireland last week, took the opposite view, and, as you probably know, the Archbishop of Cincinnati takes the same line as the Pax Society. In any case, it is Catholic teaching that the individual conscience is the final judge.

I myself think that the conditions of modern warfare and the means employed are such as to make it impossible for us to take part, though I think a very good case can be made out by those who hold that we should be quite justified in using whatever weapons are available to prevent the invasion of this country. If, for instance, you could join the Anti-Aircraft defences and could be assured that you would not be transferred to the overseas forces, I think you would be justified in joining. It is doubtless the perfect line to refuse to defend yourself against an aggressor by violent means, but it is different when it is a case of defending your family and relations. The trouble is that it will probably be impossible to make sure that your services would only be used at home.

I am sorry I cannot help you more. If you think that the hierarchy is right in its judgment and that modern warfare is justifiable, then I should not hesitate to join up, but you should remember that even hierarchies are not infallible and that in any case they are very much entangled in political considerations. Yours sincerely,   ERIC GILL

308 : TO THE REV. DESMOND CHUTE

Pigotts   20-9-1939

Dearest Desmond: As you will have heard, Walter arrived home safely. He came here for the night on Sunday the 10th and we were very glad to see him and hear all about your journey out. Things are pretty quiet here at the moment and there is no news whatever. We are carrying on with the work, and luckily have plenty to do.

I don't know if you saw the *Tablet*, but in case you didn't I enclose some cuttings herewith, which I hope you will approve of. I don't suppose you saw the *Irish Press*, (De Valera's paper) last week. Cardinal McRory, speaking at Cavan, said 'Let me say here that I hold war a disgrace to statesmen and rulers. In it is always their ambition or lust for dominion or greed to hold all they have, or a desire for revenge, or a combination of all these. That is the cause of war.' This was not quoted in any of the English Catholic papers needless to say. Walter made us an excellent translation of the passage in the O⟨sservatore⟩ R⟨omano⟩ 4th Sept., about civilian bombardment and reprisals.

We finished the carving job at Cambridge and are going to do a similar one on the Cathedral at Guildford, then we shall settle down to the Westminster Cathedral Reredos for the winter. Much love, Yours,   ERIC G.

P.S. I kept this back to include cutting from *Tablet*, 23!
All well here and no 'crusaders'.

at Guildford

Oct. 8. '39. Dearest D. Alas! This letter with the 'cuttings' was returned to me by the Censor as containing forbidden 'articles' (the cuttings I suppose!) So, reluctantly, I send it without enclosures. I'm v. sorry. I don't know what can be done about this. Anthony & I are now at Guildford doing the

carving —a coat of arms with angel supporters &
Statue of St. John Baptist (8 feet high). We
shall be here for a month or more —but I'll go
home for week-ends generally. Fortunately the
weather is lovely at present. Tell me: do you see
English papers at all? Much love   E. G.

309 : TO RALPH DOWNES

26-9-39

[. . .] No doubt whatever any Cath.ᶜ who is in doubt may
with good conscience join H.M. forces of whatever kind.
    Those *not in doubt* may:
    (a) if their certainty is that the war is right, join up with g.
        conscience.
    (b) if their certainty is that the war is *wrong, refuse* with
        equally good c. to join up. (They can truthfully say that
        many Roman Catholic clergy agree e.g. Fr. Strattmann
        O.P., Gerald Vann O.P., Abp. McNicholas O.P.
        Hierarchies have been wrong before now, e.g. at the
        Prot. Reformation.)
If you see the war in the simple-minded terms in which
most people see it —'crusade for honour and justice'
                            'defence of religion'
well and good, amen.
    If you don't see it like that —
    If you see it as a much deeper movement, in which the
shocking mistakes of Hitler, Stalin, Musso etc., are incidental
occasions rather than the real causes —
well then, you can abstain from participation with good
conscience.
    After all, *we English* invented godless commerce and godless
politics —so we can't set up to judge Russia, and *we English*
invented the 'superior race' doctrine (public school, Kipling
'The lesser breeds' . . . etc.) so we can't set up to judge Ger-

many and Nazism. Comic the way we carry on and then accuse our neighbours of our own sins.

But: seeing things as they do, our Bishops and clergy are more or less right in their judgments.

If the *quarrel* is between German anti-Catholic policy and Racism on the one hand, and English Godliness, tolerance and modest reticence on the other —well, then, of course England is right.

But these clergy and politicians and most other people are simple-minded and uninformed.

What they see isn't there!

It is not a war of the just against the unjust.

It is a war of the unjust against those who, in all sorts of unjust and mistaken ways, threaten that injustice.

German and Russian injustices and Godlessness are the excesses to which our injustice has contributed to drive them, and they make a very good excuse for our going to war with them.

Is English civilization good? or bad?

I think it's foully bad and indefensible, but if you think it's good, then defend it. [. . .]   E. G.

310 : TO LAWRENCE POWELL

Pigotts   *26-9-1939*

Dear Mr. Powell: Your very kind letter came this morning. It is exceedingly good of you and I am most grateful. We shall be most pleased to accept your hospitality. The situation is thus: as soon as the scaffold is ready (I've written to the C. of W. about this & expect to hear from him by to-morrow) my assistant, Anthony Foster, will go to Guildford &, having drawn a simplified silhouette of the carving on the wall (from scale drawing) he will set about cutting away the background. This will take him a week or thereabouts. When that is done I shall come along and between us we will do the carving —

this will perhaps take another fortnight —perhaps more. But there is no need for me to come until the cutting away of the background is finished. (Moreover I'm at this moment in bed with a bad cold, so I couldn't myself come, in any case, for a few days.) I hope I may assume that this arrangement won't be an unwarranted presumption upon your most kind invitation. After all A. F. is a jolly sight nicer chap than I am (speaking as one who knows) so I'm sure you won't mind. May I leave it thus? and as soon as I hear from the C. of W. I will dispatch A. F. and I will follow myself as soon as he's prepared the ground. Yours sincerely,　　ERIC GILL

We had 4 evac^d children here from Marylebone slum. They were perfect dears (little girl of 11, 2 younger sisters & baby brother). If yours are anything like ours, it wd. be a treat to meet them.

311 : TO MGR. JOHN O'CONNOR

Pigotts　　　　　　　　　　　　　　　　　　5-10-1939

Dear Father John: I was very much relieved and gratified to receive your letter last night.
 (1) I am very glad indeed that you approve of the design for the statue.
 (2) It is a merciful providence that supplies me with such a good job at this time.
I have quite a fine job on hand for Westminster Cathedral, viz. Reredos in St. George's Chapel, and that will last me till Christmas at least. But after that I shall be able to do your statue whole time, as far as I can see at present! I should indeed be very pleased to receive copy of the *Foolishness*[1] —it is an extraordinarily good title, let us hope it will not be too much of a 'Stumbling Block'.

[1] *The Foolishness of Father Brown*, a book of 'sermons and such' by Mgr. O'Connor.

The subject you mention about the Faith and Artistic inspiration will certainly come into the book for Cape. I've been commissioned by them to write a book 'on my opinions'! MS to be in by Aug. 1940. Many thanks for the tip.

Thank you very much for the 'Dear Angel' tune, it is very pretty and just right for children, they are learning it at this very moment in the school here. As they do not read music, two copies will be enough.

I am sorry that German broadcast was wrong about Bradford Town and Phoenix Works. There is an extremely amusing article in the *New English Weekly* (this week) on 'wishful thinking'. Yours affectionately,   E. G.

P.S. Yes, please send the drawing back, I will make a copy and return it to you without delay.

312 : TO 'THE CATHOLIC HERALD'
13 NOV. 1939

[A REPLY to the Editor's invitation to express 'a considered judgment on the issues of war and peace'.]

The general aim of the Allies is stated to be to destroy Hitlerism. What is Hitlerism? Hitler's *Mein Kampf* is the official and accepted exposition. As we read it we must envisage a vigorous and potentially expanding people, the Germans, proud of their racial vigour and intellectual attainments, but writhing under the consequences of defeat in the war of 1914-1918 and the Treaty of Versailles. We must envisage Hitler confronted by four possibilities:

1. Contraception, in order to curb the expansion of German population.
2. The extension of industrialisation and of export trade with a colonial empire (if possible) for raw materials and markets for German manufacturers.
(This was the policy of Germany before the 1914 war.)

3. Intensive cultivation of Germany by small holdings and intensive horticulture.

4. Territorial expansion into the under-cultivated and under-populated (i.e. backward and unkempt) countries of Eastern Europe.

No. 1 is rejected as unworthy of Germans.

No. 2 is rejected for the same reason. In *Mein Kampf* Hitler frequently speaks of the land and the crafts as being 'man making,' and of the factory as 'man killing.' He speaks with undisguised scorn of 'factory coolies' and of industrialisation as being only fit for inferior peoples. . . .

No. 3 is not rejected but is regarded as inadequate to meet the needs of an expanding population —not enough land to go round.

No. 4 is hailed as the only truly good solution because it meets the needs of the German people and satisfies their pride as healthy men and women, is the only solution compatible with humanity and the claims of 'the good life' —both of which are denied by Nos. 1 and 2.

But in pursuit of No. 4 Hitler is quite unscrupulous. He despises the old-fashioned politicians and all their cumbrous hypocrisies. He sees them as liars and deceivers and resolves to beat them at their own game. One thing matters and only one: territorial expansion —not as an end but as a means to the good life, the good life of Germans. He is prepared to industrialise but only in order to rearm and so win the land for the plough.

Now (1) the Allies have, naturally, no particular objection to the treaty of Versailles, and, in spite of much criticism of that treaty, have made no attempts to reverse or modify its provisions except as forced by Hitler to do so; (2) None of the Allies is officially averse to contraception; (3) None of the Allies is averse to industrialisation or to living by export trade — quite the contrary; (4) None of the Allies has made any attempt to place their peoples upon a sound agricultural basis, either at home or in their colonies. On the contrary they have neglected their home agriculture (England especially) and pursued a policy of Colonial mass-productive agriculture which, as is now at last becoming known, is causing earth-wide erosion of the soil and destruction of land fertility.

Therefore we may assume that the Allies' war aims are as follows:

1. The continuation of the policy of Versailles.
2. By implication, the imposition of contraception upon the German people (too many Germans).
3. The revival of the Bismarckian policy of German industrialisation and the regulated competition of German export trade (playing the game).
4. The abandonment of the *Mein Kampf* policy of territorial expansion in Eastern Europe.
5. 'Hitlerism' being thus destroyed the world will be safe for 19th century capitalist commercial industrial plutodemocracy — with 20th century 'big business' improvements.

Such being the Allies' obvious aims it is equally obvious that the war should be concluded as rapidly as possible — i.e., before the rank and file of the Allies' armies and their civilian populations wake up to the fact that, under the guise of fighting for 'honour and justice,' the freedom of religion and the integrity of politics (no promise to be openly broken while anybody remembers it), they are really being used as an instrument for world-industrialisation.

313 : TO GRAHAM CAREY

19-10-1939

Dear Graham: [. . .] Re war — no, I'm still at large. Certainly I don't hold with the official views — but they haven't started locking up pacifists yet. Forgive more now. Have got a lecture to give this afternoon to the architects here & must prepare. Much affection.   ERIC G.

I look forward to Lettering book with much excitement.
I will hunt up my files & see what I've got of Johnston's writing.
When you say 'informal' I'm wondering whether you mean
ordinary epistolary hand or 'semi formal'. He once wrote out
some articles of apprenticeship for me.* Fast writing but not
just epistolary. What about that?

* very beautiful too.

314 : TO GRAHAM CAREY

1-11-1939

Dear Graham: Herewith, at last, photos & notes re Gorleston
Church. I hope you'll not be disappointed. Defects, mistakes,
weaknesses are too evident. The altar, the central feature &
whole raison d'être of the building, doesn't show up in the
photo. as it does in the real thing. The drawing of plan etc. is
being sent in separate parcel. I'll be anxious to hear if these
things arrive safely & your opinion. Yours affectly ERIC GILL

315 : TO GRAHAM CAREY

At Guildford, Surrey   *29-11-1939*
*(where I'm carving Statue of St. John-B. on new Cathedral! All in the
wind & rain . . .)*

Dear Graham: Thank you very much for letter of Nov. 3,
received on Monday last (the 27th). I hasten to send, hoping
to goodness you'll receive the precious thing safely, the
Johnstonian 'Indenture'. It's a fine piece of work (the somewhat flourishy 'hand' is, he said, to make erasures & alterations
more difficult).

I am jolly glad to hear about the C. ART ASSOC^n & its
doings. (I understand about the Appalachians) You are doing
noble work. And S. Dakota too. I don't feel as tho. there's

EE

anything to be hoped for in England (or France) — but we must go on regardless of results. God only knows what we are in for. I thought Laurence Dennis' article, 'Economic Necessity of Religion', in *The Examiner*, & the Editorial preceding it, very good indeed & most useful & illuminating. I am most glad you approve of my letter in same.[1] And I liked yours very much too. We struck, I think, the same sort of notes. Poor M. Townshend! poor Mr. Richardson! I'm sad to hear that *Examiner* is finished.

I'm sure I shan't, at least I bet I won't be disappointed with your *Lettering* book. It will be most useful to have the '4 causes' brought to bear on the matter. I look forward eagerly to seeing it.

I brought the 'Indenture' thing with me here anticipating your wanting it, but didn't bring any of his 'epistolary' writing. In fact I don't know if I've got any. I'll be home again in about a fortnight & will have a hunt. I haven't had a letter from him for more than 20 years anyway! I'll send what I can find.

I will write to him now and ask for permission to reproduce. But I doubt if I'll get an answer before Christmas, if by then! He's a beggar to delay answering letters. He's getting old too —nearly 70. I'll say in my letter that if you don't hear from him you will presume permission granted.

Dear Graham — good bye for now. It's late at night & I'm having strenuous days on the scaffold in bad weather (out of doors). I hope you are well. I am. Yours   ERIC G.

1 Letter 305 here.

316 : TO GRAHAM CAREY

Pigotts   *11-12-1939*

Dear Graham: Thank you very much for your further letter of the 23rd November. I am glad the drawing and photographs arrived safely and that you are pleased with them. I shall look forward eagerly to seeing the article in the *C.A.A. Magazine.* I will send a list of addresses later. I think it is a splendid work that you and they are doing.

We are, of course, anxious for quick results, but it is obvious that while it is very easy to destroy a culture, it is a slow and difficult job building it up again. I do not know what the possibilities are in America (I gather from you that they are somewhat more hopeful than here), but it seems to me that the whole world has got to go through the industrial thing. Look at India, which is now apparently going through a phase exactly like ours of the 1840's, and I do not believe that Gandhi, for all his power both of intelligence and sanctity, can stem it. A book could be written on this matter, but I must stop, as I am dealing with a fortnight's arrears of letters, having been at Guildford, and am only home for the week-end.

I have found a letter from Johnston —a very old one, but perhaps it will suit your purpose. Please return it with the indenture when done with. I hope you get the letter safely. Yours ever,   ERIC GILL

317 : TO A. R. HINKS

16-1-1940

Dear Sir: I have just received a cutting from *The Geographical Journal* for January giving a report of the lecture and discussion on the 6th November. I am very much interested in what you said and beg you to forgive me for writing to you personally. Like many people, I have suffered much more from undeserved praise than undeserved blame, so your words do something to redress the balance.

As perhaps you know, I was a pupil of Edward Johnston and was living almost next door to him when he was designing the L.P.T.B. sans-serif. It was a revolutionary thing and, as you know, at one go it redeemed the whole business of sans-serif from its nineteenth century corruption. It was not until 1927 that I was asked by the Monotype Corporation to do a sans-serif for them. This was designed, of course, for a somewhat different purpose from that of the L.P.T.B. The latter was designed primarily for station name boards and only later became a printing type, whereas the Monotype sans-serif was designed first of all for typography, and moreover for machine punch cutting. It therefore seemed desirable to me that the forms of the letters should be as much as possible mathematically measurable and that as little reliance as possible should be placed upon the sensibility of the draughtsmen and others concerned in its machine facture. Thus the E has equal arms and the middle one is as near as possible to the middle and so throughout. I do not myself think there is much to choose between Gill Sans and Johnston Sans, but I do think that the alterations I made might be said to be an improvement from the point of view of modern methods of production, so I shall be really grateful if you will tell me in what particulars you and 'many others' think that Johnston's design is 'much superior'.

With regard to the lettering of the street names in Kensington, I have always been pleased to see these and have wondered who did them. In a general way they are very good, but I am sorry to hear that anybody thinks they are mine. The explanation doubtless is that whereas Edward Johnston confined his work almost entirely to penmanship, I did hardly anything in that line and carried his teaching on into lettering in stone, so that it has perhaps unfortunately seemed to many that anything in the way of Roman lettering in stone, which looked like deriving from the revival instigated by Johnston, must be something to do with *me*, and I dare say I did have some influence in that direction and that there would be some degree of truth in the contention that if I had not done something to improve inscriptions, a lot of the inscribed work of to-day would be worse than it is, but if you prefer you can put it all down to Edward Johnston.

But whatever may be said about that, I shall be, as I said above, glad to know what are your criticisms of Gill Sans as compared with Johnston Sans. There is always scope for improvement and the Monotype Corporation is very glad to hear of such. Yours faithfully, ERIC GILL

PS. In case you do not know the little book, may I refer you to my *Essay on Typography* (cheap edition, five shillings, Sheed & Ward), page 46?

318 : TO LAWRENCE POWELL

Pigotts *16-1-1940*

Dear Lawrence: Thank you very much indeed for your letter of the 13th. I have been meaning to write ever since my return, but have been somewhat overwhelmed with arrears of correspondence and have not quite got clear of it yet.

I am extremely glad to know that you are so pleased with the model of St. John the Baptist. I think I am glad that you can find a place for it indoors, for it is a little frail for the open air, but I should give it a good wash with toothbrush and water, unless you think it is all right as it is, but it got a bit dirty up on that scaffold. I really am extremely glad that you and Elsie are so pleased to have it.

I am glad too you had a nice Xmas up North. I look forward to my next visit, which seems to be now quite certain, for I have this morning received from Maufe drawing showing the set out of the big Crucifix stones. It is going to be a grand job and much grander than originally thought of. The figure will be 8′ 0″ high and it will be supported by two enormous hands as of God the Father holding Him up to the world (*Hic est filius meus dilectus*). I am jolly pleased that E. M. has accepted this scheme. It gives me a grand job to look forward to.

At present I am doing the Altarpiece for Westminster Cathedral, but have not got on very fast with it —extremely hard stone, very cold weather (and my big workshop is none too warm) and other jobs to be kept going. It is jolly cold up here, but I suppose it is at Guildford too.* So far we have not had any burst pipes; I hope you have not had any of that trouble either. It is terrible to think of the unfortunate labourers in that vineyard on Stag Hill —no money coming in in this cold weather. With love to you both, Yours   ERIC G.

* ice on the river! any skating?

319 : TO GRAHAM CAREY

Pigotts   *26-1-1940*

Dear Graham: Thank you very much for sending C.S.A.Q. with article on Gorleston Church. I think this has been done extremely well and we are very glad you have been able to give us so much space —still more that you have given the idea so much publicity and praise.

You said we could have some more copies, so please could you send me say twenty-five, if that is not too big a parcel. If this is all right, I will send them out to various people and not trouble you to do that.

Thank you also for your other letter of the 10th January and for cheque enclosed. I had not expected this and it comes in very handy. I look forward very much to seeing the lettering book. With best wishes from us all, Yours   ERIC G.

PS. 9.30 a.m. —your letter of the 2nd has this very moment arrived! Thank you very much for it. I am glad Johnston's letter arrived safely. I am also very glad to have your remarks about Industrialism and the chances of survival with or without catastrophe, about which I agree. I am still dallying with the thought of emigration en masse or at least en famille to the States and (thinking wildly) if we got a church to build as a result of the C.S.A.Q. it would be a good opportunity to go over and look around and talk around . . . . I won't say more than that at the moment. I am very interested to hear about Mgr. Ligutti. What a pity Fr. ——, who is so good in other ways, is so asinine about agrarianism.

My Mary gave me *Peaks & Lamas*[1] for a Christmas present. A. K. C. had told me about it. I think it is a very good book—I wish it were a lot cheaper so that more people could read it. Gerald Vann O.P. is bringing out a little book on St. Thomas Aq. in which he deals quite a lot with essential unity of East and West and quotes A. K. C. frequently.[2]   E. G.

320 : TO DR. COOMARASWAMY

Pigotts   *16-2-1940*

Dear Ananda: I have so many things to thank you for that I am ashamed not to have written before and even now I cannot write at length. I have been waiting until I finished reading *Peaks & Lamas* (which I did last night) and now I have got the galley proof of your *Nature of Mediaeval Art*, which is an admirable summary of the matter, and would make an excellent leaflet for house to house distribution, if only the subject were something to do with the war —as indeed it is, if only they knew.

As to *Peaks & Lamas*, thank you for telling me about it. It seems to me a very excellent work and I 'kid' myself I have derived great benefit from it, both materially and spiritually. I suppose it might be considered by the learned to be a

---

[1] By Marco Pallis.   [2] *St. Thomas Aquinas* (Hague & Gill, 1940).

popularizing exposition of Buddhism and the life of Tibet, but
provided the popularizer is a decent man, there is a good place
for such things and Marco Pallis does seem to me to do the
job well. [. . .]

The index at the end seems to me very inadequate —I had
to make a new one to mark the very many illuminating remarks
which more particularly bear on matters which concern you
and me. Again thank you very much for telling me of the
book. I hope you will see some results in my future efforts at
exposition.

I hope you are well —we are, as you know, in the throes of
what might be called 'the madness of Europe' —an inevitable
consummation, impossible to foretell the end. If we 'fight to
a finish', the aftermath of hate and vengeance will, I imagine,
be irreparable, but there is nothing more to be said —I mean
I can say nothing more at the moment. I am myself much
occupied by trying to help to spread about the ideas which
must be the basis of peace, if there should ever again be such
a thing, for obviously there can never be peace until the world
is rid of its allegiance to commerce and finance. I imagine all
parties would agree to this, if they recognized it, but we suffer
from an extraordinary blindness and it seems to me that very
few people indeed are even aware who their rulers really are,
or what their allegiances really are.

I hope to send you some publications shortly. I have just
written a little book on *Christianity and the Machine Age*, which
I hope contains stuff of which you will approve. Yours
affectionately,   ERIC G.

Dear Ananda: The above, dictated, seems very cold reading.
I wish I could write (a) all I want to say and (b) as I really feel.
As to the latter I can only add that I do send you much love
& deepest gratitude —the gratitude you can pass on to God to
whom it is due.   E. G.

I am sending a pamphlet herewith. I hope & pray you'll like
it but it requires interpretation to be acceptable on the higher

level of, say, Tibet! I mean: all this fuss about the human *person*! I wish I could discuss this with you. I believe there is an ultimate reconciliation between the Xtian belief in the sanctity & reality of individual personality & the ultimate impersonality of 'the void' . . . But on our level, *here* & *now*, and as confronted by our mechanical capitalism . . . What then?

321 : TO THE MARQUESS OF TAVISTOCK [1]

27-2-1940

Dear Lord Tavistock: Thank you for your letter of the 26th. I am very sorry but I shall be unable to come to the Meeting on Thursday, as I shall be in Wales. I wonder, however, if it would be possible for you to have a talk before the Meeting with Stuart Morris. I have written to him and sent him some notes with reference to a project which I think is quite 'up your street' and very much *à propos* of the matters we have been discussing. Briefly it is this (but I must not write at length):—

1. That in the natural way of things the last people one attempts to reason with during the course of a fight are the belligerents, but, on the other hand, the first people one naturally appeals to are the neighbours and on-lookers.

2. That modern war is not a war of professional armies, but of nations ('all in' totalitarian), therefore much more comparable to a fight in a slum than a fight between boxers.

3. That all the belligerents are dependent upon the neutral states for supplies of one sort or another, and therefore the neutrals have clearly a complete whip-hand by means of boycott —a boycott or blockade which could be re-

[1] Now the Duke of Bedford.

newed even after the cessation of actual fighting, if the belligerents refused to agree to the terms of settlement arrived at.

4. That the terms of settlement be arrived at by a conference in which the neutral states would be judges.

This may sound fanciful, but the more you think about it, the more obvious it seems that the situation is one in which the neutrals have not only the power but the duty of neighbours, and that the real shame of the situation is their shame even more than that of the belligerents who, God knows, have plenty of cause for quarrel —at least they think so.

As you are in touch with De Valera, it seems to me that a move in this direction might easily be made through him, as he is a more than usually honourable politician and well-known to all the neutral states. I am sorry to inflict all this on you and I do hope it will be possible for you to have a talk with Stuart Morris before Thursday. Why should not common sense, even at this late hour, come in and overrule all our worn-out diplomacies? Yours sincerely, ERIC GILL

322 : TO HIS BROTHER EVAN

Capel-y-ffin   *29-2-1940*

My dear Evan: Thank you most kindly for your birthday letter. I wish we could just go out & have a nice long confab. in a pub —you, & Donald too. At present moment I'm in bed at above address with sore throat & cough, nothing to worry about —but it gives me a chance to write a few letters. What a grief it is to be so much out of touch geographically & modern life increases the grief because it fobs us off with all sorts of ersatz for contact. In that respect the old pre-steam days were better. If chaps didn't live within a few miles of one another, they took it for granted that that was that —& looked forward to a better world. Dear Evan I hope your old guts are quite

well again. Are you pining to get back to the old battery? Or
do you, like me, take a somewhat jaundiced view of the
affair? I'm pretty well entangled in pacifist doings at present.
Free speech is still allowed but there are those who wish it
wasn't and I shd.n't be surprised if they won. PAX, as I
expect Donald has told you, is going fairly strong in its small
way at present. But it's the P.P.U. that takes most of my spare
time. Tell Donald (if he don't know it already) that we've
just printed a PAX leaflet entitled *conscience* for the benefit of
C.O.s & their judges. We copied the definition out of the
Cath. Ency. Dic. & added some notes (with theological
approval). It ought to be useful, as it's astonishing how few
know what a conscience is when asked. Does Donald remember who did that particular definition? [. . .] Your bro ERIC

323 : TO THE 'NEW ENGLISH WEEKLY'

28 MARCH, 1940

Work and Poverty

Sir: I am sorry I cannot give Mr. Kenway the definition for
which he asks. I can only say that the direction of Holy
Poverty is exactly the opposite of the direction in which the
world is moving to-day and in which 'the world,' as such,
must always move. It is obviously impossible that everyone
should embrace Holy Poverty, but at least those who do might
be held up as exemplars, their general teaching approved
instead of repudiated, and the teaching of the Gospel published and given the primacy on all occasions, whereas, at
present, it seems to be the ambition to camouflage the Church
to look as much as possible like the Ritz Hotel. What are the
national and imperial ambitions, and, following suit or *vice
versa*, what are the ordinary small business man's ambitions —
and his wife's?

I agree, of course, with very much of what Pontifex II has written (March 14), but I cannot understand why he should entangle me with the post-Renaissance artist world, and all its signature business and personal exhibitionism. He actually seems to think that we want (I mean people of my way of thinking) every workman to be like a modern artist —sign his works and have his vogue. On the contrary, I want exactly the opposite —I want to abolish 'art and artists' altogether. Now, I suppose, he will say I am contradicting myself. But look —at present we have the artists on a pedestal and the ordinary workmen simply 'hands' —not quite as simple as that, for not all artists are highly esteemed and not all workmen quite degraded, far from it. But that is the direction we are necessarily moving in —towards a still further worship of 'art' as such, and a still further degradation of work as such — in the end we shall have the Leisure State. I should like to abolish 'art' and the factory as well. Impossible? But we might move *in that direction*. No? Very well, then, the Leisure State and let us face up to it. Meanwhile, I agree entirely with Dante and his commentator, for Dante himself said that the whole object of his poem was to lead men from misery to happiness, and that he had no literary ambitions whatsoever. And I agree with all the moralists and 'doctors' that personal ambition is the devil. (Christians and Buddhists, strange to say, are at one on this.)

Pontifex II shows his misunderstanding in his paragraph about the colliery workers, from hewers to office workers. All these chaps, he says, help me to produce something to which *my name* will be put, but not theirs. He cannot see that I do not want my name put on anything —or theirs either. He cannot see that I want to be no more than a responsible workman and them *no less*. He cannot see that in a good human society there is *no* work which does not bear the imprint of its maker (a ledger clerk does not only do accurate accounting but keeps *books* —there is artistry in check-weighing, but you do not need to talk about it, you do not want the blather of art critics) and there is no work of which you can say who did it —completely human and completely anonymous.

'*He had compassion on the multitude,*' i.e. He went about trying to improve social conditions, so to say. But '*man does not live by bread alone.*' Our reformers think that the 'higher things' can be supplied 'out of working hours' —the Leisure State. (See article on the Leisure State in *The Clergy Review* for February![1]) I am in a fog because I do not know what Pontifex II wants —does he want the L.S.? Does he think there is a thing called 'Art', in the sense of the old lady who said: '*It may be art, but I don't like it,*' or in the sense of those reformers who say 'it would be a good thing to bring art to the masses'? If he say 'Yes' to both questions, I give up. My quarrel with him was on account of his distinguishing between 'end products' and others. I say all products are end products and there should be no artists' signatures.   ERIC GILL

324 : TO MGR. JOHN O'CONNOR

Pigotts   *2-4-1940*

Dear Father John: Thank you very much for your letter of last Sunday. I wish I could have been with you to talk about the matter after Mass, but the newspaper reporter who called on me on Easter Monday *as a friend* is all wrong. All I said was that the face of St. John Fisher was in a rough state at present, all the same I should be very glad to see the bust by Torreggiano. You did not say where this is to be seen, can you tell me?

I send herewith a pamphlet which I hope will meet with your approval. I am working hard at present on that line of business, politics are not my affair and Neville C and Adolf H seem to me like Tweedle Dumb and Tweedle Dee.

[1] Reprinted in *Last Essays*, pp. 64-70, and *It All Goes Together*, pp. 157-62.

I understand J— has gone all complacent, but please give him my love and I hope you will have many more years yet.

I am very sorry I have not managed to persuade Denis T to go to Bradford yet. He is engaged in other works but I still hope that he will do it. I've just seen him & he assures me he is coming to you *soon*. We all send our love. Yours affectionately,   ERIC G.

325 : TO THE REV. DESMOND CHUTE

Pigotts   *29-4-1940*

My dearest Desmond: At last I am beginning a letter to you. But the reason why I am finding myself with time available is that I am in bed with German Measles! Oh it's a bore, I do feel completely rotten — though I feel a bit better to-day. Came to bed with what I thought was 'flu' on Ap. *12th*! The next week the doctor said I'd got a bit of 'congestion' & must stay put & now this other business has developed. I don't feel like writing letters but I'll make this start & then every now & then, when I get a lucid moment to observe silver linings (it's a long worm that has no turning . . .), I'll jot a few words down. (I'm writing this double. col. way as it's easier to manipulate in bed . . .) Walter Shewring was here last week from Tues. to Sat. morn. He seemed well but looked tired and thin. I had some cheering talks with him. He is a real loving friend to both of us. René has just finished setting the type for W. S's book.[1] There seems to be very little hope of sales in commercial circles, but I do hope that won't deter them from publishing. There are some most excellent things in it. I've just got proofs of a new book of *mine — Christianity & the Machine Age*, to be published by the S.P.C.K., fancy that! Dr. Flood has been looking through it as theologl. censor on my behalf, so I live in hopes that it will not be

[1] *Topics* (Hague & Gill, 1940).

condemned at Westminster or at Rome. It's only a little book —about 70 pp. —one of a series called the 'Christian News-Letter Books (1ˢ·/). I'm wondering if I can send you a copy when it's published. I expect the publishers can manage it. I'll tell them. Dent's have just brought out (at last) my book of Essays: *Sacred & Secular* with 8 drawings by Teg★ and they are now about to produce the book of *Life* drawings! I've enlarged the preface by several paragraphs since you saw it. The latest addition being to point out to the sympathetic reader that a garden full of flowers is really a grand exhibition of sex organs. 'Well, that's fine' as the Americans say. Surely if anything on earth were calculated to allay our prudishness & nastimindedness it wd. be the realization that our organs are our flowers —pistils & stamens & petals & all. How sweet! How salutary! What a release from the privy! . . . † I don't know when the book will be published. I believe there's going to be a very big trouble about paper. So it's very likely all such 'luxury' publishing will be in-definitely postponed. Meanwhile they've sent me some proofs of the reproductions which seem to me quite good —i.e. as good as reproductions can be, and as *some* of the drawings are (I think) good —in the sense that they do communicate some-thing about our human flesh wh. is worth communicating —I am hopeful that the book when it does come out will be a not valueless contribution to charity.

Alas, I am still in bed! The G. Measles is finished but I've got a bit of congestion of right lung which the doctor insists must keep me there until it clears up. It is better —decidedly, he says. So I hope to be about again shortly. I've been feeling pretty bad, weak & weary —otherwise I wd. have gone on with this letter . . . Luckily I've got a job of work I can get on with to keep me from the despairing feeling of uselessness and waste. I suppose I told you —or didn't I? —that I was

★ complimentary but damned review of it in *T.L.S.* May 11)
† at this point I made a fresh start. 9 May.!)

under contract with Jonathan Cape to produce a book. I can't tell you all the complications (take too long) but the net result is that the book has to be of an autobiographical kind! But as I've never been to the top of Mt. EVEREST or to the S. Pole, nor done anything worth writing home about, it won't be so much an autobiography as an autopsychography.

And now it's May 14! What with one thing and another and not feeling too bright or breezy I haven't got back to this till now. For one thing I had to write a longish letter to Gordian for his birthday on May *10th*. Poor dear Gordian, God knows where he is! Somewhere in France or Belgium driving a motor ambulance car. He joined up in November and got into the R.A.S.C. (M.A. Convoy), so I hope, as he likes driving motor cars more than anything else, he's not having too bad a time, but he does not write as though he were enjoying life much. And this very morning another good letter has come from you — opened by Censor and I am sure he was edified.* Dearest Desmond thank you very much indeed for it. We rejoice to know that you are still safe. It is impossible for non-political contraptions like my mind to follow the political or military situation. I pray simply that it may end as soon as may be and before too much hate has been engendered. It is no use, because we are completely agreed, saying more. [. . .]

I've been thinking a lot about you during the last days — thinking about Ditchling and 1918-21. Because I've just got to that period in the aforementioned autopsy. I shan't have to say anything much in a historical or biographical way, because it's not that kind of book. But in as much as certain *influences* made themselves felt at that place and time they must be written about. If you were dead it would be easier because then I could tell them how much I love you & how much I owe you & how much I learnt from you & was and am inspired by you. It's a pity because I've naturally spread myself a bit

* dated May 5.

over some of the kind friends of my childhood & youth since dead and it doesn't seem fair to the friends of *now*.

Dear Desmond — now it's Wednesday 15th. and in the vague hope that it may still be possible to get this letter to you I will finish it and send it off to-day. I hope to goodness . . . that Italy keeps out of the vortex, and that we shall meet in happier times. *Orate*, meanwhile, *pro invicem*. [. . .] There is a valuable article by Denis Gwynn in the current *Irish Eccl. Record* on the Pope & the war. I was v. glad to see him quoted as having said, last August, that it is by force of *reason* . . . that justice makes progress. The implication which I have indicated by dots was actually expressed in words by H.H.[1] I wish it were possible to keep you better informed of things here by sending you cuttings — but that is apparently forbidden. We are thrown back, in spite of ourselves, upon the eternal verities. I may tell you however that Laurie and I are still working on the Westminster reredos. It wd. have been finished ere now but for this illness. Then I'm due to deliver ms. to Cape by Aug. 1st. (you remember that day in 1918?). I've got a carving of St. Hubert to do for a man who lives near here and one of *Fortuna* to go over the door of some new flats in London. (I wonder . . .) Also a statue of S. Joseph for Fr. O'C. to pair with the one of B.M.V. I did for him. Then I've got a great big crucifix to carve on the outside of the E. Wall of the new Guildford Cathl. (if nothing tran-spires to stop it) & two amorini holding emblems of History and Grammar to go over door of a new Library at Oxford. So we're *not* out of work yet — but who knows anything? Meanwhile all here are well, bar me and I soon will be. And all send you love. Petra & Joanna & their respective infants are well & cheerful & beautiful. Denis is none too busy — but he is helping me a bit with lettering work & is v. good at it as you know. As for René, he is rushed to death with work but will shortly be seriously menaced by shortage of paper. News from Capel-y-ffin continues good. Betty is having a new

---

[1] *i.e.* 'not force of arms' (Broadcast of August 24th, 1939).

FF

babe in July! (Never ain't 'eard of B-C I take it.) The *Guest House* seems to be able to keep going & they have hopes of good numbers during the Summer. [. . .]

Item: I have recently completed my translation of the Little Office of B.M.V. (Dom^n. Rite) into modern English. René is printing it for me on spec. The utmost scope of my ambition is that I shall obtain permission for its use by tertiaries for *private recitation*. But I wd. dearly love *that* much to be allowed. The existing English trans. are abominable — both nonsensical and, as regards hymns, nauseating. Walter has helped me with the hymns in *my* version — but they are in *vers libre* — as thus:

Quem	He whom earth, sea, sky,
terra	worship adore proclaim,
pontus	who rules the triple world,
aethera	is borne in Mary's womb.

He whom the moon and sun and all things
serve duly according to their times,
is carried by a maiden's womb
over which heaven's grace has poured.

Glory to you, Lord,
born of a maiden,
with Father & Holy Spirit
eternally. Amen.

And so good-bye & God bless you from your dear ERIC G.

326 : TO GRAHAM CAREY

Pigotts   *7-5-1940*

Dear Graham: Thank you very much for your letter of 17th April. It is truly kind of you to do so much to help in the matter of the lecture tour. I am very sorry I have yet not properly replied to your letter of 4th March. I have been very much rushed with work and unfortunately the war does not make things easier as I find myself obliged to do a lot of extra writing and lecturing and still more unfortunately I have gone and got ill again and have been in bed for the last three weeks. A return of the old congestion of lungs. I am much better and hope to be at work again shortly.

I have got work on hand which will last me until the end of October. After that it would be, as far as I can see, quite feasible to do a lecture tour in America as you suggest! In the first place it would be the best way of finding out whether I could breathe in the American air (you will forgive this way of putting it for I am sure you understand how difficult it is to face the thought of so big a move) and it would be giving me a splendid chance of seeing you and discussing the matter fully —which can't be done by correspondence.

It is kind of Philip Hofer to interest himself and I am grateful to him but I am very much worried by the prospect of undertaking so many lectures. I do not think I am really good at that job. I cannot stand up as a professional lecturer. There are certain matters in which, rightly or wrongly, I feel a sort of *call* e.g. the relation between industrialism and human work, and if I were invited to come to America to air my views on that subject I should feel it a duty to comply. But as you will understand it is a different matter to let it be known that you are willing to give lectures at all sorts of places on engraving and sculpture etc. I don't really feel capable of it nor 'called' to do so.

So do you think it would be possible simply to put me forward as being prepared to come and lecture (preach would be a better word) on the social and artistic problem of our time? If that were possible I shall then come with perhaps one or two lectures which I should be prepared to repeat whenever called upon to do so.

Assuming that I have enough engagements to cover the cost of the trip and a living wage as well, that is all that matters. As to expenses I have no ideas as yet but will make enquiries, nor do I know at all whether war conditions would allow of such a scheme. I suppose it is possible to get permits. That also I will enquire about.

I agree entirely with you and Hofer that it would be desirable to avoid the professional lecture manager and I shall certainly do so.

Now what do you think about it in the light of the above? If you think the matter is urgent because the various institutions will want to make up their schedules and if you think that they would be prepared to engage me on my sort of lines as suggested above then I think I may hereby authorize you to arrange a lecture tour on the assumption that I cannot leave England until the end of October, but can do so after that.

I am more grateful that I can say for your kindness in taking all this trouble. I only hope it will not involve you in a lot more work. But I should very much like to come and I am very willing to do whatever I can to help the good work. I do not mind to whom I lecture but it would be desirable not to arrange *large* affairs as I have not an orator's training. I shd. think audiences of not more than 100 to 200 wd. be my sort of capacity. I'm hurrying to post this off & must postpone more details for the present. You'll understand I *want* to come & lecture on my lines —but, except incidentally & as a sort of sideshow, I don't want to lecture on *art*.

Yes the Magazines (*C.S.A.Q.*) arrived safely, but I had to fill up endless forms to get them out of the customs. Lord! you'd think they were made of gun cotton. Love from

ERIC G.

327 : TO HIS BROTHER EVAN

Pigotts   *9-5-1940*

My dear Evan: *Thank you v. much* for your philatelic memorial envelope.[1] I am v. glad to have it —for a variety of reasons.

[1] The stamps in question were those of the issue of May 6th, 1940, commemorating the centenary of the first adhesive postage stamp.

H.M's P.O. is quite childlike in its innocence and, tho' the photogravure reproduction of the 1840 engraving goes v. badly alongside the 1940 head of G. VI,* the innocent idea is clear enough, and, as they've done me the great honour of using what, in a vague way, I may call *my* lettering, & a not too bad crown, the whole show —might be a lot worse.

Alas, I'm still kept in bed with con⟨gestio⟩n of l⟨ungs⟩. But the doc. says I'm better. I feel d. weak, that's all *I* know. I had a *long* letter from the ven. archdeacon[1] this morn. which I will shortly send on to you. Much love—   ERIC G.

    * & as thus reproduced looks v. inferior to its original.

328 : TO HIS BROTHER CECIL

Pigotts   *10-5-1940*

Dear bro Cecil: V glad to get yr letter this morn. Alas I'm in bed again. That there laryngitis-flu came back & then just when I was better of that Germhun measles appeared —& *now* the doc. says I've got a patch of congested lung & must stay in bed till it's cleared up . . . So here I am & if I did not know God was good I should think He wasn't —am consequently forced to take the blame myself —v. unfortunate. However luckily Ive got some writing work* I can get on with, so I'm not merely wasting time. (I feel rotten *weak*, that's the worst of it.) But I see no chance of getting to S. Wales yet awhile. I hope I shan't get up & have to go to gaol —but who knows. I'm v. glad R^d Bishop has made contact. He's a good & jovial soul. I'm v. sorry N. has lumbago —poor dear —I hope it's gone now. Much love to you both —I *wish* you could come & see me yr. bro.   ERIC

    * viz the Autopsy. (short for autopsychography). It's now got to the year 1913.

         [1] His brother Romney (in Papua).

Dear Sir: An answer to Father G—'s letter in your issue of
17th May seems called for. There are, I think, two points to
be considered. In the first place that a just war is not only
that fought for a just cause but also by just means, and it is,
I think, chiefly on account of the means employed in modern
warfare that many are moved to refuse military service. Very
few, if any, Catholics would maintain that the stated cause of
the Allies is not a just one, but very many are convinced that
the means employed in modern warfare are such as to make
participation undesirable or impossible and as those means are
rapidly becoming more and more inhuman and uncharitable
such refusal becomes more and more urgent.

But the second consideration is perhaps even more important in relation to Father G—'s letter. It is this: that the
Bishops' pronouncements on the justice of our cause have
primarily the effect of maintaining and confirming the good
conscience of those who have enlisted or been conscripted
and not of imputing a bad conscience to those who refuse.
For as Father G— must know full well there is a vital distinction between ⟨not⟩ disturbing a conscience and imposing a
probable opinion. He must, in the course of reading the
decisions of the Roman Congregations, have come across the
phrase *non sunt inquietandi*.

It might not be improper to point out that there are many
eminent ecclesiastics who view with sympathy the position
outlined above. I would not embarrass them by mentioning
the names of English theologians who hold that the opinion
of the 'Conscientious Objector' is a probable one, but I may
without offence mention Archbishop MacNicholas O.P. of
Cincinnati, who has himself encouraged the formation in his
diocese of a League of Conscientious Objectors. Yours faithfully,   ERIC GILL

330 : TO THE 'NEW ENGLISH WEEKLY'
25TH JULY, 1940

The True Philosophy of Art

Sir: Herbert Read, in his article in your issue of July 11th, quotes Dr. Coomaraswamy as saying that a bomb 'is only bad as a work of art if it fails *to destroy and kill* to the required extent' (italics mine). It seems to me there are difficulties here not cleared up by Herbert Read. The object of the bomb maker, *purely as such*, is to contrive a thing which (a) will burst with great violence (on contact or otherwise) and (b) is of a suitable shape for handling or hurling through the air. The bomb-maker *as such* is not concerned with destruction or killing but only with bursting-power. What this power is used for is not necessarily his affair. As a bomb-maker it's all one, to him, whether his bomb be used to smash the Dome of St. Paul's or a battleship belonging to the enemy (though perhaps hatred of 'them Germans' is a useful spur to his energies).

But there is no such thing as a bomb-maker '*purely as such;*' for the bomb-maker is a man and hatred of '*them Germans*' (or something equivalent) is a necessary part of bomb-making. So we are forced to admit that 'to destroy and kill' is the object of the bomb-maker as a man and the 'thesis' of the bomb. (But note: this paragraph is irrelevant in our world; for there are, roughly speaking, no human beings making anything, but only joint-stock companies who don't give a damn whom they sell things to.)

But I do not see how Herbert Read can maintain that the 'thesis' of the bomb is 'purely *ballistic.*' I should have thought that if it was 'purely' anything it was purely *explosive*; for a bomb is no less a bomb if you wrap it up in brown paper and place it carefully under the Prime Minister's seat.

So when we come to the application of these things to such a work as Dante's poem, we have to be exceedingly careful and I don't think Herbert Read has got it quite right. Comparing the Divine Comedy with a bomb we have to consider the two desiderata (a) and (b), bursting power and shape suitable for conveyance. The 'bursting power' of the poem is the (God help me, I hope I'm being careful) dogmatic truth of the poem and the 'suitable shape' is the versification or 'poetics.' But the point to notice is that in the poem the two are coincident – you can't have Dante's particular truth apart from Dante's particular words. You can't have the truth Dante wished to convey apart from the words Dante used to convey it, because we are creatures of flesh and blood and not disembodied spirits. But in the bomb (a) and (b) are *not* coincident – a collection of chemicals in unstable equilibrium is one thing, the thing you throw 'em about in is another, and to hurl a 'dud' through the air requires the same attention to ballistics as to hurl a 'live' one.

Dante's moral aim in writing his poem was to lead people from misery to happiness – he said so. The bomb-maker's moral aim is presumably to destroy and kill. This thing called 'moral aim' is that which spurs the artist (of whatever kind) to work. And when he's once got going his aim, as workman, is to make a good job of it. But whereas in his workshop the bomb-maker can forget all about 'them Germans;' the poet in his workshop cannot for one instant forget about the misery and happiness. And whereas Herbert Read and I can whole-heartedly agree about the beauty of the bomb, I can't for the life of me see how we can agree about the beauty of Dante's poem if he persists in saying that the meaning doesn't matter.

ERIC GILL

P.S. And if I'm not wrong in thinking that, in such works as Dante's, 'content' and shape do coincide, then I don't see how we can avoid the further conclusion that the one determines the other, that the versification is determined by the truth to be told – that the end determines the means; and that the sensational (aesthetic) quality of the means is the exact measure of the intellectual intensity and clarity with which the end has been apprehended and imagined.

331 : TO LAWRENCE POWELL

Pigotts, High Wycombe   *29-7-1940*

Dear Lawrence: I have heard from Edward Maufe this morning. The stone work will be ready for carving on the east gable by August 15th! And I am very much hoping to come to Guildford on or about that date to commence the work.

Does your kind offer of hospitality still hold good? Please don't hesitate to say if circumstances make it impossible or inconvenient, e.g. you may be full up with refugees. Of course, I should like it better than anything else, but I should hate to be a burden, and I hope you will answer frankly. Moreover, and I know I can say this without any misunderstanding, you might find it a little awkward in the present trend of public opinion,[1] although I don't suppose anybody knows me at Guildford.*

I hope Elsie is well, and things are not too difficult for you all. Unfortunately I have had a bad time, having been in bed off and on for the last three months with some sort of lung trouble following influenza, but I hope to be well by August 15th. Yours,   ERIC GILL

     * except those I met last Autumn.

332 : TO GRAHAM CAREY

Pigotts   *30-7-1940*

Dear Graham: Thank you very much indeed for your letter of July 7th. I have been expecting to hear from you, but I am sorry you have worried about it as I am afraid that the present state of affairs rather knocks the proposed trip to America on the head. I don't see how I can plan anything of the sort at present. Everything seems too confused and uncertain.

We got the box of butter, and thank you very much for it. It was extremely kind of you to send it, and as a matter of fact

[1] i.e. the anti-pacifist trend.

we wondered where it had come from. We were amused as well as pleased, because one of the few things we do manage to make on our little farm is butter, so it seemed very comic to get it supplied from three thousand miles away.

I am sending herewith the review of the book, which I hope will be useful. I am sorry for the adverse criticisms, and I hope you will think them justified.

I am sorry to have to tell you that I have been in bed more or less all the time since April with a return of the lung congestion which I had in 1936. However, I think I am getting over it now and hope to return to work very soon. I have occupied the time writing a sort of autobiography which I was commissioned to do by Jonathan Cape Ltd, the publisher, and I have now finished it . . . about a hundred thousand words. Whether or no they will be able to publish it this year as originally proposed seems very doubtful.* It is really an auto*psycho*graphy, i.e. a history of mental adventures more than physical ones, as I haven't had any of the latter worth mentioning. But I do hope if you see it you will approve of it, because it is a record of those things which concern us Catholics very much. I suppose the general theme of it is the discovery of the City of God — or my attempt to do so.

To return to the lecture tour, I think I must call this 'off' for the present, and wait until this so-called war is over. It is difficult to write about this matter. I try to preserve a strictly papal & neutral frame of mind. It does seem to me more or less disgraceful the way our Ecclesiastics carry on about crusading, putting England forward (England mind you!) as the last bulwark of Christianity.

Meanwhile, I am sure that all attempts to create cells of the good life in the form of small communities are not only much to be encouraged, but are the only hope. On this subject yesterday I read a very interesting little article in your

* I have since heard that they have decided to publish in the autumn if *poss*!

American *Catholic Digest*, not much help, but certainly some home truths. From what I have heard I should think Vermont is a good place. In any case it is to me perfectly clear that communities of lay-folk religiously cutting themselves off from the money economy are an absolute necessity if Christianity is not to go down, either into the dust or the catacombs.

I do hope you will be able to achieve something. There are lots of little attempts going on in England to-day in spite of everything. But of course they are pretty hard up against it, and they get jolly little encouragement from the ordinary population, and still less from the Catholic.

I am very glad indeed to know that you approved of the little book *Christianity and the Machine Age*. I hope shortly to send you a copy as I believe it will be published almost immediately, in fact it may already be out. I understand your point about machinery, I'm sorry I didn't elaborate that point more.

You know I am extremely grateful to you for all your offers of help, and I will not hesitate to ask for more if the occasion arises. Yours, and blessings on you & with much love ERIC G.

But apart altogether from (or in addition to) the lecturing project, I would very much like to come to America to do that job of carving for you — the 'mantel piece' or what not. I might honourably work off my debt to you and establish contacts at the same time. This is a good scheme — but it, like any other, must wait until we know whether we are to live or die. . . .

P.S. I thought the reproduction of my alphabet in the lettering book[1] was very good — I don't see what you find wrong with it. On the other hand I agree with you that the page of Johnston's writing does not really come out very well. It loses its lightness and looks gratuitously flourishy.   E. G.

Herewith *Xtianity* & *Machine Age* which is now published. . . .

[1] *The Elements of Lettering*, by J. H. Benson & A. G. Carey (1940). E. G.'s alphabet is reproduced on p. 117, Johnston's indenture on p. 115.

Pigotts   *4-8-1940*

Dearest Donald: I hope you are having a very happy feast[1] and
all the family too. It is a lovely warm day here and apart from
the passage of wandering aeroplanes all is peace & quiet. We
were very glad indeed to have your letter yesterday. Thank
you very much for it. We all send you all love & greetings.
We are all well here except me – and I am I believe on the
mend. It's been a bad summer for me in that respect – in bed
off and on since April 15, and never anything very serious –
flu, Germ[n] measles, slight bronchitis, lumbago. Old age
coming on I guess. Anyway it gave me time & opp[y] to write
book for Cape's as ordered – 100,000 words, about my so-
called 'life'. He asked for an autobiography but I told him it
could'n't be done. It wd have to be an autopsychography &
that's what it is. I sent the t-script in a few weeks ago & they
say that Adolf permitting they'll publish in the autumn. I hope
& pray the brief refs to D. A. won't give offence. There's a
good patch about Capel in it, naturally. Really it amounts to
'a search for the City of God', but of course I can't give it a
fine title like that. I wish you were here that I could discuss
innumerable points with you. Dr Flood kindly, most kindly,
did all the typing for me & kept me on the theological rails.
Leastways I don't think he passed anything that he thought
wrong – but he made very few adverse criticisms. It feels to
me as tho' I ought really to die now. I don't know how I shall
be able to face the world after stripping myself more or less
naked as I have done. I also wrote a small book for a series
called the Christian News-Letter Books – pub[d] by S.P.C.K.
This will be out soon I hope. And Dent's are about to publish
a book of 'life' drawings with a long preface on nakedness
att⟨ache⟩d [. . .] What have *you* been doing lately? Have
you got anything coming along? I hope so. Now I'm just
about – soon as I'm well enough – to do some more carving

[1] St. Dominic's.

on new Guildford Cathedral, about two months work on east wall. But I don't spect to get there till end of Aug.

Yes, by mercy of God, Gordian got home safely[1] & by skin of teeth —in a destroyer. What a business. Fancy shoving the whole B.E.F. into the sea in a week! Here again I wish we could meet to discuss things & *Pax* too. So I do hope you'll get a chance to come before I go to Guildford. [. . .] Have you heard about England and the last bulwark of Christianity? What? I suppose I.C.I. & Unilever are all part of the good old bulwarks. No, I haven't seen the Blackwell book. Please forgive this economy in paper. I'm writing in the garden —it's my 3rd day down & I'm more or less stuck in a deck-chair with a rug round me. [. . .] You ought to hear Gordian on the subject of the war & Co., & the army & its officers. [. . .] Much love from   E. G.

334 : TO LAWRENCE POWELL

Pigotts   *7-8-1940*

Dear Lawrence: I have had a letter from Edward Maufe this morning saying that he is having trouble with the Bishop and company about the design for the crucifix, and he names you as one of the persons to be placated, although he assumes that you will be on his and my side. The others being the Provost, Sir Lawrence Halsey, and Captain Tuckwell.

I don't know if you have seen the design yet, but I very much hope you approve of it, and especially of the idea of the big hands holding up the cross. The idea is that the Incarnation means, God with us —God otherwise invisible to our finite minds, unknowable, and indeed almost unloveable, so that we know and love God through Christ, and by means of Him we are able to know and love God as we are otherwise incapable of doing. That being so, God may be said to present himself to us in Christ, and so the design represents the hands of God

[1] From Dunkirk.

holding up His Son. At the top, because the church is dedicated to The Holy Spirit, and for the sake of completing the Blessed Trinity, there is the traditional symbol of the Dove. The figure on the cross is robed in an alb because the idea is not to represent Christ as victim, but as reigning or ruling.

Perhaps you will remember Maufe's original design showed two smaller figures, St. John and Our Lady, I suppose, at the foot of the cross, but he agreed with me that those figures at the great height would not be very effective, so we changed the scheme to the present one. Lord! I do hope it will go through with your kind assistance, but it looks to me as though there is going to be some delay. Yours,   ERIC G.

335 : TO DR. COOMARASWAMY

Pigotts   *8-8-1940*

Dear Ananda: I am sorry I forgot the other day to acknowledge the pamphlet *Man and Woman* by Evola,[1] and to thank you for it.

While there are of course some exaggerations, and I think spiritual defects, I think it is on the whole right and good. (What a pitiful note by the Editor on page 306!) I am very glad to have this document. It is crying for the moon to expect, at this time, the acceptance of any such views, but they are really fundamentally true and their acceptance will come again later — but not in our time! I am now enjoying myself lending it to my lady friends. . . . Yours,   ERIC [GILL!]

[1] Offprint from the *Visva-Bharati Quarterly*, February-April 1940. It is a chapter from Evola's book *Rivolta contro il mondo moderno* (1934), expounding and defending the Eastern view of woman as attaining her true self only through devoted dependence upon a man. In the note referred to the Editor says: 'The fact of our publishing it must not be taken as an indication of our endorsement of the author's thesis which, however scholarly and mentally stimulating, seems to us to carry the idealisation of traditional customs and attitudes to fantastic length . . . We are unable to sympathise either with the author's aggressive vindication of our outworn oriental ideals or with his vehement condemnation of those of his own society.' The translation from the Italian is by Zlata Llamas Coomaraswamy.

Pigotts, High Wycombe   *16-8-1940*

Dear Lawrence: Thank you very much for your letter of yesterday. I was about to write to you also. I heard from Maufe a few days ago and he told me the disappointing news about the big crucifix. Of course I am very glad if as you say 'the issue was decided on the point of finance', so I hope the job will come on say next Spring. Actually from the physical point of view the postponement is just as well, as I am by no means strong yet, and doubt if I could have come to Guildford yet-a-while. Moreover there are jobs here which have been delayed on account of my illness, and so it is a relief to my mind to be able to go on with them (though I can't go as far as that yet).

I am very glad to know that you approve of the design. I am fairly sure that it will be the right thing for the place providing I can do it anything like well. Incidentally it puzzles me to know what Maufe is doing about the stones to be let into the wall for the carving. Is he leaving a gap, or what? I have asked him this question but he hasn't vouchsafed an answer.

I am glad the price was not thought excessive, it seems plenty to me.

Item, I am glad the colours of the stones of the Diocesan Arms have come out all right in the weather.

I do hope your little scheme for coming over here one Saturday afternoon will come off. Thank you both, very much, I should very much like to come back with you for the weekend, I don't see why I shouldn't now; so come as soon as you can. But let me know because it is just possible that I may be going to see my daughter in Wales for a week's change of air before long. Love to you both,   ERIC G.

True Philosophy of Art

Sir: If you can bear more of this, may I risk a few words in reply to Herbert Read's letter (August 8th)?

He says that the dogmatic intention of Dante in writing the Divine Comedy 'has little or nothing to do with the quality of the poem as a work of art' and that this is shown 'by the simple expedient of comparing the original with any translation. The dogma remains intact, but the poetry almost entirely disappears. . . .'

Sir, even if the dogma remains intact (which is doubtful; for translations are always inexact except in pure abstractions) the point is that *it doesn't 'get across.'* It has to be clothed in words (or flesh of some sort) because we humans can only know by such means, and unless we have Dante's words we don't get Dante's meaning, and we don't get Dante's particular emphasis and his special persuasiveness (rhetoric). We must learn his language if we want to know what he said, and what he meant, and just exactly what quality and value he attached to the truths he was so keen on.

Suppose for the sake of argument we concede that 'I believe in God' is truly equivalent to 'Credo in Deum'; but Dante wanted not merely to utter a formula (however useful) but to convince us, to persuade us, to convey to us why and how we should believe, to clothe a skeleton with flesh . . . and so on, and to show how horrible and evil are meanness and fear and hate, and how incompatible with faith.

The aesthetes may revel (and we're all aesthetes —it's part of our nature) in the rhythm of Dante's lines, the richness of his imagery . . . why not? But we're not fully human and cannot be good art-critics unless we understand and share with him his vision of good or, as a result of reading him, come to do so.

In effect, it seems to me, Herbert Read wishes to narrow

the concept of art to its purely physio-psychological element —
as though poetry in essence were nothing but mellifluity
('It's not what you say that matters but how you say it, only
the damn fools don't know it' —Tennyson). This is, it seems
to me, to mistake the accident for the substance —the bread
and wine for God Himself, the temporal gift for the eternal
remedy.

Suppose that Jesus had gone about Palestine simply saying:
Trust in God, trust in God, trust in God. The people might
have said: Yes, but how, why, what's it all about? So he said:
Consider the lilies of the field, they neither labour nor spin;
yet Solomon in all his glory was not arrayed like one of
these. . . .

Should we then say, with Dr. Carlos Williams and Herbert
Read, that the meaning is of secondary importance, that the
charm of his language lent whatever value they had to the
ideas conveyed, and that the ideas themselves are no more
than a more or less unimportant vehicle for the beauty? It
seems to me, we ought to say, on the contrary, that the beauty
is the vehicle for the ideas; and the difference between bomb-
making and poetry is that in the former the beauty is the
product and proof of strict and even blind obedience to a
purely functional necessity, while in the latter the beauty is
a product of conscious and deliberate acceptance and love of
a necessity which is spiritual also.   ERIC GILL

338 : TO HEW LORIMER

[Hew Lorimer had just announced his reception into the Catholic
Church.]

Pigotts   *28-8-1940*

My dear Hugh: Your letter came on Thursday with its wonderful good news. I can't tell you how glad I am and glad with
you. If your experience turns out to be anything like mine,

GG

August 9 will be always as a real birthday to you, and so, 'Many happy returns of the day' —and God be thanked and praised.

I am very glad you are not having much unpleasantness with friends & relations. I more or less understand about your young brother. Loyalties, patriotisms, professional etiquettes are jealous gods, and as Jehovah is jealous too, it's bound to be difficult, to say the least. Let us show the patience they lack.

As to my help to you! I'm only proud to think that you think I've been any —*a Domino factum est istud*. . . .

I am most glad too that you are busy. All is well while there is work.

As to the Church & politics —'Religion is politics' as W⟨illiam⟩ B⟨lake⟩ said '& politics is brotherhood . . .' So it can't be helped even if some ecclesiastics do go off the rails a bit sometimes —a bit or a lot. But it makes no difference to the grounds of faith. What a pity, to put it mildly, that people must judge truth by its exponents. But it must always be so —for at the bottom it is a matter of knowing in *whom* we believe. So it's not a pity at all. But why must they always assume the *worst* motives? Why?

I'm really better. But somehow it's very slow & I'm not able to work much yet. I was so glad to see you & you *didn't* stay too long.

We *will* remember you at Mass, both and all of you. I send, as a small memento, the latest output.[1] Alas for the rotten cover and wrapper —Nowt to do with I. . . .

Much love & love congratulations & welcomes from us both. We are most awfully happy & glad at your news. Yours

ERIC G.

---

1 *Christianity and the Machine Age.*

Dear Sir: I am honoured by the sympathetic and under-standing review of my book *Sacred and Secular*, in your May number. I think, however, that the second paragraph calls for some comment.

I have read through the essay 'Ownership and Industrialism' and I cannot see any sentence that justifies your reviewer saying that I advocate Communism, or that I call workers' ownership by that name. The ownership of the means of production by those engaged in production can only be called Communism if you mean the total ownership of all the means of production collectively by all the workers. But the thing advocated in my essay is much more in the nature of corpora-tivism or syndicalism, or Guild Socialism, i.e. that each *group* of workers in each separate undertaking should own the under-taking whether it be large or small. This is certainly not what is nowadays understood by Communism.

As your reviewer rightly perceives I maintain the Christian doctrine of private ownership. The gist of my argument is that under industrial conditions collective ownership is an historical necessity. At present we have collective ownership by the shareholders. I advocate collective ownership by the workers — not meaning the totality of the workers in the country, but the groups of workers engaged in particular enter-prises, and include in the term 'workers' all those directors and managers who are necessary to the conduct of the work.

This is not at variance with *Rerum Novarum*, on the contrary, it enables 'as many as possible of the people to become owners,' and it implies real ownership and control, and not merely owner-ship of dividends — the irresponsible ownership of investors.

The footnote at the end of my book page 198 should, I think, have explained to your reviewer my meaning with regard to relationship between money-lender and workers. 'Labour cannot do without Capital' as Pope Leo said, but it does not follow that a capitalist should own the works. And in general I only maintain that there cannot be a full Christian collaboration between the investors, whose only desire is dividends, and the workers, who by reason both of their humanity and their occupation are interested in their work.

While it is true that an owner has the right to compensation if his property is confiscated, we must in assessing the amount of compensation consider not only his expectations of future profits, but also the amounts he has sequestered in the past. Thus many people might feel that interest on money borrowed by the Government in the time of the Napoleonic wars should no longer be paid. Obviously there must be some limit.

I am of course sorry if I seem unjustly harsh when I suggest that the clergy everywhere are inclined to bow to the rich; doubtless there are a great number of the clergy of all denominations (for of course, in my book I was not thinking only of Catholics) who think and act justly and independently, but it is equally true that there are large numbers who are moved by worldly considerations. It must be so; for the administration of property necessarily calls out worldly virtues, but instead of complaining of my exaggeration, if it be such, it does indeed seem to me desirable that we Catholics especially should recognise the fact that in the opinion of vast masses of our fellow men we have allied ourselves with the rich rather than the poor, and that the history of the last 300 years gives them much justification.

In conclusion it does seem to me that the person reading the review would get an entirely different idea of my essay from what he would get if he read the essay itself. Yours faithfully,

ERIC GILL

Pigotts, 6 Aug. 1940.

[The reviewer, the Rev. A. J. McIver, replied in turn, withdrawing one point of his criticism but maintaining others. E. G. wrote again.]

Dear Mr. McIver: I am very grateful to you for your letter of October 11th. The only possible way of establishing a reconciliation between us would be by meeting and discussing, and that I fear is not possible.

I am as anxious as you to say nothing contrary to the teachings of the Papal Encyclicals. On the other hand it is necessary to recognise that there are certain ambiguities in those Encyclicals. The attitude of Pope Pius XI to the control of industry by finance is clear; on the other hand when Pope Leo says: 'Labour cannot do without Capital nor Capital without Labour,' it is not clear whether he means capital or capitalists. Nor is it clear whether he gives his approval to the irresponsible capitalism of investors whose only concern is dividends, and who take no responsible part in the management of those enterprises in which they have invested money.

It remains clear, I think, that 'as many as possible of the people should be induced to become owners,' and this in our society can only mean co-partnership between managers and directors and 'hands.' We cannot return immediately to small ownership, but we can make an effort to eliminate irresponsible investment. As I say in my article, there is no reason why people should not borrow money, but there is much reason why the mere lender of money should not be the controller of enterprise.

Thank you again for the trouble you have taken, and for the sympathy expressed in your review. Yours sincerely,

ERIC GILL

P.S. Of course I realise that much of my writing is intemperate and insufficiently precise. I hope to improve!

P.P.S. I have now had the opportunity of referring to the book, and would like to say this much more. With regard to the incompatibility of large scale production and private ownership the point is that under capitalist management these enterprises have, as the capitalists themselves proclaim, become public services, and the only privately owned thing about them is the dividends, see pages 174-5.

With regard to expropriation and compensation, the point

is that compensation must be calculated, not only with reference to the present value of enterprises, but the amounts of profits already distributed. E.g., it does not appear to be just that people should still be paying interest on money borrowed from London bankers for financing the Napoleonic wars. This point is commonly met by scaling down the rate of interest paid. Is this just?   E. G.

Pigotts, 15 Oct. 1940.

340 : TO HIS BROTHER CECIL

at High-W. Hospital!   *12-10-1940*

The above address will find me till to-morrow. I'm in here for X ray & bronchobill I mean 'scoppy. (But there'll be a bill somewhereabouts afterwards I fear). This 'ere corf of mine won't abate so I've got a specialist on the job, or rather Mary has. The affair takes place at 2.0; its now 1.10. I've been here since Wednesday. But enough . . . I hope you are both well & undamaged. We all are so far. Work still lasts out but doesn't look as tho. it wd. do so much longer. What then? Item: The famous (but shy-making) autopsychography is 'in the press'. I am now expecting proofs. I begin to think I ought to clear out before it is published. Did you see the little ($\frac{1}{8}$/6) book on *Christianity* & *the Machine Age* pub^d by S.P.C.K.? [. . .] I hope Nonie is well & David. I never heard from the police after they raked your place over. Did they return your books? Any news of Max? I'm told a bomb dropped on the Inner Temple. I wrote to him, but no reply. Much love to you both —your bro.   ERIC

341 : TO HIS BROTHER CECIL

Pigotts   *21-10-1940*

Dearest Cecil: [. . .] It was lovely seeing you both the other day, and I really am most grateful & bucked & cheered for your kindness in making the effort. I am jolly glad you got back safely.

I will write a postscript to this as Mr. Sellors has rung up to say that he is coming to see me to-day, so then I will be able to report. Meanwhile, I am feeling quite a lot better and the cough is looser. I am very glad Nonie's back is better. I am sorry about the dugout, but I suppose in Cardiff you must have such things. I am very glad you liked ours. When I say my Office at night in there I feel as safe as houses. Your bro.

ERIC G.

P.S. Sellors came this afternoon. It is as you said —a sort of cancerous growth. But he avers that it is at present well within the powers of surgery to deal with if I don't delay —a matter of cutting out a small portion —a lobe, and he thinks the chances of really eradicating it are v. high and that a complete pneumonectomy wd. be inadvisable in the circs. . . . So that's that and I'm to go to Harefield Hospital as soon as a bed is vacant. To my great relief the fees for surgery will be nil! And as we are at present quite on our beam ends, that is a real mercy. So I must forego the pleasure of shuffling off the m. coil (I'm v. glad he's against pneumon etc. because I really shd. have jibbed at that —impious I call it, at my age.) Darling Cecil I wish you were not so far away. We'll have to meet again soon. Meanwhile much love to you both. Dear Nonie, I'm so glad her lumbago is better.   E. G.

342 : TO GRAHAM CAREY

Pigotts   *30-10-1940*

Dear Graham: Your letter of the 1st arrived the night before last —pretty good going considering. I am very much delighted to know that on the second reading you found *The Necessity of Belief* is good, and also the *Machine Age* book.

Of course I am very much interested in all you say about

Formal and Final causes. I wish we could meet and talk it out. I have written more on this subject in a book about to be published on Life Drawings, and I think I have to some extent met your criticism — although I have again rubbed in the point about the law of least resistance. I send you a proof herewith & also a proof of one of the reproductions! Of course, it is unquestionable that when God looked upon His works He saw that they were good; and the word 'good' implies appreciation of forms as well as ends. I believe the problem is really one of Method, and my view is that in God's all-seeing mind He knew that Final and Formal like Righteousness and Peace would kiss one another (Psalm 84) — if you see my meaning. Indeed I find, at least I think I do, that this is so in what I might call *my* art works. What I do jib at is the suggestion of a dichotomy; as though God could give roses five petals, or butterflies such and such pattern on their wings for any sort of separate reason, or vice versa that He could attend to the *structure* of things irrespective of *formal* results.

But alas, I can't write as much as I should like, as I am desperately trying to straighten things up before going into hospital. This long illness and persistent cough has not cleared up, and having at last taken specialist's advice I find that I have got some sort of cancerous growth in my right lung, but I am advised that it is in a very early stage, and there is every reason to suppose that what they call a 'lobectomy' will do the trick, and I don't expect I'll be away more than a few weeks. Thank goodness, I haven't had to be entirely idle all these months. I have got a certain amount of work done — even written the Autobiography book — a hundred thousand words! — about which I think I must have told you. It is to be published by Cape's if possible before Christmas. Naturally this is very shy-making, and it would be really a good thing to shuffle off this mortal coil before it appears — but I don't think it will come to that. I hope to goodness you will approve of it in a general way, and that it won't do harm to God's cause. I have tried to put down the stages of progress from Brighton to Jerusalem.

Apart from that I have been going on with the reredos for Westminster, and it is now very nearly finished. But of course, as you will easily guess, things are now getting extremely difficult financially. For not only have I done much less work this year than hitherto, but future prospects are extremely bad, and unless the war comes to an end before long I can see sculpture coming to an end instead. Moreover the Income Tax is ruining us, because we are taxed doubly as much and I have only earned half my previous income.

I don't know in the least what you could do to help — anyway they can't sell us up because this building & land is mortgaged, and if there is no money they can't take it. If your offer of help has anything to do with finance, let me know, and I'll send you a statement of debts etc. But I rely on you to do as you say, and tell me what is possible or impossible. I see no possibility of coming to America yet awhile, lovely though it would be to rest awhile under your wing. And then there are the employees here to keep in work — one faithful assistant and one apprentice.

I looked urgently through your letter to see what comments you make about my letter to you of August 3rd; but there was no mention of it — I fear it must have been lost in some torpedoed ship. It was all about your lettering book, and I wrote it with much regret at not being able to praise the book as much as I had hoped to be able to. I am very anxious to hear from you about it. If you didn't get my letter, let me know, and I will send you a copy, so I won't write more now.

Dear Graham! Thank you for all your affection and interest. Yours,   ERIC G.

I'm in bed at the moment waiting to be called to go to hospital. I don't think there's serious danger of life in this 'operation' but, just supposing the Lord God wills otherwise, please know that I love you very much & thank you dearly for *your* love. May the good work go on & may we meet in heaven. God bless you.   E. G.

343 : TO ELDRED HITCHCOCK

Pigotts   *31-10-1940*

Dear Eldred: I was glad to get your letter this morning, and to know that you are still above ground.

I am writing at once to say that my specialists have now definitely decided that what is the matter with me is an unseemly growth in my right lung, and that as it is still in a very early stage, the right and feasible thing to do is to cut it out. So I am going into hospital at Harefield near Denham for the operation, and shall be going any day, i.e. as soon as they send me notice of a vacant bed. Harefield is the M.C.C. Sanatorium, the London Chest Hospital is evacuated to it. I may say that I have got the absolutely top man on the job, which is pretty good swank. [. . .] Yours,   ERIC G.

344 : TO LAWRENCE POWELL

At Harefield Sanatorium (F Ward, Cubicle 14)
nr Uxbridge, Mdx.   *4-11-1940*

I have been hoping to see you. I never got down to Wales. My cough went on & on & now the experts have decided that 'it's no use wasting tears & incantations over a disease that needs the knife' so I'm here for 'lobectomy'. Don't know how long that means but they'll be doing it this week I think. I hope you are both well. I hear from E^d M. that he's still hopeful that the big ✠ will be done . . . & I hope I'll be here to do it. Love from   ERIC G.

GENERAL INDEX

Reference is by pages. Correspondents as such are not listed here. Some items of special interest are gathered beneath the headings: *Books and writings by E. G.; Books and writings by others; Engravings by E. G.; Sculptures by E. G.* For books illustrated by E. G., see *Engravings*.